Read this book online today:

With SAP PRESS BooksOnline we offer you online access to knowledge from the leading SAP experts. Whether you use it as a beneficial supplement or as an alternative to the printed book, with SAP PRESS BooksOnline you can:

- Access your book anywhere, at any time. All you need is an Internet connection.
- Perform full text searches on your book and on the entire SAP PRESS library.
- Build your own personalized SAP library.

The SAP PRESS customer advantage:

Register this book today at *www.sap-press.com* and obtain exclusive free trial access to its online version. If you like it (and we think you will), you can choose to purchase permanent, unrestricted access to the online edition at a very special price!

Here's how to get started:

1. Visit *www.sap-press.com*.
2. Click on the link for SAP PRESS BooksOnline and login (or create an account).
3. Enter your free trial license key, shown below in the corner of the page.
4. Try out your online book with full, unrestricted access for a limited time!

Your personal free trial **license key**
for this online book is:

vntp-u9gb-xw7d-48re

The SAP® General Ledger

SAP PRESS

SAP PRESS is a joint initiative of SAP and Galileo Press. The know-how offered by SAP specialists combined with the expertise of the Galileo Press publishing house offers the reader expert books in the field. SAP PRESS features first-hand information and expert advice, and provides useful skills for professional decision-making.

SAP PRESS offers a variety of books on technical and business related topics for the SAP user. For further information, please visit our website: *www.sap-press.com*.

Sridhar Srinivasan, Kumar Srinivasan
SAP BusinessObjects Planning and Consolidation
978-1-59229-239-4
2010, 406 pp.

Naeem Arif and Sheikh Tauseef
Integrating SAP ERP Financials
2010, 380 pp.
978-1-59229-300-1

Paul Theobald
Transitioning to IFRS in SAP ERP Financials
2009, 210 pp.
978-1-59229-319-3

Heinz Forsthuber, Jörg Siebert
SAP ERP Financials User's Guide
2009, 594 pp.
978-1-59229-190-8

Eric Bauer and Jörg Siebert

The SAP® General Ledger

Galileo Press

Bonn • Boston

Galileo Press is named after the Italian physicist, mathematician and philosopher Galileo Galilei (1564–1642). He is known as one of the founders of modern science and an advocate of our contemporary, heliocentric worldview. His words *Eppur se muove* (And yet it moves) have become legendary. The Galileo Press logo depicts Jupiter orbited by the four Galilean moons, which were discovered by Galileo in 1610.

Editors Patricia Kremer and Eva Tripp
English Edition Editor Erik Herman
Translation Lemoine International, Inc., Salt Lake City, UT
Copyeditor Pamela Siska
Cover Design Graham Geary
Photo Credit iStockphoto.com/DNY59
Layout Design Vera Brauner
Production Editor Kelly O'Callaghan
Assistant Production Editor Graham Geary
Typesetting Publishers' Design and Production Services, Inc.
Printed and bound in Canada

ISBN 978-1-59229-350-6

© 2011 by Galileo Press Inc., Boston (MA)
2nd Edition, updated and revised, 2011
2nd German edition published 2010 by Galileo Press, Bonn, Germany

Library of Congress Cataloging-in-Publication Data
Bauer, Eric.
    The SAP General Ledger / Eric Bauer, Jörg Siebert. — 1st ed.
        p. cm.
    ISBN-13: 978-1-59229-350-6
    ISBN-10: 1-59229-350-6
    1. SAP ERP. 2. Accounting—Computer programs. 3. Accounting—Data processing.
    4. Financial statements. I. Siebert, Jörg. II. Title.
    HF5679.B348 2011
    657'.3028553—dc22
    2010028733

Contents at a Glance

Contents

3   Integration in Financial Accounting 109

5   Document Splitting 293

6   Migration 355

Introduction

The aim of this book is to familiarize you with the design, configuration, and migration of New General Ledger (New G/L) in SAP® ERP Financials. New G/L brings together solutions that were previously distributed across multiple applications in SAP R/3, and fulfills requirements such as transparency and flexibility. IFRS-motivated reporting requirements, such as segment reporting and parallel accounting, are also considered.

The General Ledger in SAP R/3—the so-called classic G/L—is highly heterogeneous. In conjunction with the classic G/L, customers currently have to implement several SAP components in order to fulfill international and industry-specific accounting requirements. To remedy this problem, SAP has created a new, flexible General Ledger approach in SAP ERP.

New G/L merges the classic General Ledger with profit center accounting, special ledgers (including cost-of-sales ledger), and the consolidation staging ledger (see Figure 1).

The segment characteristic as well as the document-splitting function fulfills the increased requirements for segment reporting according to IFRS or US-GAAP. Also, New G/L uses a broad, unified data basis, so that G/L account, functional area, profit center, and segment are contained in a single data record. This feature enhances data quality and obviates the need for reconciliation measures.

Thus, using New G/L removes the need to use several separate components, as illustrated in Figure 2.

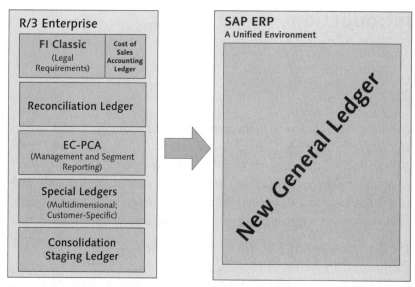

Figure 1   New General Ledger—A Unified Environment

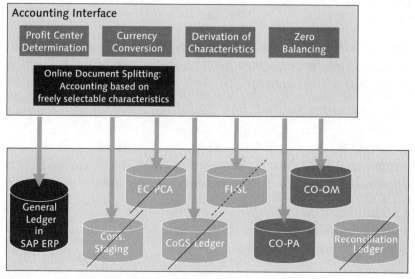

Figure 2   New General Ledger—A Unified Approach

About this Book

This book is intended for readers with a good knowledge of the SAP application Financial Accounting and of General Ledger accounting. Its goals are to provide recommendations on the design of New G/L and to explain its configuration in detail. On more than 150 additional pages, this second edition describes the new functions of Enhancement Packages 3 and 4 as well as experiences that have been gained in successfully implemented migration projects.

Target audience of this book

This book is divided into seven chapters.

Structure of this book

Chapter 1, New General Ledger in SAP ERP—An Overview, demonstrates the differences between the classic and the new General Ledger and explains the motivation behind the new solution. It additionally provides an overview of the innovations in Enhancement Packages 3 and 4.

Chapter 2, Design and Features of the Ledgers, explains the architecture of New G/L. It describes the features of the ledger and ledger groups, discusses various scenarios, and explains how to include customer-specific fields.

Chapter 3, Integration in Financial Accounting, deals with the consequences of closely integrating or merging the functions of the classic SAP R/3 modules or SAP ERP modules, Financial Accounting (FI) and Management Accounting (CO). Key phrases such as *integrated planning* (also for secondary cost elements) and *different period control for CO and FI* are some examples. This chapter focuses on the *profit center accounting including authorization check and assignment monitor* scenario in G/L and new options for integrating CO and FI in real time.

The existing local accounting standards were supplemented by new IFRS reporting requirements. SAP R/3 provided three options for mapping a parallel accounting procedure: accounts, special ledgers, and company codes. New G/L represents a fourth option: the ledger approach in New G/L.

Chapter 4, Parallel Accounting—IFRS on the Advance, focuses on the design and configuration for asset accounting, stocks, receivables, securities, and provisions.

It is possible to activate document derivation when New G/L is updated. The aim is to project account assignment objects to document line items in which they were not originally assigned; for example, to project the profit center from the revenue lines to the receivables line. These options increase the transparency of postings and enable you to create additional balance sheets. This means that you no longer need to create a collective posting in order to adjust the balance sheet and profit-and-loss statement because all the information is already available at the document level. This feature is the subject of **Chapter 5**, Document Splitting.

The transition from classic G/L to New G/L can be straightforward or very complex, depending on the initial situation and the desired outcome. **Chapter 6**, Migration, describes the migration procedure, the Migration Cockpit, and the relevant services provided by SAP.

Chapter 7, Practical Reports, describes already implemented projects providing reports of real-life scenarios from SAP Consulting, Accenture GmbH, Siemens IT Solutions and Services, ConVista Consulting AG, and J&M Management Consulting. This chapter also contains lessons learned so that you can benefit from these experiences.

The book concludes with an Appendix that provides succinct answers to some frequently asked questions.

Special Icons

To make it easier for you to use this book, we use special icons to indicate information that may be particularly important.

[!] Attention

This icon warns you about a potential problem. Take extra care when tackling this task or using the function in question.

[Ex] Example

This icon indicates an example. We use examples frequently throughout the book to illustrate the topics and functions under discussion.

[+] Note

This icon indicates a note. We use this icon to draw your attention to important information that can facilitate your work.

Acknowledgments

Writing a book is not easy; writing or revising this technical book in particular required great commitment—not just from the authors. Many friends and colleagues supported us throughout this book project by providing advice, information, and corrections. We would like to take this opportunity to thank them all sincerely. Rather than risk forgetting one by listing them all, we have decided not to make a list. However, one name that must be mentioned is Jörg Hartmann. With his passion for technical detail and his pioneering work in the area of migration tools, he was always a great support to us and provided valuable input for this book.

Of special importance to us was the support of our families: Myriam, Smilla, and Kian Schlude as well as Eva, Jennifer, and Laura Siebert. The work required for this book meant that they had to do without our presence on several occasions and not just on weekends. It is safe to say that without their patience and tolerance, the book would not have been written. They deserve our heartfelt thanks, and we dedicate this book to them.

Eric Bauer and **Jörg Siebert**

Undoubtedly, it is quite an effort to leave a familiar and known environment and meet new challenges. But it can also be possible that this new environment exceeds all expectations — in a positive sense.

1   New General Ledger in SAP ERP — An Overview

In SAP R/3, a wide range of components must be used in order to fulfill international accounting standards and industry-specific requirements. New G/L removes this fragmented approach and creates a new, unified "Financials world" that can competently handle changing requirements. It thus enables companies to meet the challenge of compliance, which requires a clear, transparent representation of business realities.

In this chapter, we will first present the changing underlying conditions that drive change in Financial Accounting, such as compliance and reporting requirements and enterprise performance management. We then will compare the functions of the "classic" General Ledger in SAP R/3 with New G/L in SAP ERP.

1.1   The Path to New G/L in SAP ERP

The new G/L solution in SAP ERP Financials replaces the solutions developed since the introduction of SAP R/3. The following sections explain the general motivation for developing the new G/L solution and describe the individual solutions of the "old Financials world."

1.1.1   Background

Any ongoing developments made to SAP ERP systems are embedded in a historical context that characterizes these systems throughout their lifecycles. The new G/L solution in SAP ERP Financials is no exception. It is the product of a Financials world that has emerged since the introduction of SAP R/3 and represents a response to certain changes (see Figure 1.1).

Figure 1.1 Changes in SAP ERP Financials

Changes in SAP ERP Financials

These changes in SAP ERP Financials reflect the following trends:

1. Consistency
2. Increased Efficiency
3. Risk Management
4. Transparency

We will now take a closer look at these four trends.

Consistency

Changes in SAP ERP Financials

The consistency referred to is most noticeable in the restructuring of external and internal accounting in SAP ERP Financials. Financial Accounting (FI) and Management Accounting (CO) now map a version of reality through New G/L. Legal reports and management reports are populated by a single data source.

The following reporting requirements are now fulfilled in New G/L by a single data source:

- Legal reporting

- Segment reporting

- Management reporting

Increased Efficiency

The second trend shown in Figure 1.1, increased efficiency, is mainly a function of an optimized financial supply chain. The financial supply chain is made up of functions and processes for internal and cross-enterprise financial transactions. It comprises all transactions that are linked to the capital flow, from the sales order to reconciliation to payment of vendors.

Financial supply chain

SAP Financial Supply Chain Management (FSCM), for its part, is an integrated approach to improving the transparency and monitoring of all cash flows. The goal of FSCM is to optimize the financial supply chain in order to maximize and maintain long-term profits. It represents an integrated approach that leads to greater transparency, control, and monitoring of all the processes associated with the capital flow. The SAP FSCM component is linked to New G/L in SAP ERP via the Accounting interface.

Financial Supply Chain Management

> **Literature Recommendation**   **[+]**
>
> For more information on SAP FSCM, refer to the book *Financial Supply Chain Management with SAP ERP*, which was also published by SAP PRESS.

Risk Management

The third change illustrated in Figure 1.1 is risk management.

The following actions are essential for all business risks that need to be managed in the context of governance, risk, and compliance management:

Governance, risk, and compliance

- Identification

- Valuation

- Monitoring

Compliance requires us to act in a way that adheres to the requirements of the law and is in accordance with regulations. Figure 1.2 provides an overview of the most important goals in terms of governance, risk, and compliance management.

Figure 1.2 Governance, Risk, and Compliance Management

The U.S. Sarbanes-Oxley Act and the German Bilanzrechtsmodernisierungsgesetz (BilMoG; in English, Accounting Law Modernization Act) are just two examples of the many legal requirements that apply to our companies.

How do we go about fulfilling these requirements? First, an enterprise needs comprehensive support to ensure that all of its employees at all levels can make decisions and take actions in accordance with the law. New G/L provides just such support by enabling data to be presented in a transparent format. It presents the complex web of relationships between different reporting characteristics as a unified whole, thus fulfilling the reporting requirements of various external and internal groups. For example, it eliminates the weak points and risks inherent in time-consuming and error-prone reconciliation work.

Transparency

The fourth change depicted in Figure 1.1 is transparency. You achieve more transparency using *Enterprise Performance Managements* (EPM) for Finance, which comprises strategy management, business planning, profitability and cost management, and business consolidation.

The latter obtains its data from the preparatory work done in the consolidation staging ledger in New G/L. The consolidation transaction type is a data field in New G/L, as shown in Chapter 2, Design and Features of the Ledgers.

This feature makes the task of integrating consolidation-relevant data from an SAP ERP system in a consolidation system much easier to manage. The business consolidation trend also involves the harmonization of platforms for external and internal reporting.

1.1.2 SAP R/3-Based Solutions for Financial Accounting

We will now take a look at the "old world," where the heterogeneity of ledgers causes the problem of having to reconcile sets of figures.

Classic General Ledger

The classic General Ledger in Financial Accounting, which was primarily a response to legal requirements, still exists in Release SAP R/3 Enterprise alongside a range of other, separate ledgers (see Figure 1.3). While the classic ledger is oriented toward legal requirements, the cost-of-sales accounting ledger is used to create a profit and loss (P&L) statement based on cost-of-sales accounting, the profit center ledger is for management and segment reporting, and the special ledgers are for customer-specific requirements.

These special ledgers, each of which is intended to fulfill specific requirements, are explained in the following.

The main purpose of the classic General Ledger is to create a balance sheet and a profit and loss statement (P&L statement).

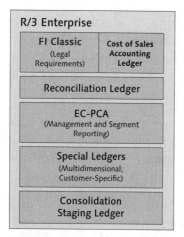

Figure 1.3 Ledgers in Release SAP R/3 Enterprise

Balance sheet
and P&L These documents have to take country-specific requirements into account. This means, for example, that the balancing entity (such as the company code for Germany, as shown in Figure 1.4) creates a balance sheet based on the local legal framework. As well as country-specific requirements, players in capital markets are also required to generate international financial statements in accordance with International Financial Reporting Standards (IFRS) or Generally Accepted Accounting Principles (GAAP), or both.

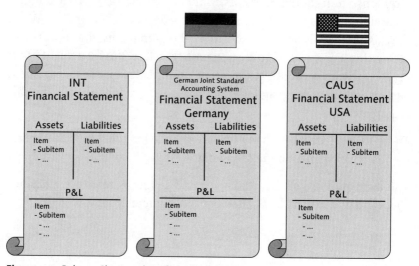

Figure 1.4 Balance Sheet and Profit and Loss Statement

Cost-of-Sales Ledger

In order to create the P&L statement based on cost-of-sales accounting as well as on period accounting, the SAP system needs the transaction figures for each functional area.

Cost-of-sales accounting

One special requirement is that the costs need to be separated into functional areas, such as production, administration, sales, and research and development. However, the classic General Ledger provides transaction figures for the entity "Account" only, with the option of reporting by business area. Thus, the functional areas have to be created individually, as shown in Figure 1.5.

Functional areas

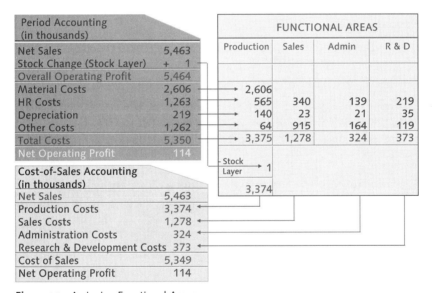

Figure 1.5 Assigning Functional Areas

Therefore, in cases where a functional area breakdown is required, you have to use another ledger: the cost-of-sales ledger. This ledger provides transaction figures per functional area, as you can see from the Sales, Administration, and Research functional areas shown in Figure 1.6.

Cost-of-sales ledger

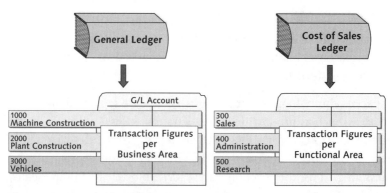

Figure 1.6 Cost-of-Sales Ledger

Special Ledgers

Besides the requirement to present the P&L statement based on the cost-of-sales accounting procedure (and thus to assign transaction figures to functional areas) as well as on the period-accounting procedure, you often need to provide transaction figures not only for existing account assignment fields, but for new account assignment fields as well. Companies often need to create reports based on markets, products, activity fields, and other criteria.

Account assignment field

SPECIAL REGION is another possible account assignment field (see Figure 1.7). This field enables users to create reports, such as P&L statements, for specific regions.

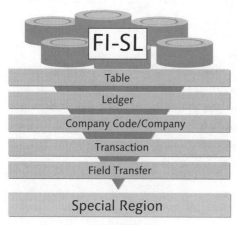

Figure 1.7 FI-SL Special Ledgers

The "special ledgers" component (FI-SL) can be used to extend the account assignment block. This extension makes it possible to provide the additional transaction figures in a special ledger.

Using special ledgers for extension purposes

Reconciliation Ledger

The Reconciliation Ledger in SAP R/3 can be used to reconcile postings from internal and external Financial Accounting. FI postings are already transferred automatically to CO in SAP R/3 (in real time).

This system is also used in the pre-SAP ERP SAP R/3 environment. However, if amounts are allocated within CO in SAP R/3 for company codes, functional areas, or business areas, this information has to be communicated back to FI.

Reconciliation Ledger

The SAP R/3 system doesn't send this data to FI automatically. While CO transactions are updated in the reconciliation ledger, the system does not at first send this information on to the FI system. Only at the end of the period is the reconciliation ledger used to transfer the data, after which FI is once again reconciled with the CO postings.

Transaction KALC is used to call the reconciliation program. Figure 1.8 shows the selection screen for inputting parameters and process control.

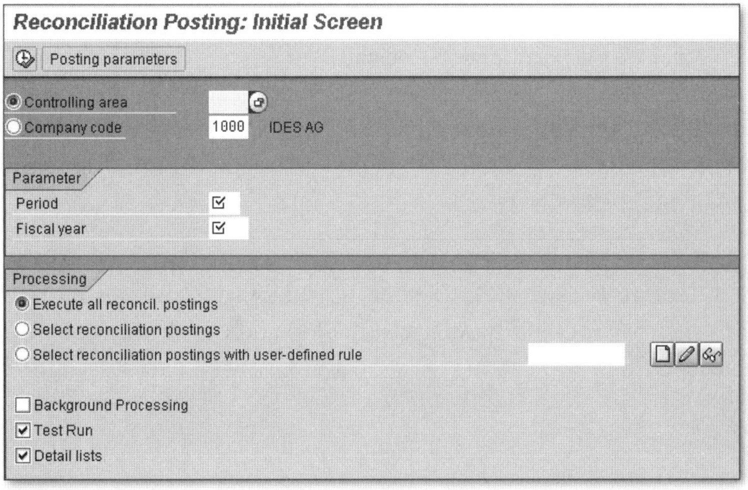

Transaction KALC

Figure 1.8 Reconciliation Posting in Transaction KALC

Profit Center Accounting

As well as being mapped in the classic revenue and cost controlling components of SAP ERP (Overhead Cost Controlling, Product Cost Controlling, Profitability Analysis), all critical business processes are also mapped in Profit Center Accounting (EC-PCA). Figure 1.9 illustrates this value flow in the direction of Profit Center Accounting.

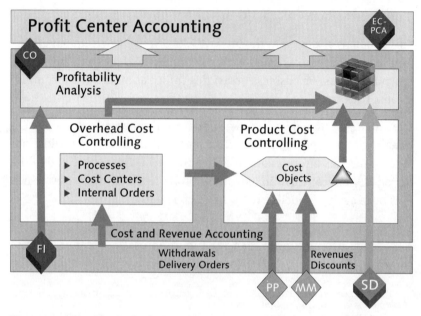

Figure 1.9 Value Flow in Profit Center Accounting

Profit Center Accounting EC-PCA

Profit Center Accounting can be regarded as a "shadow controlling" element of an overall companywide controlling concept. EC-PCA functions can now be mapped in New G/L.

New G/L not a replacement for CO

It would be incorrect to think that New G/L can replace CO. This is not the intention of New G/L. Despite its flexibility, it cannot replace functions such as Profitability Analysis (CO-PA) and Overhead Cost Controlling (CO-OM).

1.1.3   The Fragmentation Problem

The problem of sets of figures that need to be reconciled is a result of the heterogeneous ledger environment described earlier. This fragmentation goes against the requirement in modern Financial Accounting for a unified approach. New G/L renders these silo solutions obsolete and achieves the goals described below.

Problem of sets of figures that need to be reconciled

A unified solution is particularly important in terms of fast close and reducing total cost of ownership (TCO), especially when we consider that international accounting requirements and industry-specific regulations have led to the creation of a wide variety of different data storage locations.

Fast close and TCO

Veracity and reliability are central factors in Financial Accounting. New G/L incorporates these factors and fulfills the requirement for data transparency.

Reliability

The new unified approach does full justice to legal, management, and segment reporting requirements. For example, the same procedures are used for different reporting approaches, which ensures that data quality is maintained.

Data transparency

Less manual post-processing means that double maintenance of data—previously a frequent occurrence—is required to a much lesser degree. Correspondingly, the risk of illegal or non-regulation activity is reduced. This benefit in turn supports enterprises' efforts in the area of corporate governance. Section 1.3, New G/L, also discusses the added value of New G/L in terms of compliance. But first we will discuss the new technology of enhancement packages.

Low manual input

1.2   Enhancement Package Technology

One request that has been brought forward by SAP customers concerns the topical changes within the SAP ERP system. New functions are supposed to be used in financial accounting; other innovations in areas such as payroll, purchasing, and sales are not interesting initially. In the past, new functions became visible for all areas and partly directly active in case of an upgrade.

Big bang approach
SAP customers usually want to avoid this "big bang" approach. They request smaller projects with calculable comparisons of project costs and process benefit. The technology of enhancement packages is an answer to the two dimensions of these challenges, that is, innovations on the one hand and as little effort as possible on the other hand.

Stable core
Without a stable core, it becomes possible to implement process improvements without an upgrade. Small functional improvements in a business process are now possible, thereby avoiding a big bang scenario.

Retrospect—
extension sets
in SAP R/3
The idea of a stable core and functional improvements in the form of small packages are not new in the SAP environment. In Release SAP R/3 4.7, *extension sets* were provided as a similar approach. However, this attempt was not successful because the various SAP industry solutions urged changes to the SAP ERP core. Furthermore, the new basic SAP component, SAP NetWeaver, became an important infrastructure which also had to be taken into account. Experiences from this time show that it can be difficult to keep a core stable and develop innovations at the same time.

Today, the conditions are stable with regard to enhancement packages. Functional enhancements of the SAP ERP core have been offered since 2005 in the form of enhancement packages. Because these functional innovations are encapsulated topically and inactive initially, they require a separate activation in Customizing. If you select TOOLS CUSTOMIZING • IMG PROJECT PROCESSING • F5 • SAP CUSTOMIZING IMPLEMENTATION GUIDE • ACTIVATE BUSINESS FUNCTIONS, the system takes you to the *business functions sets*, which represent functional enhancements of the enhancement packages that are technically available in the SAP system.

Business
functions sets
The activation of individual business functions generates new Customizing menu paths or innovations in the SAP system, which become visible in the application. With regard to New G/L, Enhancement Packages 3 and 4 include many functional enhancements. Figure 1.10 illustrates the required business functions: FIN_GL_CI_1 and FIN_GL_CI_2.

You cannot
skip an EHP
The ⊞ icon indicates a dependency between the two business functions. The principle of Enhancement Packages (EHP) comprises a cumulated administration of the respective topic areas; that is, if you activate the FIN_GL_CI_2 business function delivered with Enhancement Package 4,

you also automatically activate the FIN_GL_CI_1 business function delivered with Enhancement Package 3. In other words, the changes of EHP4 are based on EHP3. But it is also technically feasible to activate only EHP3 without EHP4. After this description of the technical conditions, let's look at the contents of the EHPs or business functions (see Figure 1.10).

Q35 - Switch Framework: Change Business Function Status

Check Changes ‖ Activate Changes

Business Function Set

Name	Description	Planne	Depend	SFW B	Docum	Releas	Release
FIN_ACC_GROUP_CLOSE	Financials, Group Closing	Busine...		🗄	ⓘ	ⓘ	602
FIN_ACC_ILM	Information Lifecycle Management: Tax Audit...	Busine...	🔀	🗄	ⓘ	ⓘ	604
FIN_ACC_LOCAL_CLOSE	Local Close	Busine...		🗄	ⓘ	ⓘ	603
FIN_ACC_PEO	Partly Exempt Organizations	Busine...		🗄	ⓘ	ⓘ	604
FIN_ACC_XBRL	Reporting Using XBRL Standards	Busine...		🗄	ⓘ	ⓘ	603
FIN_APAR_PAYMT_ADV	FI, Enterprise Service for Sending Payment ...	Busine...		🗄		ⓘ	605
FIN_CO_COGM	CO, Parallel Valuation of Cost of Goods Man...	Busine...		🗄			605
FIN_FSCM_BCONS_CON	Billing Consolidation Connector	Busine...		🗄		ⓘ	604
FIN_FSCM_BD	SAP Biller Direct Buy Side	Busine...		🗄	ⓘ	ⓘ	602
FIN_FSCM_BD_3	SAP Biller Direct Buy Side 2	Busine...	🔀	🗄			605
FIN_FSCM_BNK	Bank Communication Management	Busine...		🗄	ⓘ	ⓘ	604
FIN_FSCM_CCD	FSCM Functions	Busine...		🗄	ⓘ	ⓘ	602
FIN_FSCM_CCD_2	FSCM Functions 2	Busine...	🔀	🗄	ⓘ	ⓘ	604
FIN_FSCM_CCD_3	FSCM-Funktionen 3	Busine...	🔀	🗄			605
FIN_FSCM_CCD_INTEGRATION	FSCM Integration 2	Busine...		🗄	ⓘ	ⓘ	604
FIN_FSCM_INTEGRATION	FSCM Integration	Busine...		🗄	ⓘ	ⓘ	602
FIN_FSCM_SSC_AIC_1	FSCM, Integration mit Financial Shared Servi...	Busine...	🔀	🗄			605
FIN_GL_CI_1	New General Ledger Accounting	Busine...		🗄	ⓘ	ⓘ	603
FIN_GL_CI_2	New General Ledger Accounting 2	Busine...	🔀	🗄	ⓘ	ⓘ	604
FIN_GL_DISTR_SCEN_1	FI-GL (New), Transfer of Totals and Single D...	Busine...		🗄		ⓘ	605
FIN_GL_REORG_1	FI-GL (New), Reorganization and FI-AA Seg...	Busine...		🗄		ⓘ	605
FIN_INHOUSE_CASH_1	FIN In-House Cash Module Enhancements	Busine...		🗄			605
FIN_LOC_CI_1	Non-HCM Localization Topic	Busine...		🗄	ⓘ	ⓘ	603
FIN_LOC_CI_2	FI Localization Topics for Japan and Portugal	Busine...		🗄	ⓘ	ⓘ	604
FIN_LOC_CI_3	RE-FX Localization Topics for Portugal	Busine...		🗄	ⓘ	ⓘ	604
FIN_LOC_CI_4	FI Localization Topics for Japan and South K...	Busine...		🗄	ⓘ	ⓘ	604

Figure 1.10 Business Functions

The FIN_GL_CI_1 business function includes the following innovations from Enhancement Package 3:

EHP3—Business Function FIN_GL_CI_1

▶ External planning data transfer to New G/L, CO integrated planning for secondary cost elements, cumulative planning data entry for balance sheet accounts (see Section 3.1.4)

▶ Authorization check for profit centers (see Section 3.1.5)

▶ Drill-down report for profit centers and segments, tool for transferring Report Writer or Report Painter reports from Profit Center Accounting; use of the fields ELIMINATION PROFIT CENTER and TYPE OF ORIGIN OBJECT in reports, and line item extractors (see Section 3.1.7).

▶ Ledger group-specific posting and clearing (see Section 4.8)

▶ Conversion from G/L accounts to open item management (see Section 4.9)

The following bullets list the innovations from Enhancement Package 4 that are included in the FIN_GL_CI_2 business function:

▶ Assignment monitor for profit center (see Section 3.1.7)

▶ Enhanced standard configuration of document splitting (see Section 3.4)

▶ Separate check of posting period for postings from CO to FI, check of posting period for non-representative ledgers (see Section 3.5)

▶ Ledger group-specific document display (see Section 4.8)

▶ Wizards for customizing the document splitting (see Section 5.6)

These functional innovations in combination with the new migration scenarios offer additional good reasons to change to New G/L. In the future, both new options, parallel accounting in CO and a formal, IT-supported process of reorganization (for instance, of profit centers), will be desirable.

[+] | **Covering Enhancement Packages in this Book**

This second edition includes all functions up to and including Enhancement Package 4, which are described based on examples from both the application and from Customizing.

1.3   New General Ledger

The following sections deal with the benefits and added value of New G/L. They also briefly present the following additional functionalities:

▶ Mapping of parallel accounting via parallel ledgers

▶ Default extension of fields in the flexible totals table FAGLFLEXT

▶ Associated segment reporting options in New G/L

▶ Document splitting

▶ Real-time integration of CO into FI

1.3.1 Additional Functionality in General Ledger

New G/L in SAP ERP features a range of improvements in the classic General Ledger in SAP R/3 Enterprise. Note that these functions are not mentioned in order of importance. Figure 1.11 shows an overview of the benefits of New G/L.

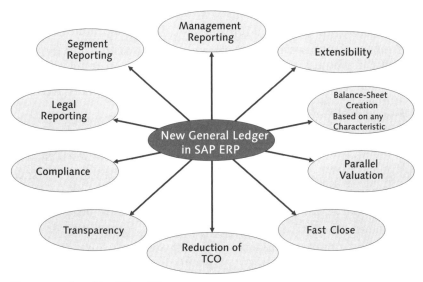

Figure 1.11 Benefits of New G/L

A look at the *architecture* will give you an initial idea of the flexibility of New G/L. The extended data structure contains new fields and optional scenarios for fulfilling external and internal reporting requirements.

Architecture

> **Presentation of Transactions**
>
> Despite the new functionality, the general structure of the transactions and reports is almost exactly the same, from the user's viewpoint, as in the classic General Ledger.

[+]

Only minor changes have been made to the interfaces of transactions and reports from SAP R/3 Enterprise and previous releases. Figure 1.12 shows an example: the balance display of G/L accounts.

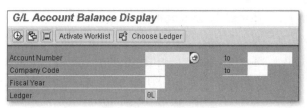

Figure 1.12 Selection Screen Interface for G/L Accounts Balance Display

User interface   When developing the system configuration, the developers also aimed at making the company-code parameter settings as recognizable as possible, in order to improve on the configuration of previous SAP R/3 releases.

1.3.2   Parallel Accounting

Transparency and disclosure requirements   To increase transparency and simplify cross-border securities transactions, the European Union (EU), among others, has decided that consolidated financial statements need to be published in accordance with International Financial Reporting Standards (IFRS). In Germany, the International Accounting Standards (IAS) and IFRS have been accepted accounting standards since 1999. These accounting standards were developed by the International Accounting Standards Board (IASB), an organization that is independent of the EU.

While most European listed companies were obliged to introduce IFRS on January 1, 2005, SAP and other European companies listed on U.S. stock exchanges received an extension until 2007. Therefore, SAP had to adhere to this standard for the first time for fiscal year 2007. SAP publishes its statements in accordance with both IFRS and U.S.-GAAP.

For the international capital and sales markets, comparable statements are becoming more and more important. IFRS consolidated financial statements are mandatory for many enterprises.

International accounting   Because no one is exempt from this trend, and individual financial statements are the basis of consolidated financial statements, it is very likely that soon all such statements will be international in nature. International accounting will not remain restricted to consolidated financial statements; it will also affect individual financial statements.

Consolidated financial statements will no longer be a matter of consolidation only. Small and mid-sized enterprises also will have to adhere to international accounting standards in the medium to long term. Moreover, the harmonization trend is now noticeable on a worldwide basis (see Figure 1.13).

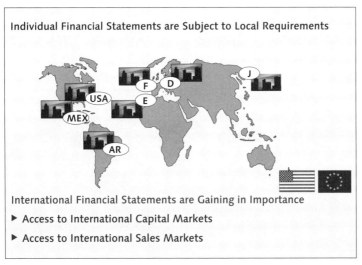

Figure 1.13 International Regulations and Standards for Financial Statements

New G/L gives users the option to map parallel accounting using parallel accounts—with which we are familiar from SAP R/3—or parallel ledgers. Both approaches—parallel accounts and parallel ledgers (not to be confused with special ledgers)—work equally well for this purpose. Users can use standard reporting for both solutions.

Parallel accounts or ledgers— equivalent solutions

Which solution is appropriate depends on the individual customer's situation. For example, in a case where the number of G/L accounts is so huge that the account is no longer an option, the ledger approach scenario in New G/L would be advisable.

If the parallel ledger approach of New G/L is used, a separate ledger is kept in New G/L for each accounting standard. Thus, multiple valuations—in accordance with the company's accounting standards, for example—can be mapped in accordance with local accounting standards and using various ledgers for taxation purposes.

Parallel ledgers

New G/L provides the functionality and flexibility needed to keep multiple ledgers within the General Ledger. These ledgers represent the display options of parallel accounting in the SAP ERP system. This approach ensures that a version of reality is encapsulated in a large but flexible ledger.

Parallel accounts

The "older" approach to parallel accounts (Figure 1.14 provides a simple illustration) is no less effective in New G/L than in the classic General Ledger. We now compare the parallel ledgers approach of New G/L to the parallel accounts approach.

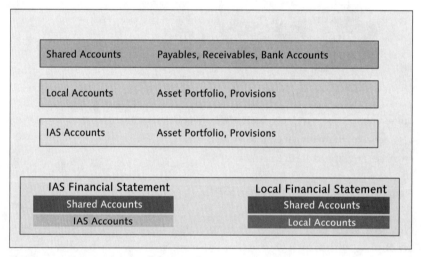

Figure 1.14 Mapping via Parallel Accounts

Local financial statement/IAS financial statement

Shared and local accounts are reported jointly as follows for a local financial statement:

▸ Joint accounts and IAS accounts are presented for the IAS financial statement.

▸ There are additional accounts for each accounting procedure. These accounts are followed by the specific postings with valuation variances for each accounting procedure.

▸ Separate retained earnings accounts also have to be created (local GAAP, US-GAAP/ IAS, joint accounts), as shown in Figure 1.15.

▶ Number assignments have to be specified for the accounts (number structure, number, or letter).

▶ An account assignment manual also has to be created.

Among other things, it is essential to keep multiple retained earnings accounts in the system (as shown in the lower part of Figure 1.15) if you want to use an accounts approach to map parallel accounting. The program for the balance carryforward then has to be re-started several times.

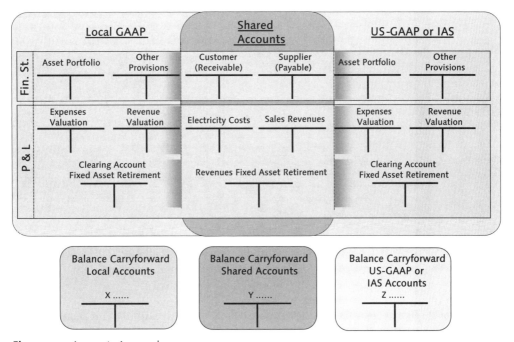

Figure 1.15 Accounts Approach

For further information on the ledger approach, see Chapter 4, Parallel Accounting—IFRS on the Advance.

1.3.3 Default Field Extension

More entities are updated in the totals table of New G/L (FAGLFLEXT) than in the classic totals table (GLT0). The new fields in New G/L are

Totals table FAGLFLEXT

COST ELEMENT, COST CENTER, PROFIT CENTER, FUNCTIONAL AREA, and SEGMENT FOR SEGMENT REPORT.

Extended data structure

If you look at the database tables (see Figure 1.16), you see how the default data structure has been significantly extended.

Classic General Ledger Totals Table GLT0		
Field	...	Short Description
...	...	...
BUKRS	...	Company Code
RYEAR	...	Fiscal Year
RACCT	...	Account Number
RBUSA	...	Business Area
...	...	...
...	...	...
...	...	...
...	...	...
...	...	...
		SE11_OLD

New General Ledger Totals Table FAGLFLEXT Some of the available fields:		
Field	...	Short Description
...	...	...
RYEAR	...	Fiscal Year
RACCT	...	Account Number
COST_ELEM	...	Cost Element
BUKRS	...	Company Code
RCNTR	...	Cost Center
PRCTR	...	Profit Center
RFAREA	...	Functional Area
RBUSA	...	Business Area
SEGMENT	...	Segment for Segment Rep.
...	...	...

Figure 1.16 Benefits in Detail—Extended Data Structure

Customer-specific fields

New G/L is extensible. Again, flexibility is crucial here; customer-specific or industry-specific fields can be incorporated, and totals for these can be updated.

Industry solutions

For industry solutions in particular—such as banking and insurance, as well as suppliers and public administration—this extensibility allows New G/L to be adapted flexibly. The example in Figure 1.17 illustrates options for an industry template for the public sector.

These new account assignment fields are available in FI G/L account postings, Materials Management (MM) inventory management, and MM purchasing, and are also updated in the CO line items.

Account assignment field and account assignment block

SAP recommends that you create the concept for your own account assignment field as early as possible, and that you make the changes in the account assignment block as well. Chapter 2, Design and Features of the Ledgers, explains how to extend the account assignment block.

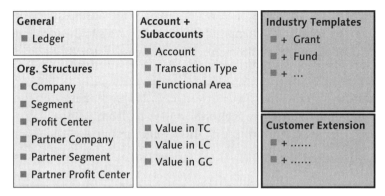

Figure 1.17 General Ledger in SAP ERP Standard Structure—Industry and Customer Extensions

1.3.4 Segment Reporting

New G/L provides the new "segment" entity for IAS and GAAP segment reporting purposes. The SEGMENT field is a standard account assignment object that enables reporting on an object level below the company code.

"Segment" entity

The aim here is to obtain a highly detailed view of business segments such as markets or products (see Figure 1.18).

Fields of activity

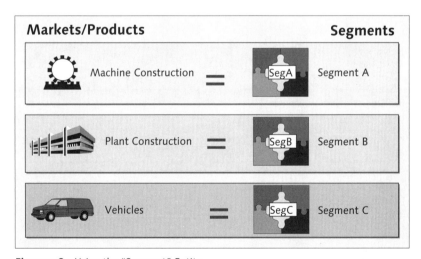

Figure 1.18 Using the "Segment" Entity

Derivation from
profit center

The segment is also available in New G/L because the business area or profit center, or both, were often used for other purposes in the past and thus had to fulfill other requirements. The segment is usually derived from the profit center, as shown in Figure 1.19.

Determining
segments
using BAdI

In the posting process, the segment can be filled in manually or the system can propose one. There is also the option of determining the segment using a Business Add-In (BAdI). The definition name of the BAdI is FAGL_DERIVE_SEGMENT.

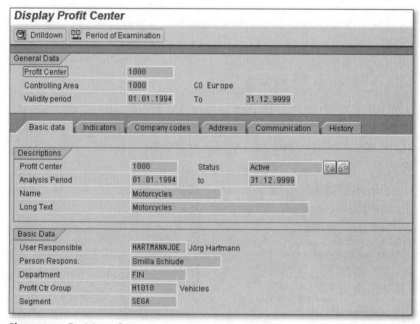

Figure 1.19 Deriving a Segment

The steps that are necessary to post, display, and evaluate the "segment" entity (see Figure 1.20) are described in Chapter 2, Design and Features of the Ledgers.

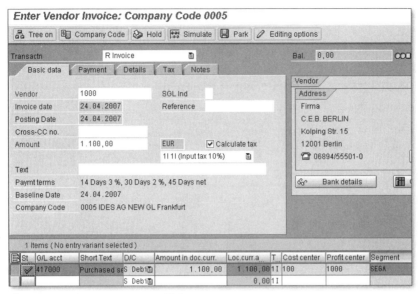

Figure 1.20 "Segment" Entity in FI Document

1.3.5 Document Online Split

In the past, it was possible to create balance sheets with a zero balance on the company code and business area levels. Profit center balance sheets could also be generated, although it was not always possible for these to have a zero balance. The new document-splitting function makes it possible for you to create balance sheets for any entity. A zero balance is then generated for the entity in question, such as a segment or profit center.

Document split

The entities that were defined in the configuration as document-splitting characteristics are projected into posting items without account assignments. See Chapter 5, Document Splitting, for details on the configuration.

Document-splitting characteristics

1.3.6 Real-Time Integration of CO into FI

Time-consuming reconciliation work between Financial Accounting (FI) and Management Accounting (CO) at the end of the period is no longer necessary because cross-entity processes in Controlling can be transferred in real time to New G/L.

Reconciliation work

Real-time integration

Real-time integration from FI to CO did exist before SAP ERP. When recording an expense item for business expenses, you have to specify a single real CO object. In the posting process, a CO document and an FI document are created. The CO document posts the costs relevant to the expense item to the real CO object (see Figure 1.21).

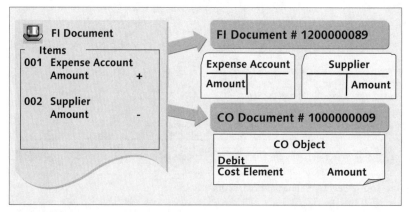

Figure 1.21 Real-Time Integration from FI to CO

Integrating in the opposite direction, from CO to FI (see Figure 1.22), was not possible in real time in previous releases. This applied, for example, to characteristics changes for processes or transactions, such as period-based allocations (assessments/distribution), manual repostings in CO, activity allocations, and the settlement of orders or projects.

Reconciliation ledger

The reconciliation ledger, which was maintained in Cost Element Accounting, always had to be used to reconcile CO with FI.

Summary standardizing entries or reconciliation postings had to be carried out per cost element or expense account over periodic program runs.

Chapter 3, Integration in Financial Accounting, uses examples to illustrate the posting process and the corresponding configuration in New G/L.

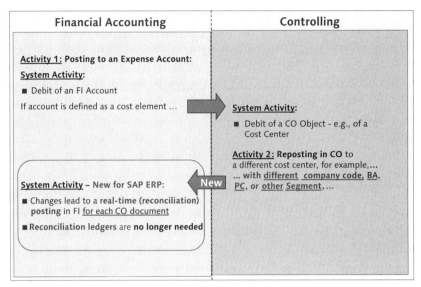

Figure 1.22 Real-Time Integration from CO to FI

1.4   Conclusion

New G/L represents a paradigm shift in Financial Accounting in SAP ERP systems. The addition of multidimensionality and customer-specific fields removes the fragmentation of previous versions. The time and effort previously required for reconciliation has become a thing of the past. Thus, using New G/L removes the need to use several separate components.

Subsequent chapters explain how to activate the various scenarios and how new G/L affects business processes.

Inventions are not always welcome — and this feeling is justified to some extent. Inventions have a right to exist not merely because they are innovations but because of the improvement they provide.

2 Design and Features of the Ledgers

New General Ledger (New G/L) has all the functions of the classic General Ledger, but it also features enhancements in the form of special ledger functions to create greater flexibility.

The following analogy illustrates this flexibility: Picture the binding of New G/L as an extendible book cover and the individual ledgers as chapters in the book. In contrast to a book with a hard cover, the extendible cover allows new chapters to be added as required. This option of adding new chapters — or ledgers — is a defining feature of New G/L. Once all of the chapters/ledgers have been put together, the result is a single thick, bound volume.

Flexibility of the General Ledger

This chapter discusses the features of the individual ledgers and the ledger groups. It also examines how the various scenarios are managed and the new "segment" entity, as well as the option of adding customer-specific fields to the coding block.

2.1 Features of the Ledgers

The principle of using different ledgers to meet different requirements was implemented in SAP R/3. These ledgers comprised the classic General Ledger (General Ledger 00) for legal requirements, the cost-of-sales ledger (Ledger 0F) for cost-of-sales accounting, the profit center ledger (Ledger 8A) for management and segment reporting, and other special ledgers for multi-dimensional, customer-specific requirements. The number of individual ledgers was reduced with the release of SAP ERP, which also alleviated the problem of reconciling different sets of figures.

Separate ledgers

This section deals with defining, assigning, and posting to the leading ledger and the non-leading ledgers. Using several ledgers allows you to apply different accounting standards. Using non-leading ledgers allows you to use different fiscal year variants within the same company code.

2.1.1 Basis of the Ledgers

Standard totals table FAGLFLEXT

Ledgers for saving and analyzing values are based on a totals table. As a rule, SAP recommends that you use the standard totals table FAGLFLEXT (the industry solution for SAP for Public Sector uses FMGLFLEXT, for example).

Ledgers for General Ledger accounting

You begin by defining the ledgers you want to use for General Ledger accounting in the Customizing settings via the navigation path: FINANCIAL ACCOUNTING (NEW) • FINANCIAL ACCOUNTING GLOBAL SETTINGS (NEW) • LEDGERS • LEDGER • DEFINE LEDGERS FOR GENERAL LEDGER ACCOUNTING.

The database table in Figure 2.1 shows the standard extension of the data structure of this table.

Classic General Ledger Totals Table GLT0 Selected fields available:			New General Ledger Totals Table FAGLFLEXT Selected fields available:		
Field	...	Short Description	Field	...	Short Description
...	...	...	...	...	...
BUKRS	...	Company Code	RYEAR	...	Fiscal Year
RYEAR	...	Fiscal Year	RACCT	...	Account Number
RACCT	...	Account Number	COST_ELEM	...	Cost Element
RBUSA	...	Business Area	BUKRS	...	Company Code
...	...	...	RCNTR	...	Cost Center
...	...	...	PRCTR	...	Profit Center
...	...	...	RFAREA	...	Functional Area
...	...	...	RBUSA	...	Business Area
...	...	...	SEGMENT	...	Segment f. Segm. Report
			...	...	...
		SE11_OLD			SE11_OLD

Figure 2.1 FAGLFLEXT Totals Table

In contrast to the classic General Ledger, the FAGLFLEXT table contains new fields, including PROFIT CENTER, SEGMENT FOR SEGMENT REPORT, and FUNCTIONAL AREA. Customer-specific enhancements are also permitted. In addition, a distinction is made between leading and non-leading ledgers.

2.1.2 Leading Ledger

In New G/L, there is one leading ledger for each client that is valid for all company codes. An important decision you need to make is which accounting standard to use in the leading ledger. This assignment cannot be deactivated once it has been defined.

One leading ledger per client

You can define only one ledger as the leading ledger (see Figure 2.2). SAP provides the leading ledger 0L as standard.

Leading ledger 0L

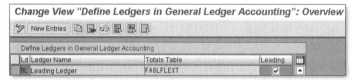

Figure 2.2 Defining a Leading Ledger

Similarly, Figure 2.3 shows the IAS ledger in client 800 as an example of a leading ledger for company codes 1000, 2000, 3000, and 4000.

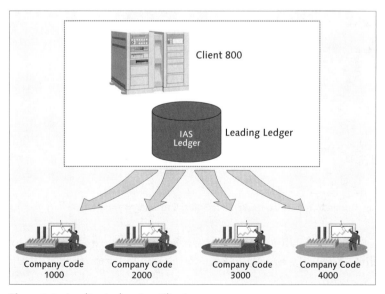

Figure 2.3 Leading Ledger in a Client

You define the leading ledger in the IMG via the following Customizing navigation path: FINANCIAL ACCOUNTING (NEW) • FINANCIAL ACCOUNTING GLOBAL SETTINGS (NEW) • LEDGERS • LEDGER • DEFINE LEDGERS FOR GENERAL LEDGER ACCOUNTING.

Accounting standard

The leading ledger normally follows the same accounting standard used to draw up the consolidated financial statements. For more detailed information, see Chapter 4, Parallel Accounting — IFRS on the Advance.

Integration with subsidiary ledgers

The leading ledger is integrated with all subsidiary ledgers (see Figure 2.4). For example, document splitting is based on integration with accounts payable accounting and accounts receivable accounting (FI-AP or FI-AR) or Asset Accounting (FI-AA), where the post-capitalization of cash discounts on assets occurs in real time.

If parallel accounting is mapped with the accounts approach, only one ledger is normally used, that is, the leading ledger. As an alternative to the accounts approach, you can use the ledger approach in New G/L.

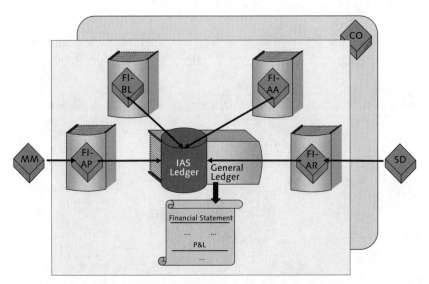

Figure 2.4 Integration of the Leading Ledger and Subsidiary Ledgers

There is thus one leading ledger, which by default posts its values to Controlling (and is the only ledger to do so).

Therefore, only the leading ledger is integrated with CO and only values from the leading ledger are sent to CO. So far, parallel valuation approaches can be mapped in CO only if you use the accounts approach described in Section 1.3.2, Parallel Accounting.

A similar principle applies to integration with Asset Accounting (FI-AA). The leading area in Asset Accounting (depreciation area 01) must be posted to the leading ledger (see Figure 2.5).

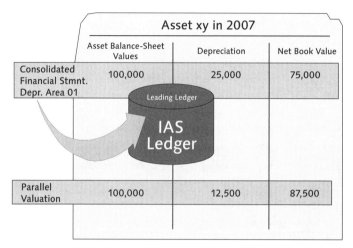

Figure 2.5 FI-AA—Depreciation Area 01 Posts to the Leading Ledger

We will now explain the settings you need to make for the leading ledger. In each company code, the settings made for the following parameters are automatically applied to the leading ledger:

▶ Currencies

▶ Fiscal year variant

▶ Posting period variant

These three parameters are discussed in more detail in the following sections.

Currencies

In New G/L, three additional (local) currencies can be mapped to the transaction currency. The leading ledger uses the (additional) local currencies assigned to the company code. For example, the leading ledger and company code shown in Figure 2.6 have a company code currency (the Japanese Yen), a group currency (the Euro) as a second local currency, and a hard currency (the U.S. dollar) as a third currency.

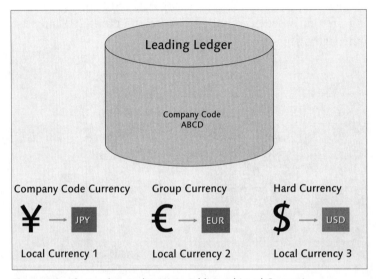

Figure 2.6 The Leading Ledger Uses Additional Local Currencies

Currencies of the leading ledger

You define the currencies of the leading ledger in Customizing via the navigation path: Financial Accounting (New) • Financial Accounting Global Settings (New) • Ledgers • Ledger • Define Currencies of Leading Ledger. Here, you specify the currency to be used in the leading ledger. The following settings must be made for each company code:

▶ **Local currency 1 (as company code currency)**
This is defined in the company code settings.

▶ **Additional local currencies**
You can define up to three additional local currencies, which are used for each company code in parallel with the first local currency.

▶ **Parallel currencies**
For the additional local currencies, you must define the currency type and the exchange rate type for each company code (see Figure 2.7).

The *currency type* reflects the "role" of the parallel currency. We can distinguish between the following currency types: Currency type

- ▶ Company code currency
- ▶ Group currency
- ▶ Hard currency
- ▶ Index-based currency
- ▶ Global company currency

The *exchange rate type* determines which exchange rate defined in the system is to be used to calculate additional amount fields. In the example shown in Figure 2.7, this is exchange rate type "M, STANDARD TRANSLATION AT AVERAGE RATE." Exchange rate type

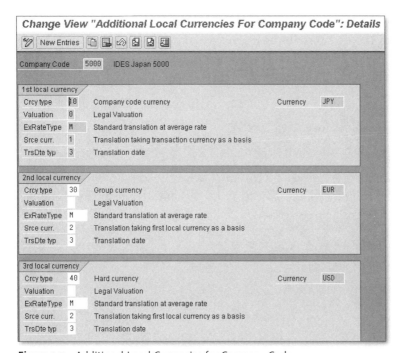

Figure 2.7 Additional Local Currencies for Company Code

You can define various *exchange rates* with different exchange rate types for each currency pair. Different exchange rates may be used for the following purposes: Exchange rates

- ▸ Valuation

- ▸ Conversion

- ▸ Currency translation

- ▸ Planning

Exchange rate types M, G, and B

For the first local currency, you can select currency type M (average rate), G (buying rate), B (bank selling rate), or another rate type of your choice.

Base currency for currency translation

This means that three local currencies plus a transaction currency are available for balance sheet evaluations. In classic General Ledger accounting, this was only possible with an additional special ledger.

Fiscal year variant and posting period variant

After you have defined the currencies as the first parameter for the leading ledger, you must configure the remaining two parameters for this ledger, namely, the fiscal year variant and the posting period variant. Here, you apply the three-step variant principle, familiar from SAP R/3:

1. Define variant

2. Define values for the variant

3. Assign objects to the variant

Variant principle

The *variant principle* is a procedure whereby certain properties are assigned to one or more objects in the system. It applies, for example, to the following three variants:

- ▸ Fiscal year variant

- ▸ Posting period variant

- ▸ Field status variant

Fiscal year variant

The first two of these variants are discussed in greater detail in the following paragraphs. The field status variant is addressed at the end of Section 2.2.5, Segmentation Scenario. We begin by looking at the *fiscal year variant* for the leading ledger.

In order for business processes to be assigned to various periods, you need to define a fiscal year with posting periods. In doing so, you must define the number of posting periods and the start and end dates of these periods and special periods. The fiscal year variant thus simply defines the number of periods as well as the start and end dates of these periods. In this way, the fiscal year is defined as a variant and the company code or company codes are assigned to the variant.

The fiscal year variant does not specify whether a posting period is open or closed. This data is managed in a separate SAP table and defined in the *posting period variant*.

Posting period variant

To prevent documents from being posted in incorrect posting periods, the relevant posting periods can be defined as closed, and the correct posting periods defined as open in the posting period variant.

The leading ledger uses the fiscal year variant and the posting period variant of the company code. Figure 2.8 shows the assignment of a fiscal year variant that corresponds to one calendar year to the IAS ledger.

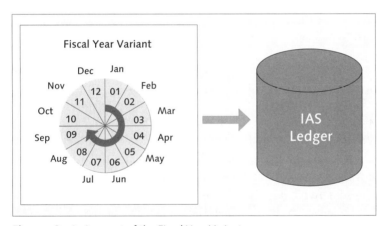

Figure 2.8 Assignment of the Fiscal Year Variant

Figure 2.9 shows the assignment of posting period variant 0001 to various ledgers.

Variants are assigned in Customizing via the navigation path: FINANCIAL ACCOUNTING (NEW) • FINANCIAL ACCOUNTING GLOBAL SETTINGS (NEW) • LEDGERS • FISCAL YEAR AND POSTING PERIODS. Exceptions to this principle are discussed in Chapter 3, Integration in Financial Accounting.

Assigning variants

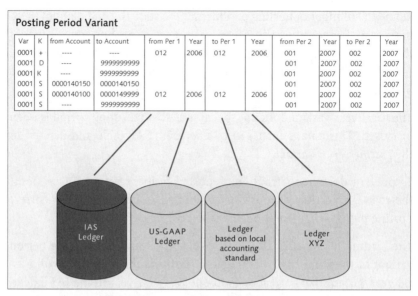

Posting Period Variant

Var	K	from Account	to Account	from Per 1	Year	to Per 1	Year	from Per 2	Year	to Per 2	Year
0001	+	----	----	012	2006	012	2006	001	2007	002	2007
0001	D	----	9999999999					001	2007	002	2007
0001	K	----	9999999999					001	2007	002	2007
0001	S	0000140150	0000140150					001	2007	002	2007
0001	S	0000140100	0000149999	012	2006	012	2006	001	2007	002	2007
0001	S	----	9999999999					001	2007	002	2007

Figure 2.9 Assignment of the Posting Period Variant

This feature allows you considerable freedom with regard to the fiscal year variant and posting year variant. You are restricted only by the use of Asset Accounting (see SAP Note 844029).

Representative ledger

One special feature must be noted in relation to the open and closed posting periods in the representative ledger. The representative ledger can be seen as the ledger with the most senior ranking within a group of ledgers. A ledger group combines ledgers that are to be handled in the same way in terms of functions and processes. If the posting period of the representative ledger is open, postings are also made in all other ledgers in the ledger group to which the representative ledger belongs, even if the periods in these ledgers are closed. The representative ledger is discussed in detail in Section 2.1.6, Defining Ledger Groups.

2.1.3 Non-Leading Ledgers

The non-leading ledgers are used as parallel ledgers together with the leading ledger. You do not need parallel ledgers to map the GLT0, GLFUNCT, and GLPCT totals tables you may be using. In the future, you will be able to combine these tables into a single ledger in New G/L.

Complete ledgers

Parallel ledgers are always managed as complete ledgers. This means that all postings without valuation variances are shown in the evaluations for the leading and non-leading ledgers.

Valuation postings that do not apply to a specific accounting standard are explicitly made in the ledger defined for that purpose. This subject will be discussed again later on in this book (section 2.1.4, Data Concept) when we describe the data concept.

Parallel ledgers

Parallel ledgers are ledgers managed in parallel within a general ledger. These can be used to apply different accounting standards, such as IAS/IFRS or U.S.-GAAP (see Figure 2.10).

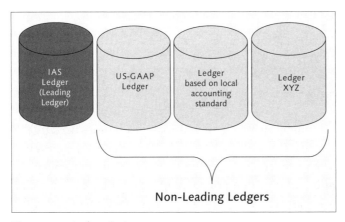

Figure 2.10 Ledger Features

You can define the non-leading ledgers (see Figure 2.11) in the Implementation Guide (IMG) via the path: FINANCIAL ACCOUNTING (NEW) • FINANCIAL ACCOUNTING GLOBAL SETTINGS (NEW) • LEDGERS • LEDGER • DEFINE LEDGERS FOR GENERAL LEDGER ACCOUNTING.

Ld	Ledger Name	Totals Table	Leading
0L	Leading Ledger	FAGLFLEXT	☑
BZ		FAGLFLEXT	☐
GF	demo	FAGLFLEXT	☐
L5	IAS	FAGLFLEXT	☐
L6	local	FAGLFLEXT	☐

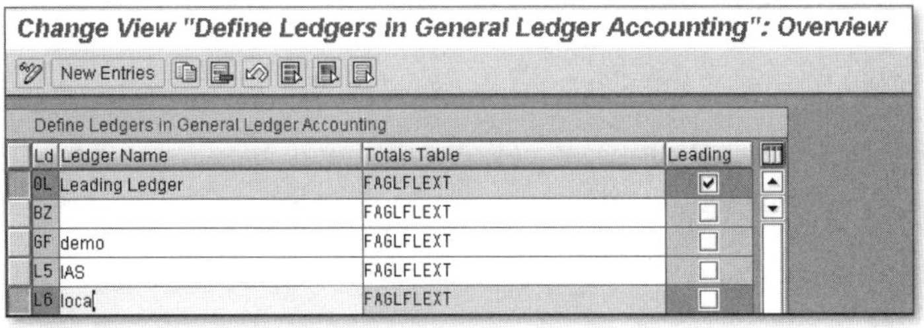

Figure 2.11 Defining Non-Leading Ledgers

Activating non-leading ledgers However, unlike leading ledgers, non-leading ledgers must also be activated for each company code. You can do this in the IMG via the path: FINANCIAL ACCOUNTING (NEW) • FINANCIAL ACCOUNTING GLOBAL SETTINGS (NEW) • LEDGERS • LEDGER • DEFINE AND ACTIVATE NON-LEADING LEDGERS. In this IMG activity, you implement the settings shown in Figure 2.12 for the non-leading ledgers for each required company code.

This setting activates the required non-leading ledger for the respective company code. Figure 2.12 shows the non-leading ledger L6, for example.

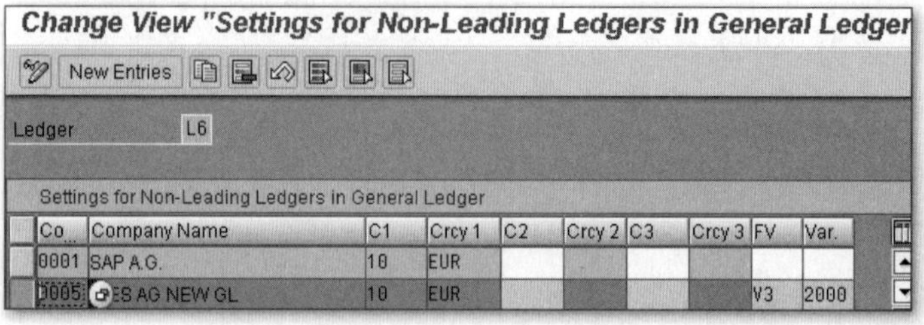

Figure 2.12 Settings for Non-Leading Ledgers

Currencies of the non-leading ledgers You can define additional currencies that deviate from those used by the leading ledger. The currency of the leading ledger — that is, the currency of the relevant company code — is always used as the first currency. As a second and third currency of a non-leading ledger, only use currency types that you have already assigned to the relevant company code for the leading ledger may be used.

You can define a fiscal year variant that differs from the leading ledger. If you do not specify a fiscal year variant, the fiscal year variant of the company code is automatically used. This means that a company code can have various fiscal year variants. For example, the leading ledger may use fiscal year variant K4 (fiscal year corresponds to the calendar year), while the non-leading ledger uses fiscal year variant V3 (a fiscal year does not correspond to the calendar year). This option is also available in the special ledgers but not in the classic General Ledger.

In addition to an alternative fiscal year variant, you can also define a posting period variant that differs from the leading ledger.

Tax assessment New G/L also allows you to map tax assessments in a separate, non-leading ledger.

If you want to use this function, note that you must specify the ledger containing the tax data for data extraction with DART (see also SAP Note 873125 from 07.08.09). Before you can use this function, you must implement the corrections and follow the manual steps in this Note.

DART data extraction

[+]

Required DART Version

To implement the corrections, you must first install DART Version 2.4.

In the selection screen of the extraction program, you can select a ledger from which the data is to be extracted. If you do not explicitly select a ledger in the selection screen—that is, no alternative ledger is selected—the leading ledger is always used for the evaluation.

If you also use the function for account balancing in segments in New G/L, certain documents may be split to ensure a balance of zero within the segments.

Postings are made to special clearing accounts for these documents. Because these clearing accounts are also selected when you use DART, but the technical document line items from document splitting are not selected, a difference will appear in the control totals. You can ignore this difference if the total of the differences amounts to zero. Each of the differences is expressed between the item total and the account balance, but in most cases differences result in a total of zero.

2.1.4 Data Concept

Due to the high degree of flexibility in New G/L, it is particularly important to design the new general ledger itself and the project associated with its implementation in such a way that New G/L can fulfill all of your business and technical requirements and achieve its full potential.

Design of New G/L

Both the scenarios and fields to be mapped and the number of individual and totals records in each table and ledger are key factors in a successful and sustainable design.

The BKPF (document header) and BSEG (document line items/item) tables—see Figure 2.13—are also available in New G/L, with slightly modified functions. Additional fields include:

Tables BKPF and BSEG

- Ledger group in BKPF

- Segment in BSEG

Individual transactions are reflected in the following three tables:

- BKPF (document header file)

- BSEG (document segment file—leading)

- BSEG_ADD (document segment file—non-leading)

The following section explains how these tables are used. Documents that are relevant for the leading ledger are written to the BKPF and BSEG tables (see Figure 2.13).

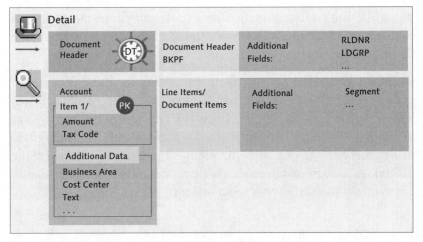

Figure 2.13   Table Names—Document Header and Document Item

Ledger group   Documents without valuation differences are posted to all ledgers (see Figure 2.14). If there are no valuation variances—for example, if the LEDGER GROUP field remains blank—the documents are posted to all ledgers. The document header data in BKPF and the document line items in BSEG are updated.

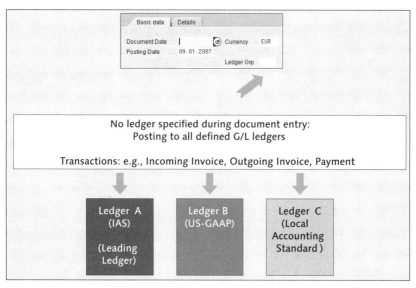

Figure 2.14 Posting to All Ledgers

Field RLDNR

The value "Initial" in the RLDNR field in the document header (see Figure 2.15) indicates that this document is relevant for all ledgers.

BKPF							
	BUKRS	**BELNR**	**GJAHR**		**RLDNR**	**LDGRP**	**BSTAT**
	0001	0017	2003		___	___	___

BSEG					BSEG_ADD			
	BUKRS	**BELNR**	**GJAHR**	**BUZEI**	**BUKRS**	**BELNR**	**GJAHR**	**BUZEI**
	0001	0017	2003	001				
	0001	0017	2003	002				
	0001	0017	2003	003				

Figure 2.15 No Valuation Variances—Posting to All Ledgers

However, if the data is posted only to the leading ledger, the ledger information is stored in BKPF. The value 0L in the RLDNR field in the document header (see Figure 2.16) indicates that this document is relevant only for the leading ledger.

BKPF							
	BUKRS	BELNR	GJAHR		RLDNR	LDGRP	BSTAT
	0001	0017	2003		0L	___	___

BSEG					BSEG_ADD			
	BUKRS	BELNR	GJAHR	BUZEI	BUKRS	BELNR	GJAHR	BUZEI
	0001	0017	2003	001				
	0001	0017	2003	002				
	0001	0017	2003	003				

Figure 2.16 Valuation Variance—Posting to Leading Ledger 0L Only

The next section explains the document structure when additional ledgers are used.

Table BSEG_ ADD—Posting to additional ledgers

The BSEG_ADD table (see Figure 2.17) is updated only if additional ledgers are used and if the documents to be posted are not relevant for the leading ledger. However, BSEG_ADD does not contain any document-splitting information. The table is irrelevant from this point of view.

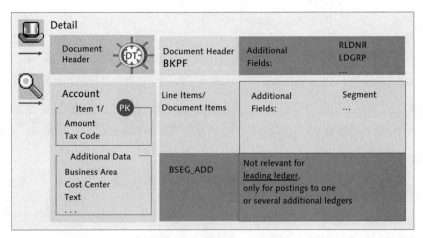

Figure 2.17 BSEG_ADD—for Posting to Additional Ledgers

Ledger group

In a standard posting transaction, which is merely "enhanced" with a field for entering the ledger (or, to be precise, the ledger group, see Figure 2.18), you explicitly specify which ledger is to be filled during posting.

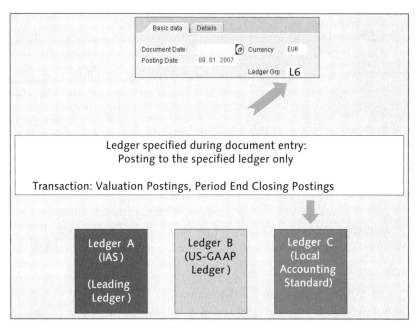

Figure 2.18 Posting to a Single Ledger

The value L6 in the RLDNR field in the document header (see the example shown in Figure 2.19) indicates that this document is relevant for non-leading ledger L6. In this case, values are written exclusively to table BSEG_ADD. The BSEG table is not filled at the same time. In the document header, this document status in the field (BSTAT) is indicated with the entry "L" — posting to a non-leading ledger.

BKPF					RLDNR	LDGRP	BSTAT
	BUKRS	BELNR	GJAHR		L6	_____	L
	0001	0017	2003				

BSEG					BSEG_ADD			
	BUKRS	BELNR	GJAHR	BUZEI	BUKRS	BELNR	GJAHR	BUZEI
					0001	0017	2003	001
					0001	0017	2003	002
					0001	0017	2003	003

Figure 2.19 Valuation Variance — Posting to Non-Leading Ledger L6

Principle of the
leading ledger

As you can see, using an additional ledger does not automatically mean that additional documents are saved. If the valuation basis is identical, the storage technique that follows the leading-ledger principle is very economical, which offers an advantage over the accounts approach. Even so, evaluations are designed as though one complete ledger was selected in each case. Documents are collected from the three tables in the background and displayed together in a unified way. In the FAGL-FLEXT standard totals table, individual postings are displayed together in aggregated form for later evaluations.

Transactions
FB50L/FB01L—
Authorizations

An authorization for posting transactions is granted only to experts with the requisite specialized background knowledge in order to ensure that the correct postings are made in the correct ledgers. Examples are FB50L (Enter G/L Account Document for Ledger Group), Enjoy transaction, or FB01L (Enter General Posting for Ledger Group).

The next section examines how the system responds to postings in special periods if you use (at least) one other ledger in addition to the leading ledger in New G/L and if this ledger has a different fiscal year variant that contains special periods.

Special periods

If you post to a special period and the period calculated from the posting date is the last "normal" period in the fiscal year, then values are similarly posted to a special period in the additional ledger.

The first special period in the fiscal year variant of the leading ledger is transferred to the first special period in the fiscal year variant of the non-leading ledger; the second special period is posted to the second, and so on. If there are not enough special periods in the additional ledger, postings are made to the last special period available.

[Ex]

Postings in Special Periods

In the company code (and thus also the leading ledger), you have fiscal year variant K4 (see Figure 2.20) with periods corresponding to calendar months and four additional special periods. In the additional ledger, you have a fiscal year variant with 53 periods as calendar weeks and two additional special periods.

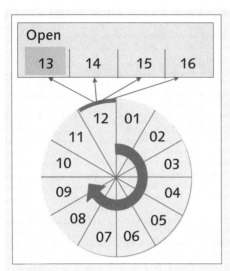

Figure 2.20 Special Periods in Fiscal Year Variant K4

If a posting is made to period 13 (with a posting date of December 31), this is posted in period 54 in the additional ledger, and periods 14, 15, and 16 are copied to period 55. However, if you had a non-calendar fiscal year variant (such as V3 in Figure 2.21) in the additional ledger, this posting would not be copied to a special period because the posting date of December 31 falls in period 9 rather than in the last normal period (12) of fiscal year variant V3.

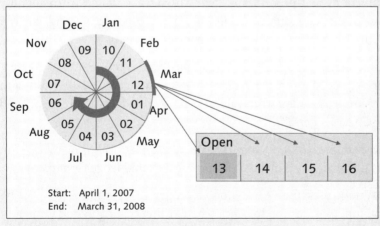

Figure 2.21 Non-Calendar Fiscal Year Variant V3

2.1.5 Changes to the Definition and Assignment of the Ledgers

Fixed valuation view
While you can add new, non-leading ledgers, you are not permitted to change the definition of the ledgers from *leading* to *non-leading* or from non-leading to leading. In contrast to other applications (Controlling, Asset Accounting, and so on), the leading ledger represents the fixed valuation view (see Section 2.1.2, Leading Ledger).

SL/profit center ledger versus ledger in New G/L
Subsequent changes to the ledgers of New General Ledger (unlike the special ledger or the profit center ledger) are not planned. Auditing is required.

Audit requirement
As a result, careful consideration must be given to the possible business effects of any changes made in the Customizing settings of New G/L in terms of documents that have already been posted.

2.1.6 Defining Ledger Groups

For each ledger you create, a ledger group with the same name is automatically generated. You can change the name of the ledger group, which is simply copied from the ledger.

Combining ledgers
A ledger group is a collection of ledgers used for joint processing within the functions and processes of general ledger accounting. To simplify the use of the individual functions in general ledger accounting, you can combine any number of ledgers into a ledger group.

Posting via ledger group
Creating ledger groups allows you to post values to more than one ledger in one posting. In the example shown in Figure 2.22, a posting to ledger group B updates the values in the two ledgers "IAS ledger" and "U.S.-GAAP ledger."

If, for example, IAS/IFRS and U.S.-GAAP are identical in many cases in terms of valuation, it makes sense to use a shared ledger group.

Representative ledger
The system uses the representative ledger to determine the posting period for a posting and to check whether this posting period is open. If the posting period for the representative ledger is open, the system posts to all ledgers in the ledger group. However, when the relevant ledgers are posted, their individual fiscal year variants are taken into account in each case.

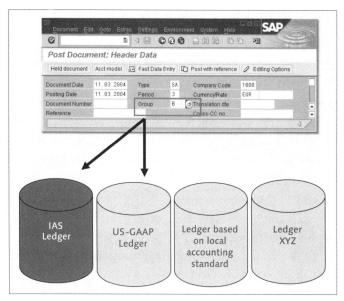

Figure 2.22   Posting to Ledger Group B

Open Posting Period of the Representative Ledger   **[!]**

In order to avoid misunderstanding, it is worth repeating our comment about the posting period variant for the representative ledger. If the posting period of the representative ledger is open, postings are also made to all other ledgers in same ledger group, even if the periods in these ledgers are closed.

You define your ledger groups by using the Customizing path: FINANCIAL ACCOUNTING (NEW) • FINANCIAL ACCOUNTING GLOBAL SETTINGS (NEW) • LEDGERS • LEDGER • DEFINE LEDGER GROUP (see Figure 2.23).

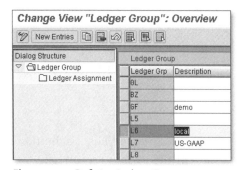

Figure 2.23   Defining Ledger Groups

The following configuration options are available:

▸ **Select the leading ledger as the representative ledger**
If the leading ledger is contained in the ledger group, you must select the leading ledger as the representative ledger.

▸ **Assign a representative ledger**
If the leading ledger is not contained in the ledger group, you must assign one of the ledgers to be the representative ledger (see Figure 2.24). If the ledger group contains only one ledger, this ledger is also the representative ledger.

▸ **Check the selection of the representative ledger**
If the ledger group contains more than one ledger, a check is performed when posting occurs by means of the fiscal year variant of the company code to determine whether the representative ledger of the ledger group has been selected correctly.

▸ **Fiscal year variant of the representative ledger**
If a fiscal year variant that differs from the company code is defined in all ledgers of the ledger group, you can select any ledger as the representative ledger.

If the same fiscal year variant defined for the company code is also defined for one of the ledgers in the ledger group, this ledger must be selected as the representative ledger.

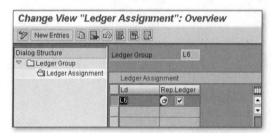

Figure 2.24 Assigning the Representative Ledger

2.2 Scenarios

The earlier sections have described general settings for ledger definition. You can find a more detailed discussion of the various scenarios in the following sections.

2.2.1 Defining and Assigning Scenarios for Ledgers

You can use scenarios to define which fields in a ledger are to be updated during posting. Figure 2.25 shows the standard scenarios provided by SAP. You cannot define your own scenarios, but you can use customer-specific fields (for more details, see Section 2.3, Customer Fields).

Scenarios

Separate data sources (for example, in the form of separate ledgers when using the special ledger approach) are no longer required to map the various scenarios. You will find the available scenarios in Customizing via the path: FINANCIAL ACCOUNTING (NEW) • FINANCIAL ACCOUNTING GLOBAL SETTINGS (NEW) • LEDGERS • FIELDS • DISPLAY SCENARIOS FOR GENERAL LEDGER ACCOUNTING.

A single data source

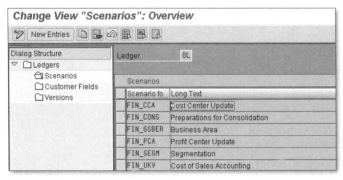

Figure 2.25 Assigning Scenarios

With the fields updated in the scenarios, you can fulfill various business requirements, for example, using Cost-of-Sales Accounting or segment reporting to produce a P&L statement.

Scenarios for New G/L accounting

You do not require a ledger for each scenario; it is not necessary to define additional (non-leading) ledgers in order to assign additional scenarios.

You can assign one or more scenarios to a ledger. All six standard scenarios can be assigned to the same ledger. Figure 2.25 shows an example of a case where all available scenarios are assigned to the 0L ledger.

Assigning a scenario to a ledger

This means, for example, that the following scenarios provided as standard by SAP may only be relevant for you in one IAS/IFRS and/or one U.S.-GAAP ledger:

▶ Segmentation (FIN_SEGM, updates the SEGMENT, PARTNER SEGMENT, PROFIT CENTER fields)

▶ Cost-of-Sales Accounting (FIN_UKV, updates the SENDER FUNCTIONAL AREA and RECEIVER FUNCTIONAL AREA fields)

Example of a totals table The following example is designed to help you understand the entries in the totals table.

The independent business transactions that are posted to account 861000 for provisions in period 12. Tables 2.1 and 2.2 show the number of data records for two different applications.

Application 1 (Table 2.1): There are no variances for ledgers 0L, L5, and L6. Identical scenarios are assigned to all ledgers.

Ledger	Fiscal Year	Period	Account	Amount	Profit Center	Segment
0L	2010	12	861000	10,000	3333	A
L5	2010	12	861000	10,000	3333	A
L6	2010	12	861000	10,000	3333	A
0L	2010	12	861000	7,500	4444	B
L5	2010	12	861000	7,500	4444	B
L6	2010	12	861000	7,500	4444	B
0L	2010	12	861000	13,000	5555	C
L5	2010	12	861000	13,000	5555	C
L6	2010	12	861000	13,000	5555	C

Table 2.1 Number of Table Entries—9

Application 2 (Table 2.2): There are no valuation variances for ledgers 0L, L5, and L6. Ledgers L5 and L6 are not assigned the *Profit Center* or *Segment* scenarios.

Ledger	Fiscal Year	Period	Account	Amount	Profit Center	Segment
0L	2010	12	861000	10,000	3333	A
0L	2010	12	861000	7,500	4444	B
0L	2010	12	861000	13,000	5555	C
L5	2010	12	861000	30,500		
L6	2010	12	861000	30,500		

Table 2.2 Number of Table Entries—5

Well-designed totals tables are essential for optimizing the performance of evaluations. The relevant fields and characteristics can be updated in the database tables only if a scenario is assigned to a ledger. Fewer fields to be transferred results in a higher degree of compression. Ledgers with a minimum number of scenarios normally generate fewer totals records, which in turn results in faster access for evaluations.

Performance

You can assign both scenarios and customer-specific fields (see Figure 2.26) as an IMG activity in Customizing via the path: FINANCIAL ACCOUNTING (NEW) • FINANCIAL ACCOUNTING BASIC SETTINGS (NEW) • LEDGERS • FIELDS • ASSIGN SCENARIOS AND CUSTOMER FIELDS TO LEDGERS.

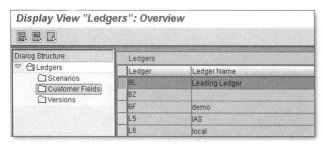

Figure 2.26 Assigning Customer-Specific Fields to Ledgers

2.2.2 Scenario Views: Data Entry View and General Ledger View

If New G/L is activated, a financial accounting document always has two views:

Two views

▶ Data entry view

▶ General ledger view

Data entry view The *data entry view* shows a document as it is normally displayed or entered in accounts receivable or accounts payable accounting or in Asset Accounting.

Compared to SAP ERP, with the New G/L, no changes have been made in terms of document entry or functions. The example below is based on the posting of an expense for services paid for in cash. The expense is posted to cost center 1000. The posting record is shown in Table 2.3:

Itm	PK	Account	Amount	Currency	Tx	Cost Center
1	40	Purchased services	50	EUR	1I	1000
2	50	Petty cash	55	EUR		
3	40	Input tax	5	EUR	1I	

Table 2.3 Expense Posting for Services Paid for (in Cash)

The data entry view is shown in Figure 2.27.

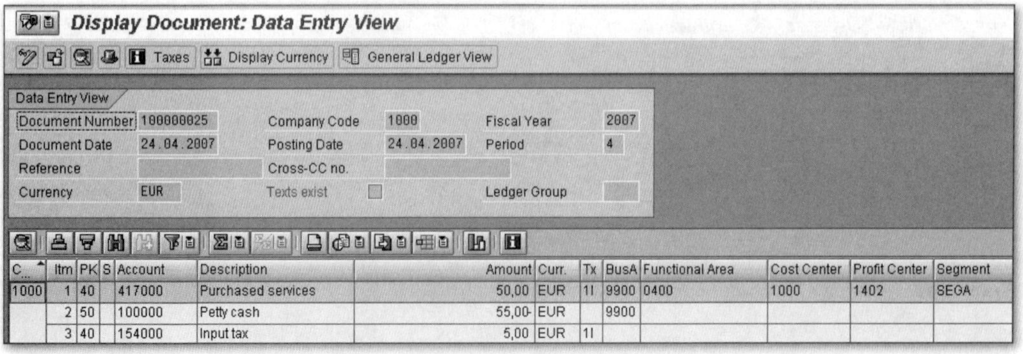

Figure 2.27 Data Entry View of a Financial Accounting Document

The interdependencies between the account assignments have also remained the same as in the data entry view. The PURCHASED SERVICES account (for example, account 417000) in Figure 2.27 is defined in CO as a primary cost element and therefore requires a cost-accounting-relevant accounting assignment (to cost center 1000 in Figure 2.27) when a posting document is entered.

Figure 2.28 shows how the profit center, business area, and functional area are derived from the CO object (for example, cost center 1000).

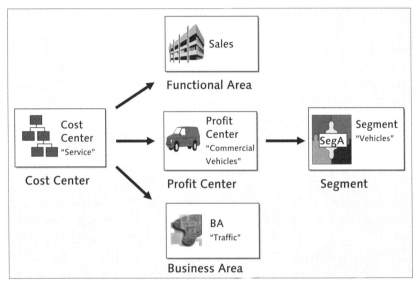

Figure 2.28 Cost Center, Business Area, Functional Area, and Segment

The only change in New G/L is that a segment can now be derived from the profit center (see also Figure 2.28). We will discuss segments in more detail below.

In contrast to the data entry view (the view shown when an accountant posts a document), the *general ledger view* shows only the elements of a document that are relevant for the general ledger. In the general ledger view, the document is shown not only in the leading ledger but in the non-leading ledgers as well (provided that it is posted to these; see Section 2.1.4, Data Concept).

General ledger view

Figure 2.29 shows the OTHER LEDGER button. This button allows you to display non-leading parallel ledgers from the general ledger view.

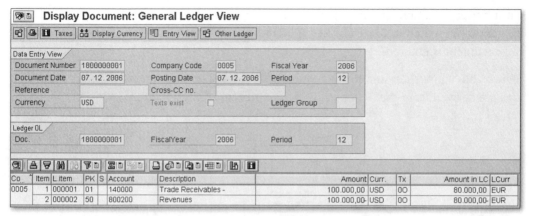

Figure 2.29 General Ledger View of Financial Accounting Document — Other Ledger

"Business Area" scenario (FIN_GSBER)

What does this general ledger view look like when the *Cost Center Update* (FIN_CCA) and *Business Area* (FIN_GSBER) scenarios are assigned?

The general ledger view of a financial accounting document with an assignment to these two scenarios shows account assignment to cost center 1000 and business area 9900. Because the *Cost Center Update* and *Business Area* scenarios are assigned to the leading ledger 0L, these two entities are written to the general ledger and displayed in the corresponding general ledger view. Figure 2.30 shows how the general ledger is updated. Business area 9900 is derived from the master record of cost center 1000.

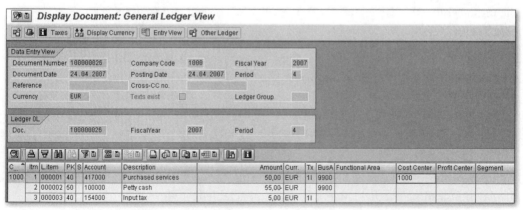

Figure 2.30 General Ledger View with Assignment of "Business Area" and "Cost Center Update" Scenarios to Ledger 0L

Other scenarios, such as *Profit Center Update* (FIN_PCA), *Segmentation* (FIN_SEGM), or *Cost-of-Sales Accounting* (FIN_UKV) are not assigned to ledger 0L and therefore are not displayed.

If the *Segmentation* scenario is assigned to another ledger, such as ledger ZZ, the general ledger view (ledger ZZ) appears as shown in Figure 2.31.

"Segmentation" scenario FIN_SEGM

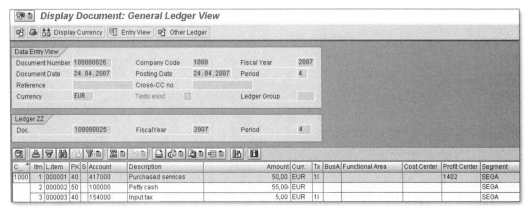

Figure 2.31 General Ledger View with Assignment of "Segmentation" Scenario to Ledger ZZ

The *Segmentation* scenario (FIN_SEGM) involves an update of the SEGMENT, PARTNER SEGMENT, and PROFIT CENTER fields. Profit Center 1402 is derived from the master record of cost center 1000, while segment A is, in turn, derived from the master record of Profit Center 1402.

Now that we have shown how documents are entered, the following sections discuss each of the individual scenarios in detail.

2.2.3 "Business Area" Scenario

The business area serves both as the company code and as a unit for external reporting for a company. The fields or industries in which a company operates can be created as individual business areas in the system in order to provide an additional evaluation level.

External reporting

Responsibility for business areas is generally shared among several company codes, for example, for lines of business or divisions. To produce

Business area for fields of activity/ industries

a business area financial statement or P&L statement, all objects from Controlling (cost center, orders, sales orders, and so on), from Logistics (for example, material master record), and Asset Accounting are assigned to the relevant business areas.

This assignment is shown in Figure 2.32, in which the PLANT CONSTRUCTION business area is assigned to the SERVICE cost center, the TRADE FAIR internal order, the material master, the sales order, and the asset from Plant and Equipment.

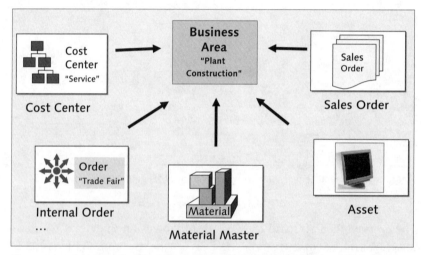

Figure 2.32 Assignment of Cost Center, Sales Order, Material Master, and Asset to Business Area

Figure 2.33 shows that the external accounting evaluations (financial statement and P&L statement) are also based on the differentiation of business areas.

Cross-company code reporting
It is particularly important to note that business areas as cross-client characteristics are essentially independent of company codes. In other words, they can be posted from any company code. If some company codes are not active in a certain industry, you can use a validation to prevent values being posted to these.

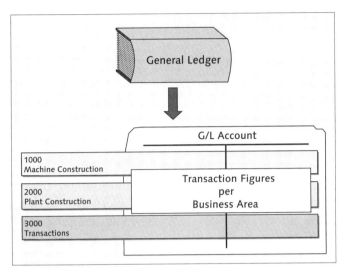

Figure 2.33 Business Area

Business areas allow you to create business area financial statements with a balance of zero in the general ledger. For more information, see Chapter 5, Document Splitting.

Business area
financial statement

The statement that the *"business area"* entity will no longer be enhanced with further development (see SAP Note 321190) has often been misinterpreted to mean that business areas could be in danger of extinction. Therefore, we repeat below the most important passages from that SAP note in relation to the business area. These passages serve to underline the fact that these fears are unfounded.

> *To meet the changing requirements, we will focus the further functional developments in Financial Accounting on the "profit center" entity. With the New G/L in release SAP ERP 2004, it is possible to create financial statements on profit centers. The business area will be retained in the present form. Data and functions will be available in future. (Source: SAP Note 321190)*

In the *Business Area* scenario (FIN_GSBER), the SENDER BUSINESS AREA and RECEIVER BUSINESS AREA fields are updated. Therefore, business area financial statements are still possible.

Update of "Sender
Business Area" and
"Receiver Business
Area" fields

2.2.4 "Profit Center Update" Scenario

A differentiation between categorization by business areas, which is based on external accounting, and classification by profit centers, which is based on internal accounting, has become less and less important as accounting and financial controlling have converged. The choice between business areas and profit centers is becoming increasingly difficult, not least for this reason.

Differentiating between external and internal accounting

Profit Center Accounting was initially designed and implemented purely to display results from an internal perspective. For this purpose, all revenue-generating and cost-generating controlling objects (cost center, orders, project, sales orders, and so on; see Figure 2.34) were mapped to profit centers and updated with the relevant data affecting net income.

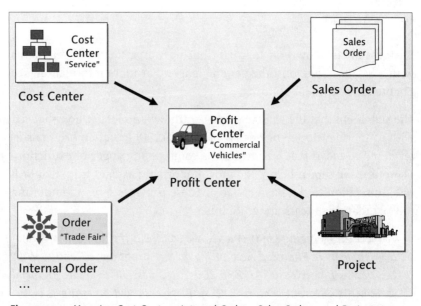

Figure 2.34 Mapping Cost Centers, Internal Orders, Sales Orders, and Projects to Profit Centers

Profit center accounting

To show profitability, key figures (return on investment, or ROI), financial statement items of the current and fixed assets, and short-term liabilities also were allocated to profit centers.

As a result, the profit center has become increasingly similar to the business area in terms of the options for assigning financial statement data and P&L data. However, Profit Center Accounting is more flexible than the business area. Options for mapping a (time-dependent) profit center hierarchy, statistical key figures, profit center assessments, and allocations at internal transfer prices represent additional developments not available with business areas.

Profit center flexibility

Profit Center Accounting is also included in New G/L. Centralized shared evaluations and reports are possible. Assessments and allocations can thus also be executed in New G/L. In the *Profit Center Update* scenario (FIN_PCA), the PROFIT CENTER and PARTNER PROFIT CENTER fields are updated.

For more detailed information about Profit Center Accounting in the general ledger, see Chapter 3, Integration in Financial Accounting.

2.2.5 "Segmentation" Scenario

Given the importance of international accounting standards (IAS/IFRS or U.S.-GAAP), the need for segment reporting that takes account of all business activities (areas) within a company is becoming more pressing. The *Segmentation* scenario (FIN_SEGM) helps you meet this need. In this scenario, the SEGMENT, PARTNER SEGMENT, and PROFIT CENTER fields are updated.

Segment reporting

Profit centers and business areas are often used to create reports at a level "below" company codes in SAP R/3 releases, as described in Chapter 1, New G/L in SAP ERP—An Overview. In SAP ERP, an additional account assignment object is provided in the SAP standard system in the form of the "segment" entity.

The SEGMENT field is contained by default in FAGLFLEXT, the totals table of New G/L. Segments are defined in Enterprise Structure Customizing rather than in the New G/L Customizing. As shown in Figure 2.35, you can define segments by following the path: ENTERPRISE STRUCTURE • DEFINITION • FINANCIAL ACCOUNTING • DEFINE SEGMENT.

"Segment" account assignment object

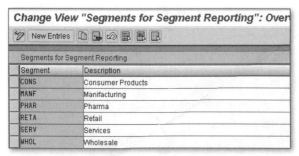

Figure 2.35 Defining Segments

Fields of activity Segment reports allow a company to obtain an accurate overview of business activities spanning a range of markets, divisions, and products (or fields of activity). As shown in Figure 2.36, various organizational levels can be mapped.

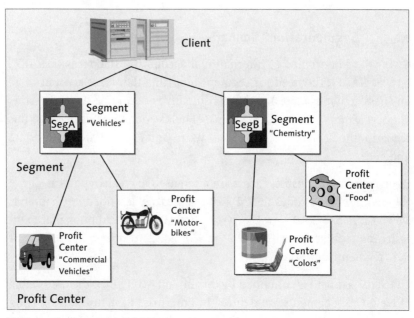

Figure 2.36 Organizational Objects

Segment reporting The segment is essentially provided as an option because the business area and profit center are frequently used for other purposes and thus need to fulfill other requirements.

As explained earlier, a segment can be defined in the master data of a profit center. The segment is derived by default from the profit center (see Figure 2.37).

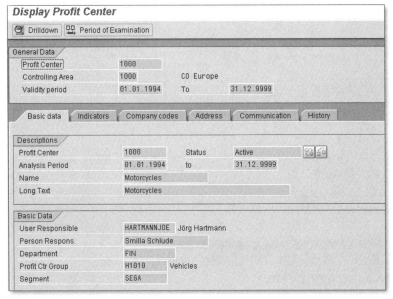

Figure 2.37 Deriving a Segment from the Profit Center Master Record

When a posting is made to the profit center, a segment is derived and the same posting is made to it. The profit center may be defined as an account assignment object, for example, in a cost center, in an order, and in Logistics master data such as the material master record shown in Figure 2.38. This is why the profit center was chosen as the object from which the segment is derived.

To add a segment to a profit center, choose the following path in the SAP application menu: ACCOUNTING • FINANCIAL ACCOUNTING • GENERAL LEDGER • MASTER RECORDS • PROFIT CENTER • INDIVIDUAL PROCESSING • CHANGE.

If you have selected the segment as an independent accounting unit, the system issues a message (see Figure 2.39) to remind you to enter the segment as an entity when creating a profit center. The appearance of the system message, message number FAGL_LEDGER_CUST052, can be controlled accordingly in Customizing.

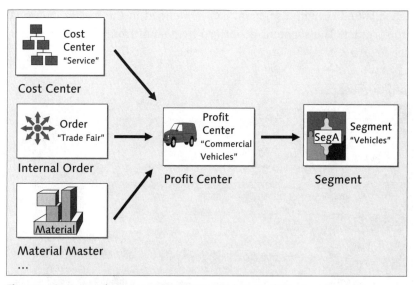

Figure 2.38 Material Master–Cost Center–Order–Profit Center–Segment

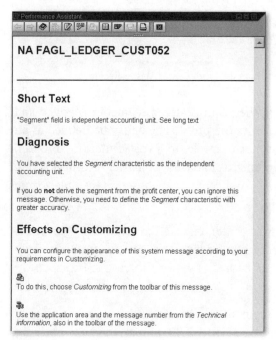

Figure 2.39 Message: "Segment" Field Is an Independent Accounting Unit

A segment entered in the profit center cannot be changed without making additional settings. The entity has a gray background in the profit center master record and cannot be changed in the default configuration (see Figure 2.40).

Figure 2.40 Segment Cannot Be Changed

In Transaction SE16, you can access the V_FAGL_SEGM_PRCT table (see Figure 2.41 and Figure 2.42) and make a setting so that the SEGMENT field can be changed in the profit center master record.

Table V_FAGL_SEGM_PRCT

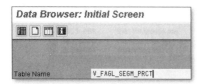

Figure 2.41 Table V_FAGL_SEGM_PRCT

Figure 2.42 Segment Can Be Changed in Profit Center Master Record

Figure 2.43 shows how this option is available after the change. This change is only possible as long as no postings have been made to the profit center that is to be changed.

Figure 2.43 Segment Can Be Changed

If you do not use Profit Center Accounting in your system, you can use a BAdI to program other solutions for deriving the segment by means of a user exit. This derivation option based on a BAdI is also useful if you use Profit Center Accounting but the profit center cannot be uniquely assigned to the segment. The definition name of the BAdI is FAGL_DERIVE_SEGMENT.

FAGL_DERIVE_ SEGMENT

You will find this IMG activity in Customizing by following the path: FINANCIAL ACCOUNTING (NEW) • FINANCIAL ACCOUNTING GLOBAL SETTINGS (NEW) • TOOLS • CUSTOMER ENHANCEMENTS • BUSINESS ADD-INS (BADIS) • SEGMENT DERIVATION • DERIVE SEGMENT. A (training) example is provided in Figure 2.44.

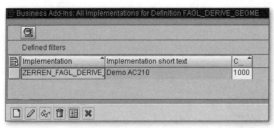

Figure 2.44 FAGL_DERIVE_SEGMENT

The GET_SEGMENT interface contains the source code that allows the SEGMENT characteristic to be derived on a customer-specific basis (see Figure 2.45 and Figure 2.46).

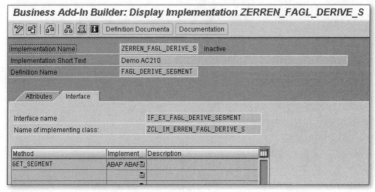

Figure 2.45 Interface GET_SEGMENT

Figure 2.46 Method IF_EX_FAGL_DERIVE_SEGMENT~GET_SEGMENT

In the BAdI implementation, you can choose to program a user exit or to create a formula.

After you define and derive the segments, you must ensure that the "segment" entity appears in the FI document.

Maintaining the segment

Figure 2.47 shows the two determinants. Note the field status of the posting key and the field status of the field status group of the FI account to which the posting is made.

Field status

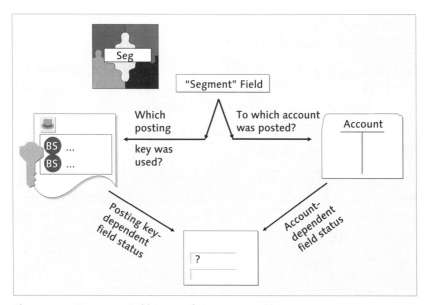

Figure 2.47 Document Field Status of "Segment" Field

During document entry, different fields are displayed, depending on the transaction and on the accounts used. For example, if you post expenses, the cost center and tax data normally are displayed. If cash is posted, however, this information is not required. These different display options for document processing are controlled by the field status.

As a rule, you set the account-dependent field status for G/L account in Customizing. As with field status control for the fields of general ledger accounts, the field status with the highest priority is used here also. The field status SUPPRESS has the highest priority, followed by the field status REQUIRED ENTRY, while OPTIONAL ENTRY is the field status with the lower priority.

[!] **"Suppress" and "Required Entry" Statuses Cannot Be Combined**

The field status SUPPRESS cannot be combined with the field status REQUIRED ENTRY. Any attempt to combine these field statuses will result in an error.

You maintain the field status in Customizing via the path: FINANCIAL ACCOUNTING (NEW) • FINANCIAL ACCOUNTING GLOBAL SETTINGS (NEW) • DOCUMENT • DEFINE POSTING KEYS.

In the posting key, the SEGMENT field must be declared as an OPTIONAL ENTRY field or as a REQUIRED ENTRY field. This is illustrated in Figure 2.48 with the example of posting key 40 for DEBIT ENTRY.

This field appears in the additional account assignments, as shown in the field check in Figure 2.49.

Field status group   The same applies to the field status groups in the field status variant. Here too, the SEGMENT field must be defined as a REQUIRED ENTRY field or as an OPTIONAL ENTRY field. The SEGMENT field is also found in the ADDITIONAL ACCOUNT ASSIGNMENTS group.

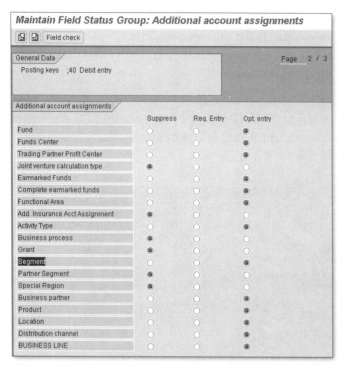

Figure 2.48 Field Status of the "Segment" Field in the Posting Key

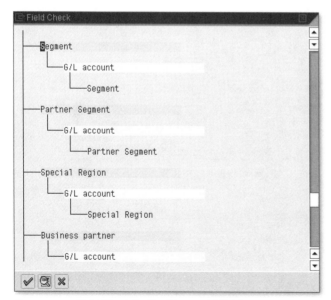

Figure 2.49 Field Check for the "Segment" Field

You maintain the field status of the field status groups (see Figure 2.50) for the relevant FI accounts via the Customizing path: FINANCIAL ACCOUNT-ING (NEW) • FINANCIAL ACCOUNTING GLOBAL SETTINGS (NEW) • LEDGERS • FIELDS • DEFINE FIELD STATUS VARIANTS.

The variant principle applies here also. Figure 2.50 shows how the field status is maintained in the field groups (here, field status group G001) within a field status variant. This is field status variant 1000 in our example (see Figure 2.51).

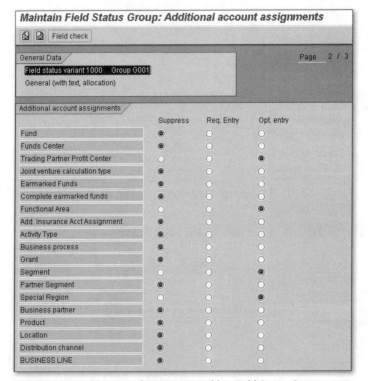

Figure 2.50 Field Status of "Segment" Field in Field Status Group

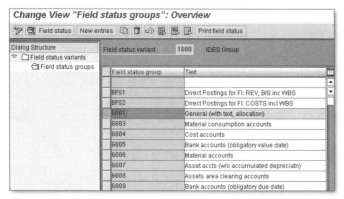

Figure 2.51 Field Status Groups in Field Status Variant

Field status variant

Company codes are then assigned to the field status variant (see Figure 2.52).

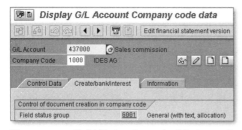

Figure 2.52 Assigning Company Code to Field Status Variant

The field status group is then assigned to the G/L account in the application. An example of this is provided in Figure 2.53, where field status group G001 is assigned to G/L account 437000 (SALES COMMISSION).

Figure 2.53 Field Status Group in G/L Account

The SEGMENT field must also be included in the document display using the layout. This inclusion is required to ensure that the field is not only available for posting, but also is shown in the document display and in the document simulation. Figure 2.54 shows the segment SEG A in a document display.

Definition of the scenarios is essential, as explained earlier. The *Segmentation* scenario must be defined for the ledger. Otherwise, the segment will be displayed in the document entry view only.

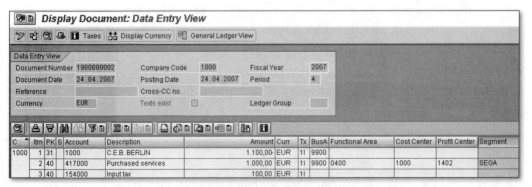

Figure 2.54 Displaying "Segment" Entity in FI Document

2.2.6 "Preparations for Consolidation" Scenario

With consolidation, individual account closings are combined in the period-end closing. Even if this step is mapped in an SAP system, preparations must be made at the level of individual account closings for subsequent consolidation.

In SAP R/3 systems, the consolidation staging ledger was often used. This was a separate data storage location where data was collected and adjusted using postings. Separate Customizing settings and reports were needed for this type of self-contained data area, which required reconciliation. These disadvantages are similar to those of the profit center ledger and cost-of-sales accounting ledger.

The data basis of New G/L allows you to access, among other things, the consolidation transaction type, and the trading partner at the level of totals records.

If the *Preparations for Consolidation* scenario is not activated, the transaction type is not updated. However, this transaction type could serve as a vehicle for the creation of changes in provisions worksheets. See the example in Chapter 4, Parallel Accounting—IFRS on the Advance.

Additional reporting dimensions, which may be required for a management consolidation, can be designed, for example, in SAP SEM-BCS.

If you update your financial data in New G/L with all necessary additional account assignments and want to set up an integrated data transfer to SEM-BCS, the structure of New G/L provides the essential fields for company and profit center consolidation as standard in the following scenarios:

> Preparations for Consolidation FIN_CONS

> Profit Center Update FIN_PCA (see Section 2.2.4, "Profit Center Update " Scenario)

These key fields are:

> CONSOLIDATION TRANSACTION TYPE (FIN_CONS)

> TRADING PARTNER (FIN_CONS)

> PARTNER PROFIT CENTER (FIN_PCA)

An extractor allows for an integrated transfer of the data to SAP NetWeaver BI, from where it is then imported into SEM-BCS.

To ensure that the consolidation-relevant fields in New G/L are updated correctly, you must take note of the requirements explained in the following paragraphs.

First, settings must be made for the preparations for a company consolidation.

1. Assign the Preparations for Consolidation scenario to all consolidation-relevant ledgers (see Figure 2.55) in Customizing via the path: FINANCIAL ACCOUNTING (NEW) • FINANCIAL ACCOUNTING GLOBAL SETTINGS (NEW) • LEDGERS • LEDGER • ASSIGN SCENARIOS AND CUSTOMER FIELDS TO LEDGERS.

Preparations for Consolidation FIN_CONS

Profit Center Update FIN_PCA

Preparations for company consolidation

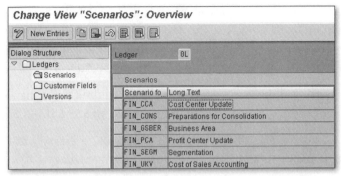

Figure 2.55 Assigning Scenarios—"Preparations for Consolidation"

2. Make sure that the relevant company is entered in the TRADING PART-NER field (see Figure 2.56) in the master records of customers and vendors belonging to affiliated companies. You will find this field in the control data of the customer or vendor master record.

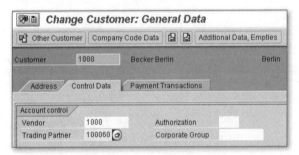

Figure 2.56 Trading Partner in Vendor Master Record

Preparations for profit center consolidation

Settings then must be made for preparations for profit center consolidation.

1. First, all settings must be made for the profit center account assignments. In particular, the Profit Center Update scenario must be assigned to all relevant ledgers.

2. The PRCTR PROFIT CENTER field must be flagged as a document-splitting characteristic for general ledgers (ZERO BALANCE column in Figure 2.57).

For more information about document splitting, see Chapter 5, Document Splitting. You make this setting in Customizing via the path:

FINANCIAL ACCOUNTING (NEW) • GENERAL LEDGER ACCOUNTING (NEW) • BUSINESS TRANSACTIONS • DOCUMENT SPLITTING • DEFINE DOCUMENT SPLITTING CHARACTERISTICS FOR GENERAL LEDGER ACCOUNTING.

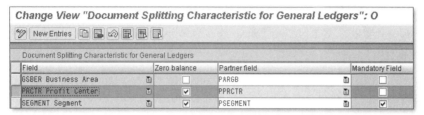

Figure 2.57 Profit Center as Document-Splitting Characteristic for General Ledger Accounting

3. Ensure that the PROFIT CENTER and SEGMENT fields in the field status of all accounts are set as ready for input. The PARTNER PROFIT CENTER and PARTNER SEGMENT fields in the field status of all accounts used to manage partner information must also be set as ready for input.

4. For the posting keys used, the PROFIT CENTER, SEGMENT, PARTNER PROFIT CENTER, and PARTNER SEGMENT fields must be set as ready for input.

Further Information **[+]**

For detailed information about deriving the partner profit center, see SAP Note 826357.

Next, we turn our attention to the data flow from New G/L to SEM-BCS in accordance with SAP Note 852971.

Data flow from New G/L to SEM-BCS

As usual, the integrated transfer of transaction data to SEM-BCS is performed by an upstream "staging" InfoProvider, which is filled from the feeder system by means of extraction.

You use the "read from data stream" data entry method for the transfer to the transactional SEM-BCS InfoProvider. You also can choose to use a remote cube as a staging InfoProvider to enable an "on demand" data transfer from the feeder system to SEM-BCS.

Transactional SEM-BCS InfoProvider

The 0FI_GL_10 DataSource is provided in SAP NetWeaver BW Business Content for the extraction of leading ledger data from New G/L

DataSource 0FI_GL_10

to SAP NetWeaver BW. However, because of the structure of the downstream data flow in BW Content, only some of the transferred fields can be updated. This limitation is due to the technical restrictions that apply to updating an operational data store (ODS) object. Therefore, the consolidation-relevant partner fields are not included in the 0FI_GL_10 InfoProvider, which then cannot be used as a staging InfoProvider for SEM-BCS.

DataSource 0SEM_BCS_10

SAP provides the 0SEM_BCS_10 DataSource (see Figure 2.58) for the transfer of data from general ledger accounting to consolidation. This feature opens up another option for data transfer to SEM-BCS, without affecting the data transfer to the InfoProvider of New G/L.

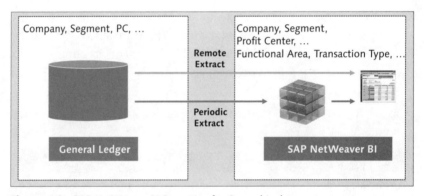

Figure 2.58 SAP NetWeaver BI Reporting for General Ledger

Note that the 0SEM_BCS_10 DataSource is provided exclusively for the transfer of data from the leading ledger to the staging InfoProvider in full update mode. Delta update using an intermediary ODS object is not possible with this DataSource.

We will now look at how this DataSource can be used to set up a relevant data transfer based on the Business Content of the EC-PCA and SEM-BCS areas.

Data transfer from non-leading ledgers to SAP NetWeaver BI

If you want to transfer data from a non-leading ledger to SAP NetWeaver BI, you must generate a DataSource for this ledger and set up the transfer to SAP NetWeaver BI in the consolidation staging cube.

> **Data Transfer for Profit Center Consolidation**
>
> When setting up the data transfer for profit center consolidation, note the following:
>
> The description follows from the assumption that the consolidation scenario is based on the standard Business Content provided by SAP for consolidation area 10 or on a copy with the same structure. The InfoProvider used here is 0BCS_C11.

The Profit Center Accounting InfoProvider, 0PCA_C01, is a suitable staging provider in this case. However, the procedure can also be adapted to suit a range of other models. For this purpose, you need to perform the following steps:

1. Create a copy of the Profit Center Accounting InfoProvider 0PCA_C01 in the customer namespace, for example, ZPCA_C01

2. Create a copy of the relevant InfoSource 0EC_PCA_1 in the customer namespace, for example, ZEC_PCA_1

3. Assign the ZPCA_C01 InfoProvider to the ZEC_PCA_1 InfoSource

4. Assign the 0SEM_BCS_10 DataSource to the ZEC_PCA_1 InfoSource. Make sure that the consolidation-relevant fields of the InfoSource are updated to the InfoProvider.

2.2.7 "Cost-of-Sales Accounting" Scenario

In period accounting, the sales revenues of a given period are compared with the total activities (including balance sheet changes) and total costs, classified according to expense types (accounts; see Figure 2.59). In cost-of-sales accounting, on the other hand, the sales revenues are compared with the costs of production for a given period (without balance sheet changes) and the costs for the period, classified according to functional area. The costs and expenses involved in making the revenue (cost-of-sales) are also shown in Figure 2.59.

There were several options for mapping Cost-of-Sales Accounting in SAP R/3:

- Accounts approach
- Mapping in Controlling
- Cost-of-sales ledger

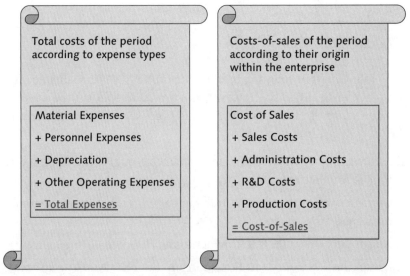

Figure 2.59 Total Costs Classified by Expense Type—Cost-of-Sales Classified by Functional Area

Accounts approach   With the accounts approach, all relevant data was mapped using accounts in general ledger accounting. This method is almost guaranteed to cause a chart of accounts to expand considerably. If we take the example of salary and depreciation, we immediately can see just how quickly the accounts multiply:

- Salary Sales
- Salary Administration
- Salary Research and Development
- Salary Production
- Depreciation Sales
- Depreciation Administration
- Depreciation Research and Development
- Depreciation Production

In this case, account determination becomes a major and costly challenge. If you prefer this solution, then you must be prepared to handle a large chart of accounts.

The requirements of Cost-of-Sales Accounting can be mapped using the Profitability Analysis in Controlling (CO-PA). In Profitability Analysis, you can use characteristics and value fields to map the dimension of the business-related source of the costs.

Mapping in Controlling

A disadvantage of this approach is that it does not enable a direct comparison with period accounting. Profitability Analysis is also somewhat less flexible because, by adding the dimension of the business-related source of the costs, an accounting aspect comes into play, in relation to which changes cannot be lightly made.

In the cost-of-sales ledger, you can use the functional area to map all postings to cost-of-sales accounting affecting net income (see Figure 2.60).

Cost-of-sales ledger

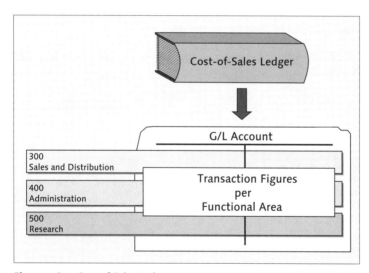

Figure 2.60 Cost-of-Sales Ledger

There are various ways—shown in Figure 2.61—to derive the functional area.

Functional area

Manual entry overrides all other options. This means that if different functional areas are proposed by all four options, the entry explicitly selected by the user is accepted by the system. Identification of the functional area in the master record of the CO object is the "weakest" option.

The CO object may be a cost center or an internal order. If a unique assignment is possible, this is a "clean" solution.

Substitution Substitutions, on the other hand, allow you to define individual rules with "if-then" relationships in order to find or derive the functional area.

Note, however, that the effort involved in creating these substitutions should not be underestimated and that additional effort is required each time a new process is added.

Many companies originally used substitution to derive functional areas, but favored the option of deriving these from CO objects, which became available with SAP R/3 Release 4.5. This method proved superior to the time-consuming creation of substitution rules, which had to be constantly updated due to evolving business processes.

Logically, the functional area can be defined in the master record of the P&L account for revenue postings or balance sheet changes.

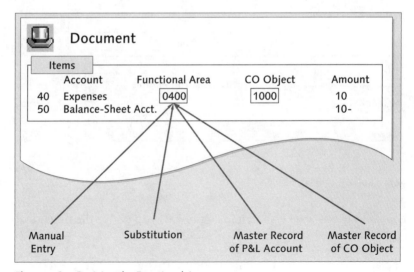

Figure 2.61 Deriving the Functional Area

In SAP R/3, a separate document is created for a relevant business transaction in the cost-of-sales ledger (the separate data storage location referred to earlier). The functional area exists at the totals record level, as shown in the example of the Sales, Administration, and Research & Development functional areas in Figure 2.60. Corresponding balances can be used for external reporting. However, separate reports must be used for evaluations. Customizing settings must be made in advance.

In New G/L, the functional area is part of the data basis. In the *Cost-of-Sales Accounting* scenario (FIN_UKV), the SENDER FUNCTIONAL AREA and RECEIVER FUNCTIONAL AREA fields are updated.

2.2.8   "Cost Center Update" Scenario

Cost Center Accounting addresses the question of where costs are incurred within your organization. When costs are incurred, they are assigned (i.e., posted) to the relevant cost center. These costs may be HR costs, rental costs or other expenses that can be assigned to a cost center. Each cost center is assigned to a cost center category (for example, administrative cost center, and production cost center).

Cost Center Accounting

Cost centers can be combined in groups if aggregated data about costs is required. A basic prerequisite for setting up comprehensive Cost Center Accounting is the creation of a standard hierarchy for a controlling area. This standard hierarchy reflects the overall structure of all cost centers in the controlling area and each node in the structure indicates cost totals.

Cost center hierarchy

In the *Cost Center Update* scenario (FIN_CCA), the SENDER COST CENTER and RECEIVER COST CENTER fields are updated.

In New G/L, it is possible to carry out "mini cost accounting" only with a small number of cost centers. Projects and internal orders are not included in this case.

In general, this scenario is also used less frequently due to its limited functional scope and Cost Center Accounting still tends to be mapped in CO (CO-OM).

2.3   Customer Fields

Customer-
specific fields In SAP R/3, the special ledger allows you to include customer-specific fields in accounting documents in the standard system. With New G/L, this option is now also available in SAP ERP. The steps involved in adding customer fields are described in this section.

2.3.1   Extending the Coding Block

In the coding block, you can add your own freely definable, customer-specific account assignment fields.

Account
assignment field These new account assignment fields are then available for FI G/L accounts in Materials Management (MM) Inventory Management and MM Purchasing, and are also updated in the CO line items. To include customer fields in the FAGLFLEXT totals table, you must first include them in the coding block (as already mentioned). Figure 2.62 shows the example of the SPECIAL REGION field in the coding block. The ZREGION data element is displayed in the Dictionary (see Figure 2.63).

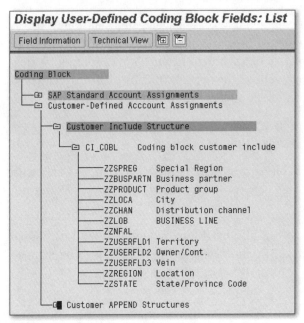

Figure 2.62   Coding Block—Displaying Customer Fields

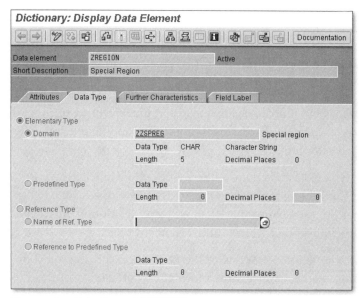

Figure 2.63 Data Element ZREGION

You can maintain the coding block in Customizing by following the menu path: FINANCIAL ACCOUNTING (NEW) • FINANCIAL ACCOUNTING GLOBAL SETTINGS (NEW) • LEDGERS • FIELDS • CUSTOMER FIELDS • EDIT CODING BLOCK.

You can add new fields to the coding block in Transaction OXK3. When you do so, central Dictionary tables are extended and entries added to cross-client tables.

Extending the coding block

When you create customer fields, these are updated by the system during automatic postings.

If you plan to add account-assignment fields, make sure you allow sufficient time for testing. These changes are transferred to the test system in a transport request and can then be transported into another system from there.

Test system

You need the following authorizations to add account assignment fields:

Authorizations

- ▸ X_COBLMOD for adding a field to the coding block
- ▸ S_TABU_CLI for maintaining cross-client tables

▸ S_DEVELOP for Dictionary authorization

▸ S_TRANSPRT for Transport authorization

The changes you make are effective in all clients in the system.

Data backup   A data backup is required before you start an update run to include a new field or make Dictionary changes in expert mode. During the update run, no other users may be working in the system and no posting transactions may be executed.

A newly added field can be removed from the coding block. However, it is very time-consuming to do so and may result in a loss of data. Subsequent changes to the field format or subsequent deletion of an account assignment field is not possible with the standard tools.

Cross-client objects are defined with the EDIT CODING BLOCK function. The definition of these objects therefore affects all clients in the system.

The information from the additional fields, which may be included in New G/L in SAP ERP, can be evaluated by a range of standard reports.

2.3.2 Adding Fields to the Totals Table

You can add new fields to a general accounting totals table in Customizing via the path: FINANCIAL ACCOUNTING (NEW) • FINANCIAL ACCOUNTING GLOBAL SETTINGS (NEW) • LEDGERS • FIELDS • CUSTOMER FIELDS • INCLUDE FIELDS IN TOTALS TABLE. The totals table in question may be FAGLFLEXT, which is the standard totals table delivered by SAP (see Figure 2.64), or a customer-specific totals table.

Figure 2.64 Customer Enhancement in the General Ledger—Initial Screen

Extending the   In the totals table, you can add standard fields from the accounting doc-
totals table   ument or customer fields with which you have already enhanced the coding block (see Figure 2.65).

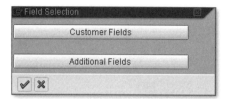

Figure 2.65 Customer Fields or Standard Fields Provided by SAP

To enhance a totals table, choose CHANGE. Under FIELD NAMES, enter the relevant fields. You can add these fields in one of the following ways:

▶ To add a customer field, double-click to select the field under CUSTOMER FIELDS.

▶ To add a standard SAP field from the accounting document, double-click to select the field under ADDITIONAL FIELDS.

You should then save your entries and activate your enhancement. Messages will then appear, indicating that the table has been activated and that the structures and programs have been generated (see Figure 2.66).

Activating the enhancement

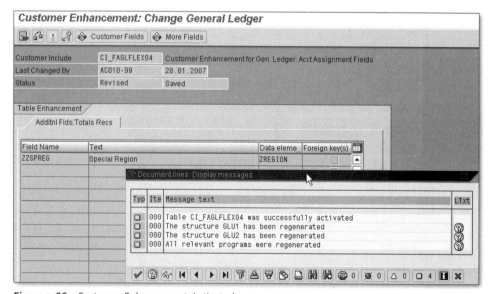

Figure 2.66 Customer Enhancement Activated

Finally, to check the overall installation, choose Cʜᴇᴄᴋ. Figure 2.67 shows the confirmation message that appears if the enhancement has been correctly defined and activated.

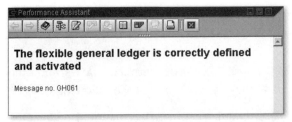

Figure 2.67 General Ledger Correctly Defined and Activated

Database indexes for totals tables
To create database indexes for the totals tables as well as the planned and actual line items, click the Dᴀᴛᴀʙᴀsᴇ Iɴᴅᴇxᴇs button as shown in Figure 2.68.

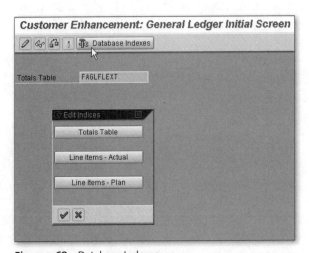

Figure 2.68 Database Indexes

It is not essential that you create these database indexes, but using an appropriate index may improve performance. Assign the fields to the relevant ledgers (see Figure 2.69 and Figure 2.70).

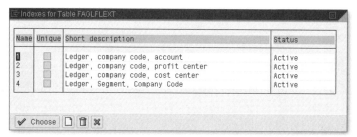

Figure 2.69 Indexes for the FAGLFLEXT Table

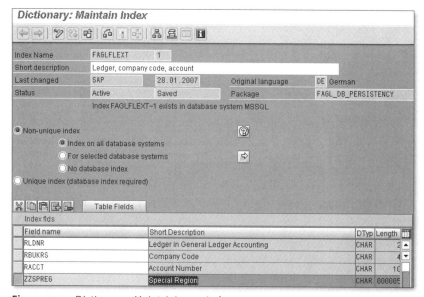

Figure 2.70 Dictionary—Maintaining an Index

Risk of Decreased Performance [!]

Note that additional data records are generated when you enhance a totals table. Each field added increases the data volume.

If you add too many new fields, this will have a negative effect on performance and increase memory consumption. Therefore, you should add customer account assignments only if they are really necessary.

In particular, fields that may have a very large number of properties may cause a dramatic increase in the data volume in certain cases. These include:

▶ INTERNAL ORDER

▶ SALES ORDER

▶ WBS ELEMENT

Data volume

The expected data volume for the design and migration concept of New G/L is an essential criterion that enables you to avoid unpleasant surprises during live operation later on. You should check in advance which additional fields are actually supposed to be used for each ledger and whether a totals table is still sufficient.

[!] **Further Information on Totals Records**

If as a consultant or as an SAP customer you are unsure about the number of totals record and their effects on the system performance and evaluations, you should read the current SAP Note 820495 or contact SAP Consulting.

If you have used a sufficiently scaled hardware for the SAP solution so far, the following general statements can be applied to the number of data records (based on the information available in August 2009).

Experiences so far

According to experiences so far, no performance problems have been detected in cases where the number of totals record did not exceed 500,000 for the largest company code per each ledger and fiscal year. Consequently, the questions arise regarding how many fiscal years the production system needs to store or whether totals records are to be archived. You must also clarify whether certain characteristics or combinations of these characteristics are required for specific accounting standards and thus ledgers. This measure directly affects the number of data records. Another criterion relates to all entries in the New G/L totals table: experience has shown that entries of fewer than ten million records in the totals table do not lead to performance problems. If one of the mentioned critical threshold values is exceeded, you should update separate table groups for each ledger.

2.3.3 Defining Customer Totals Tables

You can define your own totals table as a basis for your ledgers.

Totals tables and line item tables

The system then automatically creates both the totals table and the corresponding line item table.

SAP recommends that you use the totals table delivered in the standard system. Some functions in general ledger accounting (such as planning and reporting) are based on this standard totals table.

If the standard table does not meet your requirements and you define your own totals table (see Figure 2.71), you must ensure that these functions can access your totals table.

You can make this setting in Customizing via the path: Financial Accounting (New) • Financial Accounting Global Settings (New) • Ledgers • Fields • Customer Fields • Include Fields in Totals Table • Extras • Create Table Group.

Figure 2.71   Totals Table with FAGLFLEXT as a Template Table

If you want to add your own totals table as a customer field, you must first add it to the coding block.

2.3.4   Adding Customer Tables in Enjoy Transactions

To post manually to your customer fields in the Enjoy transactions that are available as of SAP R/3 Release 4.6 (for example, Transactions FB50, FB60, FB70), you must first assign the fields to the screen variants of the Enjoy posting transactions.

You make this setting in Customizing via the path: Financial Accounting (New) • Financial Accounting Global Settings (New) • Ledgers • Fields • Customer Fields • Include Customer Fields in Enjoy Transactions. In this IMG activity, you can assign your customer fields to a screen variant for the G/L items (screen 100 in the SAPLFSKB program) of the Enjoy posting transactions. **Screen variants**

Your customer fields are then available, for example, for manual posting for accounting assignment. This is illustrated in Figure 2.72, which shows the posting of a G/L document in Transaction FB50. **Manual posting**

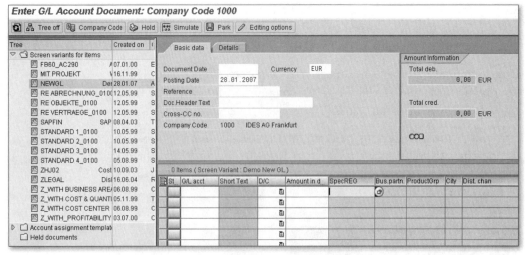

Figure 2.72 Entry Screen of Enjoy Transaction FB50

You cannot select the customer fields directly when creating a screen variant for the G/L items. You will find generic fields (ACGL_ITEM_GEN-GEN_CH and so on) as placeholders instead of your customer fields (see Figure 2.73). To create screen variants, from the SAP application menu choose ACCOUNTING • FINANCIAL ACCOUNTING • GENERAL LEDGER • POST-ING • ENTER G/L ACCOUNT DOCUMENT • EDIT • SCREEN VARIANT • CREATE SCREEN VARIANT.

Change screen variant

| GuiXT Script | | |

Screen variants for transaction   FB50

Screen values   0100 Program   SAPLFSKB

☑ Copy settings   Name of screen variant: NEW GL   ☐ GuiXT script
                             Screen variant short txt   New GL Demonstration
☐ Do not display screen

Field	Contents	W. content	Output only	Invisible	Required	Technical name
_____ 1		☐	☐	☐	☐	ACGL_ITEM_GEN-GEN_CH
_____ 1		☐	☐	☐	☐	ACGL_ITEM_GEN-GEN_CH
_____ 1		☐	☐	☐	☐	ACGL_ITEM_GEN-GEN_CH
_____ 1		☐	☐	☐	☐	ACGL_ITEM_GEN-GEN_CH
_____ 1		☐	☐	☐	☐	ACGL_ITEM_GEN-GEN_CH

Figure 2.73 Screen Variants for Including Customer Fields

At runtime, the customer fields are mapped to the generic fields on the entry screen. The following actions are therefore required: when maintaining the screen variant, you must define the maximum number of visible customer fields and their column position and sequence. You can define a maximum of five customer fields in a screen variant. In the example in Figure 2.72, these fields are SpecREG, Bus.partn., Product-Grp, City, and Dist. chan.

Customer fields in Enjoy transactions

You then must specify which fields are to be displayed in the screen variant in place of the generic fields and the sequence in which these are to be mapped to the generic fields.

If you do not make this assignment, all of the customer fields from the coding block will be displayed in the variant (up to the maximum number permitted) in the same sequence in which they appear in the coding block.

2.4   Conclusion

In SAP R/3, customers must install and implement a range of components to ensure optimal system support for meeting various legal requirements and industry-specific standards and guidelines. In industry solutions such as Public Sector, Financial Services, or Media (to name just three), financial statements must fulfill specific criteria.

New G/L allows you to keep several different ledgers within the General Ledger, thereby enabling parallel accounting (for more about this subject, see Chapter 4, Parallel Accounting—IFRS on the Advance). However, New G/L is more than just a solution to meet this one challenge. This chapter has described the enhanced data structure of New G/L and the range of possible scenarios that can be mapped. A greater number of entities can be mapped in FAGLFLEXT (the totals table of New G/L) than in the conventional totals table (GLT0).

One of the most impressive features of New G/L is its flexibility. You can, for example, include customer-specific and industry-specific fields and automatically update the totals for these fields.

Before you can reap the fruits of cooperation and closer collaboration, you must first integrate the IT systems with one another.

3   Integration in Financial Accounting

Integration or convergence of internal reporting with external reporting is particularly important. For SAP systems, this means increased dovetailing or even fusion of functions in the FI and CO components. This chapter is devoted to showing how this integration is mapped in the system, starting with the scenario of Profit Center Accounting in the General Ledger. If this scenario is active, the PROFIT CENTER and PARTNER PROFIT CENTER fields in the FAGLFLEXT totals table are updated. This data basis is then available for balance sheet evaluations and for segment reports and other management reports. The second part of the chapter concerns the periodic processes in SAP R/3 between FI and CO, which can be executed in real time in New General Ledger (New G/L) in SAP ERP.

3.1   Profit Center Accounting in New General Ledger

A key element of integration is incorporation of Profit Center Accounting into New G/L. One benefit is that it eliminates the need to reconcile reports in General Ledger accounting based on the GLT0 table and Profit Center Accounting based on the GLPCT table. The scenario of Profit Center Accounting in the General Ledger also reflects convergence of legal and management reporting. The implications of this type of structuring are examined in more detail in the following sections.

Uniform data basis

In accordance with SAP Note 826357, SAP recommends that all new customers activate the *FIN_PCA* scenario (*Profit Center Update*) in New G/L (see Chapter 2, Design and Features of the Ledgers). It doesn't make sense to activate classic Profit Center Accounting, which included the

Selecting scenarios

update of datasets in two tables, especially because doing this would require additional reconciliation.

If you are an SAP R/3 customer using classic Profit Center Accounting and you decide to switch to New G/L, you should also use this scenario. Interdependencies exist with other activities, such as document splitting and segment updating, and these cannot be activated if you do not use this scenario.

3.1.1   Financial Statement for Each Profit Center

Financial statements with a balance of zero previously could be created for each company code or business area. With Profit Center Accounting integrated with General Ledger accounting and document splitting, additional options are now available.

Company code or profit center
Note that the company code is still the most important criterion from an operational point of view. When it comes to creating dunning notices, payments, interest calculations, or advance tax-return filing on sales or purchases, the company code remains the organizational element that represents the smallest unit to be taken into account. The profit center is thus simply a new criterion for balance sheet evaluations, rather than a selection criterion that can be used for all operational activities. Figure 3.1 shows the financial statement covering various profit centers.

Object List:Data from -05.04.2007 11:27:20

Data from	05.04.2007 11:27:20
Crcy Type	00 Document currency
CoCode	1000 IDES AG
Ledger	0L Leading Ledger 0
Record Type	2 Actual assessment/di
Record Type	0 Actual
Version	1 Standard version

Cr	Crcy	Account Number	Profit Center	Segment	Functional Area	FS Item/Account	
00	EUR	INT /211100	1000/1300	Not assigned	0100	Ordinary depreciation - fixed assets	45.931,00
00	EUR	INT /211100	1000/1300	Not assigned	0400	Ordinary depreciation - fixed assets	18.372,00
00	EUR	INT /211100	1000/1400	Not assigned	0100	Ordinary depreciation - fixed assets	1.080,00
00	EUR	INT /211100	1000/1400	Not assigned	0400	Ordinary depreciation - fixed assets	433,00
00	EUR	INT /211100	1000/1402	Not assigned	0400	Ordinary depreciation - fixed assets	47.991,00
00	EUR	INT /211100	1000/1500	Not assigned	0100	Ordinary depreciation - fixed assets	5.891,00
00	EUR	INT /211100	1000/1500	Not assigned	0300	Ordinary depreciation - fixed assets	6.825,00
00	EUR	INT /211100	1000/1500	Not assigned	0400	Ordinary depreciation - fixed assets	2.356,00
00	EUR	INT /211100	1000/8110	Not assigned	0300	Ordinary depreciation - fixed assets	2.275,00
00	EUR	INT /211100	1000/8120	Not assigned	0300	Ordinary depreciation - fixed assets	2.275,00
00	EUR	INT /211100	1000/8130	Not assigned	0300	Ordinary depreciation - fixed assets	2.275,00
00	EUR	INT /211200	1000/	Not assigned		Extraordinary depreciation - fixed assets	321.732,39
00	EUR	INT /211200	1000/1000	Not assigned	0100	Extraordinary depreciation - fixed assets	39.571,00
00	EUR	INT /211200	1000/1000	Not assigned	0620	Extraordinary depreciation - fixed assets	15.830,00
00	EUR	INT /211200	1000/1010	Not assigned	0100	Extraordinary depreciation - fixed assets	70.670,00
00	EUR	INT /211200	1000/1010	Not assigned	0620	Extraordinary depreciation - fixed assets	28.268,00
00	EUR	INT /211200	1000/1100	Not assigned	0100	Extraordinary depreciation - fixed assets	8.522,00

Figure 3.1   Financial Statement for Each Profit Center

You can access this view from the application menu by following the navigation path: ACCOUNTING • FINANCIAL ACCOUNTING • GENERAL LEDGER • INFORMATION SYSTEM • GENERAL LEDGER REPORTS (NEW) • BALANCE SHEET/PROFIT AND LOSS STATEMENT/CASH FLOW • GENERAL • ACTUAL/ACTUAL COMPARISON • FIN. STATEMENT: ACTUAL/ACTUAL COMPARISON.

3.1.2 Allocations in the General Ledger

Assessments and distributions are standard procedures in classic Profit Center Accounting. Values are collected and then debited to several profit centers with a certain distribution. With Profit Center Accounting in the General Ledger, accountants must use a new procedure. Here we distinguish between two types of allocation: distributions and assessments.

Distribution is used to distribute general costs or revenues from one general cost center, profit center, or segment to others. This procedure is based exclusively on the original accounts.

Distribution

Figure 3.2 shows how a power bill is distributed from profit center XY to profit centers 1, 2, and 3 based on fixed percentages. The original G/L accounts 416100 and 416110 are used here.

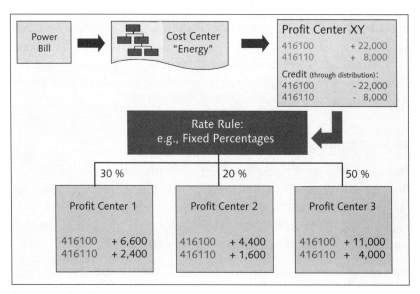

Figure 3.2 Distribution

Assessment In contrast to distribution, *assessment* uses a credit account. In Figure 3.3, profit center XY is credited with a separate assessment account 630099.

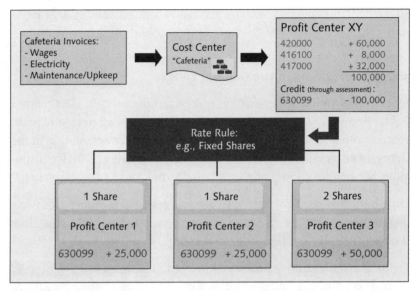

Figure 3.3 Assessment

In contrast to the classic approach, this cannot be a secondary cost element in Profit Center Accounting in the General Ledger. The credit account therefore reflects a G/L account, should result in a balance of zero on the closing key date, and should appear below the balance sheet. This is one of the key differences regarding allocations in Profit Center Accounting in New G/L.

3.1.3 Planning in the General Ledger

Planning based on the new Profit Center Accounting is also possible in this scenario. Some new transactions for plan data entry are provided for this purpose. You will find these in the application menu via the path: ACCOUNTING • FINANCIAL ACCOUNTING • GENERAL LEDGER • PERIODIC PROCESSING • PLANNING • PLANNED VALUES • ENTER (NEW).

Planning in connection with an account Figure 3.4 shows an example of planning in profit center PC18 in connection with account 400000, CONSUMPTION, RAW MATERIALS 1.

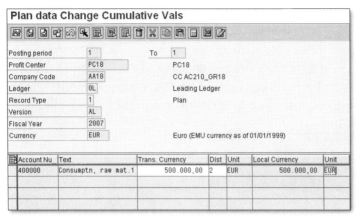

Figure 3.4 Changing Plan Data

Before you can execute Profit Center Planning in the application menu, you must first make the following settings in Customizing:

1. **Activate the totals table**

   Activate the FAGLFLEXT totals table for planning via the following menu path: FINANCIAL ACCOUNTING (NEW) • GENERAL LEDGER ACCOUNTING (NEW) • PLANNING • TECHNICAL HELP • INSTALL SUMMARY TABLE.

2. **Import a planning layout**

   The system requires a layout so that you can enter plan data. You can import the standard layouts provided in source client 000 via: FINANCIAL ACCOUNTING (NEW) • GENERAL LEDGER ACCOUNTING (NEW) • PLANNING • TECHNICAL HELP • IMPORT PLANNING LAYOUTS. Figure 3.5 shows the planning layouts to be imported in the FAGL namespace.

SAP			
Execute in Background	Execute		

Obj. Type	Object	Description	
Planning layout	0FAGL-01	Profit Ctr, Account	
Planning layout	0FAGL-02	PrCtr Group, Account	
Planning layout	0FAGL-03	Segment, Account	
Planning layout	0FAGL-04	PrCtr,Func.Area,Acct	
Planning layout	0FAGL-05	PrCtr,PartPrCtr,Acct	
Planning layout	0FAGL-06	Cost Center, Account	
Planning layout	0FAGL-07	Account	

Figure 3.5 Planning Layouts

3. **Set planner profile**

You set the planner profile via the following menu path in the SAP Easy Access menu (application): ACCOUNTING • FINANCIAL ACCOUNTING • GENERAL LEDGER • PERIODIC PROCESSING • PLANNING • SET PLANNER PROFILE. Here you can find the SAPFAGL planner profile. Figure 3.6 shows how to set the SAPFAGL planner profile.

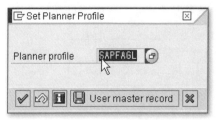

Figure 3.6 SAPFAGL Planner Profile

4. **Create a planning document type**

The plan data you enter is stored in the system as a posting. As with actual postings, you need a valid document type; in this case, you need one that is used exclusively for planning. You must define this document type in Customizing via the menu path: FINANCIAL ACCOUNTING (NEW) • GENERAL LEDGER ACCOUNTING (NEW) • PLANNING • DEFINE DOCUMENT TYPES FOR PLANNING. Figure 3.7 shows the defined document type P0 with the assigned number range interval 01.

[+] **Also Required If Plan Line Items Are Not Entered**

You should note that this step in configuration is also necessary if you don't want to enter any plan line items using this type.

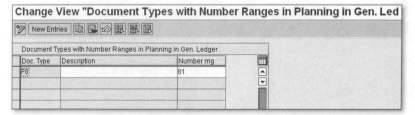

Figure 3.7 Change View "Document Types with Number Ranges in Planning in General Ledger"

5. **Define a number range**

A number range is required, in particular if you want to save line items for plan data entry to ensure greater traceability. You can make the necessary settings via the menu path: Financial Accounting (New) • General Ledger Accounting (New) • Planning • Define Number Ranges for Plan Documents. Figure 3.8 shows number range interval 01. To access this view, click the Maintain Groups button.

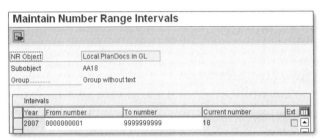

Figure 3.8 Number Range Interval

6. **Define a plan version**

As a rule, various scenarios have to be taken into account in planning. These scenarios can be mapped with versions in Customizing via the menu path: Financial Accounting (New) • General Ledger Accounting (New) • Planning • Plan Versions • Define Plan Versions.

The *version key* is particularly important when planning for subsequent integration with cost accounting. In the example shown in Figure 3.9, ledger 0L is defined with version AL for manual planning in General Ledger accounting and for integration planning.

If an identical AL version is defined in CO-OM, its plan values are updated from primary processes into the General Ledger in real time. In contrast, the plan values are transferred from the CO-PA component using a program run rather than online processing. The restriction relating to secondary cost elements, which was not transferred in integration planning prior to Enhancement Package 3 (or considering SAP Note 1009299), does not apply here. For more information, refer to Section 3.1.4, Enhancements for Planning with Enhancement Package 3.

At this time, plan values cannot be transferred from New G/L to other components. In addition, the data is transferred in one direction only.

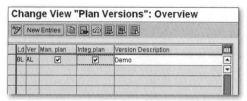

Figure 3.9 Plan Version

7. **Assign a plan version to a fiscal year**

Finally, you must assign the ledger and the version to a company code and fiscal year. You can make this setting via the menu path: FINANCIAL ACCOUNTING (NEW) • GENERAL LEDGER ACCOUNTING (NEW) • PLANNING • PLAN VERSIONS • FISCAL YEAR-DEPENDENT VERSION PARAMETERS.

Figure 3.10 shows the assignment of ledger 0L and version AL to company code AA18 for fiscal year 2007. You can also decide whether line items are to be updated (Line item column). From a technical perspective, these plan documents are stored in the FAGLFLEXP table.

Figure 3.10 Assigning Company Code and Fiscal Year

3.1.4 Enhancements for Planning with Enhancement Package 3

Business Function
FIN_GL_CI_1

With Enhancement Package 3 (FIN_GL_CI_1 business function) you can find, in the planning area, enhancements that provide new options in addition to the standard functions. We focus on the following three aspects:

► CO plan data integration for secondary cost elements

► Cumulative plan data entry for balance sheet accounts

► Plan data transfer from an external data source

Let's start with CO plan data integration for secondary cost elements.

CO Plan Data Integration for Secondary Cost Elements

This planning integration of secondary costs has been available as of ECC 6.0 with Enhancement Package 3 or considering SAP Note 1009299. Taking into account this SAP note, you can use the FAGL_PLAN_ACT_SEC program for plan data integration for secondary cost elements already in SAP ERP 2004 or in ECC 6.0 without Enhancement Package 3.

This function supplements the planning integration for primary cost elements, which was already described. It increases the consistency between plan data in controlling and plan data in financial accounting.

For planning, you have the option to transfer plan data for secondary cost elements from controlling to New G/L accounting. The accounts are determined during the transfer to FI analogous to the real-time integration of controlling with financial accounting. In Customizing (under FINANCIAL ACCOUNTING (NEW) • GENERAL LEDGER ACCOUNTING (NEW) • PLANNING • ACTIVATE PLANNING INTEGRATION FOR SECONDARY COST ELEMENTS) you can activate the planning integration from Overhead Cost Controlling (CO-OM) for secondary cost element for New G/L Accounting.

Transfer of plan data

Figure 3.11 shows the setting in Customizing before the activation, Figure 3.12 after the activation.

Activate planning integration

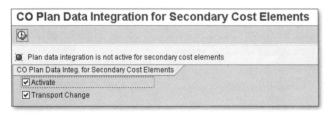

Figure 3.11 Plan Data Integration is Inactive for Secondary Cost Elements

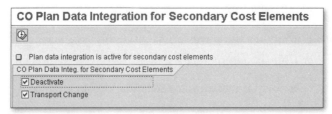

Figure 3.12 Plan Data Integration is Active for Secondary Cost Elements

For versions with planning integration, the plan data on secondary cost elements is updated or transferred to General Ledger accounting. But the system doesn't update this plan data under the secondary cost element in the General Ledger; rather—like for real-time integration in actual—the account determination defines a valid G/L account.

This means that you must first set up the account determination for the real-time integration for the desired planning transactions. Figures 3.13 and 3.14 illustrate this process.

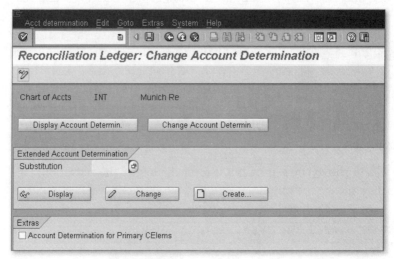

Figure 3.13 Account Determination—Initial Screen

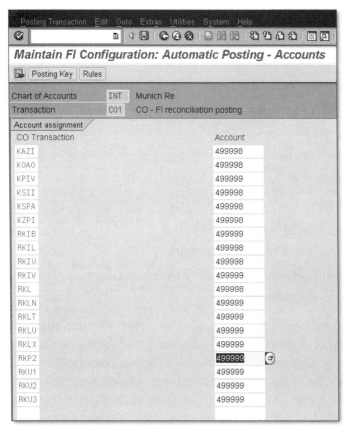

Figure 3.14 Configuration Accounting—Automatic Postings to Accounts (Reconciliation CO-FI)

For secondary cost elements with which you work in CO for secondary planning processes, you require corresponding reconciliation accounts in FI. You must assign these in account determination. You can find the Customizing setting under Financial Accounting Basic Settings (new) • Ledgers • Real-Time Integration of Controlling with Financial Accounting • Account Determination for Real-time Integration • Define Account Determination for Real-Time Integration. Here you can also define the account determination for the following secondary planning transactions:

Assigning reconciliation accounts in account determination

Considering
various planning
transactions

- ▸ KSPB—Plan Assessments In Result

- ▸ KZPP—Periodic Plan Overhead Rates

- ▸ RKP2—Planning Activities

- ▸ RKP3—Planning Secondary Costs

- ▸ RKP7—Activity-Dependent Planning Secondary Costs

- ▸ RKP8—Planning Settlement Costs

- ▸ RKP9—Activity-Dependent Planning Settlement Costs

- ▸ RKPL—Plan Indirect Activity Allocation

- ▸ RKPS—Plan Secondary Costs with Template

- ▸ RKPU—Plan Overhead Cost Assessment

- ▸ RKPW—Secondary Order Cost Planning

- ▸ RKPX—Activity-Dependent Secondary Order Cost Planning

- ▸ RKPZ—Planning Overhead Rates

Additionally, you have the option to achieve a higher level of detail in the assignment of transactions if you add an assigned substitution rule to the enhanced account assignment function. This way, you can achieve an assignment for each planning transaction—for instance, a reconciliation account for each planning of activity-dependent secondary costs—and also a reconciliation account for each planning of the respective individual activity-dependent secondary cost elements.

What does this mean for practical use? In the planning of activities or activity allocations, you can use many different activity types (for instance, consulting, repair, machine setup, and so on) in CO. This requirement on the system can be met using such a substitution rule.

New report for
plan line items

With Enhancement Package 3, you are provided with a new report for plan line items. Using Transaction code FAGLP03, which you can find in the SAP application menu under FINANCIAL ACCOUNTING • GENERAL LEDGER • PERIODIC PROCESSING • PLANNING • PLAN VALUES • DISPLAY PLAN LINE ITEM, you can call the report for the plan line items. Figure 3.15 shows the report selection screen.

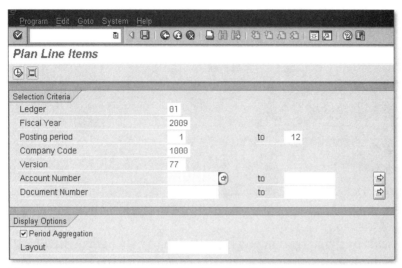

Figure 3.15 Transaction FAGLP03 — Plan Line Item (Selection Screen)

Figure 3.16 shows the evaluation report in accordance with the selections made.

Year	DocumentNo	Crcy	Ld	R	Ver	Account	CoCd	LnItm	Period	Trans.cur.	LC Amount	Key	User
2009	1	EUR	0L	1	77	400000	1000	000001		12.000,00	12.000,00	EUR	JOE
2009	1	EUR	0L	1	77	400001	1000	000002		24.000,00	24.000,00	EUR	JOE
*		EUR								36.000,00	36.000,00	EUR	

Figure 3.16 Transaction FAGLP03 — Plan Line Item (Report Display)

Of course, this report is relevant only if you previously activated the plan line item update. You can find this Customizing setting, which is illustrated in Figure 3.17, via the menu path: FINANCIAL ACCOUNTING (NEW) • GENERAL LEDGER ACCOUNTING (NEW) • PLANNING • PLAN VERSIONS • FISCAL YEAR-DEPENDENT VERSION PARAMETERS • ACTIVATE LINE ITEMS FOR PLANNING.

Customizing for plan line item

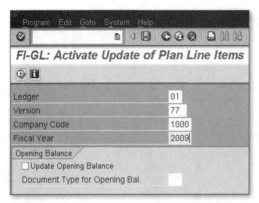

Figure 3.17 FI-GL—Activate Update of Plan Line Items

Saving in the FAGLFLEXP table

Consequently, you can find the plan values not only in the FAGLFLEXT table: the system also stores a plan line item for each individual transaction in planning in the FAGLFLEXP table.

In the previously discussed step or in the menu path in Customizing, FINANCIAL ACCOUNTING (NEW) • GENERAL LEDGER ACCOUNTING (NEW) • PLANNING • PLAN VERSIONS • FISCAL YEAR-DEPENDENT VERSION PARAMETERS • ASSIGN AND ACTIVATE PLAN VERSION FISCAL YEAR, you can view the flag for writing line items (Line item column) within the scope of planning in fiscal year-dependent version parameters (see Figure 3.18).

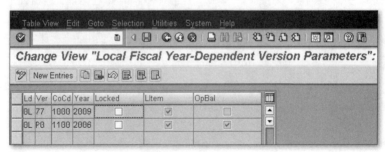

Figure 3.18 Fiscal Year-Dependent Version Parameters

Comparing classic and new planning

You can find the menu paths for CO plan assessment in the application in the SAP Easy Access menu under ACCOUNTING • CONTROLLING • COST CENTER ACCOUNTING • PLANNING • ALLOCATIONS • ASSESSMENT.

Overall and in comparison with the classic General Ledger accounting, you can determine that you can use plan data from two areas of the CO component for planning in New G/L accounting:

▶ Overhead Cost Controlling: primary and secondary cost elements

▶ Profitability Analysis: primary cost elements

The following figures indicate the differences with regard to the transfer of plan data from Overhead Cost Controlling and Profitability Analysis between the "classic" (SAP R/3) environment compared with the "new" (SAP ERP) environment of New G/L Accounting.

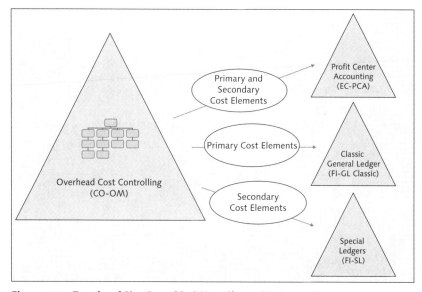

Figure 3.19 Transfer of Plan Data CO-OM to Classic G/L Accounting

Figure 3.19 illustrates the old transfer process of plan data without an active New G/L. Values of Overhead Cost Controlling (CO-OM) can be transferred to various areas. Only primary cost elements are to be considered for G/L. If additional plan data of secondary cost elements needed to be transferred, this was possible only for Profit Center Accounting or Special Ledger.

Data transfer without New G/L

The transfer of primary and secondary plan data in Profitability Analysis (CO-PA) is analogous to Overhead Cost Accounting (CO-OM) (see Figure 3.20).

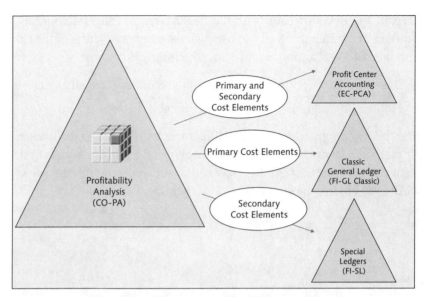

Figure 3.20 Transfer of Plan Data CO-PA to Classic G/L Accounting

Figure 3.21 shows that New G/L closes the functional gap with regard to CO-OM.

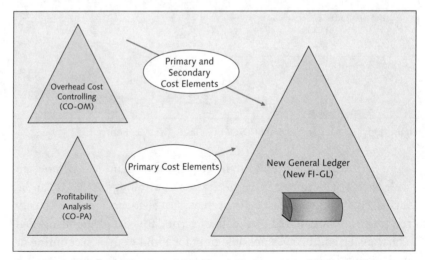

Figure 3.21 Transfer of Plan Data CO-OM and CO-PA to New G/L Accounting

Table 3.1 shows that the planning of cost elements is directly stored in New G/L. Planning in Profit Center Accounting or in Special Ledgers, as was necessary in the classic G/L environment, is no longer required in New G/L Accounting.

Data transfer with New G/L

	Overhead Cost Controlling (CO-OM)	Profitability Analysis (CO-PA)
Primary Cost Elements	Yes	Yes
Secondary Cost Elements	Yes	No

Table 3.1 Transfer Options for Plan Data

You can find the appropriate paths for transferring plan data from CO-OM or from CO-PA to New G/L Accounting in Customizing under the following two menu paths:

▶ FINANCIAL ACCOUNTING (NEW) • GENERAL LEDGER ACCOUNTING (NEW) • PLANNING • TRANSFER PLAN DATA FROM CO-OM

▶ FINANCIAL ACCOUNTING (NEW) • GENERAL LEDGER ACCOUNTING (NEW) • PLANNING • TRANSFER PLAN DATA FROM CO-PA

After the CO plan data integration for secondary cost elements, we will now describe the cumulative plan data entry for balance sheet accounts.

Cumulative Plan Data Entry for Balance Sheet Accounts

In the manual planning of balance sheet accounts in FI, you can select at client level whether you want to plan balance sheet changes or cumulative asset values. You must make the necessary setting in Customizing via the menu path: FINANCIAL ACCOUNTING (NEW) • GENERAL LEDGER ACCOUNTING (NEW) • PLANNING • ACTIVATE CUMULATIVE PLAN DATA ENTRY FOR BALANCE SHEET ACCOUNTS.

Here you can activate—Figure 3.22 shows the corresponding checkbox— the cumulative plan data entry for balance sheet accounts.

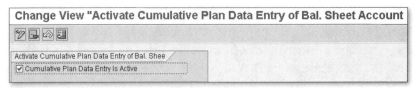

Figure 3.22 Activate Cumulative Plan Data Entry of Balance Sheet Account

If the cumulative plan data entry for balance sheet accounts is activated, the system shows planned asset values instead of the planned changes to asset values.

The activation of cumulative plan data entry is relevant for the following functions:

▶ Manual planning

▶ Microsoft Excel upload

▶ Transfer of external plan data using BADI_FAGL_PLANNING_POST

But what is the effect of activating this checkbox? A short example:

1. Assume that you've activated the cumulative plan data entry. Using Transaction GP12N, you plan a value of EUR 12,000.00 with balance sheet account 140000 and distribution key 2 (DISTRIBUTION COLUMN), for example. Figure 3.23 shows this planning step.

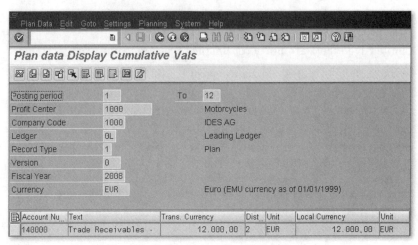

Figure 3.23 Change Plan Data in Cumulative Plan Data Entry

2. If you then have the system display the period screen, it shows periods 1 through 12 with EUR 12,000.00 for each period (see Figure 3.24). This is a special feature of cumulative planning, where EUR 12,000.00 is displayed for each period (Distribution Key 2)—EUR 12,000.00 from Period 1/January. If you plan with further receivables of additional EUR 6,000.00 in the second half of the year, the system displays a value of EUR 18,000.00 from July to December in cumulative planning.

<aside>Practical effect of this planning method</aside>

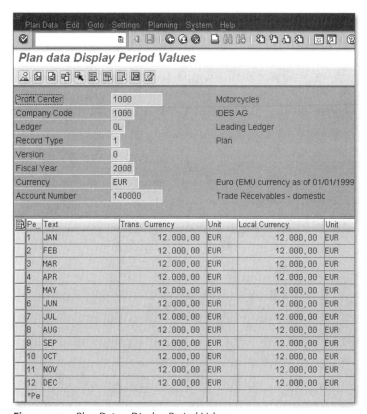

Figure 3.24 Plan Data—Display Period Values

3. Also assume that you haven't activated any cumulative plan data entry and plan EUR 12,000.00 for the entire year to a balance sheet account using Transaction GP12N. Figure 3.25 shows this planning step.

<aside>Alternatively, no cumulative entry is active</aside>

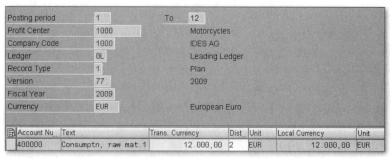

Figure 3.25 Change Plan Data Without Cumulative Plan Data Entry

▶ *Without cumulative plan data entry*

Without a cumulative plan data entry, the period screen displays EUR 1,000.00 for every period with default values, as illustrated in Figure 3.26. This means that the asset on the account increases by EUR 1,000.00 in every period—EUR 12,000.00 are distributed to the periods.

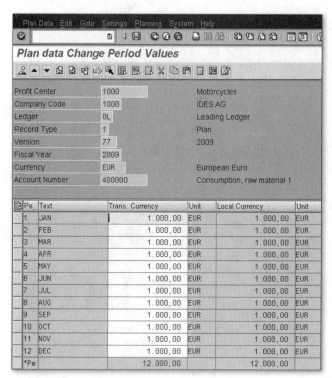

Figure 3.26 Change Plan Data—Period Values Without Cumulative Plan Data Entry

Conclusion 2—activated cumulative entry

- *With cumulative plan data entry*
  Only if you plan cumulative asset values can you execute a balance carryforward for plan data. This is done using Transaction FAGL_PLAN_VT; Figure 3.27 shows the selection screen and Figure 3.28 the result log. You can find the menu path in the application, FINANCIAL ACCOUNTING • GENERAL LEDGER • PERIODIC PROCESSING • PLANNING • PLANNING VALUES • CARRYFORWARD.

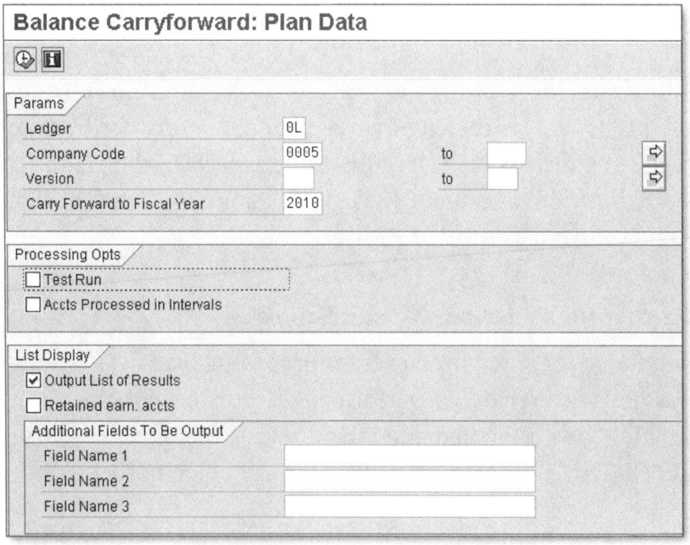

Figure 3.27 Balance Carryforward: Plan Data—Selection Screen

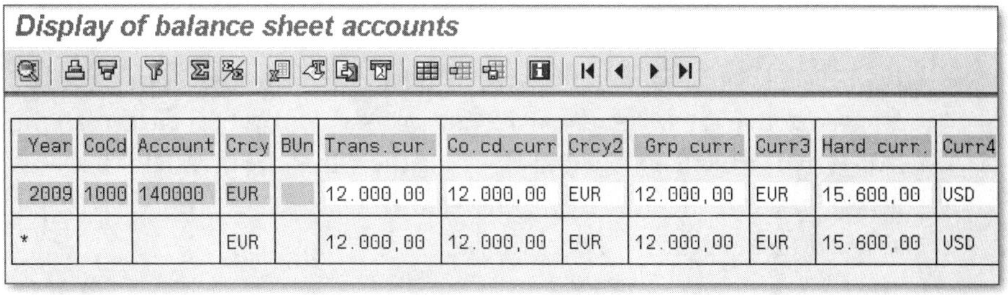
Display of balance sheet accounts

Year	CoCd	Account	Crcy	BUn	Trans.cur.	Co.cd.curr	Crcy2	Grp curr.	Curr3	Hard curr.	Curr4
2009	1000	140000	EUR		12.000,00	12.000,00	EUR	12.000,00	EUR	15.600,00	USD
*			EUR		12.000,00	12.000,00	EUR	12.000,00	EUR	15.600,00	USD

Figure 3.28 Balance Carryforward: Plan Data—Result Log

Considering balance carryforward values

The system considers balance carryforward values in the determination of asset values for the individual periods; however, it doesn't indicate them separately. In contrast to the balance carryforward for actual data (the SAPFGVTR balance carryforward program), you need to run the program repeatedly as long as the planning periods of the old fiscal year are open for plan data entry. Postings to the previous fiscal year are not automatically carried forward to the current fiscal year, even if you've already run the balance carryforward for the current fiscal year.

Configuring the cumulative plan data entry

If required, you can activate the function of cumulative plan data entry independent of the other functions of the *New General Ledger Accounting* business function in Customizing. The function is not automatically activated when you activate the business function.

Now that you're familiar with the CO plan data integration for secondary cost elements as well as the cumulative plan data entry for balance sheet accounts, we'll discuss the last of the three aspects of the planning topic for New G/L in Enhancement Package 3: Plan data transfer from an external data source.

Plan Data Transfer from an External Data Source

The background here is the requirements for uploading plan data, among others, challenges with regard to performance, and the possible total number of data records to be uploaded. Up to now, the flexible upload of Transaction GLPLUP has often been used for the upload process.

To enable you to transfer the plan data from an external data source to New G/L Accounting, New G/L provides you with a *Business Application Programming Interface* (BAPI).

You can find the new BAPI called BAPI_FAGL_PLANNING_POST in the SAP Easy Access menu via the BAPI Explorer under TOOLS • ABAP WORKBENCH • OVERVIEW • BAPI EXPLORER. There you can access the BAPI_FAGL_PLANNING_POST BAPI via the tab of the hierarchical search under FINANCIAL ACCOUNTING • GENERAL LEDGER ACCOUNTING • NEW GL PLANNING (see Figure 3.29).

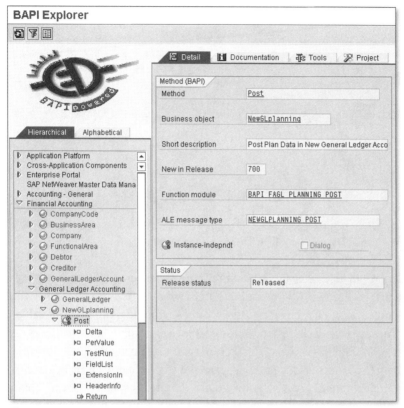

Figure 3.29 BAPI_FAGL_PLANNING_POST

For the upload of external data sources, you can also use this method (BAPI) to run a mass upload of plan data. The transfer is possible per call for a plan version, a company code, and a fiscal year as well as to a ledger of New G/L. Here you can also transfer values for selected periods of a fiscal year. Only amounts in the company code currency are transferred. If you have parallel local currencies for the company code in the appropriate ledger, the respective conversion method (see Figure 3.30) converts the amounts provided in the company code currency into the parallel local currencies. You can find the Customizing path under FINANCIAL ACCOUNTING (NEW) • GENERAL LEDGER ACCOUNTING (NEW) • PLANNING • EXTERNAL PLAN DATA TRANSFER • DEFINE EXCHANGE RATE TYPE AND DOCUMENT TYPES FOR PLAN VERSION.

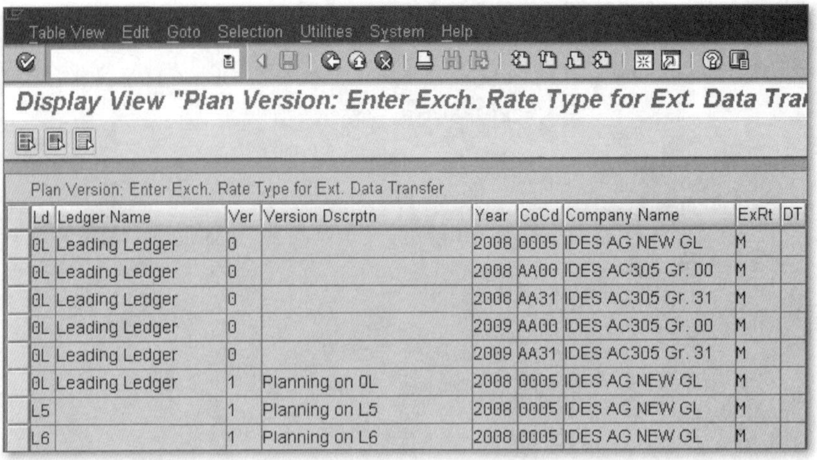

Ld	Ledger Name	Ver	Version Dscrptn	Year	CoCd	Company Name	ExRt	DT
0L	Leading Ledger	0		2008	0005	IDES AG NEW GL	M	
0L	Leading Ledger	0		2008	AA00	IDES AC305 Gr. 00	M	
0L	Leading Ledger	0		2008	AA31	IDES AC305 Gr. 31	M	
0L	Leading Ledger	0		2009	AA00	IDES AC305 Gr. 00	M	
0L	Leading Ledger	0		2009	AA31	IDES AC305 Gr. 31	M	
0L	Leading Ledger	1	Planning on 0L	2008	0005	IDES AG NEW GL	M	
L5		1	Planning on L5	2008	0005	IDES AG NEW GL	M	
L6		1	Planning on L6	2008	0005	IDES AG NEW GL	M	

Figure 3.30 Exchange Rate Type for External Data Transfer

The data in the external data source must correspond to your settings for displaying periodic planning values when it is transferred for the periods. If you plan change to asset values, you must provide the values in this form for each period. But if you select cumulative asset values, as was described in the previous section, you must provide the cumulated values for each period. Existing plan data is overwritten in this transaction. This means that if you transfer data for a specific feature (plan version, company code, fiscal year, and ledger in New G/L) for which values are already defined, the existing data is overwritten with the new values.

The plan data to be transferred using BAPI can be provided as target values (this is the default) or as delta values. In case of the delta values, the system adds the delta values to the already existing plan data. Figure 3.31 describes the BAPI_FAGL_PLANNING_POST function module; you can call it via Transaction SE37.

In summary: the function of external plan data transfer facilitates the process and considerably shortens the step of plan data transfer.

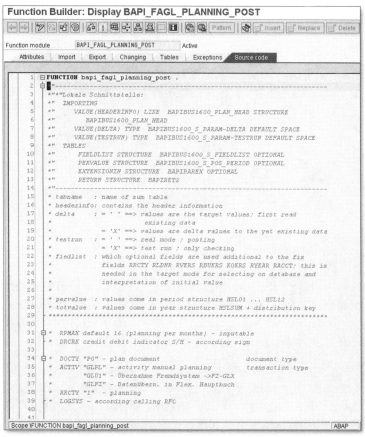

Figure 3.31 BAPI_FAGL_PLANNING_POST Function Module

3.1.5 Authorization Check for Profit Center

With Enhancement Package 3, you can now also use an authorization check for profit centers in New G/L in addition to the check of authorizations for entities like "company code" or "ledger." This development is motivated by the fact that profit centers increasingly assume the role of an "internal" company code and therefore must be protected against unauthorized access—especially considering the *compliance* aspect.

Before you can run an authorization check for the profit center, you must activate the *Profit Center Update* scenario for at least one ledger in Customizing under FINANCIAL ACCOUNTING (NEW) • FINANCIAL ACCOUNT-

Prerequisites

ing Basic Settings (new) • Ledgers • Ledger • Assign Scenarios and Custom Fields to Ledger (see Figure 3.32, Ledger 0L).

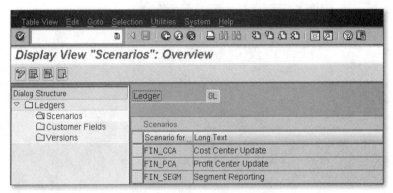

Figure 3.32 Assignment of Profit Center Update

You also need to assign the authorizations for the required profit centers in the profile for the user. You can assign these authorizations in the Customizing path: Financial Accounting (new) • Financial Accounting Basic Settings (new) • Authorizations • Manage Authorizations.

Authorization management— initial screen

The following figures illustrate authorization management. Figure 3.33 illustrates the initial screen of authorization management and shows, among other things, that the new authorization check uses the "K_PCA" authorization object, which had already existed before Enhancement Package 3.

"K_PCA" object

You can also see the "K_PCA" object in Figure 3.34, where you can also find the authorization check for relevant CO actions.

Figure 3.35 shows the restriction of the responsibility area within controlling area 1000 to profit centers 1000 through 5000.

Authorization management— maintenance

You can find the authorization management/check for profit centers via the menu path: Financial Accounting (New) • Financial Accounting Basic Settings (New) • Authorizations • Activate Authorization Check for Profit Centers.

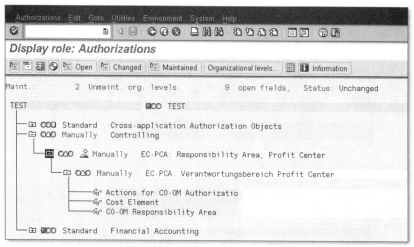

Figure 3.33 Authorization Management

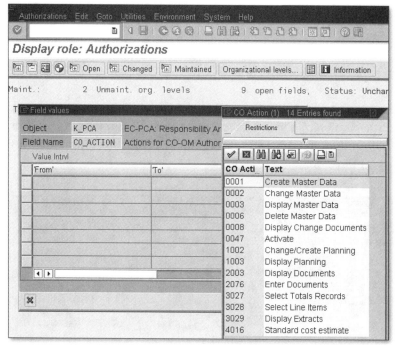

Figure 3.34 Actions of the Authorization Check

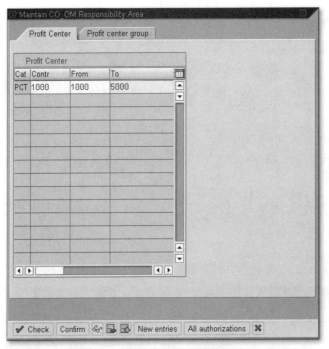

Figure 3.35 Maintenance of the Responsibility Area

In this step, you can specify whether the system is supposed to check the authorization of a user for the profit center. This setting is made for each controlling area, as is also shown in Figure 3.36 for controlling area 1000 (COAR column).

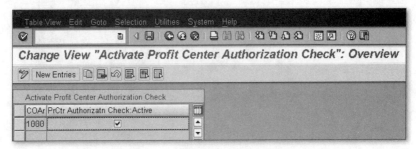

Figure 3.36 Activate Profit Center Authorization Check

Once the authorization check for profit centers has been activated, this check affects three actions:

Effects of the authorization check

- Posting
- Clearing
- Document display

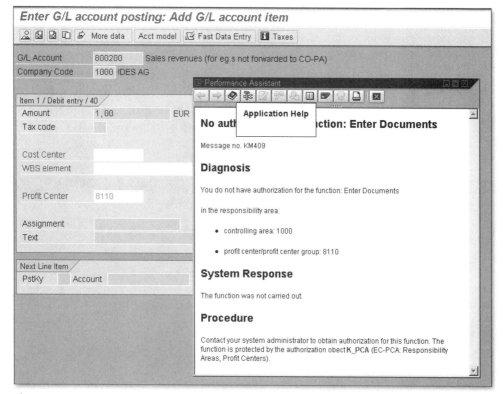

Figure 3.37 Message—No Authorization for Function: Enter Documents

You can post only if you as the user have the authorization for all profit centers posted in the document. The authorization check is run during the document entry and not during posting. During document entry and document clearing, action 2076 (Enter Documents) is checked. Figure 3.37 illustrates that when you enter documents for profit center

8110, the system displays the message that no authorization exists for the ENTER DOCUMENTS function for PROFIT CENTER 8110 in CONTROLLING AREA 1000. (Figure 3.37 refers to the restriction of the responsibility area to profit center 1000 through 5000 in controlling area 1000 as shown in Figure 3.35.)

Clearing   In manual clearing, the system selects only open items that—according to the General Ledger view—post to profit centers for which you have authorizations as the user or that are initial. The authorization check is run against only the leading ledger. In Figure 3.38 you can view two items in the line item display of account 7930, which you can access via the SAP application menu ACCOUNTING • FINANCIAL ACCOUNTING • GENERAL LEDGER • ACCOUNT • DISPLAY ITEMS; these two items include a document with the amount of EUR 400,000.00, posted to profit center 1000, and another document with EUR 399,999.00, posted to profit center 8110.

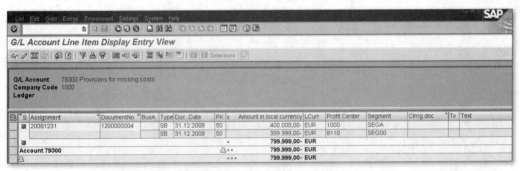

Figure 3.38   Line Item Display of Account 79300

When you call Transaction FB1SL via the SAP application menu ACCOUNTING • FINANCIAL ACCOUNTING • GENERAL LEDGER • ACCOUNT • CLEAR • SPECIFIC TO LEDGER GROUPS (see Figure 3.39), the system offers only the document with EUR 400,000.00 posted to profit center 1000 because you have the authorization for profit center 1000 only. The document with the amount of EUR 399,999.00, posted to profit center 8110, is not displayed; Figure 3.40 shows only the first document.

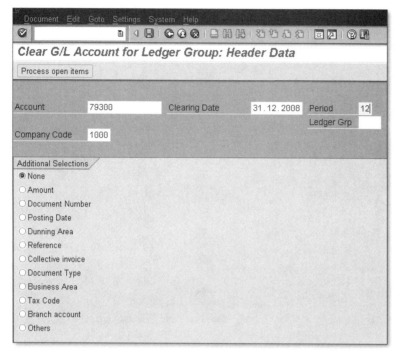

Figure 3.39 Manual Clearing—Transaction FB1SL (Selection Screen)

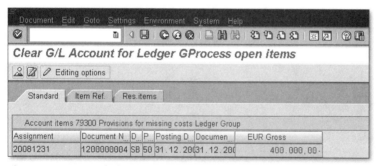

Figure 3.40 Manual Clearing—Transaction FB1SL ("Profit Center" Field)

The authorization also includes the Profit Center selection field in the clearing transaction:

1. You add the field in Customizing under Financial Accounting (new) • Accounts Receivable and Accounts Payable Accounting • Vendor Accounts • Line Items • Edit Open Items • Select Selection Fields. Figure 3.41 shows the corresponding Customizing setting.

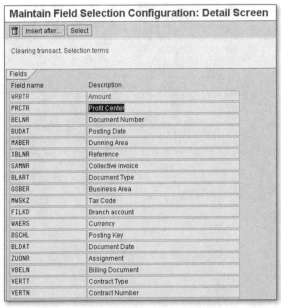

Figure 3.41 Making the "Profit Center" Selection Field Available in Selection

2. After you've added the field, the Profit Center field is provided in the selection screen of the application (see Figure 3.42).

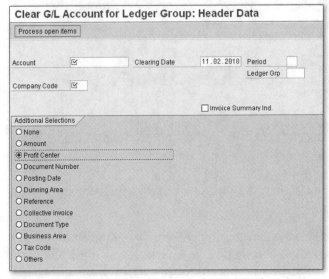

Figure 3.42 "Profit Center" Selection Field Available for Selection

3. If you enter only *one* profit center, the authorization check is performed with reference to the user. If you enter *no* profit center, the authorization check is performed against the corresponding General Ledger line items (technically speaking, against table FAGLFLEXA).

However, the authorization check for profit centers doesn't offer transaction processing that is completely oriented toward profit centers. This means, for example, that automatic payment processes such as the payment program and automatic clearing—also for activated authorization check for profit centers—are performed centrally and not specifically for profit centers.

Implement checks centrally

In the document display using Transaction FB03 in the SAP application menu ACCOUNTING • FINANCIAL ACCOUNTING • GENERAL LEDGER • DOCUMENT • DISPLAY, the system shows only line items for which the profit centers are initial or in which authorized profit centers were posted. Action 3028 (Display Line Item) is checked in the document display.

Figure 3.43 shows a document of a customer invoice posted to revenue account 800200 with one item assigned to profit center 1000 and a second item assigned to profit center 8110.

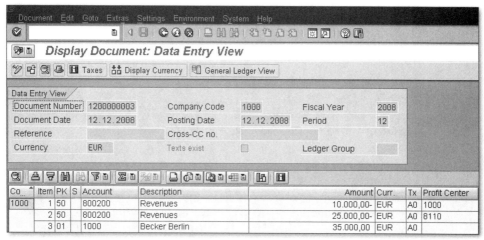

Figure 3.43 Customer Invoice with Two Revenue Items Posted to Different Profit Centers

Assuming that you have no authorization either for profit center 1000 or for profit center 8110, the system displays the error messages shown in Figure 3.44.

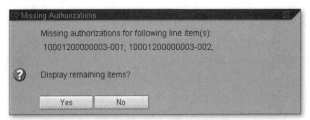

Figure 3.44 Error Message—Missing Authorizations

Then the system displays only the receivable item posted to customer 1000 (line item 3) in the document display (see Figure 3.45).

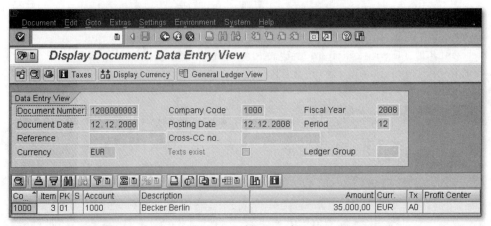

Figure 3.45 Document 3—Receivable Posted to Customer 1000

[+] **Other Evaluations**

One more comment on other evaluations: For reporting in the area of profit centers, the authorization check already existed prior to Enhancement Package 3. For Transaction FAGLL03 (Line Item Display), for example, the authorization check already existed and is therefore not related to the activation of the authorization check for profit centers in Customizing.

3.1.6 Evaluations

The integration of Profit Center Accounting into New G/L also has implications for standard reporting. A new subfolder in the information system does not simply represent all new profit center reports. Rather, additional selection options for the profit center have been incorporated into existing reports. The OPEN ITEMS report for receivables in Figure 3.46 shows the additional selection criteria of CONTROLLING AREA and PROFIT CENTER.

Standard reporting

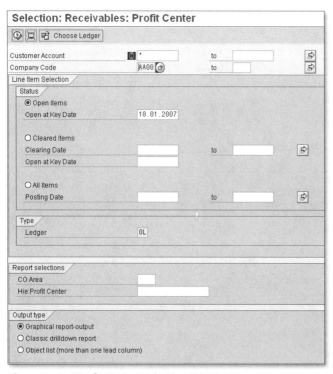

Figure 3.46 "Profit Center" Selection Criterion

You will find this report in the application menu via the path: ACCOUNTING • FINANCIAL ACCOUNTING • GENERAL LEDGER • INFORMATION SYSTEM • GENERAL LEDGER REPORTS (NEW) • LINE ITEMS • OPEN ITEMS • PROFIT CENTER RECEIVABLES. Figure 3.47 shows accounting document 1800000000 for the fiscal year 2006.

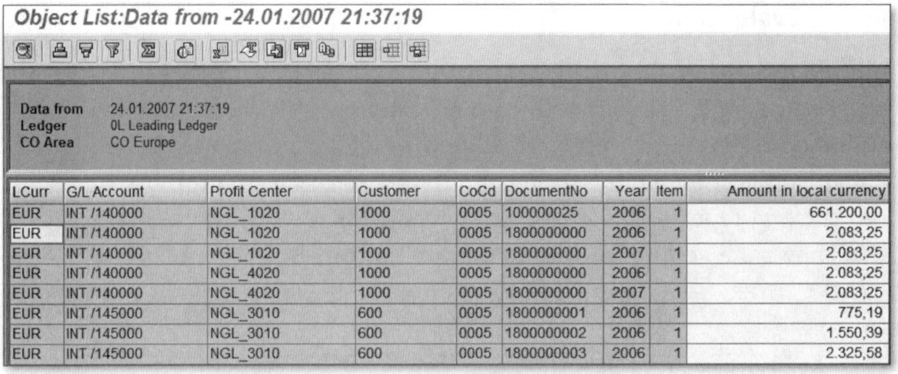
Object List:Data from -24.01.2007 21:37:19

Data from 24.01.2007 21:37:19
Ledger 0L Leading Ledger
CO Area CO Europe

LCurr	G/L Account	Profit Center	Customer	CoCd	DocumentNo	Year	Item	Amount in local currency
EUR	INT /140000	NGL_1020	1000	0005	100000025	2006	1	661.200,00
EUR	INT /140000	NGL_1020	1000	0005	1800000000	2006	1	2.083,25
EUR	INT /140000	NGL_1020	1000	0005	1800000000	2007	1	2.083,25
EUR	INT /140000	NGL_4020	1000	0005	1800000000	2006	1	2.083,25
EUR	INT /140000	NGL_4020	1000	0005	1800000000	2007	1	2.083,25
EUR	INT /145000	NGL_3010	600	0005	1800000001	2006	1	775,19
EUR	INT /145000	NGL_3010	600	0005	1800000002	2006	1	1.550,39
EUR	INT /145000	NGL_3010	600	0005	1800000003	2006	1	2.325,58

Figure 3.47 List of Line Items for Each Profit Center

If document splitting is activated, the report selects only the relevant document line items. Figure 3.48 clearly shows that several profit centers were assigned in the business transaction, but only the value EUR 2,083.25 of the selected profit center is displayed in the open items (Amount column).

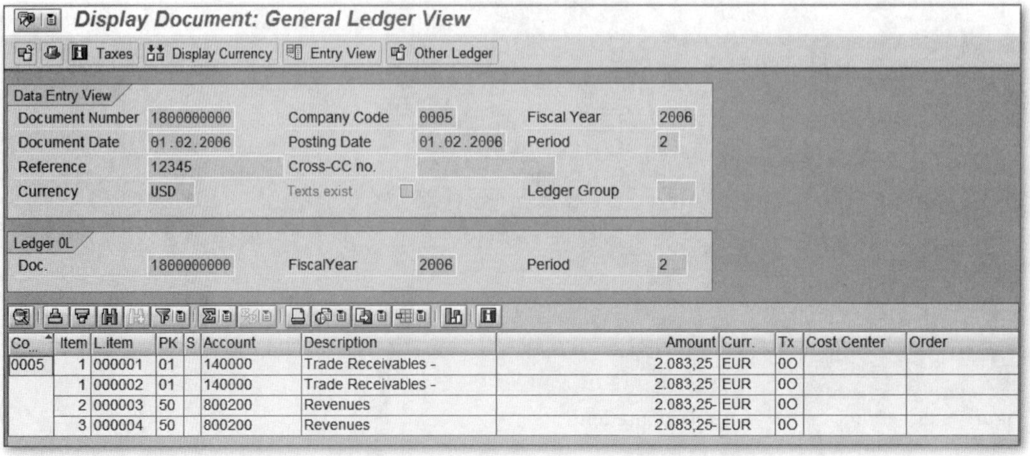
Display Document: General Ledger View

Taxes | Display Currency | Entry View | Other Ledger

Data Entry View

Document Number	1800000000	Company Code	0005	Fiscal Year	2006
Document Date	01.02.2006	Posting Date	01.02.2006	Period	2
Reference	12345	Cross-CC no.			
Currency	USD	Texts exist		Ledger Group	

Ledger 0L

Doc.	1800000000	FiscalYear	2006	Period	2

Co...	Item	L.item	PK	S	Account	Description	Amount	Curr.	Tx	Cost Center	Order
0005	1	000001	01		140000	Trade Receivables -	2.083,25	EUR	00		
	1	000002	01		140000	Trade Receivables -	2.083,25	EUR	00		
	2	000003	50		800200	Revenues	2.083,25-	EUR	00		
	3	000004	50		800200	Revenues	2.083,25-	EUR	00		

Figure 3.48 Document with Several Profit Centers

Hierarchy

This example clearly indicates a selection including output at the level of one or more profit centers. The familiar profit center hierarchy is not used in the FI standard configuration. A modification of the standard report allows hierarchical lists to be mapped as output or profit center nodes for selections as part of sets. Note also that existing customers may already have a large number of customer-defined reports based on profit centers. Currently, no conversion routines are available to allow these customer-specific evaluations to be converted at the touch of a button. Therefore, considerable effort may be required in order to create new evaluations.

3.1.7 Assignment Monitor for Profit Centers

The option to directly view which objects you've assigned the PROFIT CENTER characteristic to has been available since Enhancement Package 4. These different evaluation views have been necessary because the profit center has increasingly gained importance as an evaluation characteristic. One specific goal is to determine missing or incorrect assignments at an early stage.

> **Missing Assignments are Difficult to Correct** [+]
>
> The PROFIT CENTER characteristic is updated when you post in the transaction data of the documents. This data can be used by other functions, for instance, by passive document splitting, to split the business transactions automatically. Subsequently, making a correction is possible only with a lot of effort. For this reason, you should deploy these new reports intensively in advance.

Both in Profit Center Accounting and in New G/L Accounting you can call the assignment monitor via the application menu in Customizing. One possible menu path via the application in G/L Accounting is the following: ACCOUNTING • FINANCIAL ACCOUNTING • GENERAL LEDGER • MASTER DATA • PROFIT CENTER • CURRENT SETTINGS.

The various evaluations contain assignment monitors ranging from the PROFIT CENTER characteristic to other characteristics such as the following:

Assignment monitors

▶ Orders

▶ Business Processes

▶ Cost Centers

▶ Cost Object

▶ Materials

▶ Work Breakdown Structures

▶ Sales Order Items

▶ Real Estate Objects (RE-FX)

This list indicates that the PROFIT CENTER characteristic is an extremely integrative object. If you take these interdependencies into account, you can generate information from various SAP applications for Profit Center Accounting.

[!]

Significance of Master Data Maintenance
It is mandatory that you carefully maintain the master data in advance.

So that you can understand these new reporting options in detail, the following section discusses a comprehensive example.

Example of an Assignment Monitor Between Cost Centers and Profit Centers

Let's look at an example of an assignment monitor between cost centers and profit centers. Figure 3.49 shows the initial screen of the report. In this case, the Cost Centers characteristic is selected as the object to be checked. Three reporting variants are available:

▶ **Display Objects Without Profit Centers**
Using this variant, the system displays only cost centers whose master data doesn't refer to any profit center.

▶ **Display Objects for Profit Center/Profit Center Group**
Using this version, the system displays all current assignments between cost centers and profit centers or profit center groups.

▶ **Display Profit Centers Without Cost Centers**
Using this option, the system shows the PROFIT CENTER VIEW, displaying all profit centers for which no derivation from the COST CENTERS characteristic exists.

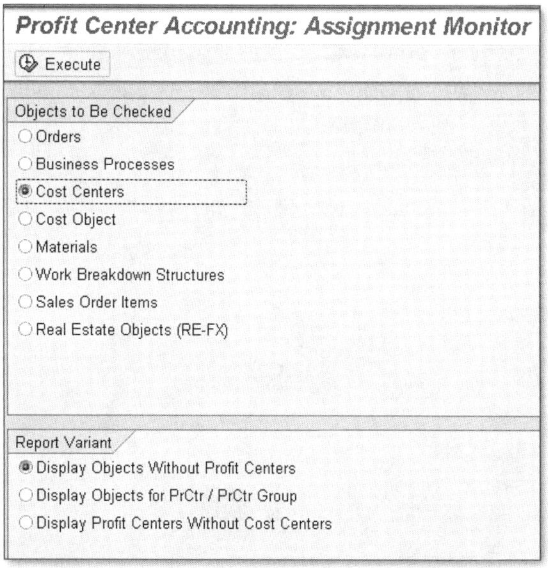

Figure 3.49 Objects to Be Checked—Cost Center

If you run the assignment report using the DISPLAY OBJECTS WITHOUT PROFIT CENTERS variant, the system displays the overview screen illustrated in Figure 3.50. In this context, you must also select the cost center category for a defined date. In this example, you selected all production cost centers that are valid as of 04/15/2009.

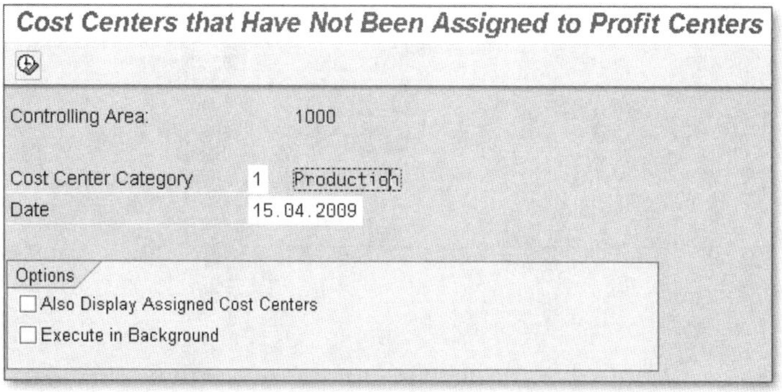

Figure 3.50 Selecting the Cost Center Category

Figure 3.51 shows all cost centers whose master data doesn't refer to any profit center. This situation could lead to an error message in the document entry for the document splitting with the PROFIT CENTER characteristic as a mandatory field, for example.

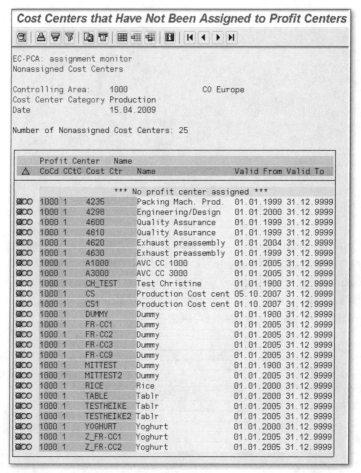

Figure 3.51 Nonassigned Cost Centers

You can make corrections by double-clicking the respective entry, and you can directly navigate from the list to the transaction for master data changes (see Figure 3.52).

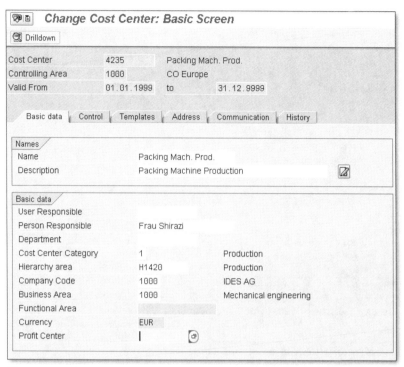

Figure 3.52 Cost Center Master Record

The number of missing assignments is not always as clear as in this case. If a manual revision cannot be made purposefully due to the scope, the SAP system also offers transactions for mass maintenance of data at some locations. In the next example, which is shown in Figure 3.53, such a transaction exists for the assignment maintenance between the characteristics, PROFIT CENTER and MATERIAL MASTER.

Of course, you should use such a transaction only with due care. After you've pressed the F8 key for execution, the system displays an overview screen for the mass maintenance of material master data. In this example, you've selected the "ID_PRCTC" variant to enable a fast entry for each material and profit center (see Figure 3.54).

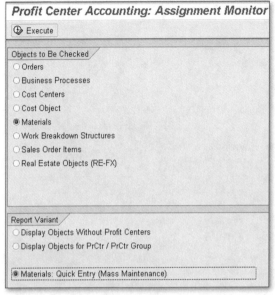

Figure 3.53 Selecting "Profit Center" and "Materials"

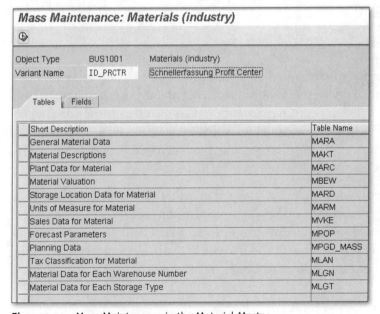

Figure 3.54 Mass Maintenance in the Material Master

To be able to select which material master data is supposed to be changed, press F8 again to go to the next selection screen. Figure 3.55 illustrates that in this example, only materials of material type FERT in Plant 1000 with profit center 1000 are supposed to be changed.

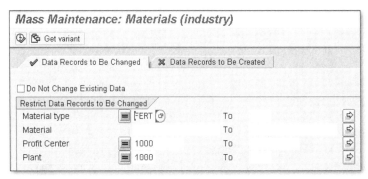

Mass Maintenance: Materials (industry)

📀 ⿻ Get variant

| ✔ Data Records to Be Changed | ✖ Data Records to Be Created |

☐ Do Not Change Existing Data

Restrict Data Records to Be Changed

Material type	▣ FERT ⿻	To	⇨
Material		To	⇨
Profit Center	▣ 1000	To	⇨
Plant	▣ 1000	To	⇨

Figure 3.55 Selecting the Data to Be Changed

Press F8 to select the data; this selection can run in the foreground or in the background. This decision should be based on the quantity of data to be selected. Then the system displays a worklist, which you can edit manually (see Figure 3.56).

Mass Maintenance: Materials (industry)

⿻ | ⿻ Restrictions ⿻ Old Values | ⿻

| General Material Data | ✔ Plant Data for Material |

⿻ ⿻⿻⿻⿻ ⿻⿻ ⿻⿻ ⿻ ⿻ 62 Entries

Material	Plant	Description	Profit Center
New Values			1010
Replace Only			1000

◀ ▶

Material	Plant	Description	Profit Center
1250	1000	Test mat · ERP05-PPBD-FG	1000
1817	1000	Test mat · ERP05-PPBD-FG-MTO	1000
AG1000	1000	Configurable product	1000
AM2-301	1000	MOTOR	1000
AM2-701	1000	Dashboard	1000
AM2-GT	1000	SAPSOTA FUN DRIVE 2000GT	1000
AM3-GT	1000	SAPSOTA 3000GT	1000
AT_FERT1	1000	finished product	1000
AT_PFERT	1000	finished product · Process Material	1000
CRP_FERT1	1000	finished product	1000

Figure 3.56 Manual Processing of the Worklist

In this example, profit center 1000 is replaced with a new value 1010. If you click the ▦ icon, the new value is transferred to the respective data records of the worklist. The actual change of the material master record takes place upon saving.

[+]

> ### Changes are Possible Only Partly from a Business Viewpoint
>
> If dependent transaction data and evaluations on the basis of Profit Center Accounting already exist, it is not useful from a business viewpoint simply to enter a new profit center value in the material master data using the mass data maintenance as in this example. If the time of data conversion is within one year and if segment balance sheets are used on the basis of Profit Center Accounting, stock transfer postings are mandatory.
>
> The segment balance sheet of profit center 1000 is therefore credited and the one of profit center 1010 is debited directly. Otherwise, a technical data conversion can lead to incorrect results within the segment balance sheets.

The new evaluation options for the PROFIT CENTER characteristic account for the increased significance of the entity and provide critical findings on the integrative assignment of this characteristic.

Scenario "Profit Center Accounting"

If you activate the Profit Center Accounting scenario in the General Ledger, you should take note of the following new options and their effects:

▶ **New balance sheet entity**
The profit center can be used as a new balance sheet entity for evaluations. Operational processes such as dunning notices, payments, or interest calculations are still controlled by the "company code" entity.

▶ **Allocations and distributions**
Allocations can be executed in the General Ledger, and distributions are supported. There are no secondary cost elements in the General Ledger.

▶ **Planning**
Planning based on the Profit Center Accounting scenario is possible. Integration of CO-OM and CO-PA exists as well.

▶ **Reporting**
The options available with the new standard reporting can now be

compared with those in classic Profit Center Accounting to a large extent.

Enhancement Package 3 offers a migration tool for transferring Report Writer and Report Painter reports to New G/L Accounting, which emerged on the basis of table GLPCT, the totals table of classic Profit Center Accounting. In future, you can use these reports on the basis of table FAGLFLEXT. This is possible for both standard reports and custom reports. The following section describes the options available here.

Transfer of Report Writer and Report Painter Reports

How do you classify Report Writer/Report Painter reports in the reporting landscape of the SAP ERP system? Figure 3.57 provides an overview of the reporting tools in the SAP ERP system.

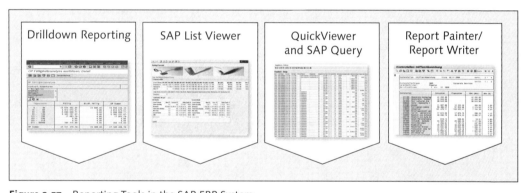

Figure 3.57 Reporting Tools in the SAP ERP System

SAP's drill-down reporting is a dialog-oriented information system that contains convenient functions for navigating in the dataset. This information system is able to evaluate the dataset according to all characteristics contained in the data description. You can use any key figures for description in this interactive drill-down reporting.

Drill-down reporting

The *SAP List Viewer* is a generic display tool that generates a standard list formatted by user-friendly aspects from the data provided. The SAP List Viewer standardizes and simplifies the handling of lists in the SAP system. You are provided with a standardized user interface and list formatting for all lists. This way, you can have the system display both

SAP List Viewer

153

simple and hierarchically sequential lists; moreover, you are provided with a multitude of interactive functions such as SORTING, SUMMATION, FILTER, and so on. You can change the presentation of lists without prior selection of data and save the changed list layout in variants.

Quick Viewer and SAP Query

Quick Viewer and *SAP Query* are tools that enable you to create lists using a menu. The SAP Query offers an extensive range of options to define reports and create various forms of reports, such as basic lists, statistics, and ranked lists. You can select the data that you require for your list from any tables of the SAP system.

Report Painter

By means of the *Report Painter* you can report on data from different applications. Because of the form layout, during definition you can view the structure of the report as it will be displayed when you output the corresponding data. The graphical user interface of the Report Painter can be used for various issues (see Figure 3.58):

▸ Definition of planning layouts

▸ Definition of drill-down reports, and

▸ Definition of Report Writer reports

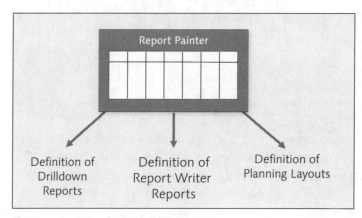

Figure 3.58 Using the Report Painter

WYSIWYG principle

The Report Painter is based on the principle of WYSIWYG; it uses a graphical reporting structure as illustrated in Figure 3.59, which forms the basis of report definition and in which the rows and columns of the report are displayed as they will be output in the report later on. The

Report Painter is the interface between the user and the Report Writer. The system converts reports, which are created in the Report Painter, to Report Writer and executes them.

[+]

> **Report Painter and Report Writer**
>
> The Report Painter fulfills a similar function as the Report Writer, but it is much easier to use—you don't need to be familiar with the set concept of the Report Writer to be able to create reports in the Report Painter.

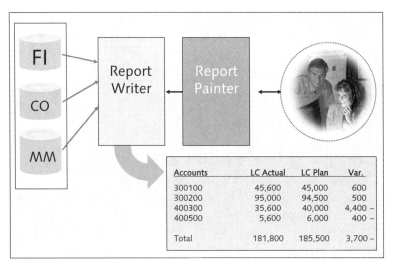

Accounts	LC Actual	LC Plan	Var.
300100	45,600	45,000	600
300200	95,000	94,500	500
400300	35,600	40,000	4,400 –
400500	5,600	6,000	400 –
Total	181,800	185,500	3,700 –

Figure 3.59 Report Painter—WYSIWYG Principle

A reporting table serves as the transfer structure of the Report Painter or Report Writer; this reporting table is specified by the SAP ERP system and cannot be changed. The reporting table summarizes all characteristics, basic key figures, and key figures. All reports are contained in libraries; a library, in turn, is a collection of characteristics, basic key figures, and key figures which were selected from the entries of a Report Writer table. Figure 3.60 illustrates these components.

Components

You have the following options when working with libraries:

Libraries

- ▸ Separation of development reports and production reports
- ▸ Subdivision of reports according to user groups
- ▸ User authorization assignment for each library

155

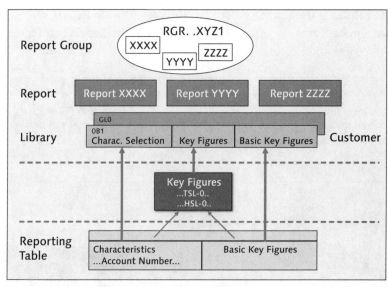

Figure 3.60 Report Writer Components

In Customizing, you can create a library via the following menu path: FINANCIAL ACCOUNTING (NEW) • GENERAL LEDGER ACCOUNTING (NEW) • INFORMATION SYSTEM • REPORT WRITER/REPORT PAINTER REPORTS • MAINTAIN LIBRARIES (see Figures 3.61 and 3.62).

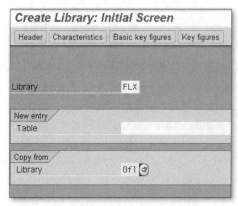

Figure 3.61 Create Library—Initial Screen

When you create a library, you must decide which characteristics, basic key figures, and key figures (see Figure 3.63) are supposed to be added to this library.

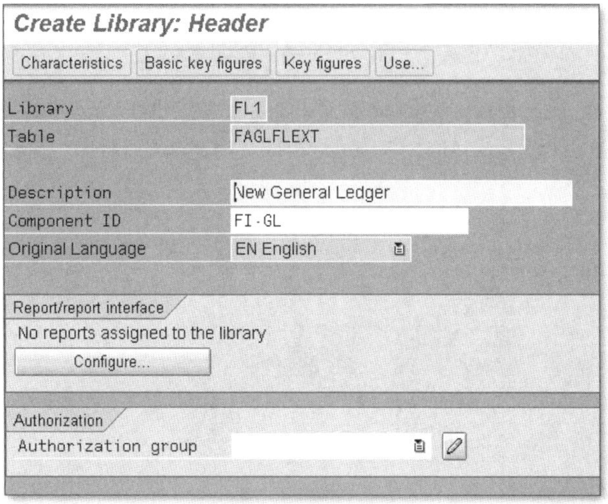

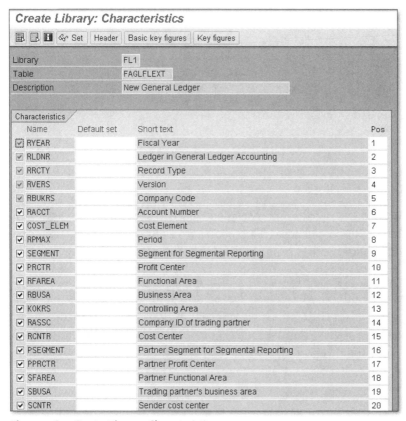

Figure 3.62 Create Library—Header

Figure 3.63 Create Library—Characteristics

Characteristics

Characteristics are criteria for selecting database records, for instance, ACCOUNT NUMBER, BUSINESS AREA, or CURRENCY KEY.

Basic key figures

Basic key figures are value and quantity fields in selected database records, for instance, LOCAL CURRENCY or TRANSACTION CURRENCY (see Figure 3.64).

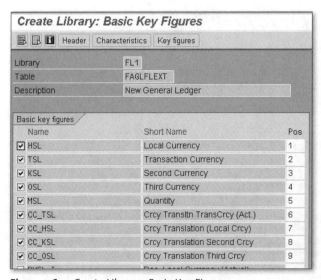

Figure 3.64 Create Library—Basic Key Figures

Key figures

Key figures consists of a basic key figure and one or more characteristics such as LOCAL CURRENCY, LOCAL CURRENCY (ACTUAL), or LOCAL CURRENCY (PLAN) (see Figure 3.65).

When you create the library, either you can specify a table and then select the desired characteristics, basic key figures, and key figures from this table, or you can simply copy an already existing library.

Defining Report Painter reports

By means of a graphical report structure, which forms the basis of the report definition, you define the Report Painter reports. This graphical structure maps the report rows and columns in such a way that they can be output in the report later on. Figure 3.66 shows the structure of the Report Painter report.

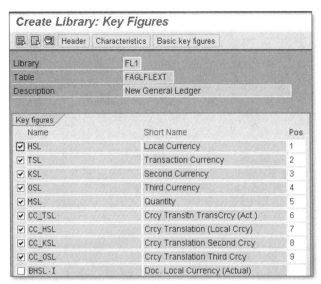

Figure 3.65 Create Library—Key Figures

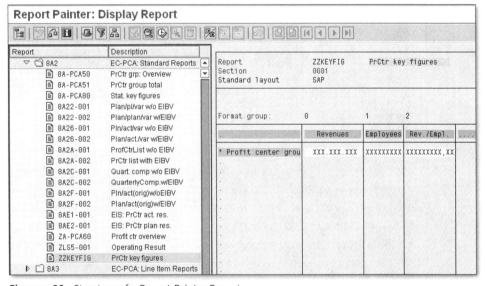

Figure 3.66 Structure of a Report Painter Report

When you run a Report Painter report, the system automatically converts it to the Report Writer format. To output reports, you must integrate them with a *report group*. Using a report group, you summarize the reports of a library that access similar data but format it differently.

Figure 3.67 provides an overview of the applications in which Report Writer and Report Painter reports are used. Figure 3.67 also shows that standard reports and custom reports exist in classic Profit Center Accounting (EC-PCA), which you may want to copy to New G/L.

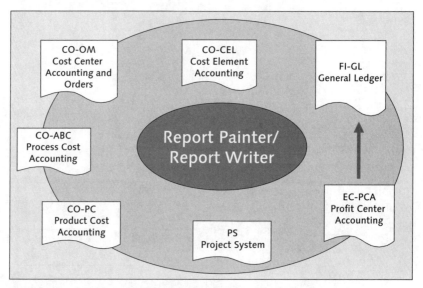

Figure 3.67 Overview of Report Painter/Report Writer Applications

Copying EC-PCA reports

If standard reports and/or custom reports exist in the classic EC-PCA environment that you want to copy, in the first step—which you already know from another enhancement within the scope of Enhancement Package 3, the authorization check for profit centers—you must activate the *Profit Center Update* scenario for at least one ledger in Customizing via the following menu path: FINANCIAL ACCOUNTING (NEW) • FINANCIAL ACCOUNTING BASIC SETTINGS (NEW) • LEDGERS• LEDGER • ASSIGN SCENARIOS AND CUSTOM FIELDS TO LEDGERS.

The tool supports you in all subsequent steps, which you can find in Customizing via the following menu path: FINANCIAL ACCOUNTING (NEW) • GENERAL LEDGER ACCOUNTING (NEW) • INFORMATION SYSTEM • REPORT

WRITER/REPORT PAINTER REPORTS • TRANSFER OF REPORTS FROM PROFIT CENTER ACCOUNTING • TRANSFER REPORTS.

Figure 3.68 shows, as an example, how to take a Report Painter report in the area of classic Profit Center Accounting EC-PCA as the starting point.

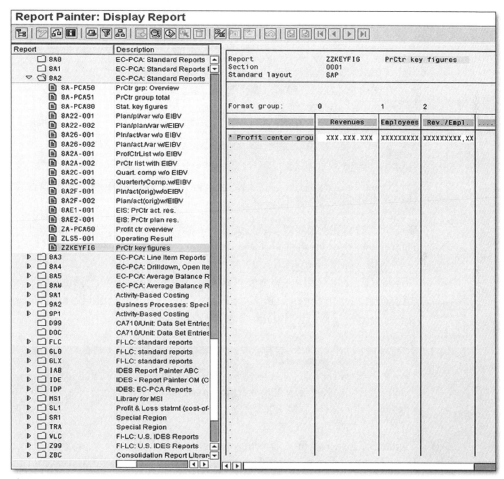

Figure 3.68 Report Painter Report ZZKEYFIG (Profit Center Key Figures in classic Profit Center Accounting EC-PCA)

The ZZKEYFIG PrCTr key figures report is supposed to be copied to New G/L. You can find such a report in the application under ACCOUNTING • CONTROLLING • COST CENTER ACCOUNTING • INFORMATION SYSTEM • TOOLS • REPORT PAINTER • DISPLAY (more precisely, in the standard EC-PCA reports in library 8A2). Proceed as follows:

First select a source and a destination library. Figure 3.69 shows this selection.

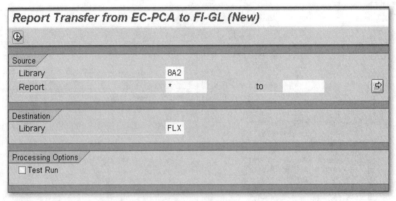

Figure 3.69 Selecting the Source and Destination Library

The system copies the reports as well as dependent objects, such as sets and variables, to the new environment. This copying could be necessary, for example, if the field name has changed.

[+] | **Sets and Variables**

A set is an object that you use to combine specific values or value intervals in one set name. The set values exist in one or more dimensions of a database table.

Sets Figure 3.70 shows an example of sets and their usage; you can view a basic set that contains values (single values or value intervals) using the same characteristic. In this example, January, February, and March are combined in one *Basic Set Quarter 1*.

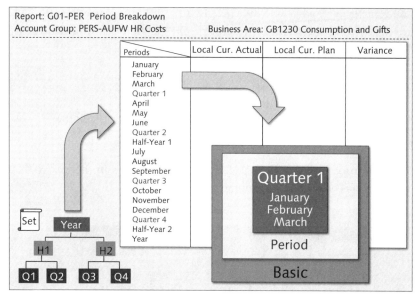

Figure 3.70 Sets

When you define reports, you can also use variables instead of fixed val-   Variables
ues. When you run the report group, the system displays an input-ready
field for each used variable in the report's selection screen. Figure 3.71
shows an example for variables.

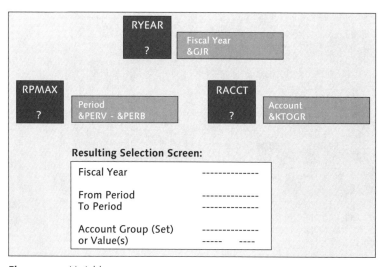

Figure 3.71 Variables

Test run for transfer

The transfer of reports to New G/L can also be done in the test run. Figure 3.72 shows the result of the test run in the analysis. In this process, the reports to be transferred are categorized as follows:

- Reports that can be transferred without any problems (green traffic light)
- Reports that may require postprocessing (yellow traffic light)
- Reports that cannot be transferred (red traffic light)

The system does not update any Customizing entries in the test run. It only displays a transfer log, which is not stored.

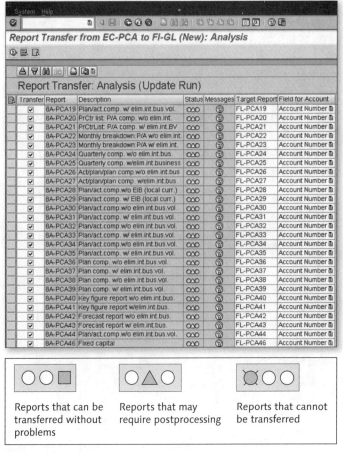

Figure 3.72 Analysis Through Test Run

You can use the substitution for the ACCOUNT field in the report: You can use it to replace the account number from the EC-PCA environment (GLPCT table, RAACCT field) in New G/L Accounting with the ACCOUNT field (by default, FAGLFLEXT table, RACCT field) or with the cost element (FAGLFLEXT table, COST_ELEM field). Figure 3.73 provides a graphical illustration of substitution.

Substitution

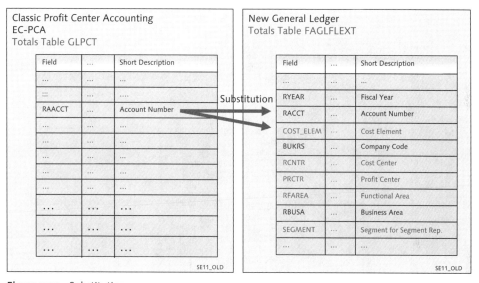

Figure 3.73 Substitution

In the update run, the system checks whether the report to be transferred already exists in the destination library and issues a warning message if necessary. The report transfer is evaluated in detailed logs, which are also saved during an update run.

System check

You can find the logs on report transfer in Customizing via the following menu path: FINANCIAL ACCOUNTING (NEW) • GENERAL LEDGER ACCOUNTING (NEW) • INFORMATION SYSTEM • REPORT WRITER/REPORT PAINTER REPORTS • TRANSFER OF REPORTS FROM PROFIT CENTER ACCOUNTING • DISPLAY LOGS OF REPORT TRANSFERS.

Now let's go back to the starting point: a Report Painter report, which you transferred from the area of classic Profit Center Accounting EC-

PCA (Report ZZKEYFIG PrCTr key figures) to New G/L Accounting in this example.

You can find the report after transfer in the application under ACCOUNT-ING • CONTROLLING • COST CENTER ACCOUNTING • INFORMATION SYSTEM • TOOLS • REPORT PAINTER • DISPLAY: more precisely, in the reports in library FLX (see Figure 3.74).

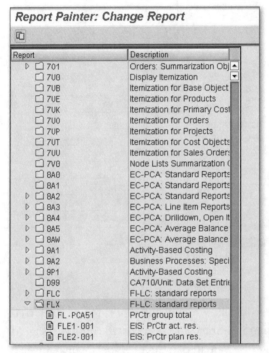

Figure 3.74 Report in the New Library FLX

[+] | **Changed Report Name**

During the report transfer, the system proposes a name for the destination report. This name was changed in this example.

Figure 3.75 shows a directory of the reports, which you can now find in library FLX.

Directory: Report

Lib	Report	Description	Table	Changed By	Changed on	Created By	Created on	Origin
☐FLX	FL-PCA47	Qtrly plan comp. w/o elim.int.bus.	FAGLFLEXT	ACCOUNTANT1	04.02.2009	**SAP**	04.02.2009	
☐FLX	FL-PCA48	Qtrly plan comp. w/ elim.int.bus.	FAGLFLEXT	ACCOUNTANT1	04.02.2009	**SAP**	04.02.2009	
☐FLX	FL-PCA51	PrCtr group total	FAGLFLEXT	ACCOUNTANT1	04.02.2009	**SAP**	04.02.2009	P
☐FLX	FL-PCA60	Plan/act.comp.w/o elim.int.bus.vol.	FAGLFLEXT	ACCOUNTANT1	04.02.2009	**SAP**	04.02.2009	
☐FLX	FL-PCA61	Plan/act.comp. w/ elim.int.bus.vol.	FAGLFLEXT	ACCOUNTANT1	04.02.2009	**SAP**	04.02.2009	
☐FLX	FL-PCA62	Plan/act.comp.w/o elim.int.bus.vol.	FAGLFLEXT	ACCOUNTANT1	04.02.2009	**SAP**	04.02.2009	
☐FLX	FL-PCA63	Plan/act.comp. w/ elim.int.bus.vol.	FAGLFLEXT	ACCOUNTANT1	04.02.2009	**SAP**	04.02.2009	
☐FLX	FL-PCA64	PrCtr list: P/A comp. w/o elim.int.	FAGLFLEXT	ACCOUNTANT1	04.02.2009	**SAP**	04.02.2009	
☐FLX	FL-PCA65	PrCtrList: P/A comp. w/ elim.int.BV	FAGLFLEXT	ACCOUNTANT1	04.02.2009	**SAP**	04.02.2009	
☐FLX	FL-PCA66	Qtrly act. comp. w/o elim.int.bus.	FAGLFLEXT	ACCOUNTANT1	04.02.2009	**SAP**	04.02.2009	
☐FLX	FL-PCA67	Qtrly act. comp. w/ elim.int.bus.	FAGLFLEXT	ACCOUNTANT1	04.02.2009	**SAP**	04.02.2009	
☐FLX	FL-PCA68	Qtrly plan comp. w/o elim.int.bus.	FAGLFLEXT	ACCOUNTANT1	04.02.2009	**SAP**	04.02.2009	
☐FLX	FL-PCA69	Qtrly plan comp. w/ elim.int.bus.	FAGLFLEXT	ACCOUNTANT1	04.02.2009	**SAP**	04.02.2009	
☐FLX	FL-PCA70	Plan/act.comp.w/o elim.int.bus.vol.	FAGLFLEXT	ACCOUNTANT1	04.02.2009	**SAP**	04.02.2009	
☐FLX	FL-PCA71	Plan/act.comp. w/ elim.int.bus.vol.	FAGLFLEXT	ACCOUNTANT1	04.02.2009	**SAP**	04.02.2009	
☐FLX	FLE1-001	SAP-EIS: Actual PrCtr result	FAGLFLEXT	ACCOUNTANT1	04.02.2009	**SAP**	04.02.2009	P
☐FLX	FLE2-001	SAP-EIS: Plan PrCtr result	FAGLFLEXT	ACCOUNTANT1	04.02.2009	**SAP**	04.02.2009	P

Figure 3.75 Directory of Reports in Library FLX

This chapter has already introduced the reporting tools available in SAP ERP including drill-down reporting. Enhancement Package 3 comprises drill-down reports for profit centers and segments. The motivation for the new drill-down reports is customers' requests for standardization in reporting for the most critical profit center reports in New G/L Accounting. Previously, the drill-down in secondary cost elements was not possible in New G/L. The interface to CO reports was also missing. Let's take another look at the architecture of drill-down reports in Figure 3.76.

As you can see in Figure 3.76, characteristics, key figures, and forms can be included in the definition of reports.

▶ A form describes the basic content and formal structure of report lists and can be considered as a semifinished product for a report, which is then completed with characteristics and key figures in the report definition.

▶ Characteristics are included in both the form and the report itself.

▶ Key figures can be selected either in the form or in the report.

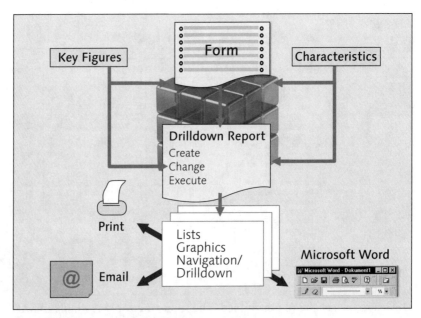

Figure 3.76 Architecture of Drill-down Reporting

Drill-down reporting functions A report results in a multitude of interactively selectable report lists and graphics, which are displayed in the screen. Drill-down reporting itself contains user-friendly functions for navigating in the dataset (for instance, next level, next object within the level, hiding a level, detail list/drill-down list). Additionally, it includes a variety of other functions for interactive report processing (sortings, requirement specifications, ranked lists, and so on): You can, for example, send report lists (for instance, by fax), provide them on the Internet, or transfer them as a file to Microsoft Word and Excel.

Printing reports Besides the dialog functions for displaying reports, drill-down reporting also includes functions for printing reports. You are provided with various print formatting functions specifically for printing reports; they enable you to visually design your reports according to your requirements (for instance, page break, header and footer, underscore).

Prerequisites To create drill-down reports, you must first create some prerequisites, which are comparable to the prerequisites for profit center authorization check and for the transfer of profit center reports from EC-PCA to New G/L:

1. First, you must activate the scenarios *Profit Center Update* or *Segment Reporting* (see Figure 3.77).

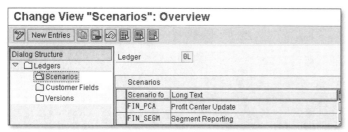

Figure 3.77 Assigning the "Profit Center Update" or "Segment Reporting" Scenarios to Ledger 0L

2. Then import the new default drill-down reports from client 000. You can find this option in Customizing under FINANCIAL ACCOUNTING (NEW) • GENERAL LEDGER ACCOUNTING (NEW) • INFORMATION SYSTEM • DRILL-DOWN REPORTS (G/L ACCOUNTS) • REPORT • IMPORT REPORT FROM CLIENT 000.

3. Here the system also queries the report type, as shown in Figure 3.78; in one of the next steps, you can select the individual reports (see Figure 3.79).

Figure 3.78 Specify the Report Type for the Import of Reports from Client 000

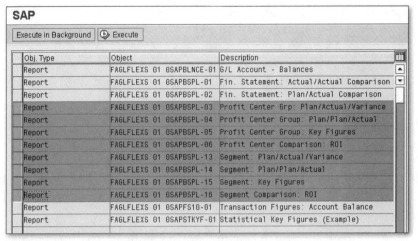

Figure 3.79 Specify the Report for the Import of Reports from Client 000

4. After the import, you can find the reports in the application (see Figure 3.80), which is available via the following menu path: ACCOUNTING • FINANCIAL ACCOUNTING • GENERAL LEDGER • INFORMATION SYSTEM • GENERAL LEDGER REPORTS (NEW) • REPORTS FOR PROFIT CENTER ACCOUNTING.

5. The following eight standard reports are available (four for profit centers, four for segment reports):

- OSAPBSPL-03: Profit Center Group: Plan/Actual/Variance

- OSAPBSPL-04: Profit Center Group: Plan/Plan/Actual

- OSAPBSPL-05: Profit Center Group: Key Figures

- OSAPBSPL-06: Profit Center Comparison: ROI

- OSAPBSPL-13: Segment: Plan/Actual/Variance

- OSAPBSPL-14: Segment: Plan/Plan/Actual

- OSAPBSPL-15: Segment: Key Figures

- OSAPBSPL-16: Segment Comparison: ROI

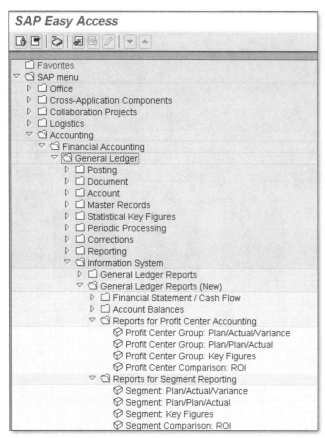

Figure 3.80 Drill-down Reports For Profit Center and Segment Reporting in the Information System of the Application

You are provided with standard drill-down reports for profit center and segment reporting. The structure of these reports is similar to the underlying reports from Profit Center Accounting (8A-PCA001G, 8A-PCA004G, and 8A-PCA011).

You can call the reports just mentioned for a single profit center, for a profit center interval, for a profit center group, or for an individual segment or a segment interval. Figure 3.81 shows the selection screen of a drill-down report for Profit Center Accounting, which illustrates these options.

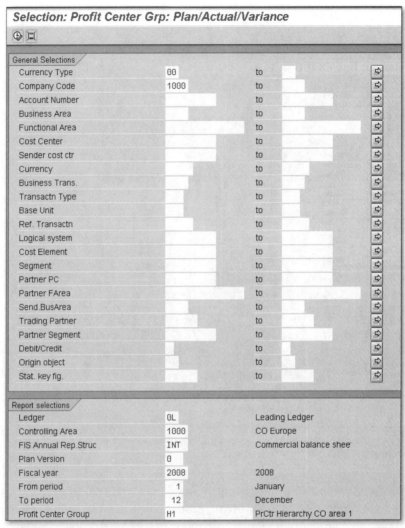

Figure 3.81 Selection Screen of the Drill-down Reports For Profit Centers in the Information System of the Application

Drill-down options

Figure 3.82 provides an overview of the drill-down options. The reports enable a drill-down according to profit center, partner profit center, or segment and partner segment.

Execute Profit Center Grp: Plan/Actual/Variance: Overview

Number format...

Profit Center Grp: Plan/Actual/Variance   Current data (04.02
┌Navigation
Account Number   ▲   ▣ Currency Type   ▲ ▼ ⊝ 00   Document currency
Cost Element   ▣ Currency   ▲ ▼ ⊝ EUR   Euro
Segment
Profit Center   ▼
⊠ ⟲ ✖

FS Item/Account Displayed in	Plan 1 EUR	Actual 1 EUR	Variance 1 EUR	Var. % 1
◇— Commercial balance sheet	0,00	59.391.853,43	59.391.853,43	●/○
◇—— A S S E T S	12.000,00	41.912.583.339,75	41.912.571.339,75	349.271.428
◇ ┌→ Fixed assets	0,00	7.271.463,69	7.271.463,69	●/○
◇ └→ Current assets	12.000,00	41.905.311.876,06	41.905.299.876,06	349.210.832
◇—— L I A B I L I T I E S	12.000,00-	41.912.583.339,75-	41.912.571.339,75-	349.271.428
◇ ┌→ Capital and reserves	12.000,00-	39.669.005.522,51-	39.668.993.522,51-	330.574.946
◇ ├→ Special items with reserves	0,00	2.294.610,96-	2.294.610,96-	●/○
◇ ├→ Provisions	0,00	4.247.038,13-	4.247.038,13-	●/○
◇ ├→ Payables	0,00	2.237.030.168,15-	2.237.030.168,15-	●/○
◇ └→ Prepaid expenses and deferred	0,00	6.000,00-	6.000,00-	●/○
◇ ─→ Profit and loss statement	0,00	2.378.680,73-	2.378.680,73-	●/○
◇ ─→ Extraordinary result	0,00	0,00	0,00	●/○
◇ ─→ Financial statement usage	0,00	9.471.181,73	9.471.181,73	●/○
◇ ─→ Accounts not assigned	0,00	59.391.853,43	59.391.853,43	●/○
◇ ─→ Supplement	0,00	7.092.501,00-	7.092.501,00-	●/○

Figure 3.82 Navigation in the Drill-down Report

You can navigate from a drill-down report to the G/L account line item display to an original Controlling document. Figure 3.83 illustrates this procedure.

Navigating to the CO document

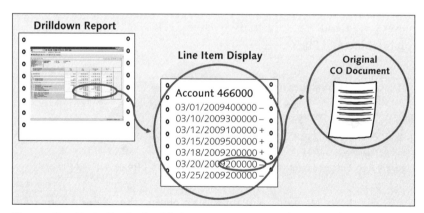

Figure 3.83 Navigation in the G/L Account Line Item Display/Original Controlling Document

You can also run a drill-down for secondary cost elements. Moreover, you can navigate from a drill-down report to a plan line item display.

It's also possible to navigate to the totals reports from Controlling (cost element and cost center reports); however, this is useful only if you've previously restricted to the cost center origin type in the drill-down report. Another option immediately associated with this topic is provided with the enhancements of Enhancement Package 3: adding the HOART and EPRCTR fields in reports.

Adding the "HOART" and "EPRCTR" Fields

This option involves the use of the Type of origin object field (ZZHORAT) in Report Writer or Report Painter reports and, in drill-down reports, the use of the Elimination Profit Center field (ZZEPRCTR) in Report Writer or Report Painter reports with elimination of internal business volume. Because it is not possible to define drill-down reports with elimination of internal business volume, it doesn't make sense to add the latter field to the drill-down reports.

Prerequisite

As a prerequisite for adding the fields to reports, you must first include the additional fields in the totals table. You must make this setting in Customizing via the path: Financial Accounting (New) • Financial Accounting Basic Settings (New) • Ledgers • Fields • Customer Fields • Include Fields in Totals Table. This applies to both fields, that is, to ZZEPRCTR and ZZHOART.

Figures 3.84 and 3.85 illustrate that the ZZHOART field is included in totals table FAGLFLEXT.

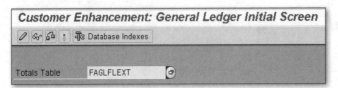

Figure 3.84 Enhancement General Ledger Initial Screen—Totals Table FAGLFLEXT

Implementing the BAdI

For the ZZEPRCTR field, you must implement the *Derive Elimination Profit Center* BAdI in Customizing via the following menu path: Financial Accounting (New) • General Ledger Accounting (New) • Information System • Report Writer/Report Painter Reports • Set Elimination Profit Center for Reports with Elimination of Internal Business Volume.

Customer Enhancement: Display General Ledger

⟦ ⟧ Customer Fields ⟦ ⟧ More Fields

Customer Include	CI_FAGLFLEX04	Customer Enhancement for Gen. Ledger: Acct Assignment Field
Last Changed By	HARTMANNJOE	12.12.2008
Status	Active	Saved

Table Enhancement

Additnl Flds:Totals Recs

Field Name	Text	Data element	Foreign key(s)	
ZZHOART	Type of origin object (EC-PCA)	HOART	☐	▲
			☐	▼
			☐	

Figure 3.85 "ZZHOART" Additional Field in the Totals Table FAGLFLEXT

Figure 3.86 shows the inclusion of the ZZEPRCTR field.

Change View "Report Writer: Special Fields": Overview

⟦ ⟧ New Entries ⟦ ⟧⟦ ⟧⟦ ⟧⟦ ⟧⟦ ⟧⟦ ⟧

Table	Orig. table	Field Name	Typ	O	O	Fil	Def.field	Filler routine	
FAGLFLEXT		GCURR		☐	☐	☑	RLDNR	E03_GET_CURRENCY_2	▲
FAGLFLEXT		HSL*	3	☐	☐	☐			▼
FAGLFLEXT		KSL*	3	☐	☐	☐			
FAGLFLEXT		LCURR		☐	☐	☑	RLDNR	E03_GET_CURRENCY_1	
FAGLFLEXT		MSL*	3	☐	☐	☐			
FAGLFLEXT		OCURR		☐	☐	☑	RLDNR	E03_GET_CURRENCY_3	
FAGLFLEXT		OSL*	3	☐	☐	☐			
FAGLFLEXT		PRCTR		☐	☐	☐			
FAGLFLEXT		RACCT		☐	☐	☐			
FAGLFLEXT		RBUKRS	2	☐	☐	☐			
FAGLFLEXT		RBUSA		☐	☐	☐			
FAGLFLEXT		RCLNT	3	☐	☐	☐			
FAGLFLEXT		RCNTR		☐	☐	☐			
FAGLFLEXT		RLDNR	1	☐	☐	☐			
FAGLFLEXT		RRCTY	1	☐	☐	☐			
FAGLFLEXT		RVERS	2	☐	☐	☐			
FAGLFLEXT		RYEAR	2	☐	☐	☐			
FAGLFLEXT		SEGMENT		☐	☐	☐			
FAGLFLEXT		TSL*	3	☐	☐	☐			
FAGLFLEXT		WSL	3	☐	☐	☐			
FAGLFLEXT	☐	ZZEPRCTR		☐	☐	☐			
FILC		ASL*	3	☐	☐	☐			
FILC		GCURR		☐	☐	☑		E03_GET_CURRENCY_2	
FILC		HSL*	3	☐	☐	☐			▲
FILC		KSL*	3	☐	☐	☐			▼

Figure 3.86 "ZZEPRCTR" Additional Field—Elimination Profit Center

"ZZHOART" field

The transaction data can be categorized by the account assignment object on which posting was implemented. The type of the origin object determines whether the transaction data originate from cost centers, internal orders, or other account assignment objects. To include the field in the drill-down reports, you must create the required report in Customizing via FINANCIAL ACCOUNTING (NEW) • GENERAL LEDGER ACCOUNTING (NEW) • INFORMATION SYSTEM • DRILL-DOWN REPORTS (G/L ACCOUNTS) • REPORT • SPECIFY REPORT and select the ZZHOART field from the list of available characteristics.

"ZZEPRCTR" field

You can use the elimination profit center in Report Writer or Report Painter reports with elimination of internal business volume. It is based on the partner profit center. The partner profit center is used to map business relationships between two profit centers of the same enterprise. However, the elimination profit center is updated only if the partner profit center is used in the elimination of internal business volume.

To include the ZZEPRCTR field (and the ZZHOART field) in the Report Writer and Report Painter reports, use the following menu path: FINANCIAL ACCOUNTING (NEW) • GENERAL LEDGER ACCOUNTING (NEW) • INFORMATION SYSTEM • REPORT WRITER/REPORT PAINTER REPORTS • MAINTAIN LIBRARIES.

You must activate the ZZHOART and ZZEPRCTR characteristics in change mode. Figure 3.87 illustrates that the ZZHOART field is included in library FLX/totals table FAGLFLEXT.

If you want to transfer reports from the classic profit center environment, EC-PCA, to New G/L Accounting, the system runs a mapping for the two fields provided that the two fields were used in the source report and that they are activated in the destination report.

The following presents another enhancement in the area of evaluations for New G/L provided by Enhancement Package 3.

Library	FLX		
Table	FAGLFLEXT	General Ledger: Totals	
Description	New GL		

Characteristics

Name	Default set	Short text	Pos
☑ RYEAR		Fiscal Year	1
☑ RLDNR		Ledger in General Ledger Accounting	2
☑ RRCTY		Record Type	3
☑ RVERS		Version	4
☑ RBUKRS		Company Code	5
☑ RACCT		Account Number	6
☑ COST_ELEM		Cost Element	7
☑ RPMAX		Period	8
☑ SEGMENT		Segment for Segmental Reporting	9
☑ PRCTR		Profit Center	10
☑ RFAREA		Functional Area	11
☑ RBUSA		Business Area	12
☑ KOKRS		Controlling Area	13
☑ RASSC		Company ID of trading partner	14
☑ RCNTR		Cost Center	15
☑ PSEGMENT		Partner Segment for Segmental Reporting	16
☑ PPRCTR		Partner Profit Center	17
☑ SFAREA		Partner Functional Area	18
☑ SBUSA		Trading partner's business area	19
☑ SCNTR		Sender cost center	20
☑ DRCRK		Debit/Credit Indicator	21
☑ AWTYP		Reference Transaction	22
☑ RMVCT		Transaction Type	23
☑ LOGSYS		Logical system	24
☑ ACTIV		FI-SL Business Transaction	25
☑ RTCUR		Currency Key	26
☑ RUNIT		Base Unit of Measure	27
☑ ZZHOART		Type of origin object (EC-PCA)	28
☐ TIMESTAMP		UTC Time Stamp in Short Form (YYYYMMDDhhmmss)	

Figure 3.87 Inclusion of the "ZZHOART" Field in the FLX Library

Line Item Extractor

The *line item extractor* (0FI_GL_14) enables you to extract documents from the leading ledger in New G/L Accounting for BI reporting. In addition, you can generate extractors for non-leading ledgers. Each of the generated extractors is named 3FI_GL_XX_SI, whereas XX is the name of the ledger.

The documents are extracted using the delta method. With this method, the system considers only data that is new or has been changed since the last time data was extracted.

You generate the additional line item extractors for non-leading ledgers using Transaction FAGLBW03.

Enhanced maintenance transactions

The functional scope of the transactions for maintaining extract structures and DataSources was enhanced. You now have the option to generate extractors not only for FI-SL totals records but for line item tables. Figure 3.88 illustrates the data flow.

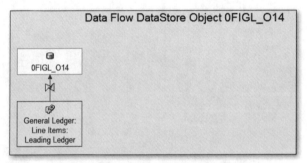

Figure 3.88 Data Flow of the "0FIGL_O14" Object

Before you call Transaction FAGLBW03, you must update two tables (T800AIS_PI and T881IS_PI) with the data of your previous extract structures and DataSources. An order is read for transporting the newly generated table entries. SAP recommends conversion of the order. In general, this conversion takes only a few seconds. Select YES to update the tables. As long as you haven't converted the order, you cannot use the enhanced functionality. Therefore, the conversion of tables is necessary.

Section 3.2, Reposting in Controlling, discusses reposting in Controlling, which was not transferred to FI in real time in SAP R/3. This flaw has been eliminated.

3.2 Reposting in Controlling

Let's take a look back: With an architecture based on distributed data storage as in SAP R/3, dependencies always arise between individual components. For example, if the costs of running the company cafeteria are distributed among various cost centers in CO, this produces the following scenario: Cost Center Accounting (CO-OM) credits the company cafeteria cost center by debiting other cost centers and thus also other functional areas. This procedure is unique to Controlling. The functional area change cannot be transferred to Financial Accounting in real time in SAP R/3. The system temporarily stores the information from Cost Center Accounting in a reconciliation ledger. All Controlling changes and effects on FI are normally transferred together at the end of the period with Transaction KALC.

In New G/L, separate data storage is retained in the form of Cost Center Accounting. Two documents are still produced for FI and CO. A reconciliation ledger can now be activated that prompts you in real time whether the document is to be posted to Financial Accounting. This feature can result in FI-CO real-time integration in the case of:

Reconciliation ledger

▶ Company code changes

▶ Business area changes

▶ Functional area changes

▶ Profit center changes

▶ Segment changes

Figure 3.89 shows a manual transaction for reposting in Controlling. The system responds in the same way with automatic procedures such as assessments or distributions. Cost center 5_1000 is credited, while cost center 5_2200 is debited.

This procedure incorporates a segment change and a profit center change. In this example, they automatically produce a document for external accounting (FI). Figure 3.90 shows the reposting from profit center ADMIN to profit center 2200 in the General Ledger.

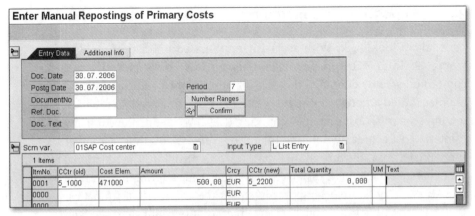

Figure 3.89 Cost Center Reposting

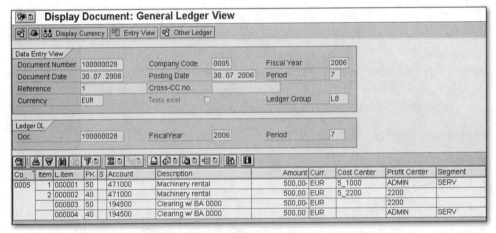

Figure 3.90 Real-Time FI Integration

This means that reconciled reporting is available to the company at all times. Locking the posting period in FI therefore has an immediate effect on CO. Conversely, having legal and management reporting that is always coordinated also means having identical time frames for the period-end closings.

A variant is defined with a key date, as shown in Figure 3.91. It should be possible logically to identify transactions that are posted with CO-FI real-time integration by a separate document type. You find this via the menu path: FINANCIAL ACCOUNTING (NEW) • BASIC SETTINGS • LEDGERS • REAL-TIME INTEGRATION. The ledger group indicates the ledgers to which you want to save the CO values. Note that Controlling is supplied by default with values from the leading ledger 0L. You can decide on a case-by-case basis whether integration is required. Field changes in customer fields are also possible with a BAdI. It is theoretically possible for all CO documents to be mapped in General Ledger accounting. The idea of also mapping streamlined Cost Center Accounting in New G/L is based on this approach.

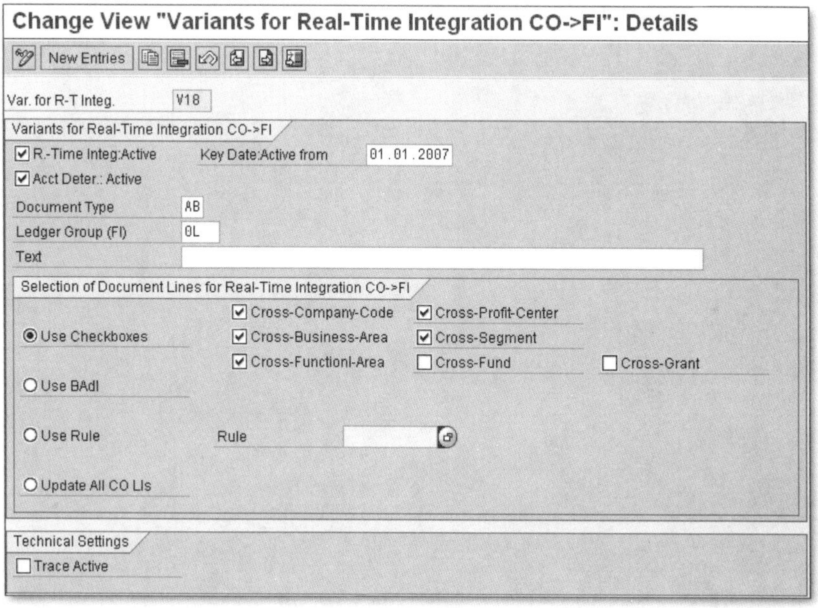

Figure 3.91 Defining a Variant for Real-Time Integration

TRACE provides access to detailed logging. The Trace Active checkbox in Customizing has a global effect on all transactions and users. Therefore, its use is not generally recommended. Transaction FAGLCOFITRACEAD-MIN provides user-specific logging (see Figure 3.92).

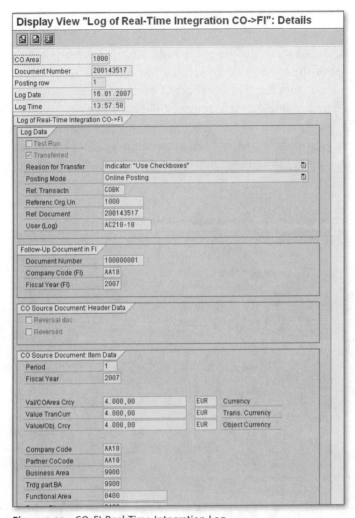

Figure 3.92 CO-FI Real-Time Integration Log

You must always map assessments based on secondary cost elements to primary accounts, using transfer tables. Figure 3.93 shows an example of a transfer table.

Updating of secondary cost elements partly not possible

The secondary cost element cannot be derived and updated under the following circumstances:

► If the CO-FI real-time document was created with the classic General Ledger. This is because the CO document is not read into New G/L as part of the migration.

► If an ALE scenario with distributed cost accounting is active. Real-time integration is maintained in the sending system but cannot be transferred with an IDoc because the information cannot be mapped there.

► A currency conversion in New G/L means a deletion of the current year and reposting via the migration programs.

► The cost element is not saved in the data entry view (table BSEG). If several secondary cost elements in a document are posted, aggregation is performed in the FI document.

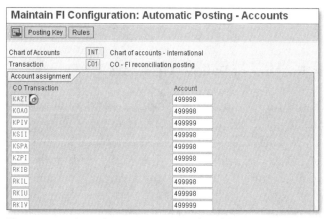

Maintain FI Configuration: Automatic Posting - Accounts

| Posting Key | Rules |

| Chart of Accounts | INT | Chart of accounts - international |
| Transaction | C01 | CO - FI reconciliation posting |

Account assignment

CO Transaction	Account
KAZI	499998
KOAO	499998
KPIV	499999
KSII	499998
KSPA	499998
KZPI	499998
RKIB	499999
RKIL	499998
RKIU	499998
RKIV	499999

Figure 3.93 "Secondary Accounts" Transfer Table

Outside of these exceptional cases, real-time integration can be activated for each company code. Figure 3.94 shows activation for company codes 0005, 0006, 0007, and 0008. It is particularly important that there be an entry in Customizing for each company code in case the company code should change. Even if the boundaries between different legal entities can be crossed, the question remains whether this is a viable solution from a business perspective. The legal situation must be clarified up front in consultation with a head accountant or auditor.

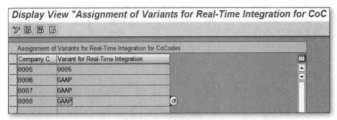

Figure 3.94 Activating Real-Time Integration

The system only creates reposting. This type of internal document may not meet certain legal requirements, which means that complete incoming or outgoing invoices including tax may be needed. Neither the old reconciliation ledger nor the new real-time integration architecture is equipped to deal with these kinds of transactions. By definition, the assessments and distributions that result from these legal infractions are not permitted.

3.3 Online Posting of Follow-Up Costs

Follow-up costs arise if the company does not receive the full amount due on the original invoice. Various posting situations in accounts receivable and accounts payable accounting and in Asset Accounting give rise to follow-up costs. These adjustments were previously made at the end of the period by means of adjustments to the financial statement and P&L statement (the reports SAPF180 and SAPF181). Two examples are provided below to illustrate the new options available with real-time postings.

3.3.1 Accounts Receivable and Accounts Payable Accounting

Correcting profit center values in real time

In accounts receivable and accounts payable accounting, follow-up costs include deductions of cash discounts, for example. Take, for example, an outgoing invoice of EUR 110,000.00 with tax charged at 10 %. This revenue is posted in SAP R/3 as EUR 100,000.00 when the invoice is posted. This amount would normally be posted not only to Financial Accounting but to the income statement in Profit Center Accounting, for instance, as EUR 80,000.00 for profit center A and EUR 20,000.00 for profit center B. If the customer pays with a cash discount of 3 %, a prorated amount of EUR 3,000.00 must be taken into account in Profit Center Accounting. This does not occur in real time in SAP R/3. Instead, a monthly reconciliation posting is executed, which readjusts the profit and loss statement SAPF181. In New G/L, the online distribution of follow-up costs is related to the *document splitting* technique. The original document itself contains information about how amounts are to be proportionately deducted from CO objects in the case of a cash discount. For example, if a customer invoice is paid with a cash discount, the cash discount amount must also adjust the relevant CO objects (that is, profit centers A and B in our example) in real time.

Figure 3.95 shows an outgoing invoice with two revenue lines and various segments or profit centers.

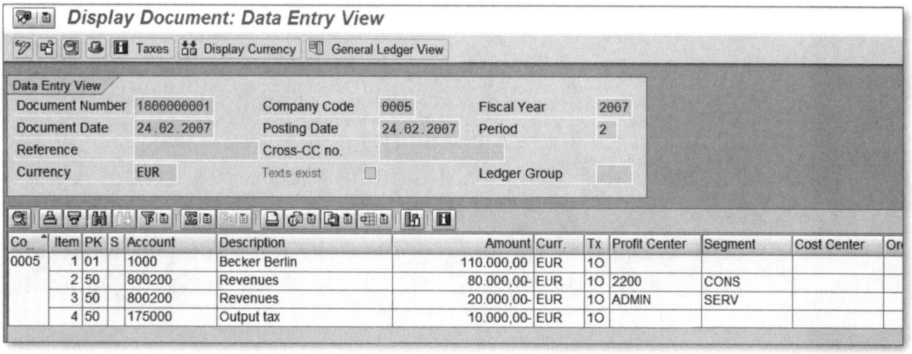

Figure 3.95 Outgoing Invoice with Various Segments or Profit Centers

An incoming payment is then posted, including the cash discount deduction (see Figure 3.96). In the data entry view, the relevant segments and profit centers are adjusted in real time in accordance with the original document.

Incoming payment inclusive of cash discount deduction

Therefore, you no longer need to readjust the profit and loss statement. Complete and correct account assignment characteristics can be determined and posted to in real time when the incoming payment is posted.

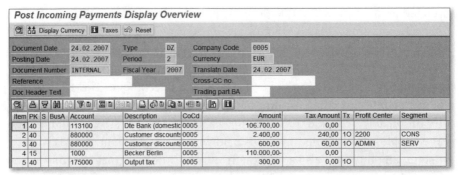

Post Incoming Payments Display Overview

🔍 ⬛ Display Currency | 🅸 Taxes | ↩ Reset

Document Date	24.02.2007	Type	DZ	Company Code	0005
Posting Date	24.02.2007	Period	2	Currency	EUR
Document Number	INTERNAL	Fiscal Year	2007	Translatn Date	24.02.2007
Reference				Cross-CC no.	
Doc.Header Text				Trading part.BA	

Item	PK	S	BusA	Account	Description	CoCd	Amount	Tax Amount	Tx	Profit Center	Segment
1	40			113100	Dte Bank (domestic	0005	106.700,00	0,00			
2	40			880000	Customer discounts	0005	2.400,00	240,00	1O	2200	CONS
3	40			880000	Customer discounts	0005	600,00	60,00	1O	ADMIN	SERV
4	15			1000	Becker Berlin	0005	110.000,00-	0,00			
5	40			175000	Output tax	0005	300,00	0,00	1O		

Figure 3.96 Incoming Payment Reflecting Segment and Profit Center in Real Time

3.3.2 Asset Accounting

Cash discount reduces acquisition and production costs

Cash discount deductions are not only reflected in outgoing invoices. If a company purchases a complex fixed asset, this gives rise to a purchasing document, which enables a cash discount deduction with the outgoing payment of the incoming invoice. In many countries, the cash discount amount reduces the acquisition and production costs of the complex fixed asset. Therefore, this must be taken into account in Asset Accounting. Previously, the entire invoice amount was activated during the gross procedure in SAP R/3. For example, if the complex fixed asset costs EUR 100,000.00 and the input tax is EUR 10,000.00, the total amount payable is EUR 110,000.00 (see Figure 3.97).

Display Document: Data Entry View

📝 📄 🔍 ⬛ 🅸 Taxes | ⬛ Display Currency | 🅴 General Ledger View

Data Entry View

Document Number	1900000003	Company Code	0005	Fiscal Year	2007
Document Date	24.02.2007	Posting Date	24.02.2007	Period	2
Reference		Cross-CC no.			
Currency	EUR	Texts exist	☐	Ledger Group	

Co	Item	PK	S	Account	Description	Amount	Curr.	Tx	Profit Center	Segment	Cost Center	Or
0005	1	31		1000	C.E.B. BERLIN	110.000,00-	EUR	1I				
	2	70		38000	000070000004 0000	100.000,00	EUR	1I	ADMIN	SERV		
	3	40		154000	Input tax	10.000,00	EUR	1I				

Figure 3.97 Purchase of an Asset—Gross Procedure

In the case of outgoing payments (see Figure 3.98), cash discounts can be posted only in certain cases and in certain amounts. A manual posting is shown here to provide a clearer overview. However, this transaction is normally posted automatically with an electronic account statement.

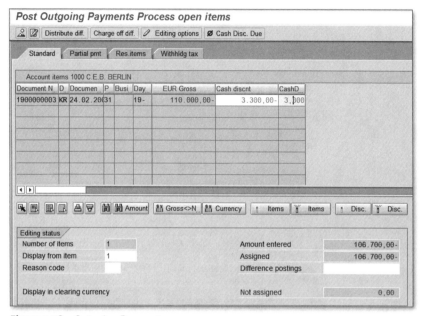

Figure 3.98 Outgoing Payment

A cash discount of 3 % would reduce the amount payable by EUR 3,300.00 to EUR 106,700.00. The net price of the complex fixed asset is accordingly reduced by EUR 3,000.00 and the input tax by EUR 300.00. In SAP R/3, however, the complex fixed asset is still listed as amounting to EUR 100,000.00 in Asset Accounting, even though it should be only EUR 97,000.00 after the outgoing payment. In SAP R/3, the acquisition and production costs were not reduced until adjustment postings were made, that is, adjustments made at the end of the period. The SAPF181 program previously was used for this purpose. As shown in Figure 3.99, new options are available in New G/L, thanks to document splitting. Accordingly, the old program can no longer be executed.

Instead, the original document itself contains information about how amounts are to be proportionately deducted from complex fixed assets in the case of cash-discount deductions. When the outgoing payment is posted, the complex fixed asset is reduced directly to EUR 97,000.00 in Asset Accounting. The result is shown in Figure 3.100.

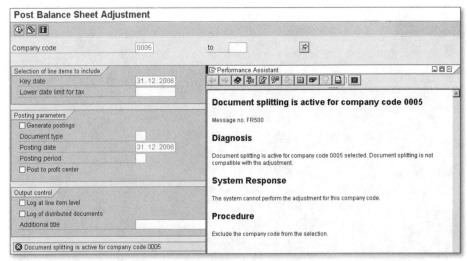

Figure 3.99 Error Message Issued by "Post Balance Sheet Adjustment" Program

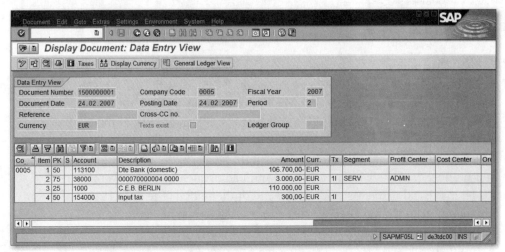

Figure 3.100 Outgoing Payment with Adjustment of Complex Fixed Asset

Two settings must be made in Customizing:

▶ First, the splitting method must support follow-up costs. This is the case in the standard configuration with method 0000000012. You can find the splitting methods in Customizing by following the menu path: FINANCIAL ACCOUNTING (NEW) • GENERAL LEDGER ACCOUNTING (NEW) • BUSINESS TRANSACTIONS • DOCUMENT SPLITTING • EXTENDED DOCUMENT SPLITTING • DEFINE SPLITTING METHODS.

▶ Second, an entry must be made in the configuration for Asset Accounting (see Figure 3.101). This entry must exist when the complex fixed asset is posted. At this point, the original document is enhanced for a subsequent outgoing payment. Online post-capitalization is not possible until this has been done.

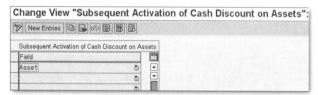

Figure 3.101 Post-Capitalization of Cash Discount to Assets

You make this setting in Customizing via the path: FINANCIAL ACCOUNTING (NEW) • GENERAL LEDGER ACCOUNTING (NEW) • BUSINESS TRANSACTIONS • DOCUMENT SPLITTING • DEFINE POST-CAPITALIZATION OF CASH DISCOUNTS ON ASSETS.

Besides the follow-up costs previously described, the next section describes the integration aspect for materials management in more detail.

3.4   Integration with Materials Management

The invoice verification is a process step that takes place directly at the interface of financial accounting and materials management. In SAP ERP, the transactions of the Materials Management (MM) component are assigned. The following pages present an integrated consistent process from the purchase order to invoice receipt. In this process, the function of document splitting of New G/L is active in the background. In the context of this example, Enhancement Package 4 included enhancements or improvements in account assignment logic.

Enhanced function of document splitting

The example considers the function of document splitting without and with the functional enhancements. The business process comprises the following steps:

1. Create purchase order
2. Post goods receipt with purchase order reference
3. Check incoming invoice with purchase order reference
4. Reduce and post vendor invoice
5. Display accounting documents

Because the result of the split accounting documents depends on the previous process steps, the focus is on the purchase order initially.

3.4.1 Create Purchase Order

Multilevel purchase order to different profit center

In the first step, you create a multilevel purchase order, that is, a purchase order that is supposed to include multiple purchase order items. In the SAP ERP system, you create a multilevel purchase order via the menu path: Logistics • Materials Management • Purchasing • Purchase Order • Create • Vendor/Supplying Plant Known, or using Transaction ME21N (see Figure 3.102).

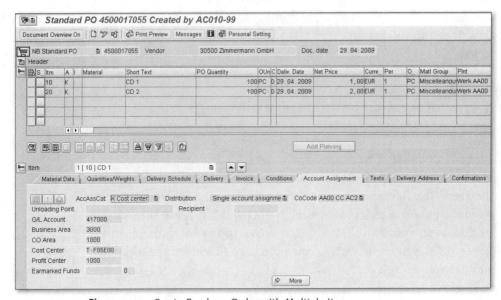

Figure 3.102 Create Purchase Order with Multiple Items

In Figure 3.102, you can clearly see that two purchase order items exist including account assignment values for profit center accounting.

For subsequent document splitting, the example is selected in such a way that reference is made to different profit center account assignments, respectively. In total, the articles CD 1 (100 pieces at EUR 1.00 each) and CD 2 (100 pieces at EUR 2.00 each) are ordered with a net value of EUR 300.00.

3.4.2 Post Goods Receipt

In the second step, you post the goods receipt in accordance with the purchase order. For this purpose, you use Transaction MIGO in the SAP menu: LOGISTICS • MATERIALS MANAGEMENT • INVENTORY MANAGEMENT • GOODS MOVEMENT • GOODS RECEIPT • FOR PURCHASE ORDER.

No quantity variance

In goods receipt, the ordered 100 pieces of the two articles, CD 1 and CD 2, are delivered, respectively. Consequently, there is no quantity variance. Figure 3.103 illustrates this transaction.

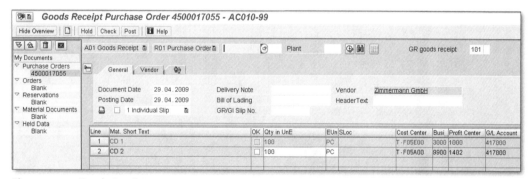

Figure 3.103 Goods Receipt

Accounting documents are updated for the material stock in the background. The document splitting now accesses the stored purchase order's profit center information.

3.4.3 Check Incoming Invoice with Purchase Order Reference

In the third step, you perform the invoice verification. In accordance with the purchase order, an invoice with an amount of EUR 440.00 for

Variance between invoice and purchase order

articles, CD 1 and CD 2, is available. You can edit it using Transaction MIRO or in the SAP menu: LOGISTICS • MATERIALS MANAGEMENT • INVENTORY MANAGEMENT • LOGISTIC INVOICE VERIFICATION • DOCUMENT ENTRY • ADD INCOMING INVOICE. After you've entered the invoice and linked it with a purchase order number, the SAP ERP system determines a discrepancy of EUR 110.00 between the invoice and the purchase order (see Figure 3.104).

This is where the actual work of the invoice verification clerk begins. It must be specified where this difference emerged and how the entire transaction is to be handled.

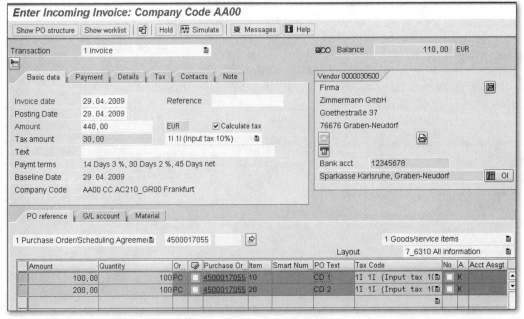

Figure 3.104 Check Invoice

Quantity difference In this example, the quantities ordered of the respective articles were delivered. So a quantity difference can be excluded at first glance. The invoice values of the articles, CD 1 and CD 2, with EUR 330.00 include 10 % tax, respectively, resulting in a gross value of EUR 110.00 for CD 1 and EUR 220.00 for CD 2. Because the difference between the purchase order amount and invoice amount is identical to the order value of article CD 1, you can assume that this item was invoiced twice.

3.4.4 Reduce and Post Vendor Invoice

Depending on the respective relation to the vendor, incorrect vendor invoices are often returned with a comment without posting or paying a value. In this example, the "incorrect" invoice is supposed to be posted nevertheless in the SAP ERP system, based on the assumption that article CD 1 was invoiced twice. To avoid an overpayment, the invoice is simultaneously reduced by the disputable amount of EUR 110.00.

Invoice reduction with Transaction MIRO

Document Principle   **[+]**

It should be a matter of course that a posting never occurs without a document. If the invoice amount is set too high, it is tempting to post the "correct" amount solely and exclusively. But then the system would post something that doesn't correspond to the vendor invoice—a posting without a document. You require two posting documents to avoid this situation: the original invoice and a document on the invoice reduction. Only then does the transaction remain transparent and reproducible.

With Transaction MIRO on invoice verification, the entry and reduction of the invoice is very simple. The previously entered data of the invoice check remains.

Figure 3.105 illustrates the additionally required columns for the second step of the invoice reduction. The error correction indicator applies to the first line item of article CD1; the second line item with article CD2 has no errors. Moreover, you require additional information for the invoice amount according to the vendor.

Because an invoice reduction in this example occurs for only one of the items, the document splitting must differentiate which profit center information is forwarded to the second posting document. This is where the changes or improvements of Enhancement Package 4 apply.

Reduction affects a profit center

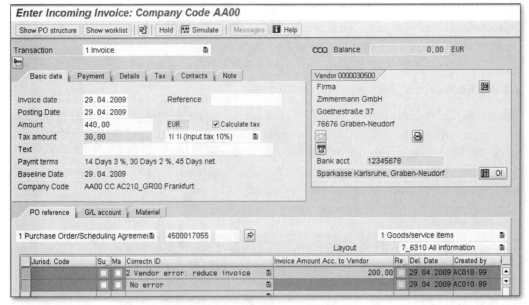

Figure 3.105 Reduce Invoice

3.4.5 Display Accounting Documents

Let's now first consider the accounting documents without the new functions of Enhancement Package 4. Figure 3.106 shows the entry view of the vendor invoice. For the amount payable of EUR 440.00, a clearing line for the invoice reduction of EUR 100.00 already exists.

Display Document: Data Entry View

| | Taxes | Display Currency | General Ledger View |

Data Entry View

Document Number	5100000005	Company Code	AA00	Fiscal Year	2009
Document Date	29.04.2009	Posting Date	29.04.2009	Period	4
Reference		Cross-CC no.			
Currency	EUR	Texts exist	☐	Ledger Group	

Co	Item	PK	S	Account	Description	Σ	Amount	Curr.	Tx	Cost Center	Profit Center	Segment	BusA
AA00	1	31		30500	Zimmermann GmbH		440,00-	EUR	1I				
	2	86		191100	Goods Rcvd/Invoice R		100,00	EUR	1I	T-F05E00	1000	SEGB	3000
	3	86		191100	Goods Rcvd/Invoice R		200,00	EUR	1I	T-F05A00	1402	SEGA	9900
	4	40		154000	Input tax		40,00	EUR	1I				
	5	40		191120	Clrg-invoice reduct.		100,00	EUR	1I				
						*	0,00	EUR					

Figure 3.106 Entry View

Additional account assignment information on the original purchase order reflects for article CD 1 in the amount of EUR 100.00 and in profit center 1000. The goods received/invoice receipt clearing account for article CD 2 shows the amount of EUR 200.00 and profit center 1402. With the General Ledger view it becomes more interesting. This view shows how additional account assignment information is projected to other line items (see Figure 3.107).

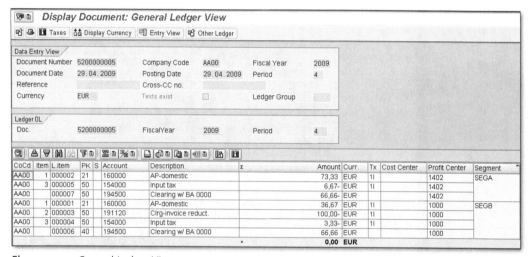

Figure 3.107 General Ledger View

Line items for the amount payable and the input tax are split with a ratio of 1:2 according to the original article information. It is remarkable here that the line item for an upcoming invoice reduction is already assigned to profit center 1000 of article CD1 in this first invoice document.

New document line item for the upcoming invoice reduction

This is the point where the function of document splitting used to be blurring prior to Enhancement Package 4.

Former functional blurring

The second posting document with the actual invoice reduction didn't receive the complete account assignment information.

Rather, the invoice reduction document of EUR 110.00 referred to the original purchase order information and split the line items for the two profit centers with a ratio of 1:2, as shown in the example in Figure 3.108.

No reduction by
profit center

The fact that only one profit center is responsible for the invoice reduction is ignored here. Enhancement Package 4 provides an alternative to this splitting logic.

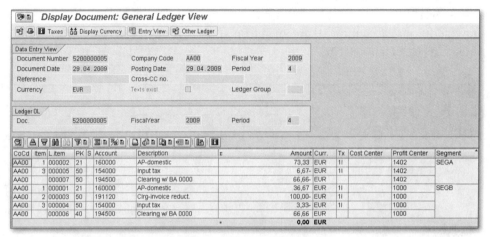

Figure 3.108 Invoice Reduction Prior to EHP4

You can find the alternative in Customizing by following the menu path: FINANCIAL ACCOUNTING (NEW) • GENERAL LEDGER ACCOUNTING (NEW) • BUSINESS TRANSACTIONS • DOCUMENT SPLITTING • EXTENDED DOCUMENT SPLITTING • DEFINE DOCUMENT SPLITTING RULES (see Figure 3.109).

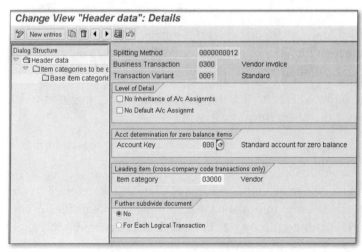

Figure 3.109 Invoice Reduction—For Each Logical Transaction

For the example shown, you must select the VENDOR INVOICE business transaction. Here you are provided with the setting option FURTHER SUB-DIVIDE DOCUMENT. Choose the FOR EACH LOGICAL TRANSACTION option to obtain a reduction document similar to the one shown in Figure 3.110. Only the profit center information of the faulty invoice items are now transferred to the reduction document.

New: document splitting for each logical transaction

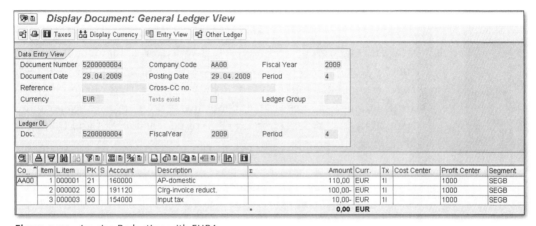

Figure 3.110 Invoice Reduction with EHP4

This new function will not be used in all usage cases directly. Some prerequisites must be met to use this function: New G/L with the *document splitting* scenario, multiple purchase order items for different profit centers, and also the use of the invoice reduction function in Transaction MIRO for invoice verification. But if these prerequisites are met, Enhancement Package 4 is worthwhile because of this enhancement alone.

Invoice reduction by cause

3.5   Period-End Closing

This section is supposed to present some exceptions in period control. Both the posting method using representative ledgers and a control using posting period 3 are new functions that are delivered with Enhancement Package 4. Another control on the basis of the General Ledger account assignment object involves a function that is based on the industry solution for public administration.

3.5.1 Representative Ledger

Prior to Enhancement Package 4, the period check was performed only on the basis of the representative ledger. The definition was made using a ledger group via the Customizing path: FINANCIAL ACCOUNTING (NEW) • FINANCIAL ACCOUNTING BASIC SETTINGS (NEW) • LEDGERS • LEDGER • DEFINE LEDGER GROUP.

Figure 3.111 illustrates how you define ledger N1 as representative within ledger group N1. The system always creates this 1:1 assignment between ledger group and representative ledger as the default value if a new ledger is defined. In some cases, SAP customers define their own ledger groups that contain more than one ledger. If, for example, U.S.-GAAP and IFRS postings entail identical valuation approaches, it can be useful to use a new ledger group IU to provide ledgers IA and U.S. with postings at the same time.

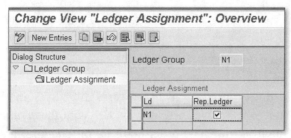

Figure 3.111 Defining a Representative Ledger

The next pages describe the function of period control prior to Enhancement Package 4 with the leading ledger 0L and the non-leading ledger N1 in more detail (see Figure 3.112).

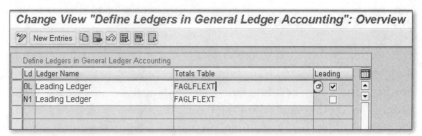

Figure 3.112 Ledger Definition

The period control of the respective company code is always assigned to the leading ledger. Alternatively, for non-leading ledgers you can define a separate variant for the period control in Customizing. Figure 3.113 illustrates this based on ledger N1 and period variant 0001 for company code AA00. Variant 1000 that is essential for the leading ledger is defined in the global data of the company code.

Period control prior to EHP4

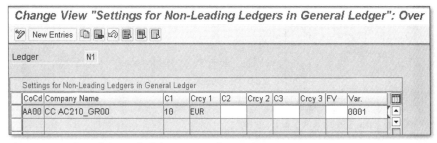

Figure 3.113 Period Control of the Non-Leading Ledger

In real life, there are definitely different time specifications to close periods for the international and local financial statement. In the example selected, the non-leading ledger stands for the international financial statement because it usually can be finalized more quickly than local financial statements. In this case, period 03.2009 within variant 0001 is already closed for the period control.

By contrast, leading ledger 0L with variant 1000 still permits this period. If you use Transaction FB50L to enter ledger-specific postings for N1 and period 3, the system displays the error message shown in Figure 3.114. The posting period is already closed.

Posting in a "closed" period

As already mentioned, the period control always uses the representative ledger before Enhancement Package 4. In this case, ledger N1 is representative within ledger group N1. But if you execute a posting using Transaction FB50, this applies to ledger group "blank." The leading ledger 0L is representative in this example, and posting period 3 is still open. Values are updated in all ledgers (see Figure 3.115).

Representative ledger is leading

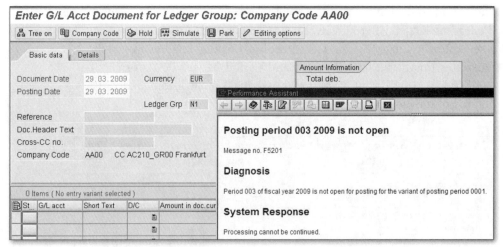

Figure 3.114 Posting Period is Closed

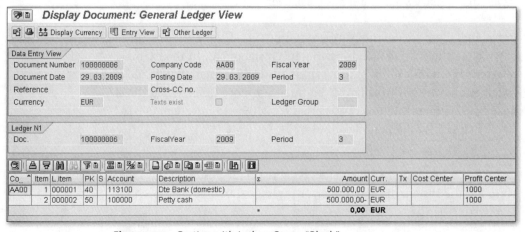

Figure 3.115 Posting with Ledger Group "Blank"

New parameters in global company code data
The selected example is intentionally designed in such a way that a contradiction arises between the settings selected (closing of period 3) and the postings made (Transaction FB50 with ledger group "blank" in precisely this period 3, which is allegedly "closed"). With this knowledge, you can now understand the development in Enhancement Package 4.

The goal was to provide an option to omit the representative ledger for period control in this constellation. For this purpose, a new parameter was added to the global data of the company code – the Manage Posting Period parameter (see Figure 3.116).

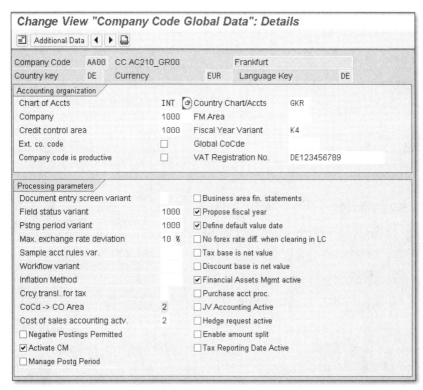

Figure 3.116 Company Code "Global Data"

If this parameter is set and if you run, for example, a posting using Transaction FB50 with ledger group "blank," the SAP system checks, for all non-leading (not representative) ledgers, whether their posting periods are open. In the example selected, the system would display an error message similar to the one shown in Figure 3.117.

If you require this ledger-specific period check per company code, this function is available with the activation of Enhancement Package 4.

Postings using the period control from EHP4

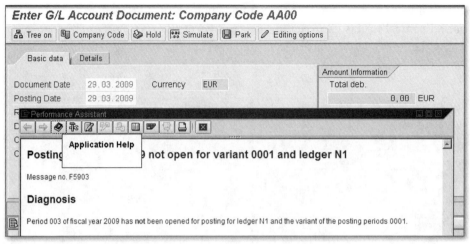

Figure 3.117 Checking all Posting Periods Concerned

3.5.2 Period Control with Three Periods

Up to now, the current settings included two configuration options to open or close posting periods:

▸ From period 1, To period 1

▸ From period 2, To period 2

In period control, you could use these columns to manage both the current periods and the special periods. Enhancement Package 4 now includes a new option: From period 3, To period 3.

Third column This third column enables you to control the real-time integration of CO in FI individually after the FI period-end closing. Concretely, this means that repostings in CO (for instance, allocations for cost centers) also entail repostings in FI for profit center, segments, or functional areas, even despite the already closed FI posting period (see Figure 3.118).

Posting from CO to FI This period control loosens the "forced" real-time integration and consequently the periodic synchronization between FI and CO. This may be required in some customer cases from an organizational viewpoint. But the effects on external reporting (segment reporting/cost of sales accounting) are obvious. This new option of period control is an instrument whose significance as a potential error source should not be underestimated.

Display View "Posting Periods: Specify Time Intervals": Overview

Posting Periods: Specify Time Intervals

Var.	A	From account	To account	From per.1	Year	To per. 1	Year	AuGr	From per.2	Year	To per. 2	Year	From Per.3	Year	To Per. 3	Year
0001	+			1	2009	12	2010		13	2009	16	2009	0		0	
0001	A		ZZZZZZZZZZ	1	2009	12	2010		13	2009	16	2009	0		0	
0001	D		ZZZZZZZZZZ	1	2009	12	2010		13	2009	16	2009	0		0	
0001	K		ZZZZZZZZZZ	1	2009	12	2010		13	2009	16	2009	0		0	
0001	S		ZZZZZZZZZZ	1	2009	12	2010		13	2009	16	2009	0		0	

Figure 3.118 New Period Control

3.5.3 Periods for each General Ledger Account Assignment Object

The processes involved in month-end closing must also be taken into account in this integrated architecture. Profit Center Accounting takes place in the General Ledger and also generates primary postings in the case of assessments. In addition, periodic values no longer arise for reconciliation in the case of reposting in Controlling. Instead, real-time account assignments are made in General Ledger accounting. While these postings to a prior period may have been allowed to "slide" in the past, the FI relevance and thus the open posting period variant is now checked when the reposting is made in CO. The settings defined in the application menu path: ACCOUNTING • FINANCIAL ACCOUNTING • GENERAL LEDGER • ENVIRONMENT • CURRENT SETTINGS • OPEN AND CLOSE POSTING PERIODS, acquire an additional significance in relation to the enhanced integration in accounting. For more information, see Chapter 2, Design and Features of the Ledgers.

Clearly, then, the existing period locks in General Ledger accounting only partly meet the requirements of the new integration (see Figure 3.119). Therefore, for the public sector industry solution (SAP for Public Sector), a transaction was created for an account assignment-dependent period lock. If you have an active EA-PS extension, you find this transaction in the application menu path: ACCOUNTING • FINANCIAL ACCOUNTING • GENERAL

LEDGER • ENVIRONMENT • CURRENT SETTINGS • OPEN AND CLOSE POSTING PERIODS ACCORDING TO GENERAL LEDGER ACCOUNTING OBJECTS.

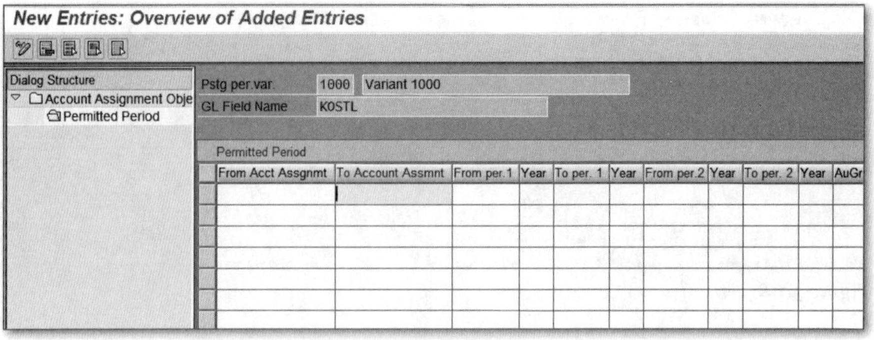

Figure 3.119 Period Lock for Account Assignment Objects

This transaction currently works only for this particular industry and its dedicated table area: FMGLFLEX. It enables flexible opening and closing of the posting periods for each account assignment object.

3.6 Conclusion

In addition to integrating Profit Center Accounting into the General Ledger, the enhanced functions of New G/L also ensure more real-time options than in SAP R/3. As a result, tasks can be completed on a daily basis that otherwise would be postponed until the end of the period, when they would be subject to greater time pressure. This ensures a transparent and accurate view of accounting at all times, simplifies reconciliation within a period, and supports the fast-close process. The sets of figures available also provide a more accurate picture of a company's current assets, finances, and revenue.

Every innovation, every possible progress, is based on a simple idea. This idea can be, for example, the imagination of globally uniform, comparable accounting standards.

4 Parallel Accounting — IFRS on the Advance

In this chapter, we look at use cases and system configurations for parallel accounting, focusing on the ledger approach in New G/L. Creating parallel financial statements does not mean that the entire body of accounting data has to be replicated simultaneously. Rather, the objective is to set priorities. Previously, either accounts, special ledgers or—in exceptional cases—company codes were used as storage locations for parallel valuation approaches. New G/L in SAP ERP now provides a fourth option for parallel accounting. This chapter compares the accounts approach and the ledger approach in New G/L on the basis of business requirements. Company codes or special ledgers are not recommended for this purpose, and are therefore not dealt with in this chapter. The next few sections focus on the configuration of the solution in New G/L. The last sections cover posting and clearing specific to ledger groups as well as the transition to open item management.

However—as already mentioned at the beginning of this chapter—the increasing use of the IFRS accounting standard is described first.

4.1 Approaching Uniform Accounting Standards

The idea of uniform, globally comparable accounting standards is an idea which is and could be used as the basis of progress.

The *International Financial Reporting Standards* (IFRS) has already come quite close to the realization of this idea. After a transition period, IFRS

IFRS in Europe

became mandatory for the consolidated financial statements of enterprises listed on the German stock exchange in Europe in 2005. This requirement affected not only the publication of these statements but also strategic and operational control processes.

Assessments and valuations of business transactions according to IFRS are therefore implemented at the operational level at which the business transactions are originally posted: the individual financial statement. This major effect on the transaction system presented a great challenge for the introduction of parallel accounting: especially because European enterprises that were listed on the U.S. Stock Exchange had to provide a statement according to U.S.-GAAP—in addition to statements according to the local standard and according to IFRS. At this point, the exchange supervisory authority did not approve IFRS.

IFRS in the U.S.

Today, the U.S. is more open to IFRS. The story of IFRS in Europe seems to be repeating itself in the U.S. In 2009, the U.S. exchange supervisory authority concluded a binding schedule for the introduction of IFRS in the U.S. For enterprises with market capitalization of more than $700 million, IFRS will be mandatory as of 2014. Enterprises with market capitalization between $75 million and $700 million have until 2015 to implement IFRS. All other listed enterprises must introduce IFRS by 2016.

Other countries introducing IFRS

Consequently, IFRS de facto has become the future financial statement standard in the U.S. Fifty other countries plan to introduce IFRS until 2011. These include Japan, Brazil, Chile, India, Canada, Malaysia, Mexico, Pakistan, and South Korea: countries whose accounting systems sometimes significantly differ from IFRS. The greater the differences between the individual accounting systems, the more important the subject of parallel accounting.

LIFO valuation

Based on fiscal law, many U.S. enterprises use inventory valuations according to the LIFO (Last In First Out) method. When purchase prices increase, this method valuates the material that is already in stock too low, and hidden reserves are accumulated. However, you can compare the financial statements of two enterprises only if hidden reserves are eliminated to a large extent and if the figures provide transparent net assets, financial positions, and results of operations.

Therefore, a valuation of inventory assets using the LIFO method is not permitted by IFRS. For enterprises in the U.S., a general IFRS implementation would have considerable taxation consequences, which probably would lead to a parallel balancing of valuations. To enable the SAP system to determine and store these valuation approaches, various options are available.

Parallel balancing

4.2 Leading Valuation Approach

Irrespective of your SAP release, the leading valuation issue assumes a critical role for the design. Creating parallel financial statements does not mean that the entire body of accounting data has to be replicated simultaneously.

The following aspects must be considered:

- **IFRS month-end closing required**
  If an enterprise must produce a month-end closing according to IFRS, for example, it often makes sense to post the primary version of this closing according to IFRS and to determine the valuation approaches separately only if the circumstances change.

- **Leading valuation as the basis for corporate decisions**
  A real-time connection to the MM (Materials Management), FI (Financials), CO (Controlling), and SD (Sales & Distribution) components is useful only for a leading valuation, which lays the foundation for corporate decisions. Other configurations, such as the determination and use of parallel prices in CO, are complex and involve a lot of effort.

If you want to accelerate the closing procedure (fast close), it is particularly important to select the appropriate leading accounting standard. If you work with operational (i.e., real-time) valuations and postings according to IFRS, the individual financial statements and the consolidated financial statements can be created and issued significantly faster than if numerous individual financial statements according to national standards had to be adapted to IFRS.

Fast close

4.3   Basic Principles

Posting method/ storage location

The posting method and subsequent storage location of reports form the basic framework of parallel accounting.

If an enterprise is required to produce a month-end closing for IFRS or U.S.-GAAP, for example, it often makes sense to post the primary version of this closing and to separately calculate values only if circumstances change. The "complete values" posting method is useful in such cases.

[Ex] **Delta Technique**

You need to valuate a provision at EUR 800.00 in accordance with IFRS, while local GAAP. requires a valuation of EUR 1,000.00. The delta method dictates that EUR 800.00 and—later—EUR 200.00 be posted. However, this method can create transparency and traceability problems. The situation can be explained fully only if both account assignment methods are used. In other words, if complete values are used, two separate, independent posting records of EUR 800.00 and EUR 1,000.00 are created for each business transaction.

International influence

The example above indicates the influence of international accounting regulations. Today, this influence is so strong that it directly affects the operational level of local financial accounting. The following example illustrates how the international group reporting standards, IFRS and U.S.-GAAP, affect the operational level of country subsidiaries in real time.

[Ex] **Example of the Influence of International Accounting Standards**

A contract completed in the Netherlands leads to sales revenues in business segments A and B. Business segment B has been recently restructured and is cross-subsidized by the highly profitable segment A. Theoretically, the revenues are to be divided in accordance with the discounts. However, in order to be able to present investors with a positive picture of growth and success, it may be a better idea to divide revenues in favor of the new segment B. In other words, the contract is structured so that cross-subsidies are neither possible nor necessary in accordance with U.S.-GAAP or IFRS. No questions are asked about this, provided that for segment A and—later—segment B, a period of at least six months elapses between the signing of the contract and the delivery of the service. You can thus see how the group-reporting requirement comes into play at this early operational level and prevents any subsequent conflict in segment reporting.

Nonetheless, local requirements still form the basis of taxation assessments. Parallel financial statements as part of accounting are facts of life
in most enterprises. Additional manual calculations in Microsoft Excel
are becoming obsolete because of intensifying requirements in terms
of transparency and thoroughness in financial statements (the audit
trail). Compounding this situation are the shorter time periods available to complete financial statements in accordance with the fast-close
principle.

4.4   Data Storage Location

But where and how can you efficiently enter, store, and provide the
valuation approaches of the various accounting standards for reporting?
Until SAP-Release R/3 4.7, there were three options: parallel accounts
approach, special ledgers, and parallel company codes. New G/L provides
a new fourth option for parallel accounting in SAP ERP. The following
sections discuss these four options in detail.

4.4.1   Mapping via Parallel Accounts

The idea behind mapping via parallel accounts is to use a storage location—namely, the account—within an overall concept by means of
complete postings. Most enterprises use a chart of accounts with account
numbers of five or six digits. However, because the SAP account number
consists of up to ten digits, you can easily extend it from six to seven
digits, for example. If you already work with ten digits, SAP SLO (*System
Landscape Optimization*) provides support for the data conversion.

Let's continue the example of extending your chart of account from six to
seven digits. Zero is prefixed to every account internally. At first glance,
nothing changes for the account determination and manual posting processes. The accounts are subdivided into several categories. There are no
valuation variances for joint accounts, which include receivables, payables, bank accounts, and a lot of P&L expense accounts, such as energy
consumption costs. If there are valuation variances, IFRS accounts and
local accounts are created.

Posting method

In real life, prefixes are assigned to the accounts:

- 0 for joint accounts
- 1 for local GAAP accounts
- 2 for IFRS accounts

You can also apply this concept to parallel accounting within a corporate group in which account class 1 reflects the corresponding local legal framework.

- Company code segment 1000 Germany: local GAAP
- Company code segment 3000 UK: local GAAP
- Company code segment 5000 Spain: local GAAP
- For local balance sheets, the system maps account class 0 (joint accounts) together with account class 1 (local accounts) in valuations within a balance sheet and P&L structure. All other accounts show a balance of 0.

System support is already provided for most of the valuation processes today. Consequently, the additional effort involved in parallel accounting is limited to the initial configuration of these programs. However, there are manual postings to accounts of the categories "local" and "IFRS," for example, in the provisions area.

Account assignment model

So as not to forget one of the two sides of valuation variances in real life, some customers have created an account assignment model. In the case of parallel accounting, manual postings involve permanent, usually manageable additional effort. Table 4.1 provides an overview of the advantages and disadvantages of the accounts approach.

Advantages	Disadvantages
Easy to implement	Multiple valuation approaches in the General Ledger
Easy to understand	Increased number of accounts
Consistent	
Audit-proof	
Standard reporting available	

Table 4.1 Conclusion—Overview of the Accounts Approach

4.4.2 Mapping via Parallel Company Codes

One of your first ideas may be to use company codes as the storage location. However, it might make sense to consider this mapping variant for parallel accounting.

On the one hand, the authorization concept enables you to implement defined and controlled access to an IFRS company code and a local company code. On the other hand, this storage location has the advantage that you don't have to add numerous customized IFRS accounts and local accounts to the chart of accounts for valuation variances. Only the company code segment for new IFRS company codes is necessary because Asset Accounting supports this mapping option.

However, there are no further advantages. If you take a second look, the disadvantages of this approach become apparent. Do you really want to double the number of company codes for IFRS purposes or even triple it for U.S.-GAAP purposes? The A segment of the accounts exists only once. Therefore, differentiations in the account name (whether it is a local or an IFRS account) are basically visible for all company codes.

The essential argument against the use of the company code approach is the consistency of this approach. Besides Asset Accounting, there is no automatic SAP valuation program that supports this parallel company code technology.

SAP does intend to implement further developments here. Thus, you can not map parallel accounting via company codes.

Table 4.2 provides an overview of the advantages and disadvantages of using company codes as the storage location.

Advantages	Disadvantages
No additional accounts required	Number of company codes doubles
Easy authorization management of valuation approaches	The account text exists only in the chart of accounts segment; that is, there is only one name for each client language and not for each company code

Table 4.2 Conclusion—Overview of the Company Code Approach

Advantages	Disadvantages
Easy to implement if valuation variances solely result from manual postings and from FI-AA	Approach is supported consistently from Asset Accounting only
Standard reporting for balance sheet and P&L statement available	No further developments planned

Table 4.2 Conclusion—Overview of the Company Code Approach (Cont.)

4.4.3 Mapping via Special Ledgers

You can also use Special Ledger (FI-SL) as the storage location for parallel accounting. This method is based on the idea of limiting the number of accounts and working with specific ledgers to map the various valuation approaches in the system.

Management requirements

This area was designed to provide a flexible and efficient tool for the management requirements.

Depending on the settings in the Customizing, postings from G/L accounting are transferred to customer-specific ledgers—special ledgers. In this separate area (for example, IFRS, U.S.-GAAP), you can work with manual standardizing entries, assessments, distributions, planning, and aggregation via roll-up. As of SAP Release R/3 4.7, automatic valuation programs can update the values directly to the Special Ledger area using a defined accounting standard, without involvement of the General Ledger.

Consequently, this additional calculation, which was actually only supposed to be a tool for management requirements, has increasingly become legally relevant.

Restrictions of Special Ledger

However, Special Ledger is a one-way street. It is not connected to Cost Center Accounting or Profit Center Accounting. You have to implement the standardizing entries, which were described for the second requirement in case 2, using a specific transaction. The field status group for optional and mandatory fields that are defined in the accounts does not apply to this transaction. One-sided postings are possible for the management due to flexibility reasons. This feature has a rather negative effect on audit assurance.

However, the overall idea of the FI-SL technology provided in Release R/3 4.7 can be considered positive. This Special Ledger technology aims at customized, self-contained ledgers for IFRS and U.S.-GAAP.

Nevertheless, this approach is tarnished by some disadvantages, such as missing cost centers and profit center integration or the existence of one-sided posting transactions within a specific posting screen. Table 4.3 provides an overview of the advantages and disadvantages of using special ledgers as the storage location.

Advantages	Disadvantages
No increased number of accounts	Additional component (FI-SL) necessary
Consistent, separate ledger for each accounting procedure	Other posting transaction than in the General Ledger (no field status validation)
Standard reporting for balance sheet and P&L statement available	No CO integration
Mapping of various fiscal year variants	Audit assurance not ensured consistently on the system side

Table 4.3 Conclusion—Overview of the Special Ledger Approach

4.4.4 Mapping via New General Ledger

New G/L in SAP ERP is based on the FI-SL technology. The new field, LEDGER GROUP, in the document header is responsible for the selection of the ledger that is supposed to be populated in case of postings. If values are determined from subledger accounting, for example, in the Transaction Manager of SAP Treasury and Risk Management, the system determines different valuation approaches for each valuation area or accounting standard and transfers them to the respectively assigned ledger group of New G/L. Here, you can map multiple ledgers, manually provide content using a standardized posting transaction (for example, FB50), or evaluate balance sheet and P&L statement (RFBILA10), for example, via standardized reporting

"Ledger Group" field

If the LEDGER GROUP field is not populated because a shared posting without valuation variances is made, the system updates all ledgers. You

Field not populated

don't have to define for certain postings such as provisions which ledger is supposed to be populated. Creating shared ledger groups, such as ledger group AB, allows you to post values to more than one ledger in one posting.

Table 4.4 provides an overview of the advantages and disadvantages of storing values in New G/L.

Advantages	Disadvantages
No increased number of accounts	The leading ledger mainly defines the integration with CO-OM, CO-PA, and FI-AA
Consistent, separate General Ledger for each accounting procedure	
Standard reporting for balance sheet and P&L statement available	

Table 4.4 Conclusion—Overview of the Special Ledger as the Storage Location

4.4.5 Storage Location—Conclusion

Mapping options in the SAP system

This historic data leads to the question of which storage location an SAP customer should use if working with the current SAP ERP release. Parallel accounts approach, special ledgers, and parallel company codes—these were the alternatives between 2001 and 2005, up to SAP Release R/3 4.7. In 2005, parallel accounting became relevant due to the European IFRS-driven wave of transition.

In light of the experiences gained here and the relation to current events in the U.S. or the 50 other countries that face the challenges of IFRS, parallel accounting needs to be considered again. With SAP's ERP releases, different ledgers can be used in New G/L as storage locations for parallel accounting. Although several of the principles of the two solutions are structured in the same way, the new solution approach should not be confused with the existing special ledger approach in SAP R/3. Rather, New G/L makes frequent reference to the ledger approach.

SAP's recommendation

Also, New G/L can still map different accounting regulations using the accounts approach. SAP Note 779251 recommends two equally valid mapping methods for parallel accounting in SAP ERP:

▶ Accounts approach

▶ Ledger approach in New G/L

In the following sections, we will describe in more detail the ledger approach as a storage location in New G/L.

4.5 Fixed Assets

The Asset Accounting (FI-AA) subledger uses as many as 99 depreciation areas to calculate different valuations that arise from a variety of acquisition and costs of production, depreciation keys, useful-life values, and replacement values. This information can be administrated and evaluated in the "Asset Accounting" subledger. You also need to consider integration when it comes to parallel accounting for financial statements. With New G/L, SAP ERP also provides integration for the ledger approach. We will look at this approach in detail in the next few pages, based on a specific scenario.

Subledger in SAP ERP Financials

4.5.1 Valuation Variances Scenario

The parallel valuation scenario should contain the entire lifecycle of a complex fixed asset, from purchase (acquisition) to use (depreciation) to sale (retirement). If two valuation approaches—IFRS and local GAAP—are used, the result should be parallel accounting that includes integration. The storage location in this case is the ledger approach in New G/L.

Lifecycle

The leading valuation in this example is IFRS. Therefore, this valuation approach is reflected in depreciation area 01 of Asset Accounting and is transferred to Controlling. Parallel accounting does not mean that all postings are made simultaneously. Only depreciation area 01 is also posted to SAP ERP 6.0 in real time.

Leading valuation

4.5.2 Asset Acquisition

In this scenario, our test company IDES in company code 0005 capitalizes two complex fixed assets that belong to the asset class "fixtures and fittings." The assets are software and hardware. To begin with a simple case, Table 4.5 shows the acquisition of hardware as a complex fixed

Software and hardware as complex fixed assets

asset, based on IFRS and local accounting standards. A vendor invoice for EUR 20,000.00 (without tax, for the sake of simplicity) has been issued. There are no valuation variances.

Account	Description	Debit	Credit	IFRS	Local GAAP
21000	Fixtures and fittings	EUR 20,000.00		0L	L6
160000	Payables		EUR 20,000.00	0L	L6

Table 4.5 Acquisition of Hardware as Complex Fixed Asset

As the posting record (see Table 4.1) clearly shows, a single posting document updates both ledgers. The acquisition is posted using the "Blank" ledger group as the common valuation approach. The value EUR 20,000.00 is displayed for balance sheet evaluations for the leading ledger 0L (IFRS) or for the ledger L6 (local GAAP).

Different acquisition costs The acquisition process for software as a complex fixed asset is a little different in this scenario. In this case, different acquisition and costs of production are used as a basis. EUR 100,000.00 is spent on external activities to develop the software, of which 80 % is recognized as an asset in accordance with IFRS and 100 % is recognized as an asset in accordance with local GAAP. Table 4.6 shows a vendor invoice for the total amount and all ledgers.

Internal order The expense item "External activity" is posted with the Controlling object "Internal order." This ensures that it is possible to create settlements for different accounting procedures at a later stage.

Account	Description	Debit	Credit	IFRS	Local GAAP
471000	External activity	EUR 100,000.00		0L	L6
160000	Payables		EUR 100,000.00	0L	L6

Table 4.6 Acquisition of Software as Complex Fixed Asset (1)—Posting via Internal Order

In the first step of creating a settlement, a shared posting is made that populates both ledgers with values for reporting purposes. In the next step, the posting record for the settlement of the internal order to the object "Asset under construction" (AuC) is displayed in Table 4.7. Amounts of 80 % for IFRS and 100 % for local GAAP are stored as the investment support key.

Settlement

Account	Description	Debit	Credit	IFRS	Local GAAP
21000	Fixtures and fittings	EUR 80,000.00		0L	L6
299999	Other costs	EUR 20,000.00		0L	L6
471000	External activity		EUR 100,000.00	0L	L6

Table 4.7 Acquisition of Software as Complex Fixed Asset (2)—Settlement of Internal Order

At this point, you might expect that a dedicated document with EUR 80,000.00 for 0L (IFRS) and EUR 100,000.00 for L6 (local GAAP) would be created for each ledger. This is not the case. Although complete valuation approaches are stored in the parallel accounts, a delta posting is also made in Asset Accounting. In practice, this means that the valuation approach of the leading depreciation area 01 is always transferred to all ledgers. Only when you make a second periodic APC values posting is the valuation approach adjusted; in our example, that is EUR 100,000.00 for fixtures and fittings. Table 4.8 shows the delta posting for the complex fixed asset and values reset to the "Other costs" account.

Posting method

Account	Description	Debit	Credit	IFRS	Local GAAP
21000	Fixtures and fittings	EUR 20,000.00		No posting	L6
299999	Other costs		EUR 20,000.00	No posting	L6

Table 4.8 Acquisition of Software as Complex Fixed Asset (3)—Execution of Periodic APC Values Posting

The two documents with EUR 80,000.00 and EUR 20,000.00 are not shown in subledger accounting. Figure 4.1 shows the Asset Explorer, the tool for displaying asset values in Asset Accounting. The correct values are visible in subledger FI-AA as early as the settlement stage for the internal order (see Table 4.7). A special delta posting method is then used to integrate this subledger with the ledger approach in New G/L.

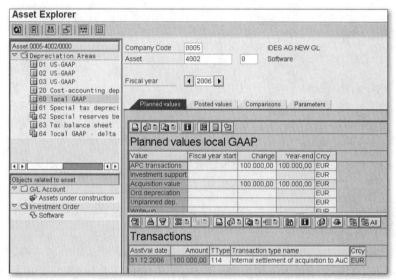

Figure 4.1 Asset Explorer

4.5.3 Depreciation Posting Run

Different useful life values

In accordance with IFRS regulations, the complex fixed assets hardware and software are depreciated over 10 years; that is, their values are corrected by 10 % every year. For IFRS, costs of acquisition and production of EUR 20,000 for hardware and EUR 80,000 for software equals depreciation amounts of EUR 2,000 and EUR 8,000, respectively. A shorter depreciation period of five years applies under local GAAP. With costs of acquisition and production of EUR 20,000.00 for hardware and EUR 100,000.00 for software, the resulting depreciation amounts are EUR 4,000.00 and EUR 20,000.00. Table 4.9 shows the corresponding posting records that the depreciation posting run creates for each ledger. The leading ledgers are ledger 0L for IFRS and ledger L6 for local GAAP.

Account	Description	Debit	Credit	IFRS	Local GAAP
211100	Depreciation of tangible fixed assets	EUR 2,000.00 EUR 8,000.00		0L	No posting
21010	Accumulated depreciation of fixtures and fittings		EUR 2,000.00 EUR 8,000.00	0L	No posting
211100	Depreciation of tangible fixed assets	EUR 4,000.00 EUR 20,000.00		No posting	L6
21010	Accumulated depreciation of fixtures and fittings		EUR 4,000.00 EUR 20,000.00	No posting	L6

Table 4.9 Depreciation of Hardware and Software as Complex Fixed Assets

The posting records clearly show that the ledger approach in New G/L uses identical accounts for different valuation approaches. This makes the structure of the chart of accounts clean and clear. FI-CO integration is possible only for the leading ledger, however; in our case, that is 0L (IFRS).

4.5.4 Asset Retirement with Revenue

The next stage in the lifecycle is the sale of the hardware as a complex fixed asset. In our example, this represents an asset retirement with revenue. This prompts the next question: Is this is a positive or a negative transaction; or to put it another way, will the sale value be greater or smaller than the posting value? We have selected this example so that

Sales greater or smaller than posting value

the answer depends on the point of view, that is, on the accounting procedure in question. After a year, the hardware has a valuation approach of EUR 18,000 in the IFRS financial statement. In the local valuation approach, because of its shorter depreciable life, the hardware has a valuation approach of EUR 16,000. The complex fixed asset is now sold for EUR 17,000, which in IFRS terms is a negative transaction (loss), and in local GAAP is a positive transaction (gain). Table 4.10 shows the asset retirement scenario in the form of a posting record.

Account	Description	Debit	Credit	IFRS	Local GAAP
21010	Accumulated depreciation of fixtures and fittings	EUR 2,000.00		0L	L6
825000	Allocation of asset retirement	EUR 17,000.00		0L	L6
200000	Loss due to asset retirement	EUR 1,000.00		0L	L6
21000	Fixtures and fittings		EUR 20,000.00	0L	L6

Table 4.10 Sale of Hardware as Complex Fixed Asset (1)

Posting method in Asset Accounting The original acquisition value of EUR 20,000.00 is reversed in balance sheet account 21000 as a credit item. The same posting logic applies to the accumulated depreciation account and the debit posting of EUR 2,000. The valuation variance between the IFRS depreciation and local GAAP depreciation does not have any effect at this point on integration with General Ledger, and the amounts are posted to both ledgers. The delta posting method in Asset Accounting adjusts the situation represented in the General Ledger during the periodic APC values posting, using the posting shown in Table 4.11.

Gain and loss In local GAAP, a total of EUR 4,000.00 in depreciation needs to be corrected in the accumulated depreciation account 21010. EUR 2,000.00 has already been shown in the posting record in Table 4.10. The difference of another EUR 2,000.00 is posted later in a periodic APC values posting (see Table 4.11). From the viewpoint of the local valuation approach, the sale of the hardware for EUR 17,000.00 at a posting value of EUR 16,000.00 represents a profitable deal. The result is a gain of EUR 1,000.00, which is then posted to account 250000. It also makes sense to set to zero the balance of account 200000 for the loss in ledger L6 (local GAAP). The debit item created in Table 4.10 is then balanced by the credit item in Table 4.11. In the next section, we will explain how this kind of posting procedure or the derived depreciation area is set up in the configuration process.

Account	Description	Debit	Credit	IFRS	Local GAAP
21010	Accumulated depreciation of fixtures and fittings	EUR 2,000.00		No posting	L6
200000	Loss due to asset retirement		EUR 1,000.00	No posting	L6
250000	Gain due to asset retirement		EUR 1,000.00	No posting	L6

Table 4.11 Sale of Hardware as Complex Fixed Asset (2)—Execution of Periodic APC Values Posting

4.5.5 Configuring Asset Accounting

Now that you have traced the lifecycle of two complex fixed assets in Asset Accounting, let's look at how to configure the system in Customizing, so that the system can map the business transactions discussed in the previous sections. Choose the following menu path to open the FI-AA Implementation Guide (IMG) for parallel valuation in Asset Accounting: FINANCIAL ACCOUNTING • ASSET ACCOUNTING • VALUATION • DEPRECIATION AREAS • SET UP AREAS FOR PARALLEL VALUATION.

Seven configuration steps

The guide (see Figure 4.2) helps you carry out the seven configuration steps.

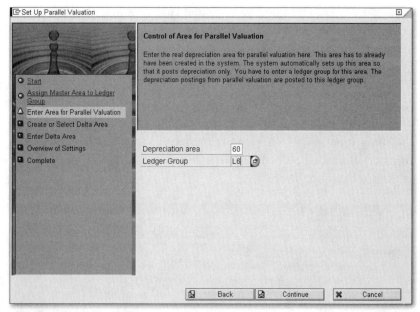

Figure 4.2 Guide for Parallel Valuation in FI-AA

Let's take a closer look at the individual steps of this guide (see Figure 4.2):

1. **Start**
   The system informs you that the guide is suitable only for parallel accounting with the ledger approach in New G/L. Other solutions, such as parallel accounts, are not relevant here. Furthermore, ledger groups must already have been set up. These groups are then assigned to the Asset Accounting depreciation areas.

2. **Assign Master Area to Ledger Group**
   In this step, you assign the depreciation area 01 to the leading ledger 0L. In our scenario, this is the IFRS accounting standard.

3. **Enter Area for Parallel Valuation**
   A non-leading ledger is assigned to the area for parallel valuation. In our case, this is ledger L6 (local GAAP).

4. **Create or Select Delta Area**
   We have already explained the delta posting method in Asset Accounting using the cases of software acquisition and hardware retirement.

A derived depreciation area (also known as delta area) for stock postings is required so that these cases can be mapped in the system.

5. **Enter Delta Area**

In this step, link the ledger group for parallel valuations to the derived depreciation area.

6. **Overview of Settings**

In our scenario, we make the settings shown in Table 4.12.

Depreciation Area	Description	Post in General Ledger	Ledger group
01	IFRS	1—real time	OL
60	Local GAAP	3—depreciations	L6
64	Delta—local GAAP	6—stocks	L6

Table 4.12 Settings for Each Depreciation Area

7. **Complete**

Before the system saves the settings you have made and places them in a transport request, it displays some final notes on the configuration (see Figure 4.3).

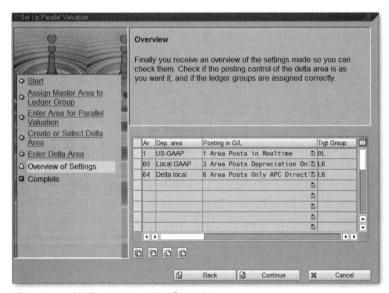

Figure 4.3 Guide—Notes on Configuration

You have now made the most important of the parallel accounting settings for the ledger approach in New G/L.

Now we look at the scenario of asset acquisition with different costs of acquisition and production. This topic was described above in relation to *software as a complex fixed asset*. In this scenario, internal and external activities are posted with the "Investment order" account assignment object, which is then settled to the "Asset under Construction (AuC)" object with different percentage rates for each accounting standard. You can find the relevant settings in Customizing via the path: INVESTMENT MANAGEMENT • INTERNAL ORDERS AS INVESTMENT MEASURES • SETTLEMENT.

First, maintain as many capitalization versions as you like. In our *software* scenario, this was version 1 for local GAAP and version 3 for the leading valuation according to IFRS. As shown in Figure 4.4, you then link the capitalization versions to the depreciation area in Asset Accounting.

Change View "Assign capitalization version to deprec. area"

Chart of dep. 1DE   Sample chart of depreciation: Germany

Ar.	Name of depreciation area	Cap. vers.	Text
01	US-GAAP	3	Group
02	US-GAAP	3	Group
03	US-GAAP	3	Group
20	Cost-accounting depreciation		100 % capitalization
51	Investment support posted to liabilities		Capitalization is not possible
60	local GAAP	1	Book depreciation
61	Special tax depreciation for APC in fin.statem		
63	Tax balance sheet		

Figure 4.4 Capitalization for Each Depreciation Area

In this next step, you tell the system which valuation approach should be used for a capitalization. You have the option of defining different percentage rates for each capitalization version based on the organizational unit level "company code," differentiated by cost element. In Figure 4.5, the two entries for company code 0005 are significant for the purposes of our scenario. The plus signs in the COST ELEMENT column serve as placeholders for all accounts in the range 400000 to 499999 for which the entire amount is capitalized for local GAAP from period 1 in the year 2006.

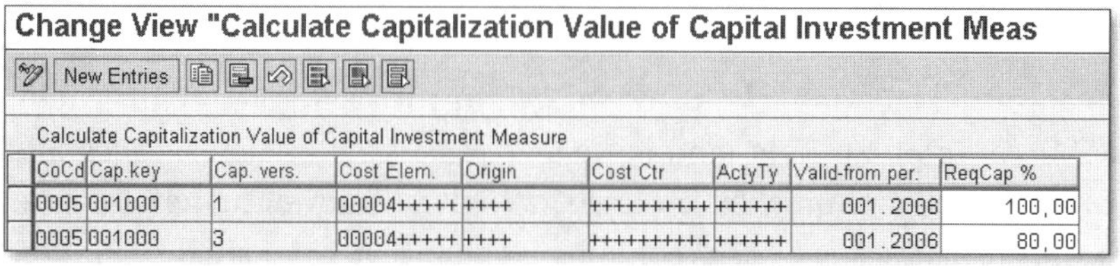

CoCd	Cap.key	Cap. vers.	Cost Elem.	Origin	Cost Ctr	ActyTy	Valid-from per.	ReqCap %
0005	001000	1	00004+++++	++++	++++++++++	++++++	001.2006	100,00
0005	001000	3	00004+++++	++++	++++++++++	++++++	001.2006	80,00

Figure 4.5 Capitalization with Different Percentage Rates

Customizing concludes with the setting for determining accounts for nonoperating expenses. This sub-point is required in cases of incomplete capitalization. In our scenario, postings for non-operating expenses under IFRS are made to the account 299999 (other costs), which is an element of account determination or FI-AA/General Ledger integration, or both.

4.6 Current Assets

Areas of valuation

Besides the valuation variances in fixed assets, which are mapped by means of the FI-AA component, you also need to take into account different valuation approaches in current assets where parallel accounting is used. Different aspects need to be emphasized, depending on the type of company: Materials valuation will not be of great importance to a service provider, for example. A repetitive make-to-order manufacturer, on the other hand, will be interested in revenue realization for long-term production orders. The topic of work in progress alone could take up half a book. In this section, our aim is to provide a general overview and not to go into detail on specific topics that are relevant only to specific industries.

Thus, we focus on three areas of valuation:

- Inventory valuation
- Receivables valuation
- Securities valuation

The sections below contain examples and Customizing settings for parallel accounting in current assets.

4.6.1 Inventory Valuation

Material master record

Inventory valuations take place in SAP in the Materials Management (MM) component. This module manages raw materials, supplies and consumables, and finished products, all in the form of material master records. This master record contains a value that is updated online for inventory management purposes.

This value can have two concrete types:

- Moving average price
- Standard price

A single type is assigned to every material master record for online inventory management:

- The moving average price is assigned to raw materials, supplies and consumables.
- The standard price, which is the result of an internal calculation based on direct costs and overhead costs, is assigned to finished products.

Figure 4.6 shows the ACCOUNTING 1 tab of the material master record.

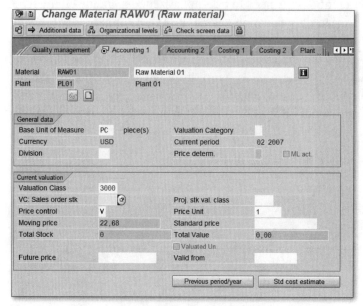

Figure 4.6 Material Master Record—Online Valuation

Raw Materials, Supplies, and Consumables

This example demonstrates from a business viewpoint what it means to carry out online inventory management with the moving average price, and what steps you then need to take in the SAP system for parallel accounting on the balance sheet date. Table 4.13 shows a goods receipt for raw materials with a value of EUR 50,000. All updates are made in real time to all ledgers.

Parallel accounting on balance sheet date

Account	Description	Debit	Credit	IFRS	Local GAAP
300000	Raw material	EUR 50,000.00		0L	L6
191100	Goods receipt—invoice receipt		EUR 50,000.00	0L	L6

Table 4.13 Purchase of Raw Materials, Supplies, and Consumables

If an identical quantity is then purchased for EUR 55,000.00 without anything being consumed, the result is a moving average of EUR 52,500.00. The valuation approach is also reflected in the balance sheet account 300000 (raw materials).

In the run-up to the balance sheet date, our raw material is consumed, which raises the question of value determination in accordance with various procedures, such as LIFO and FIFO. Also, it may be that too many items that are no longer fast-moving are still in storage. Another possibility is that the current market price has decreased or increased significantly.

Different value determination methods

Thus, you can see that there is room to maneuver in parallel accounting that can be used in very different ways. If a local financial statement is to be used as a basis for taxation later on, a company will attempt to minimize its profits as much as possible. IFRS and U.S.-GAAP, on the other hand, represent a company as realistically as possible for the benefit of investors. Thus, valuation variances arise, as the example in Table

4.14 shows. The existing valuation variance means that two postings are required for each ledger. A value adjustment of EUR 5,000.00 is made in the leading ledger 0L for IFRS, and an adjustment of EUR 20,000.00 is made in ledger L6 for local GAAP.

Account	Description	Debit	Credit	IFRS	Local GAAP
500001	Expense— accumulated depreciation	EUR 5,000.00		0L	No posting
300001	Accumulated depreciation— raw materials		EUR 5,000.00	0L	No posting
500001	Expense— accumulated depreciation	EUR 20,000.00		No posting	L6
300001	Accumulated depreciation— raw materials		EUR 20,000.00	No posting	L6

Table 4.14 Valuation of Raw Materials, Supplies, and Consumables

Besides online inventory management, the SAP material master record also provides six additional fields for key date valuation. The information shown in Figure 4.7 is contained on the Accounting 2 tab.

Integration of MM and FI

The Logistics • Material Management • Valuation • Balance Sheet Valuation SAP menu path provides several ways of automatically populating these six information fields using various valuation procedures. Previously, there was no further integration of MM and FI at this point. Instead, information about revaluations was provided in the form of a list, and postings like those in Table 4.14 were made by hand.

A small addition was made in SAP ERP 2005: The SAP menu now contains a small-scale integration option under Logistics • Material Management • Valuation • Balance Sheet Valuation • Results • Balance Sheet Values per Account.

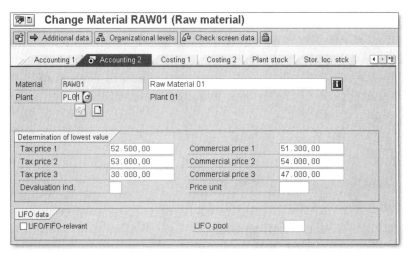

Figure 4.7 Material Master Record—Key Date Valuation

Figure 4.8 shows that, besides the price update, an additional window is opened for delta postings. An accounting standard is used to support parallel accounting including a ledger approach in New G/L.

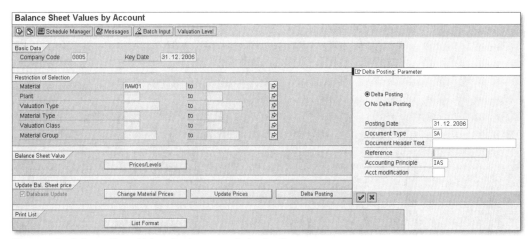

Figure 4.8 Balance Sheet Values by Account—Delta Posting

This function is still in the design phase, and integrated postings are not possible yet.

Finished Products

Standard price
Unlike raw materials, supplies, and consumables, finished products are usually mapped using the standard price for online inventory management. The standard price is calculated on the basis of direct costs and overhead costs in CO. In the next few pages, you will see how to make the required settings for inventory costing for finished products. This process consists of the following steps:

1. Define costing sheet

2. Assign valuation variant to a costing sheet

3. Assign costing variant to a valuation variant

4. Carry out inventory costing using costing variant

It becomes clear as early as the costing sheet definition stage that the balance sheet item "Finished products" is calculated in CO on the basis of cost elements and the valuation approach.

Costing sheet
Figure 4.9 shows the structure of this kind of costing sheet. As you can see, it consists of direct costs such as materials, wages, and salaries, and overhead rates for materials, manufacturing, administration, and sales. The general definition is found via the menu path: CONTROLLING • PRODUCT COST CONTROLLING • COST OBJECT CONTROLLING • PRODUCT COST BY ORDER • OVERHEAD RATES • DEFINE COSTING SHEET.

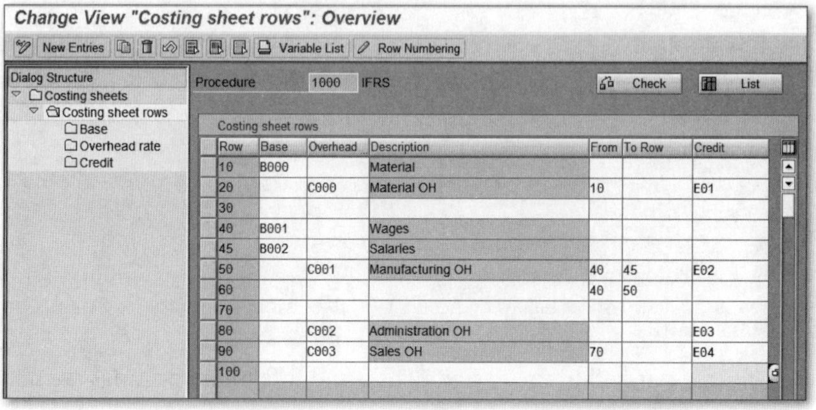

Figure 4.9 Costing Sheet Rows

Overhead rates, such as those shown in row 20 (MATERIAL OVERHEAD COSTS), contain a defined percentage rate, which is calculated on the basis of the cost elements in row 10. Figure 4.10 shows calculation base B000 with its defined cost elements and cost element groups or hierarchy node points. In our example, all cost elements are found in the interval from 400000 to 419999.

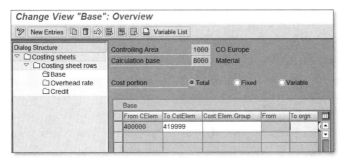

Figure 4.10 Changing the Base

By defining a costing sheet, you have taken the first step toward inventory costing. This step is important in terms of parallel accounting, because it is there that the major disadvantage of the ledger approach in New G/L becomes noticeable. Next, we will define the valuation variant. The first step is contained in Customizing via the menu path: CONTROLLING • PRODUCT COST CONTROLLING • MATERIAL COST ESTIMATE WITH QUANTITY STRUCTURE • COSTING VARIANTS: COMPONENTS • DEFINE VALUATION VARIANT.

Valuation variant

Change View "Valuation Variants": Details

| Valuation Variant/Plant | | ZZZ | Production order - IFRS |

Material Val. | ActivityTypes/Processes | Subcontracting | Ext. Processing | Overhead | Misc.

Overhead on Finished and Semifinished Materials
Costing Sheet — IFRS

Overhead on Material Components
Costing Sheet —

☐ Overhead on Subcontracted Materials

Figure 4.11 Valuation Variant—Costing Sheet

As you can see in Figure 4.11, the previously defined costing sheet, IFRS, is assigned to the valuation variant ZZZ PRODUCTION ORDER—IFRS. The second step of this is contained in Customizing under CONTROLLING • PRODUCT COST CONTROLLING • MATERIAL COST ESTIMATE WITH QUANTITY STRUCTURE • DEFINE COSTING VARIANT.

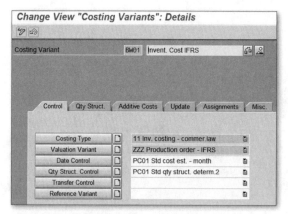

Figure 4.12 Valuation Variant—Costing Variant

Costing variant   As you can see in Figure 4.12, valuation variant ZZZ PRODUCTION ORDER—IFRS is assigned to the costing variant BW01 INVENTORY COSTING IFRS. Both figures illustrate the highly flexible and complex settings options. These setting options are less relevant for parallel accounting, which is why we will not go into further detail on this subject. In CO, the Customizing settings operate in the background if you call up the application via the menu path: FINANCIAL ACCOUNTING • CONTROLLING • PRODUCT COST CONTROLLING • PRODUCT COST PLANNING • MATERIAL COST ESTIMATE • COST ESTIMATE WITH QUANTITY STRUCTURE • CREATE.

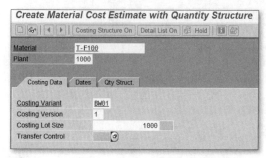

Figure 4.13 Selecting Material Cost Estimate with Quantity Structure

The selection screen shown in Figure 4.13 contains the material to be produced, the lot size, and the costing variant. In our example, the price for 1,000 items of the finished product T-F100 (pump) is to be calculated within the costing variant BW01. Costing variant BW01 is based on the valuation variant ZZZ PRODUCTION ORDER—IFRS with the direct and overhead costs of the IFRS costing sheet. Also, the lot size is a central consideration in distributing the fixed costs to the individual pump.

Figure 4.14 shows a costing structure for the material cost estimate. The material "pump" in our example is made up of individual items in a bill of material: casing, fly wheel, hollow shaft, electronic drive, and hexagon head screws. Their direct and overhead costs are included in the costing, and amount to a total value of EUR 576,288.00 for 1,000 produced items. If the "pump" finished product is still in storage, it can be valuated at a unit price of EUR 576.29 in accordance with IFRS.

Create Material Cost Estimate with Quantity Structure						
Costing Structure Off Detail List Off Hold						
Costing Structure	E	Total value	Curren	Quantity	Unit of Meas	Resource
Pump PRECISION 100	▢	576.288,01	EUR	1.000	ST	1000 T-F100
Casing	▢	138.103,00	EUR	1.000	ST	1000 T-B100
Slug for spiral casing	▢	5.110,00	EUR	1.000	ST	1000 T-T100
Flat gasket	▢	23.410,00	EUR	1.000	ST	1000 T-T200
Hexagon head screw M10	▢	4.080,00	EUR	8.000	ST	1000 T-T300
Fly wheel	▢	103.870,00	EUR	1.000	ST	1000 T-B200
Slug for fly wheel	▢	51.100,00	EUR	1.000	ST	1000 T-T000
Hollow shaft	▢	251.699,00	EUR	1.000	ST	1000 T-B300
Slug for Shaft	▢	24.510,00	EUR	1.000	ST	1000 T-T400
Electronic TURBODRIVE	▢	33.838,00	EUR	1.000	ST	1000 T-B400
Casing for electronic drive	▢	5.110,00	EUR	1.000	ST	1000 T-T500
Hexagon head screw M10	▢	4.080,00	EUR	8.000	ST	1000 T-T300

Figure 4.14 Result of Material Cost Estimate with Quantity Structure

You also need to manually enter the required accumulated depreciation postings in the same way you did for raw materials, supplies, and consumables.

One of the weaknesses of the ledger approach in New G/L is the fact that only the valuation approach of the leading ledger 0L is transferred to the CO component. With this approach, only one accounting standard can be used in CO, with the result that parallel accounting is not possible considering today's status of Enhancement Package 4 and the ledger approach in New G/L.

Material cost estimate

Leading ledger

Unlike the ledger approach, the accounts approach has the advantage that it can use additional accounts and cost elements to transfer multiple valuation approaches to CO. This option delivers significantly more flexibility in some situations, for example, if you need to determine different valuation approaches for finished products.

4.6.2 Receivables Valuation

Two valuation programs are particularly important in the following periodic tasks of receivables valuation:

▸ Flat-rate individual value adjustment (SAPF107)

▸ Foreign currency valuation (SAPF100)

In this section, we will look in more detail at these two programs in the context of parallel accounting, using the ledger approach to create a storage location.

Flat-Rate Individual Value Adjustment

Empirical values | The term *flat-rate individual value adjustment* refers to a group of customers whose receivables are to be devalued in a batch using predefined rules. Unlike individual value adjustments, flat-rate individual value adjustments do not involve any missed payments or insolvency. What do you have to do in these cases? Proceed as follows:

1. In the first step you need to post these cases manually.

2. In the second step, the program for flat-rate individual value adjustments then selects all active receivables, calculates the required adjustment on the basis of empirical values or the reliability of the accounting standard, and then automatically assigns these receivables to an account.

In the next few pages, an example explains in more detail exactly how this works and what Customizing settings you need to make.

The first requirement for making a valuation is a receivable in the accounts receivable accounting area. Table 4.15 shows a posting of EUR 10,000.00 that is valid for all accounting standards. For the sake of simplicity, no additional account assignment for output tax is included.

Account	Description	Debit	Credit	US-GAAP	Local GAAP
140000	Receivables	EUR 10,000.00		0L	L6
800200	Revenues		EUR 10,000.00	0L	L6

Table 4.15 Posting a Receivable

Before this receivable can be automatically valuated, the master data has to be maintained in accounts receivable accounting. There, the data has to be grouped for the purposes of subsequent flat-rate individual value adjustment. Figure 4.15 shows a grouping characteristic in the form of the value adjustment key 01.

Automatic valuation

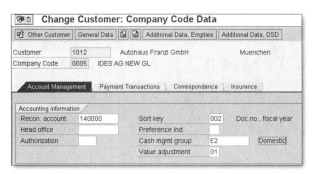

Figure 4.15 Customer Master Record

If it makes sense to group the customers by region, you could use the following keys:

▶ 01 = East

▶ 02 = West

▶ 03 = South

▶ 04 = North

The value adjustment key can be freely defined. In this section, we will look at the specific settings and functions associated with the value adjustment key. You can use other characteristics groupings for industries or for customer companies of certain sizes. Past events are used as

Value adjustment key

a basis for deciding how best to group characteristics and then to make flat-rate individual value adjustments. Auditors often have specific ideas about how flat-rate individual value adjustments should be used. Don't forget that every Euro that you include in this value reduces your company's profits and therefore its tax liability.

Valuation run The procedure for flat-rate individual value adjustment is carried out periodically and the system processes it as part of the valuation run. The program is located in the SAP application menu via the menu path: FINANCIAL ACCOUNTING • FINANCIALS • CUSTOMERS • PERIODIC PROCESSING • FINANCIAL STATEMENTS • VALUATE • OTHER VALUATIONS.

You may well guess from this generic description that the program has several application areas. For example, it can also be used to carry out discounting and other customer-specific valuations. As well as some important selection parameters and posting parameters, Figure 4.16 shows valuation method 3 FLAT-RATE INDIVIDUAL VALUE ADJUSTMENT after it has been selected. In our example, this is carried out for company code 0005 on the key date 12/31/2006. The valuated amount is required for valuations on this date only, so the program automatically corrects or cancels it on 01/01/2007.

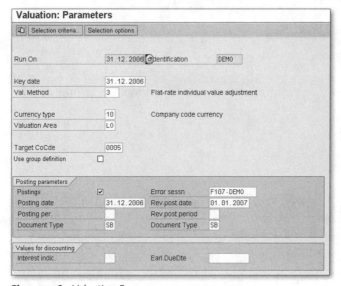

Figure 4.16 Valuation Run

The valuation run is a two-stage procedure, like the payment run and the dunning run. It is defined as follows:

1. First, the system produces a proposal that can be processed as part of a dialog list.

2. Then, in the second step, posting adjustments are made in the system.

The example in Table 4.16 shows a value adjustment to the original receivable of EUR 10,000.00 on the basis of the value adjustment key in the customer master record and on a selection of selection parameters and posting parameters in the valuation run. Let us now assume that an adjustment of 5 % will be made on the key date 12/31/2006 for the local accounting standard. Customers also use the program to determine the exact adjustment requirements. In this case, the POSTINGS checkbox is not checked, as this option is not required. Because the receivables account 140000 in the SAP system is usually defined as the reconciliation account, it cannot be posted directly.

Account	Description	Debit	Credit	US-GAAP	Local GAAP
210100	Expenses from value adjustments to receivables	EUR 500.00		No posting	L6
142100	Value adjustments to receivables		EUR 500.00	No posting	L6

Table 4.16 Adjustment to Receivables

Table 4.16 shows the generated posting record with the directly postable balance sheet account 142100 (value adjustments to receivables). This is reflected in the balance sheet as a total (EUR 10,000.00 – 500.00) in a joint financial statement item. For parallel accounting, you need to run the program for each accounting standard.

Configuration Now that you have a clearer idea of how flat-rate individual value adjustments work from the viewpoint of the application, let's take a closer look
at the Customizing. It has only two menu items and is very clear.

First you need to define the value adjustment key. To do this, open the
menu path: FINANCIALS (NEW) • ACCOUNTS RECEIVABLE AND ACCOUNTS
PAYABLE ACCOUNTING • BUSINESS TRANSACTIONS • FINANCIAL STATEMENT •
VALUATE • VARIOUS VALUATIONS • MAINTAIN VALUE ADJUSTMENT KEY.

Figure 4.17 shows the value adjustment key 01, which is valid for the
accounting standard LO (local GAAP). Thus, all receivables of customers
in country DE (Germany) whose payments are more than 30 days overdue need to be adjusted by 5 %. A general prerequisite here is that value
adjustment key 01 is stored in the customer master record.

Change View "Maintain Accumulated Depreciation Key":

Maintain Accumulated Depreciation Key

Value adjust.	Valuation	Co	Days	Future	Debit int. rate	Va
01	LO	DE	30	☐	5,000	

Figure 4.17 Customizing the Value Adjustment Keys

From a business point of view, the amount of a flat-rate individual value
adjustment always reflects empirical values based on past experiences.
It may therefore make sense to further subdivide the value adjustment
percentages, for example, into items that are overdue to various degrees,
as follows:

- 30 days—5 %
- 60 days—7 %
- 90 days—10 %

In this case, multiple entries for the value adjustment key 01 would be
required in Customizing. Next, you need to make the account determina-
tion settings in Customizing. To do this, open the menu path: FINANCIALS
(NEW) • ACCOUNTS RECEIVABLE AND ACCOUNTS PAYABLE ACCOUNTING •
BUSINESS TRANSACTIONS • FINANCIAL STATEMENT • VALUATE • VARIOUS VAL-
UATIONS • DETERMINE ACCOUNTS.

Figure 4.18 shows that accounts for Transaction B03 (FLAT-RATE INDIVID-UAL VALUE ADJUSTMENT) have to be created for each accounting standard, in our case LO (local GAAP).

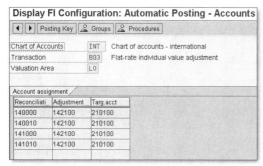

Figure 4.18 Customizing Account Determination

It is also clear from the account-assignment screen that a directly post-able adjustment account (balance sheet account) is required for each of the reconciliation accounts 140000, 140010, 141000, and 141010. The value adjustment is also reflected in the P&L statement in the target account. For a ledger approach in New G/L, the depreciation area LO is assigned to the local ledger L6 in the basic settings.

Directly postable adjustment account

Foreign Currency Conversion

Besides the flat-rate individual value adjustments, receivables in different currencies also can affect parallel accounting. If a company that submits its balance sheet in Euros makes a sale to a U.S. company in U.S. dollars, this receivable may have to be handled differently on the balance-sheet key date for local and international accounting standards. Under the IFRS and U.S.-GAAP standards, the key date principle involves valuation using the exchange rate that is valid on the key date. This practice contrasts with local regulations, which allow devaluation and forbid upward revaluation. For accounting departments, valuation determination and posting is an automatic process that can be executed for each accounting standard.

Key date principle

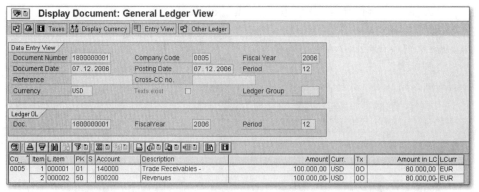

Figure 4.19 Posting Receivable in USD as Document Currency and EUR as Local Currency

In our example, a European company makes a sale at an exchange rate of EUR/USD 1.25 to a U.S. company. Figure 4.19 shows the associated posting record of USD 100,000.00 or EUR 80,000.00. This document is always updated for all accounting standards in the existing ledgers.

Valuation on balance sheet key date

On the balance sheet key date, a valuation is made of the receivables in foreign currencies. In our example, this valuation is made for U.S.-GAAP at the key date exchange rate of EUR/USD 1.35. Because the dollar has decreased in value, only about EUR 74,000.00 is required, while the receivable amount of USD 100,000.00 remains in the local balance sheet. Figure 4.20 shows the log of the valuation run.

```
Foreign Currency Valuation
[K] [◀] [▶] [K] 2 Postings  □ Messages  [⅋] [△] [▽] [▼] [▦] [▤] [▦] [▩] [⊡]

Mal for BOB                          Foreign Currency Valuation                    Time 13:05:54
Bergen                                        █                          FAGL_FC_VALUATION/D035500
Key Date 31.12.06
Valuation in Company code currency (10)
Method DEMO Valuation w/ Exchange Rate Type M
Ledger Group OL
```

Ld	AccTy	G/L	Acco	Amount in	Crcy	Amount in	Local Curr	Exch. Rat	S	Exch.rate	Typ	Valuation diff.	New Difference
*	D	140000	1001	100000,00	USD	80.000,00	EUR	/1,35000		/1,25000	DR	0,00	5.925,93-
*		140000		100000,00	USD	80.000,00	EUR					0,00	5.925,93-
**				100000,00	USD	80.000,00	EUR					0,00	5.925,93-

Figure 4.20 Foreign Currency Valuation Log

The new foreign currency valuation program is located under FINAN-CIAL ACCOUNTING • FINANCIALS • CUSTOMERS • PERIODIC PROCESSING • FINANCIAL STATEMENTS • VALUATE • FOREIGN CURRENCY VALUATION OF OI (NEW). If you are using an active New G/L, the transaction has to have the suffix "New". Otherwise, the program only can use the classic General Ledger.

New program for foreign currency valuations

If there are valuation variances in parallel accounting, more valuation runs are required for each valuation area. In our example, the foreign currency program creates a batch input folder with two postings for the U.S.-GAAP accounting standard (see Figure 4.21).

Posting method

The document thus created is automatically withdrawn or canceled in the same run on the first day of the next month. A different procedure is used in countries where the valuation cannot be withdrawn at the end of the business year.

Foreign Currency Valuation

```
Mal for BOB    Mal for BOB                           Forei   Time 13:12:06      Date  07.12.2006
Bergen                          Bergen               FAGL_FC_VALUATION/D035500 Page          1
Ledger Group OL Posting Proposal

Ledger CoCd DocumentNo Document Header Text    Typ Pstng Date Crcy  LCurr LCur2 LCur3 Text
Itm PK G/L           Amount in LC    LC2 amount      LC3 amount Text

      0005           FC valuation              31.12.2006 USD   EUR   EUR   USD
 1 40 230010         5.925,93        5.925,93          0,00  140000 · Valuation on 20061231
 2 50 140099         5.925,93        5.925,93          0,00  140000 · Valuation on 20061231

      0005           Reverse posting           01.01.2007 USD   EUR   EUR   USD
 1 50 230010         5.925,93        5.925,93          0,00  140000 · Valuation on 20061231
 2 40 140099         5.925,93        5.925,93          0,00  140000 · Valuation on 20061231
```

Figure 4.21 Automatic Posting of Foreign Currency Valuation

[+]

Valuation Posting in the Document-Splitting Scenario

If the document-splitting scenario is active, the valuation posting is carried out for each splitting characteristic. See Section 5.7, Periodic Processing, for an example.

Using the example illustrated here as a basis, we will now look at Customizing in more detail in the next few sections. You can find the

Customizing settings under the menu path: FINANCIALS (NEW) • GENERAL LEDGER (NEW) • PERIODIC PROCESSING • VALUATE.

Different valuation methods

Figure 4.22 illustrates a multi-level configuration. In the first step, different valuation methods are defined, such as method INT (key date principle) and DEMO (principle of prudence). These are assigned to relevant valuation areas and make it possible to map valuation variances. A valuation area has one valuation method, but a valuation method can be assigned to multiple valuation areas. This is one of the main differences between foreign currency valuation in SAP R/3 and in SAP ERP 2005. In SAP R/3, the valuation methods were assigned only when the foreign currency valuation program itself was started.

In the next step, an accounting standard is assigned to the valuation area. Finally, the accounting standard is assigned to the ledger in which the postings are to be made.

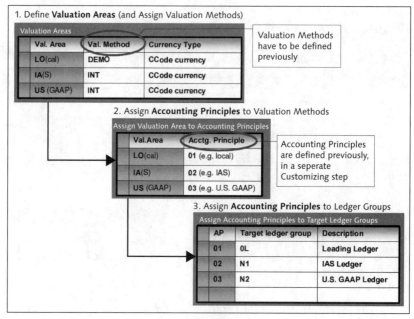

Figure 4.22 Foreign Currency Valuation Customizing with "New G/L" as Storage Location

[+]

Configuring New G/L

Because the different ledgers also post identical accounts, one entry is sufficient for the ledger approach in New G/L (see Figure 4.23).

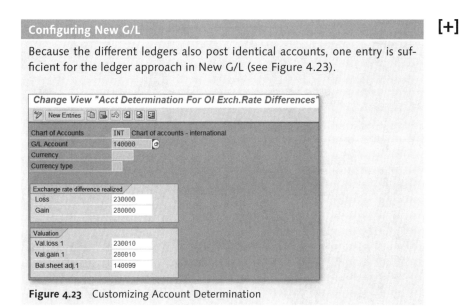

Figure 4.23 Customizing Account Determination

4.6.3 Securities Valuation

Shares, bonds, loans, and derivatives are administrated in the "Treasury" subledger. For parallel accounting, a valuation is made in accordance with different accounting standards on the key date. In SAP ERP 2005, the relevant valuation program is located via the SAP menu path: FINANCIAL ACCOUNTING • FINANCIAL SUPPLY CHAIN MANAGEMENT • TREASURY AND RISK MANAGEMENT • TRANSACTION MANAGER • SECURITIES • ACCOUNTING • VALUATION • EXECUTE VALUATION.

Figure 4.24 shows a list of the positions to be valuated for company code 1000. The key date is the year end. Similar to Asset Accounting, valuation areas are also used in the "Treasury" subledger. As you can see in Figure 4.24, there are two columns relating to valuation under IFRS and local GAAP: "VA," which contains either valuation area 001 or 002, and "VA name," which contains either "Operational" (for local GAAP) or "IFRS." Two important pieces of information are stored here:

Position valuation similar to Asset Accounting

▶ Valuation methods for each valuation area

▶ Accounting standards for account assignment to General Ledger for each valuation area

Display Positions to be Valued

⊕ Execute valuation | 🔍 | 🖨 🖶 | 🖸 🗔 🖉

Valuation Cat. Year-End Valuation
Key Date 28.12.2006

CoCd	VA	VA name	PTyp	ValCl	ID number	Short name	Sec. Acct	SAcGr	Portfolio	Contract	Fut. Acct	Trans.	Status
1000	002	Operational	01A	3	US7427181091	Procter Gamble	JPMOR_01						
1000	001	IFRS	01A	4	DE0007100000	Daimlerchrysler	DEUBA_01		PORTFOLIO1				
1000	002	Operational	01A	3	GB0006107006	Cadb. Schweppes	DEUBA_01						
1000	002	Operational	01A	3	GB0031348658	Barclays	JPMOR_01						
1000	002	Operational	01A	5	DE0005190003	BMW AG	DEUBA_01						
1000	002	Operational	01A	3	DE0005151005	BASF AG	DEUBA_01						
1000	001	IFRS	01A	3	CH0012005267	Novartis	DEUBA_01		PORTFOLIO1				
1000	002	Operational	01A	4	DE0007614406	E.ON AG	DEUBA_01						
1000	002	Operational	01A	4	US4592001014	IBM	DEUBA_01						
1000	001	IFRS	01A	3	CH0008742519	Swisscom	DEUBA_01		PORTFOLIO1				
1000	001	IFRS	01A	4	US4592001014	IBM	DEUBA_01		PORTFOLIO1				
1000	001	IFRS	01A	5	DE0007100000	Daimlerchrysler	DEUBA_01		PORTFOLIO1				
1000	002	Operational	01A	3	DE0007100000	Daimlerchrysler	DEUBA_01						
1000	001	IFRS	01A	3	GB0031348658	Barclays	JPMOR_01		PORTFOLIO1				
1000	001	IFRS	01A	5	DE0005190003	BMW AG	DEUBA_01		PORTFOLIO1				
1000	001	IFRS	01A	5	CH0012056047	Nestlé SA	DEUBA_01		9000000000				
1000	001	IFRS	01A	2	AT0000720008	Telekom AT	DEUBA_01		PORTFOLIO1				
1000	001	IFRS	01A	1	CH0012056047	Nestlé SA	DEUBA_01		PORTFOLIO1				
1000	002	Operational	01A	4	DE0007100000	Daimlerchrysler	DEUBA_01						
1000	002	Operational	01A	2	AT0000720008	Telekom AT	DEUBA_01						

Figure 4.24 Displaying Positions To Be Valued

Valuation types for each accounting standard The business transactions to be posted are listed in the posting log for each valuation area (see Figure 4.25). Posting keys 40 and 50 indicate debit and credit postings, respectively. The GENERAL LEDGER column contains the security class with the key 01A (stocks). Different valuation types for each accounting standard can be seen in the text for G/L account. There is a foreign currency gain of EUR 957.98—a gain from exchange rate fluctuation due to a favorable exchange rate between the Euro and the British pound—for both valuation areas. Although the valuation amount is the same under both IFRS and local accounting standards, different accounts are shown in the posting log.

The stocks have to be grouped for IFRS and recorded in the balance sheet in accordance with their intended purpose. There are three categories of purpose:

► Held to maturity

► Available for sale

► Trading

Posting Log: Posted Business Transactions

```
IDES-ALE: Central FI Syst                                            Time 13:56:58    Date 28.12.2006
Frankfurt · Deutschland                    Posting Log          RTPM_TRL_VALUATION/D035500 Page        1
```

Company code	1000	Valuation area001 IFRS		Valuation		General ledger	28.12.2006

```
V200    Valuation two steps:       Valuation class 0003 IFRS/US-GAAP: Delibera Product type    01A Stocks
ID number    GB0006107006  Cadb. Schweppes Sec. account JPMOR_01    JP Morgan Chase

40         6.565,83  GBP      9.787,33  EUR  10045000   Equities Designated Trading
50         6.565,83· GBP      9.787,33· EUR  10253000   Appreciation of equities Designated Trading

V202    Valuation two steps:       Valuation class 0003 IFRS/US-GAAP: Delibera Product type    01A Stocks
ID number    GB0006107006  Cadb. Schweppes Sec. account JPMOR_01    JP Morgan Chase

40             0,00  GBP       957,98  EUR  10045000   Equities Designated Trading
50             0,00  GBP       957,98· EUR  10280000   Gains from exchange rate fluctuations Desig. Trad.
```

Company code	1000	Valuation area002 Operational		Valuation		General ledger	28.12.2006

```
V202    Valuation two steps:       Valuation class 0003 IFRS/US-GAAP: Delibera Product type    01A Stocks
ID number    GB0006107006  Cadb. Schweppes Sec. account DEUBA_01    Dt. Bank 01

40             0,00  GBP     1.600,80  EUR  22045000   Equities fixed Assets
50             0,00  GBP     1.600,80· EUR  22280000   Gains from exchange rate fluctuations FA
```

Company code	1000	Valuation area002 Operational		Valuation		General ledger	28.12.2006

```
V202    Valuation two steps:       Valuation class 0003 IFRS/US-GAAP: Delibera Product type    01A Stocks
ID number    GB0006107006  Cadb. Schweppes Sec. account JPMOR_01    JP Morgan Chase

40             0,00  GBP       957,98  EUR  22045000   Equities fixed Assets
50             0,00  GBP       957,98· EUR  22280000   Gains from exchange rate fluctuations FA
```

Figure 4.25 Posting Log

Local accounting standards may permit or require a different kind of balance sheet (see Figure 4.25). Under IFRS, postings are made partly to current assets and partly to fixed assets. Local GAAP requires only one balance sheet item. This practice, which is typical in an accounts approach, could also be used in the ledger approach in New G/L. Whenever there are different results in the balance sheet or P&L statement for different accounting standards, additional accounts can or have to be used, even if there are no other valuation variances.

Mapping valuation variances—ledger approach

In our example, the valuation program posts documents for the valuation areas 001 (IFRS) and 002 (local GAAP) to ledgers L5 (IFRS) and L6 (local GAAP). Figure 4.26 shows a document for the IFRS accounting standard. In this case, the stock value has been entered on the basis of the current exchange rate and the foreign currency gain has been realized.

Several settings have to be made in Customizing so that account assignments can be made properly within the ledger approach in New G/L.

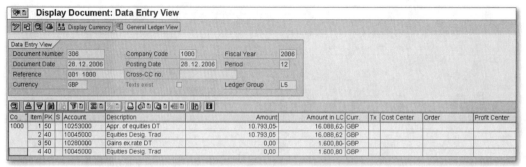

Figure 4.26 Display Document—General Ledger View

These settings are made in the following steps:

1. Define valuation areas

2. Assign accounting codes

3. Assign valuation areas to accounting codes

4. Account determination: Assign update types

5. Account determination: Posting specification

6. Account determination: G/L accounts

The first three steps are located in Customizing via the menu path: FINANCIAL SUPPLY CHAIN MANAGEMENT • TREASURY AND RISK MANAGEMENT • TRANSACTION MANAGER • GENERAL SETTINGS • ACCOUNTING • ORGANIZATION.

Defining Valuation Areas

Treasury (FI-TR)   You can maintain various valuation areas in the Treasury subledger (FI-TR), within which you can valuate financial transactions in accordance with different accounting standards. Unlike Asset Accounting (FI-AA), there can be as many as 999 valuation areas in FI-TR. Figure 4.27 shows three defined valuation areas.

Display View "Valuation Areas": Overview

Valuation Areas

VA	Valuation area
001	IFRS
002	Operational
003	US-GAAP

Figure 4.27 Defining Valuation Areas

Assigning Accounting Codes

The accounting code is an organizational unit of FI-TR. As you can see in Figure 4.28, there is a 1:1 relationship between this unit and the G/L element, the company code.

Display View "Accounting Code": Overview

Accounting Code

AC	Accounting code	CoCode
0001	SAP A.G.	0001
0100	IDES Japan 0100	0100
0110	IDES Japan 0110	0110
1000	IDES AG	1000
1002	Singapore Company	1002
2000	IDES UK	2000
2100	IDES Portugal	2100
2200	IDES France	2200
2300	IDES España	2300
2400	IDES Italia	2400
2500	IDES Netherlands	2500
2700	IDES Schweiz	2700
3000	IDES US INC	3000

Figure 4.28 Assigning Accounting Codes

Assigning Valuation Areas to Accounting Codes

Integrating FI-TR and FI-GL

When assigning the valuation area to the accounting code, you need to define whether and how the accounting code is to be integrated into the General Ledger. Figure 4.28 shows that postings should be made to Financial Accounting for the accounting code 1000 and the valuation area 001 (IFRS). You should use the account standard—IAS in our example—to specify the ledgers in which the documents are to be updated. You make the basic settings for the accounting standard in advance by following the menu path: Financials (New) • Financials General Settings (New) • Ledgers • Parallel Accounting • Assign Accounting Standard to Ledger Group.

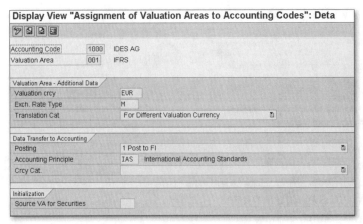

Figure 4.29 Assigning Valuation Areas to Accounting Codes

Account determination

The second part of the account determination settings can be found in Customizing via the menu path: Financial Supply Chain Management • Treasury and Risk Management • Transaction Manager • General Settings • Accounting • Connection to Other Accounting Components • Define Account Determination.

Account determination: Assigning Update Types

Posting specification

Update types are used to classify the business transactions that are about to be valuated. In the posting log of our example in Figure 4.30, the left-hand column, Update Type, contains the key V200. This stands for a two-level exchange rate valuation for security write-ups. Figure 4.30 shows that V200 has been assigned to posting specification 15100.

Account Determination: Posting Specification

The posting specification specifies how debit and credit postings are carried out. In Figure 4.31, symbolic accounts are used to assign the account symbol 4.9.4.4 to the posting specification 15100 for the posting key 50, Credit postings.

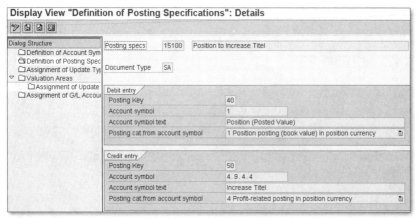

Display View "Assignment of Update Types to Posting Specs": Overview

Dialog Structure
- Definition of Account Sym
- Definition of Posting Spec
- Assignment of Update Ty
- ▽ Valuation Areas
  - Assignment of Update
  - Assignment of G/L Accou

Assignment of Update Types to Posting Specs

UpdateType	Update Type Text	P	Posting specs	Posting specifications text
V200	Valuation two steps: increase Titel	☐	15100	Position to increase Titel
V200_OCI	Valuation two steps: create pos. OCI-Position (Titel)	☐	23100	Position to Reserve new valuation T
V201	Valuation two steps: decrease Titel	☐	15500	Decrease Titel to Position
V201_OCI	Valuation two steps: create neg. OCI-Position (Titel)	☐	23200	Reserve new valuation Titel (negativ
V202	Valuation two steps: increase FX	☐	15300	Position to Increase FX
V202_OCI	Valuation two steps: create pos. OCI-Position (FX)	☐	23300	Position to Reserve new valuation F
V203	Valuation two steps: decrease FX	☐	15700	Decrease FX to Position
V203_OCI	Valuation two steps: create neg. OCI-Position (FX)	☐	23400	Reserve new valuation FX (negative
V204	Valuation two steps: cost increase Titel	☐	15100	Position to Increase Titel
V204_OCI	Valuation two steps: create pos. OCI-Position (Cost Titel)	☐	23100	Position to Reserve new valuation T
V205	Valuation two steps: cost decrease (Titel)	☐	15500	Decrease Titel to Position
V205_OCI	Valuation two steps: create neg. OCI-Position (Cost Titel)	☐	23200	Reserve new valuation Titel (negativ
V206	Valuation two steps: cost increase (FX)	☐	15300	Position to Increase FX
V206_OCI	Valuation two steps: create pos. OCI-Position (Cost FX)	☐	23300	Position to Reserve new valuation F
V207	Valuation two steps: cost decrease (FX)	☐	15700	Decrease FX to Position
V207_OCI	Valuation two steps: create neg. OCI-Position (Cost FX)	☐	23400	Reserve new valuation FX (negative
V220	Special increase Titel: obligation	☐	15100	Position to Increase Titel
V221	Special decrease Titel: obligation	☐	15500	Decrease Titel to Position
V230	Special increase Titel: mandatory	☐	15100	Position to Increase Titel
V231	Special decrease Titel: mandatory	☐	15500	Decrease Titel to Position
V241		☐	26001	

Figure 4.30 Account Determination—Assigning Update Types

Display View "Definition of Posting Specifications": Details

Dialog Structure
- Definition of Account Sym
- Definition of Posting Spec
- Assignment of Update Ty
- ▽ Valuation Areas
  - Assignment of Update
  - Assignment of G/L Accou

Posting specs   15100   Position to Increase Titel

Document Type   SA

Debit entry
- Posting Key   40
- Account symbol   1
- Account symbol text   Position (Posted Value)
- Posting cat.from account symbol   1 Position posting (book value) in position currency

Credit entry
- Posting Key   50
- Account symbol   4.9.4.4
- Account symbol text   Increase Titel
- Posting cat.from account symbol   4 Profit-related posting in position currency

Figure 4.31 Account Determination—Posting Specification

Account Determination: G/L Accounts

The relevant G/L account is determined from the symbolic account 4.9.4.4 in accordance with each business transaction, as shown in Figure 4.32. Our example contains account 10253000 for stock write-ups.

Symbolic accounts

The multi-level architecture of account determination enables a high degree of flexibility, but this does not mean that the architecture is easy to configure.

Figure 4.32 Account Determination—G/L Accounts

4.7 Provisions

In this section, we will compare the account and ledger approaches to provisions in New G/L. We will use business transactions such as transfer, disbursement, and write-off of provisions to explain the new options.

Provision types and probabilities

Valuation variances arise in parallel accounting because of different provision types and probabilities:

▶ **Probable**
For example, if an event such as a warranty case is regarded as probable, it is included in the U.S.-GAAP balance sheet. Under IFRS, an event is regarded as probable if its probability is categorized as greater than 50 %.

▶ **Reasonably probable**
If an event's probability is between 30 % and 70 %, a provision ban applies under U.S.-GAAP, because the event is then categorized as reasonably probable. Local regulations can also vary.

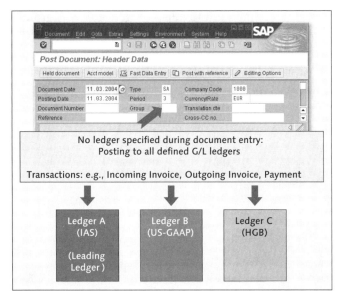

Figure 4.33 Posting to All Ledgers

In the accounts approach, you create dedicated accounts for each provision type and accounting standard. Anything more than three different standards—local, U.S.-GAAP and IFRS—results in an unmanageable block of G/L ledgers. The ledger approach in New G/L solves this problem because there is no need for multiple G/L accounts for each provision type. Rather, valuation variances are stored using the ledger method. This also makes document entry much more user-friendly (see Figure 4.33).

Accounts approach and ledger approach

If the GROUP field in the document header is empty, the system uses a joint valuation approach for all ledgers. Table 4.17 illustrates this example. In the case of valuation variances, the individual ledgers 0L for US-GAAP postings or L6 for local GAAP postings are used.

Different valuation approaches in document header

Account	Description	Debit	Credit	US-GAAP	IFRS	Local GAAP
445000	Pension expenses	EUR 100,000.00		0L	L5	L6
089000	Other provisions		EUR 100,000.00	0L	L5	L6

Table 4.17 Creating Provision for US-GAAP and IFRS

Creating ledger
groups In Customizing, you can combine individual ledgers to form groups via the menu path: FINANCIALS (NEW) • FINANCIALS GENERAL SETTINGS (NEW) • LEDGERS • DEFINE LEDGER GROUPS. In practice, it makes sense to have no valuation variances between U.S.-GAAP and IFRS and to make one posting only. Figure 4.34 shows the definition for the group ZZ for the ledgers 0L (US-GAAP) and L5 (IFRS). There is one representative ledger in this group, and this ledger handles period control.

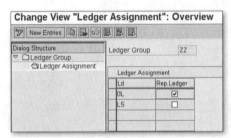

Figure 4.34 Defining Ledger Groups

If the posting period of the representative ledger is open, postings are made to all other assigned ledgers, even if their posting periods are closed.

Technical offsetting
account Previously in account determination, a disbursement always led to postings that attracted many queries. The concept of joint accounts and accounts with valuation variances reaches its limits in such cases. In Figure 4.35, the starting point is a provision of EUR 20,000.00 under local GAAP and EUR 10,000.00 under IFRS. This provision is then subject to a disbursement of EUR 8,000.00 in posting 3. The bank account is defined as the joint account, and therefore only one disbursement posting can be used. Because one account is required for each accounting standard, an additional technical offsetting account now needs to be defined. This special account is listed underneath the balance sheet and is therefore often subject to queries from auditors.

Disadvantage
of the accounts
approach exists
no longer The disadvantage of the accounts approach does not exist in the ledger approach in New G/L. Table 4.18 shows that the disbursement procedure produces values for all existing ledgers, making a technical offsetting account superfluous.

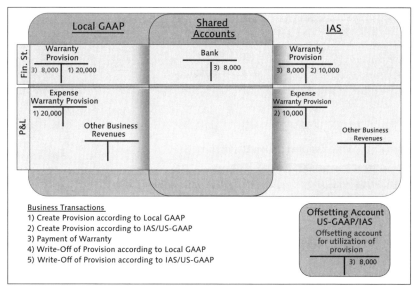

Figure 4.35 Provisions—Accounts Approach

Account	Description	Debit	Credit	US-GAAP	IFRS	Local GAAP
160000	Vendor		EUR 8,000.00	0L	L5	L6
089000	Other provisions	EUR 8,000.00		0L	L5	L6

Table 4.18 Payment of Warranty

A provision is written off at the end of its lifecycle. Because there are different provision types and different definitions of the term *probability*, different posting procedures usually take place at this stage for separate accounting standards. In the example in Table 4.19, the remaining amount for the local accounting standard is written off in ledger L6. There should be no postings to the leading ledger 0L (US-GAAP) or L5 (IFRS). In the same way, the ledger group L6 has to be included in the document header in the document entry process.

Provision

Account	Description	Debit	Credit	US-GAAP	IFRS	Local GAAP
299000	Other business revenues		EUR 25,000.00	No posting	No posting	L6
089000	Other provisions	EUR 25,000.00		No posting	No posting	L6

Table 4.19 Write-Off of Provision Under Local GAAP

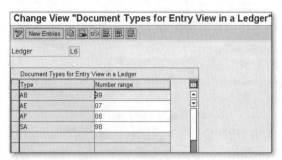

Figure 4.36 Define Document Type for Entry View

If the ledger group consists of one or more non-leading ledgers, document types have to be specified for the entry view in a ledger. You do this in Customizing via the menu path: FINANCIALS (NEW) • FINANCIALS GENERAL SETTINGS (NEW) • DOCUMENT • DOCUMENT TYPES • DEFINE DOCUMENT TYPES FOR ENTRY VIEW IN A LEDGER.

Custom document types and number range intervals

With evaluations, you need to consider the issue of custom document types and their custom number range intervals. Postings without valuation variances are contained in other number range intervals as postings with valuations variances. In this example, variances are posted in only one ledger with a custom document type and number range interval. The reason for this is to avoid document gaps within an interval, which is illegal in some countries, including Italy.

[+] **Restriction for the Ledger Approach in the General Ledger**

When it comes to restriction for the ledger approach in General Ledger, as a rule, you also need to take into account that a posting with valuation variances can be made only in combination with G/L accounts that do not permit open items. Enhancement Package 3 eases this situation.

Figure 4.37 shows a posting screen with the associated error notification. Conversely, this means that a G/L account that contains open items always accepts postings to all ledgers. If other combinations are permitted, as in provision transactions, the master record may not contain this entry. Enhancement Package 3 includes a modification of this logic. You can find more details on this later on in this chapter.

Enter G/L Acct Document for Ledger Group: Company Code 0005

| Tree on | Company Code | Hold | Simulate | Editing options |

| Basic data | Details |

					Amount Information
Document Date:	31.12.2006	Currency	EUR		Total deb.
Posting Date	31.12.2006				0,00 EUR
		Ledger Grp	L6		
Reference					Total cred.
Doc.Header Text					25.000,00 EUR
Document Type	SA	G/L account document			
Cross-CC no.					
Company Code	0005	IDES AG NEW GL Frankfurt			

1 Items (No entry variant selected)

St	G/L acct	Short Text	D/C	Amount in doc.curr.	Loc.curr.amount	T	Tax jurisdictn code
✔	299000	Other operating inco	H Cre	25.000,00	25.000,00		
	89000		S Deb	25.000,00	0,00		
					0,00		
					0,00		
					0,00		
					0,00		
					0,00		
					0,00		

❌ Postings to G/L accounts with open item management are not permitted

Figure 4.37 Posting to a Single Ledger

This restriction does not exist in parallel accounting using the accounts approach. Because of the open items, completed transactions can be cleared and are no longer displayed in the line item display. To reflect the same level of clarity in the ledger approach, you will need to set certain selection parameters, sorting criteria, and filter criteria in New G/L up to Enhancement Package 3. Figure 4.38 shows a new selection option for ledgers and accounting standards.

Advantages of the accounts approach

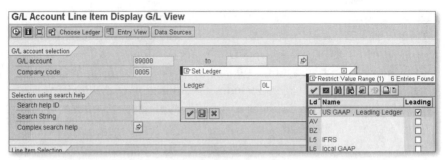

Figure 4.38 Evaluating Line Items in a Ledger

Provisions report Now that you have seen the whole lifecycle of the transfer, use, and write-off of provisions, be aware this process has to be reflected in the reporting system. Previously, the SAP standard contained no transaction for creating a provisions report. SAP ERP 2005, in contrast, can do this quickly and conveniently with its Report Painter reporting tool. The reporting specification is illustrated in Figure 4.39.

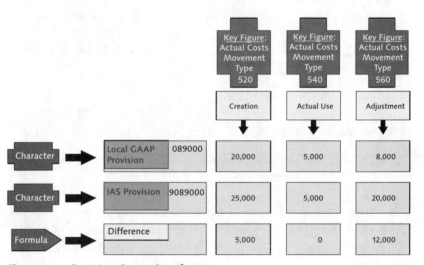

Figure 4.39 Provisions Report Specification

Fully save field information for transaction type Each provision type is saved in the rows as the characteristic ACCOUNT or LEDGER. The historical development is saved in the columns in the form of the transaction type. However, some basic settings have to be made in advance. In the field status group, define the TRANSACTION TYPE field for the provisions accounts as a mandatory field. You do this by following the menu path: FINANCIALS (NEW) • ACCOUNTS RECEIVABLE AND ACCOUNTS PAYABLE ACCOUNTING • BUSINESS TRANSACTIONS • INTERNAL TRANSFER POSTING • EXECUTE AND CHECK DOCUMENT SETTINGS • DEFINE FIELD STATUS VARIANTS • FIELD STATUS GROUPS • CONSOLIDATION. To ensure that the document information is also available in the totals table in New G/L, you have to activate the *consolidation preparation* scenario under FINANCIALS (NEW) • FINANCIALS GENERAL SETTINGS (NEW) • LEDGERS • ASSIGN SCENARIOS AND CUSTOMER-SPECIFIC FIELDS • SCENARIO: FIN_CONS. Otherwise, the characteristic will not be transferred to the totals table and will not appear in the provisions report. You should also remember that the Report Painter report must be based on this new table. You can accomplish this by linking a new library to the reporting table FAGLFLEXT. These settings are found via the menu path: INFORMATION SYSTEMS • AD-HOC REPORTS • REPORT PAINTER • REPORT WRITER • LIBRARY. If no values are displayed in your provisions report, you must have overlooked one or more of the steps described above.

4.8 Posting and Clearing Specific to Ledger Groups (Enhancement Package 3)

This section introduces an enhanced function in New G/L—another innovation that is available with Enhancement Package 3 and thus included in the FIN_GL_CI_1 business function—posting and clearing specific to ledger groups.

4.8.1 Business Context

Ledger group-specific clearing should be used for the ledger approach for parallel accounting in New G/L but it doesn't make sense for the accounts approach.

Ledger group-specific posting and clearing processes are mainly used for closing activities and focus on documents that are valuated differently in the various ledgers due to multiple valuation approaches in parallel accounting standards and thus need to be posted separately.

Ledger approach in New G/L

Section 4.7 described an example of provisions in detail. Ledger group-specific posting and clearing can be particularly useful for the posting and writing-off of provisions (examples include provisions for commissions, provisions for warranties, and provisions for future legal costs/risks).

4.8.2 Indicators in the Master Record

First of all, the CLEARING SPECIFIC TO LEDGER GROUPS indicator needs to be selected. You can find it under ❶ in Figure 4.40 in the control data/the account management data in the company code of G/L account 79300.

Activation suspends other indicators

This indicator replaces the OPEN ITEM MANAGEMENT and LINE ITEM DISPLAY INDICATORS ❷, which you can also find in this figure. Figure 4.40 consequently demonstrates that you cannot select any of these two indicators, OPEN ITEM MANAGEMENT and LINE ITEM DISPLAY, IF the CLEARING SPECIFIC TO LEDGER GROUPS indicator is set.

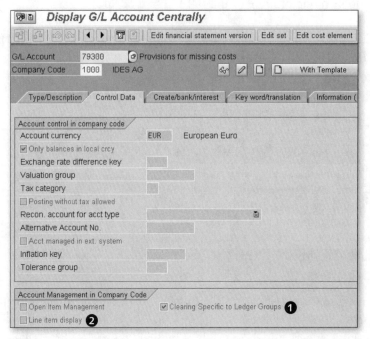

Figure 4.40 "Clearing Specific to Ledger Groups" Indicator in the Master Record of a G/L Account

Figure 4.41 shows the error message that the system outputs when you try to select the open item management option in addition to the CLEARING SPECIFIC TO LEDGER GROUPS indicator.

Figure 4.41 Message—"Clearing Specific to Ledger Groups" or "Open Item Management" Indicator in the Master Record of a G/L Account

4.8.3 Required Customizing Settings

To view the indicator, more than one ledger needs to be defined for the company code. You can do this in the Customizing of the system via the following IMG path: FINANCIAL ACCOUNTING (NEW) • FINANCIAL ACCOUNTING GLOBAL SETTINGS (NEW) • LEDGERS • LEDGER • DEFINE LEDGERS FOR GENERAL LEDGER ACCOUNTING. Figure 2.11 in Chapter 2, Design and Features of the Ledgers, illustrates this setting in the system Customizing.

Displaying indicators

You also need to define the field status appropriately using the field status control of the account group (account group-dependent field status) and using the field status control of Transaction FS00 to create or change G/L accounts (transaction-dependent field status). This process is also shown in Figure 4.42, where the field status control of the GL ACCOUNTS GROUP in the INT CHART OF ACCOUNTS is used.

Defining the field status

You implement this setting in Customizing via the IMG path: FINANCIAL ACCOUNTING (NEW) • GENERAL LEDGER ACCOUNTING (NEW) • MASTER DATA • G/L ACCOUNTS• PREPARATION • DEFINE ACCOUNT GROUP.

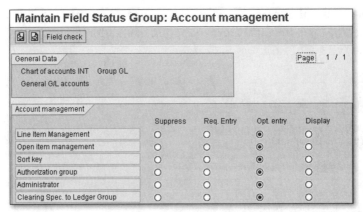

Figure 4.42 Field Status of the "Clearing Specific to Ledger Groups" Field for G/L Accounts of the GL Accounts Group in the Customizing

4.8.4 "Ledger Group-Specific Clearing for G/L Accounts" Indicator — Restrictions of Use

Let's now look at the restrictions of the use of the "Ledger Group-Specific Clearing for G/L Accounts" indicator.

[!] | **Using the "Clearing Specific to Ledger Groups" Indicator for Balance Sheet Accounts Only**

It is critical to note at this point that you mustn't select the CLEARING SPECIFIC TO LEDGER GROUPS indicator for any kind of G/L account. You should use the CLEARING SPECIFIC TO LEDGER GROUPS indicator for balance sheet accounts only.

As already mentioned, it makes sense to use the business scenario of creating or writing off provisions as an example. However, you cannot set the CLEARING SPECIFIC TO LEDGER GROUPS indicator for the following accounts:

- ▶ Goods receipt and invoice receipt accounts
- ▶ Accounts for cash discounts
- ▶ Reconciliation accounts
- ▶ Tax-relevant accounts
- ▶ P&L accounts

4.8.5 Process of Posting and Clearing Specific to Ledger Groups

The following sections describe the individual steps of posting and clearing specific to ledger groups.

Ledger Group-Specific Posting and Document Display—Usage

Once you've set the Clearing Specific to Ledger Groups indicator for a G/L account with open items, you can post documents to the respective account with referring to the specific ledger groups. You can enter these postings via Transaction Enter G/L Account Document for Ledger Group (FB50L). You can find this transaction in the SAP application menu under Accounting • Financial Accounting • General Ledger • Posting • Enter G/L Account Document.

Alternatively, you can also enter the ledger group-specific document using Transaction General Posting (FB01L) for a specific ledger group.

The document display in Figure 4.43 and Figure 4.44 displays the result of the creation of provisions for the specific ledger group.

Figure 4.43 first shows the document for ledger group A1 (ledger A1 could represent the IFRS, for example) with document number 9900000000 and an amount of EUR 1,000.00 posted in fiscal year 2008 (according to the posting record, which is illustrated in Table 4.20).

Ledger group A1

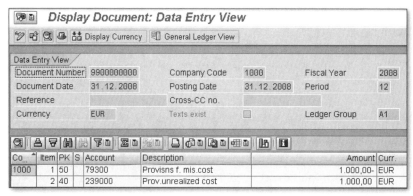

Figure 4.43 Document Display: Result of the Posting Specific to Ledger Groups in Ledger Group A1

Account	Description	Debit	Credit	Ledger Group	Fiscal Year
239000	Provisions unrealized cost	EUR 1,000.00		A1	2008
79300	Provisions		EUR 1,000.00	A1	2008

Table 4.20 Posting Specific to Ledger Groups in Ledger Group A1

The document contains a ledger group-specific view of the account. If you used the accounts approach, you would have needed additional accounts to map the business context here!

Ledger group N1

Figure 4.44 shows the document for ledger group N1 (ledger N1 could represent the US-GAAP, for example) with document number 1 and an amount of EUR 1,500.00 posted in fiscal year 2008 (according to the posting record, which is illustrated in Table 4.21).

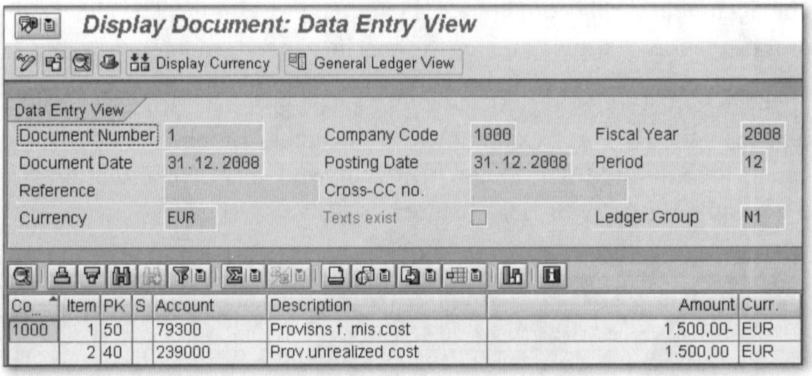

Figure 4.44 Document Display—Result of the Posting Specific to Ledger Groups in Ledger Group N1

Account	Description	Debit	Credit	Ledger Group	Fiscal Year
239000	Provisions unrealized cost	EUR 1,500.00		N1	2008
79300	Provisions		EUR 1,500.00	N1	2008

Table 4.21 Posting Specific to Ledger Groups in Ledger Group N1

Our example is based on a (of course, ledger group-specific) vendor invoice from February 2009 of the vendor LEITZ 1 with an amount of EUR 1,200.00. You could post this invoice using Transaction FB60 (Enter Vendor Invoices), for example. You can find this transaction in the SAP application menu under ACCOUNTING • FINANCIAL ACCOUNTING • VENDOR • POSTING • ENTER VENDOR INVOICE.

Figure 4.45 shows the resulting posting document, 1900000001 (according to the posting record illustrated in Table 4.22).

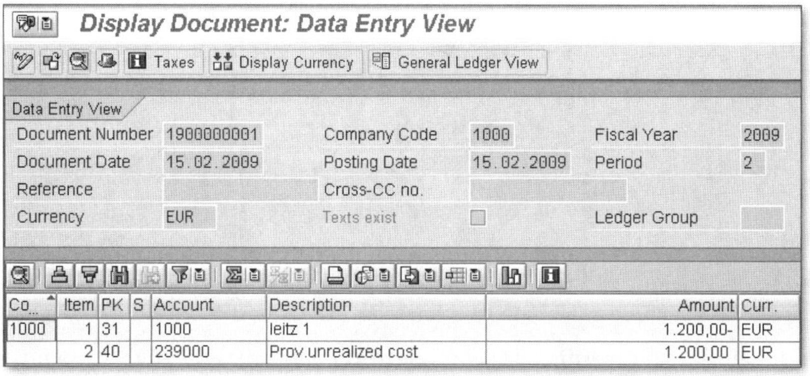

Posting document

Figure 4.45 Document Display of the Vendor Invoice in February 2009

Account	Description	Debit	Credit	Ledger Group	Fiscal Year
239000	Provisions unrealized cost	EUR 1,200.00			2009
160000	Vendor leitz 1		EUR 1,200.00		2009

Table 4.22 Posting of the Vendor Invoice in February 2009

The following deals with the use and write-off of the provision: the resulting transfer posting in the use case, posted in ledger A1 with EUR 1,000.00, described in Table 4.23, and the transfer posting of EUR 1,200.00 in ledger N1, illustrated in Table 4.24.

Writing off provisions

Account	Description	Debit	Credit	Ledger Group	Fiscal Year
79300	Provisions	EUR 1,000.00		A1	2009
239000	Provisions unrealized cost		EUR 1,000.00	A1	2009

Table 4.23 Transfer Posting Specific to Ledger Groups in Ledger Group A1

Account	Description	Debit	Credit	Ledger Group	Fiscal Year
79300	Provisions	EUR 1,200.00		N1	2009
239000	Provisions unrealized cost		EUR 1,200.00	N1	2009

Table 4.24 Transfer Posting Specific to Ledger Groups in Ledger Group N1

You can find the posted documents in the system as shown in Figure 4.46 and Figure 4.47.

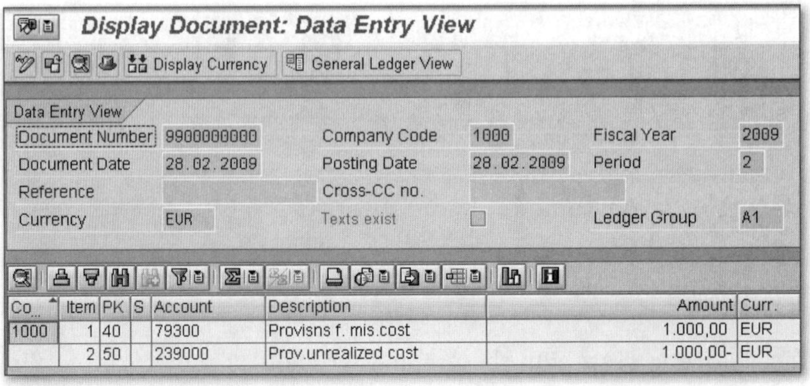

Figure 4.46 Document Display: Result of the Transfer Posting Specific to Ledger Groups in Ledger Group A1

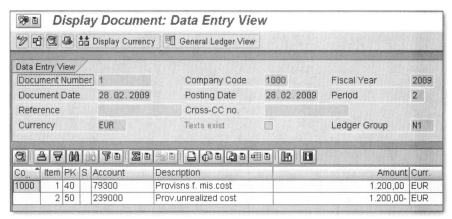

Figure 4.47 Document Display: Result of the Transfer Posting Specific to Ledger Groups in Ledger Group N1

Ledger group N1 also includes a posting of a writing-off of EUR 300.00 on an account for revenues from the writing-off of the accruals/deferrals (see Table 4.25).

Writing off accruals/deferrals

Account	Description	Debit	Credit	Ledger Group	Fiscal Year
79300	Provisions	EUR 300.00		N1	2009
290000	Income – provisions		EUR 300.00	N1	2009

Table 4.25 Transfer Posting Specific to Ledger Groups in Ledger Group N1

This posting is the delta amount between the amount of EUR 1,500.00, which was originally posted to ledger N1 as a provision in 2008 (see Table 4.21), and the amount of the vendor invoice from February 2009 (see Table 4.22). You can view this posting in Figure 4.48.

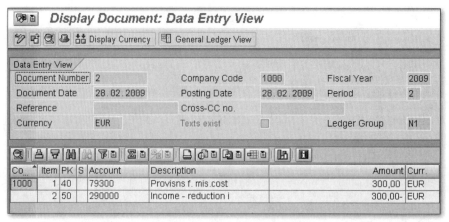

Figure 4.48 Document Display—Result of the Transfer Posting Specific to Ledger Groups (Difference) in Ledger Group N1

Ledger group A1

So how does the system map the ledger-specific balance display on G/L account 79300 from February 2009 in ledger group A1 or ledger group N1? Figure 4.49 for ledger group A1 and Figure 4.50 for ledger group N1 demonstrates this; both figures show that the cumulated balance of the posted accounting documents amounts to zero.

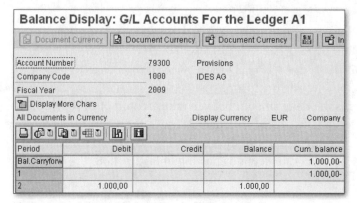

Figure 4.49 Balance Display—Result of the Transfer Postings Specific to Ledger Groups in December 2008 and in February 2009 in Ledger Group A1

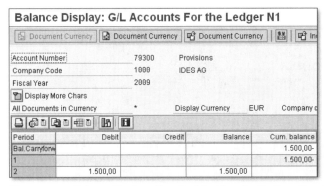

Figure 4.50 Balance Display—Result of the Transfer Postings Specific to Ledger Groups in December 2008 and in February 2009 in Ledger Group N1

The following sections continue with the description of this process to obtain a (closing) clearing specific to ledger groups.

Existing Accounts for Postings Specific to Ledger Groups

First, let's look at SAP's recommendation.

> **SAP's Recommendation** [+]
>
> SAP recommends creating new accounts for clearing specific to ledger groups.

However, you can use existing accounts instead of creating new accounts. You must consider that this option of using existing accounts is available under certain circumstances only:

If no postings have been made to the G/L account, you can set the CLEARING SPECIFIC TO LEDGER GROUPS indicator for this account retroactively. This is certainly the easiest implementation variant.

Variant 1— no postings

If postings have already been made but neither the Line Item Display indicator nor the Open Item Management indicator has been set, proceed as follows:

Variant 2—postings have been made

1. **Generating line items retroactively**

   First, you need to generate the line items retroactively using the RFSE-PA01 report, as shown in Figure 4.51.

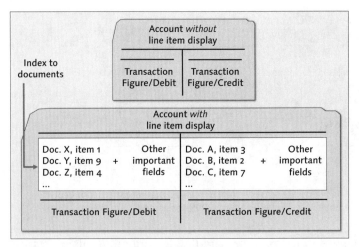

Figure 4.51   Generating Line Items Retroactively

2. Starting the report

When changing an account (setting the Line Item Display indicator, here in Figure 4.52 the indicator in account 79360), the system prompts you to start the RFSEPA01 report.

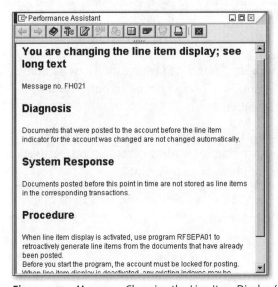

Figure 4.52   Message—Changing the Line Item Display (Activation)

3. **Locking an account**

Figure 4.53 shows the selection screen of the RFSEPA01 report, which you are supposed to start. To ensure a consistent state during the report runtime, you need to lock the account against postings.

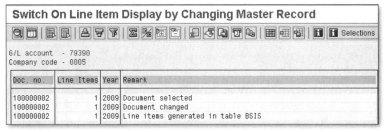

Switch On Line Item Display by Changing Master Record

Company code	0005
G/L account	79360
Document number	to

Additional log
☑ List log

Figure 4.53 Switch On Line Item Display—Selection Screen RFSEPA01

4. **Releasing an account**

After the items have been converted, you can release the lock.

5. **Log**

Figure 4.54 shows the log: The report lists the selected documents and logs the number of generated line items as well as the number of documents that have been changed. The list log allows for outputting a log for each document.

Switch On Line Item Display by Changing Master Record

G/L account - 79390
Company code - 0005

Doc. no.	Line Items	Year	Remark
100000002	1	2009	Document selected
100000002	1	2009	Document changed
100000002	1	2009	Line items generated in table BSIS

Figure 4.54 Log—Switch On Line Item Display with RFSEPA01

6. **Setting the "Open Item Management" indicator retroactively**

In addition, you need to set the indicator for ledger group-specific open item management retroactively using a report. You can find the corresponding IMG menu path under FINANCIAL ACCOUNTING (NEW) • GENERAL LEDGER ACCOUNTING (NEW) • MASTER DATA • G/L ACCOUNTS • CREATE AND PROCESS G/L ACCOUNTS • DEFINE ACCOUNT CONTROL • ACTIVATE OPEN ITEM MANAGEMENT FOR ACCOUNTS MANAGED VIA LINE ITEMS.

7. **Calling the selection screen**

You can find the selection screen, which you can also call using Transaction FAGL_SWITCH_TO_OPEN_ITEM (FAGL_SWITCH_TO_OPEN_ITEM is the corresponding report name), in Figure 4.55.

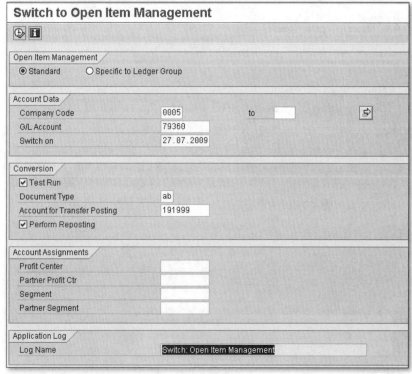

Figure 4.55 Switch On (Ledger Group-Specific) Open Item Management—Selection Screen

8. **Test run log**

During the test run, the system already provides a detailed log (see Figure 4.56).

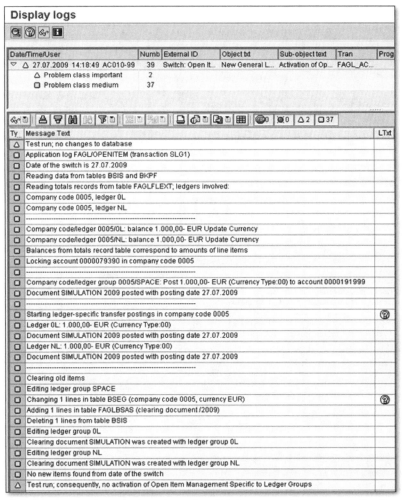

Figure 4.56 Switch On (Ledger Group-Specific) Open Item Management—Test Run Log

9. **Update run log**

The system also provides a detailed log for the update run. Figure 4.57 shows a log with the postings that are made during the update run.

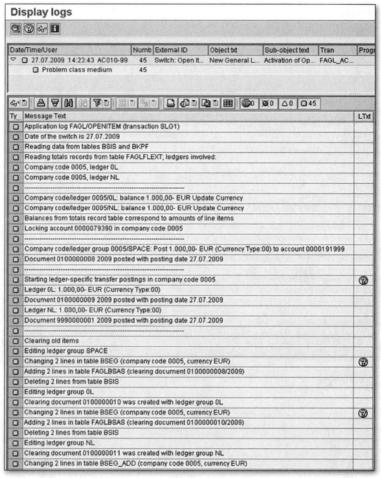

Figure 4.57 Switch On (Ledger Group-Specific) Open Item Management—Update Run Log

[+] **Further Information**

In this context, the following section should be noted: It provides additional information on the process of switching from G/L accounts to open item management.

Report
FAGL_SWITCH_
TO_OPEN_ITEM

If the account uses line item management or open item management as illustrated in Figure 4.58 and postings have already been made to the account, you can set the indicator in the same way, that is, using the previously mentioned report, FAGL_SWITCH_TO_OPEN_ITEM.

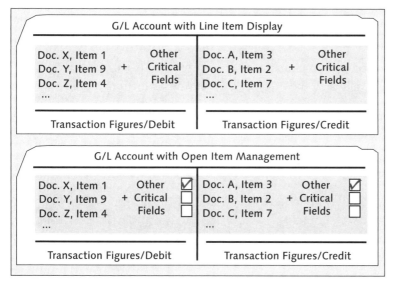

Figure 4.58 Account with Line Item Management or Open Item Management

---

After the First Posting a Decision for Ledger Group-Specific OI Management is Irreversible

You also have to consider the "one-way street principle." After having converted a G/L account to an account with ledger group-specific OI management and made postings to this account, you can no longer reset the account to the "state" of a "common" G/L account with ledger group-specific open item management.

[+]

Clearing Specific to Ledger Groups—Usage

Let's return to the core of clearing specific to ledger groups.

Clearing specific to ledger groups

You are already familiar with postings specific to ledger groups, so it seems logical that the clearing process also needs to be ledger group-specific. What would you expect in this case? That open items that were posted in a specific ledger group are also separately cleared in exactly this ledger group! This means that documents that you posted in a specific ledger group can be processed only in this ledger group. If you—as in this example—posted provisions in a specific ledger group, you must also post their writing-off in this ledger group.

Transactions For balance sheet accounts, several new transactions are available for clearing specific to ledger groups. You can clear the accounts manually or automatically.

To clear accounts manually, two new transactions are available—after you have activated the FIN_GL_CI_1 business function:

▶ Posting with Clearing—for Ledger Group (Transaction FB05L); works like Transaction FB05

▶ Clear G/L Account—for Ledger Group (Transaction FB1SL); works like Transaction FB1S

You can find Transactions FB05L and FB1SL in the SAP application menu under ACCOUNTING • FINANCIAL ACCOUNTING • GENERAL LEDGER • ACCOUNT • CLEAR • SPECIFIC TO LEDGER GROUPS or TRANSFER POSTING WITH CLEARING SPECIFIC TO LEDGER GROUPS.

"Posting with Clearing" function When using the POSTING WITH CLEARING function, you enter the clearing amount and then select the open items that you want to clear. This procedure is illustrated in Figure 4.59.

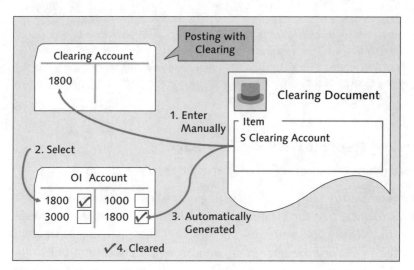

Figure 4.59 Posting with Clearing

If the overall amount of the selected open items is identical to the clearing amount entered, the system clears the open items by generating clearing items.

If you use the CLEAR ACCOUNT function, you select the open items of an account that amount to zero. The system marks them as cleared and generates a clearing document. The number of the clearing document and the clearing date are entered in the cleared items. The clearing date can be the current date or any selected date. This process is illustrated in Figure 4.60.

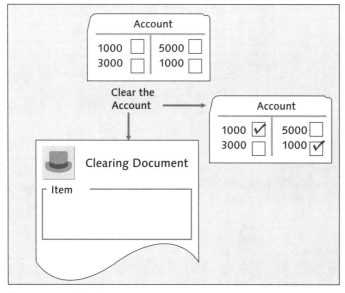

Figure 4.60 Clear Account

The new transactions are very similar to the old transactions. The statement emphasized in Chapter 2, Design and Features of the Ledgers, can be applied again: To keep the training for the users to a minimum, the transactions for entering reports and the selection screens of the corresponding reports and programs were designed in such a way that they are as similar to the "classic" transactions as possible.

The following figures show screenshots that illustrate the CLEAR ACCOUNT function using the ledger group-specific clearing process of ledger group A1 or ledger group N1 as an example.

In Figure 4.61, G/L account 79300 and ledger group A1 are selected for the clearing process. After the header data has been entered, the open items are selected (see Figure 4.62). The item with EUR 1,000.00 on the debit side is assigned an item with the same amount on the credit side.

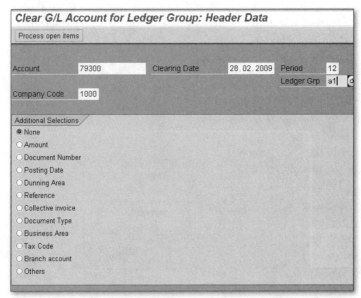

Figure 4.61 Ledger Group-Specific Clearing of a G/L Account—Ledger Group A1 (Header Data)

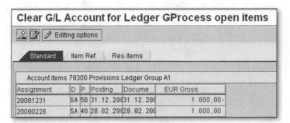

Figure 4.62 Ledger Group-Specific Clearing of a G/L Account—Ledger Group A1 (Processing Open Items)

Let's now compare the conditions for ledger group N1: In Figure 4.63, G/L account 79300 but ledger group N1 is selected for the clearing process. After the header data has been entered, the open items are selected (see Figure 4.64). The item with EUR 1,200.00 and EUR 300.00 on the debit side is assigned an item with EUR 1,500.00 on the credit side.

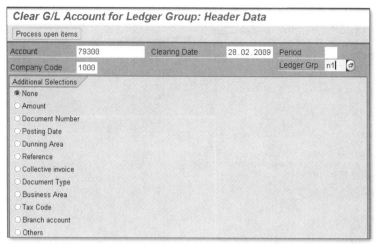

Figure 4.63 Ledger Group-Specific Clearing of a G/L Account—Ledger Group N1 (Header Data)

Clear G/L Account for Ledger GProcess open items

⌖ ▨ ✎ Editing options

| Standard | Item Ref. | Res.items |

Account items 79300 Provisions for missing costs Ledger Group N1

Assignment	Document N.	D.	P.	Posting Date	Document Date	EUR Gross
20081231	1	SA	50	31.12.2008	31.12.2008	1.500,00-
20090228	1	SA	40	28.02.2009	28.02.2009	1.200,00
20090228	2	SA	40	28.02.2009	28.02.2009	300,00

Figure 4.64 Ledger Group-Specific Clearing of a G/L Account—Ledger Group N1 (Process Open Items)

Clearing— classic transactions

If you try to use a "classic" transaction, for example, F-03 or FB1S, for the clearing process for an account that is defined by specific ledger groups, the system outputs a message that says that clearing specific to ledger groups is possible with Transactions FB1SL or FB05L only (see Figure 4.65).

Clearing— automatic

To clear an account automatically, you can use Transaction F13L—it works just like Transaction F.13. You can find the corresponding program, SAPF124, in the application's menu path under ACCOUNTING • FINANCIAL ACCOUNTING • GENERAL LEDGER • PERIODIC PROCESSING • CLEARING • AUTOMATIC CLEARING • G/L ACCOUNTS—SPECIFIC TO LEDGER GROUPS.

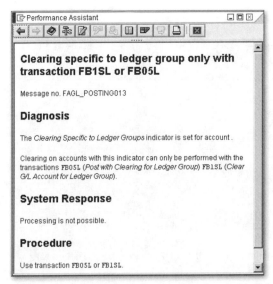

Figure 4.65 Clearing Specific to Ledger Groups Possible with Transaction FB1SL or FB05L Only

Figure 4.66 shows the selection screen of the automatic clearing program; Figure 4.67 presents the log.

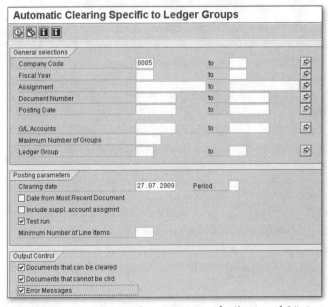

Figure 4.66 Automatic, Ledger Group-Specific Clearing of G/L Accounts

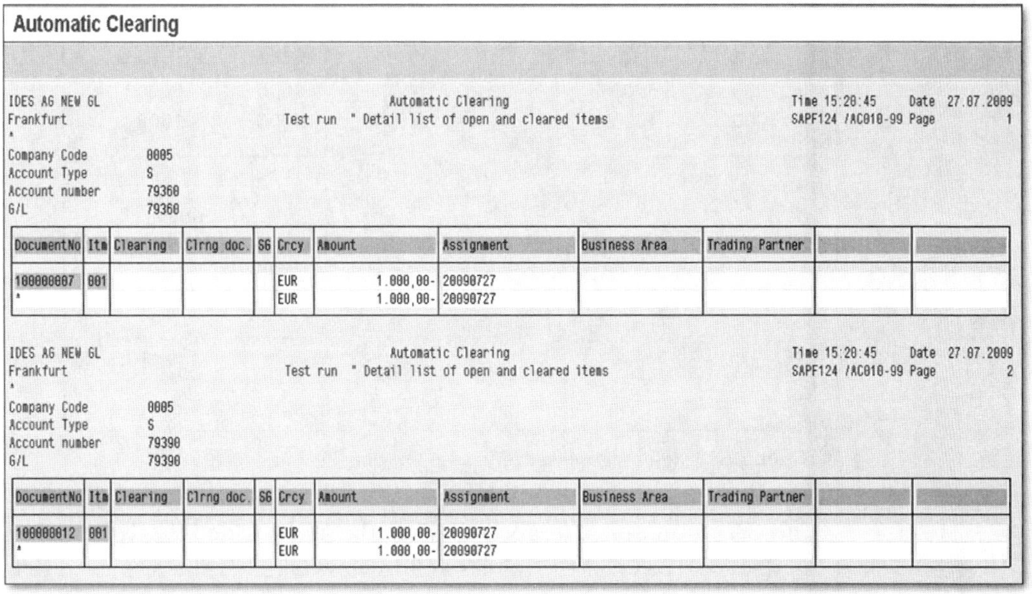

Figure 4.67 Automatic Clearing of G/L Accounts

Resetting a ledger group-specific clearing process is similar to resetting a clearing process that is not ledger group-specific. For example, if you have cleared an item accidentally, you can use Transaction FBRA to reset the clearing. This is done by resetting the clearing document and the cleared items. Figure 4.68 illustrates this option. The system removes the clearing data from the items. In addition, the system logs these changes; you can have the system display them in the change documents, for example, via Transaction FB04.

Reset cleared items

Posting and Clearing Specific to Ledger Groups—Reporting

We now look at the aspects of posting and clearing specific to ledger groups in the context of evaluations: The reporting at G/L account level as well as document level or item level provides new display and selection options.

Clearing specific to ledger groups

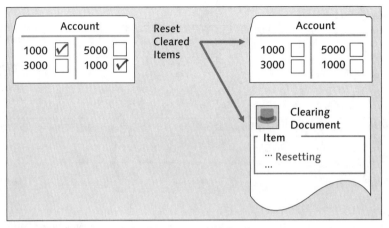

Figure 4.68 Resetting the Ledger Group-Specific Clearing Process

The G/L account list (report RFSKVZ00, can be called via Transaction S_ALR_87012328) now enables you to view whether the displayed G/L account uses ledger group-specific open item management. Figure 4.69 illustrates this display option.

G/L Account List

```
IDES-ALE: Central FI Syst                        G/L Account List                    Time 14:38:11     Date  08.07.2009
Frankfurt - Deutschland                                                              RFSKVZ00/AC010-99 Page           1

ChartofAccts:   INT = Chart of accounts - international
Sort:           G/LAccount, CompanyCode

Name 1           Contents 1        Name 2         Contents 2    Name 3         Contents 3   Name 4         Contents 4
G/L acct  0000079300 Company Code      Company Code Name
Section          GENERAL DATA
Long Text     Provisions for missing costs                     Account Group   GL
Section          STATUS IN CHART OF ACCTS
Creation block                     Posting Block               Planning block               Deletion flag
G/L acct  0000079300 Company Code   0005  Company Code Name       IDES AG NEW GL
Section          ACCOUNT CONTROL
Tax category                       Reconcil.ID                 E/R diff. key                Acct currency  EUR
Balances in LC  X                  W/o tax                     Account extern.
Section          ACCOUNT MANAGEMENT
Line items                         OI management               LG-SpecClg     X             Sort key       001
Section          DOCUMENT ENTRY CONTROL
Field status gp G001               Auto. posting               Supplement                   Rec.act ready
```

Figure 4.69 Display in the G/L Account List—Ledger Group-Specific Clearing

Selecting G/L accounts

To select all G/L accounts with ledger group-specific open item management, you can use ledger group-specific clearing as the selection criterion for the free selection of the RFSKVZ00 report. Figure 4.70 shows this selection option.

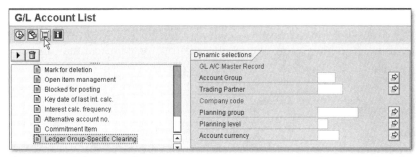

Figure 4.70 Selection in the G/L Account List—Accounts with Ledger Group-Specific Clearing

You have to fulfill the prerequisite for the selection according to SAP Note 1086335 and implement the necessary settings in the logical database, SDF. Figure 4.71 presents the corresponding selection view with the SKB1 table and XLGCLR field.

Selection—
prerequisites

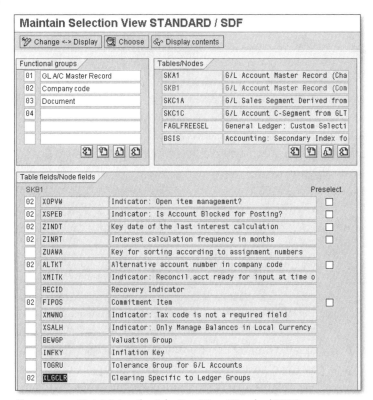

Figure 4.71 Maintaining the Selection View "Standard/SDF"

"Account Detective" report

You can use the ACCOUNT DETECTIVE report (report RFAUDI30), which you can call via Transaction S_ALR_87101048, for example, to solve audit-specific issues and obtain information for external auditors and internal audits. Figure 4.72 shows the report's selection screen.

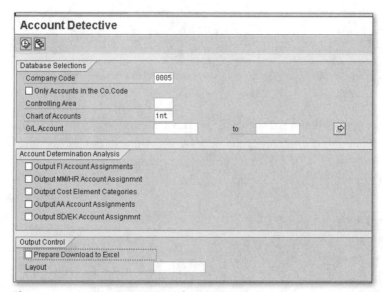

Figure 4.72 Account Detective—Selection Screen

For the evaluation of G/L account master records, the report includes the column for ledger group-specific clearing (LEDGER GROUP-SPECIFIC CLEARING column, see Figure 4.73).

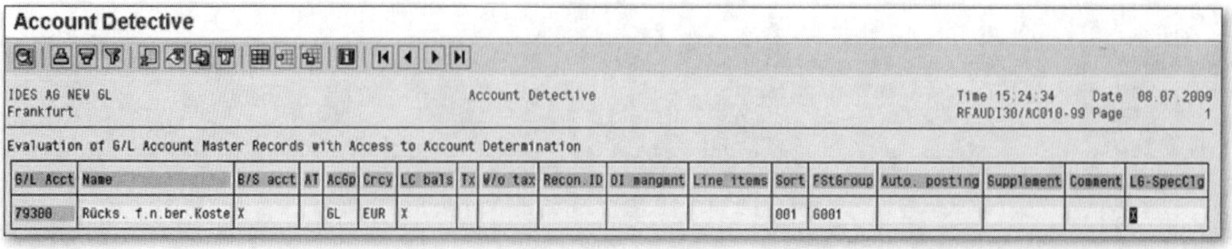

Figure 4.73 Account Detective—"Ledger Group-Specific Clearing" Column

Line item display

In the line item display, you can use Transaction FAGLL03 to view the items that were posted to an account with ledger group-specific open item management. The entry view merely displays the items that were

posted to the leading ledger or to a ledger group in the leading ledger. The G/L view lists all items that were posted to the corresponding G/L account in the respective ledger (see Figure 4.74). The line item display also contains the ledger group column (CLEARING SPECIFIC TO LEDGER GROUPS column, see also Figure 4.74).

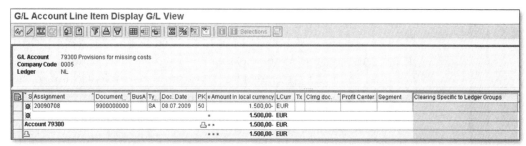

Figure 4.74 G/L Accounts Line Item Display G/L View—"Clearing Specific to Ledger Groups" Column

You can also sort the line items by ledger group.

Please note that you cannot use the "classic" G/L account line item display from classic G/L Accounting (Transaction FBL3N) for G/L accounts with ledger group-specific OI management; if you try to do this, the system outputs the message shown in Figure 4.75.

Line item display— classicGeneral Ledger

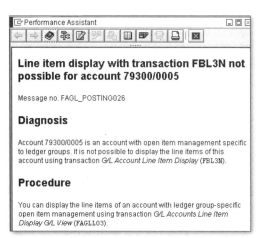

Figure 4.75 Error Message—Line Item Display with Transaction FBL3N Not Possible for Account

4.8.6 Restriction — Sample Accounts for Posting and Clearing Specific to Ledger Groups

There is one restriction you have to consider when using sample accounts. Let's look at the background: Sample accounts are used if the head office of a corporate group wants to control the account data for the company codes centrally. For this purpose, the head office creates sample accounts with the data that the company code segments are supposed to contain. The number of the sample account to be used is entered in every chart of accounts segment. When creating the company code segment via the company code, the system copies data from the sample account to the account fields. Figure 4.76 illustrates this process.

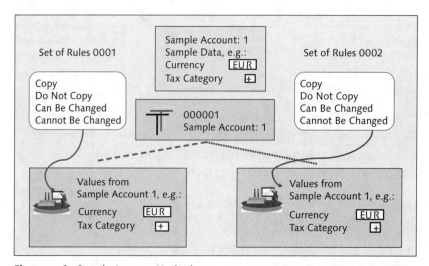

Figure 4.76 Sample Account Method

Sample account method A rule variant (set of rules) assigned to the company code determines whether a value is copied from the sample account to the company code segment and whether this value is a fixed value or can be changed. This *sample account method* (Transactions FSM*) as well as the copy process for G/L account master data using Transactions FS15 (RFBISA10 program for sending the G/L account master records) and FS16 (RFBISA20 program for receiving the G/L account master records) unfortunately do not support the Clearing Specific to Ledger Groups indicator because these transactions use an older dynpro technology. Therefore, you must set the indicator manually after having processed the master records of the respective accounts.

4.9 Switching from G/L Accounts to Open Item Management

The previous sections briefly touched upon the retroactive switch-on of open item management. This section introduces an additional function: the switch from G/L accounts to open item management in New G/L, which is available with Enhancement Package 3 and thus included in FIN_GL_CI_1 the business function.

The following sections discuss the prerequisites for the switch from G/L accounts to open item management and provide a posting example from the application for illustration purposes.

4.9.1 Customizing Settings

As of Enhancement Package 3, Transaction FAGL_ACTIVATE_OP provides you with the option of a retroactive activation for open item management for G/L accounts. Here, the indicator for ledger group-specific open item management is replaced by a report; you can find the corresponding IMG menu path under FINANCIAL ACCOUNTING (NEW) • GENERAL LEDGER ACCOUNTING (NEW) • MASTER DATA • G/L ACCOUNTS • CREATE AND PROCESS G/L ACCOUNTS • DEFINE ACCOUNT CONTROL • ACTIVATE OPEN ITEM MANAGEMENT FOR ACCOUNTS MANAGED VIA LINE ITEMS.

Transaction FAGL_ ACTIVATE_OP

This display is based on the existing line item display option, which enables you to create an evaluation using the report for listing the line items—Figure 4.77 illustrates this by means of account 79200.

Line item display

The line item display must be activated in the company code in the account management of the account. Figure 4.78 shows the master record of the G/L account with the corresponding fields/checkboxes LINE ITEM DISPLAY, OPEN ITEM MANAGEMENT, and CLEARING SPECIFIC TO LEDGER GROUPS.

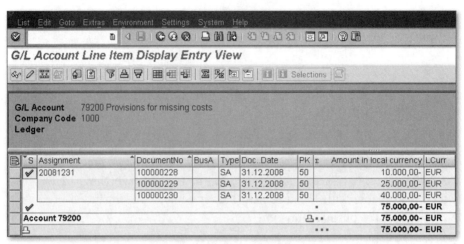

Figure 4.77 Line Item Display of Account 79200

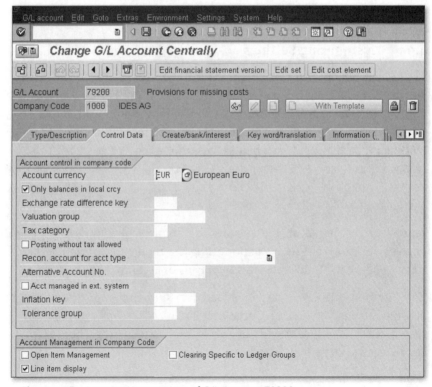

Figure 4.78 Account Management of G/L Account 79200

Basically, the transaction provides three options, which were already mentioned in Section 4.8, Posting and Clearing Specific to Ledger Groups (Enhancement Package 3):

▶ Switching from line item display to open item management

▶ Switching from line item display to ledger group-specific open item management

▶ Switching from open item management to ledger group-specific open item management

As already noted, the G/L account needs to be managed with line items. If you want to activate ledger group-specific open item management, the G/L account may already work with open item management. Because the SAP system needs to post documents, the selection screen provides mandatory fields and entries for the account assignment.

SAP recommends creating separate accounts. The documents posted with Transaction FAGL_ACTIVATE_OP do not represent an "actually existing" business transaction. As you can see in Figure 4.79, you can define the character of the open item management—STANDARD or SPECIFIC TO LEDGER GROUP.

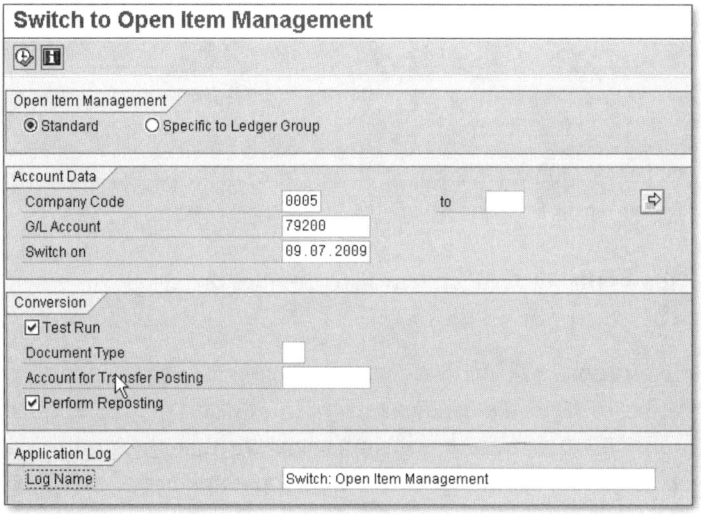

Figure 4.79 Selection Screen of Transaction FAGL_ACTIVATE_OP

Log A detailed log shows possible error messages, such as the error message from Figure 4.80. Here, the balance of ledger OL differs from the account balance.

This log also lists the restriction that an automatic activation of open item management is not possible because ledger group-specific postings have already been made so that the balances of the G/L account in the various ledgers are no longer identical. This detailed log is provided during the test run.

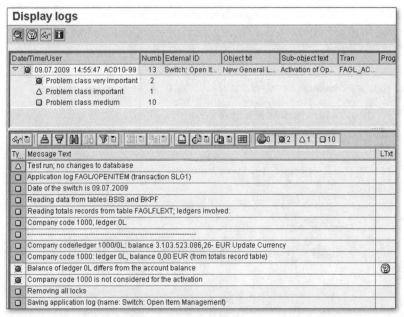

Figure 4.80 Report for the Switch to Open Item Management—Log

Figure 4.81 shows that the SAP system also provides this diagnosis when you double-click the error message.

Making postings If the basic conditions are met, the system makes the corresponding postings in order to receive a balance of zero in any currency as a result for the account. In this context, you must ensure that the permitted value for exchange rate difference in the global parameters of the company code is not set too low, because this can result in the process being canceled.

Figure 4.81 Diagnosis—Error Message

Figure 4.82 shows an excerpt from the table that you can call via the IMG menu path FINANCIAL ACCOUNTING (NEW) • FINANCIAL ACCOUNTING BASIC SETTINGS (NEW) • GLOBAL PARAMETERS FOR COMPANY CODE • CURRENCIES • MAXIMUM DIFFERENCE BETWEEN EXCHANGE RATES • DEFINE MAXIMUM DIFFERENCE BETWEEN EXCHANGE RATES FOR EACH COMPANY CODE to define the maximum difference between exchange rates for each company code.

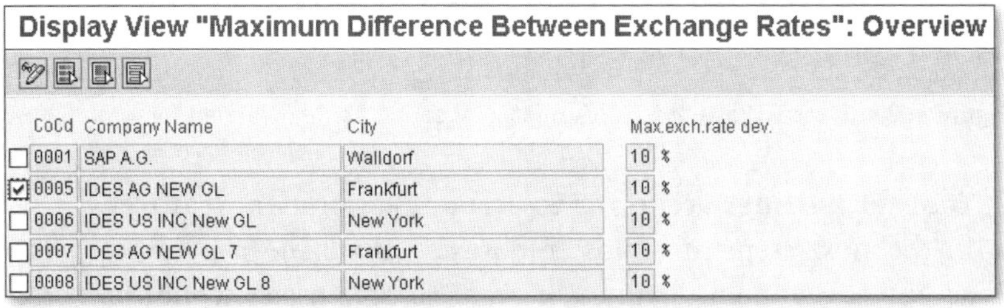

Display View "Maximum Difference Between Exchange Rates": Overview

CoCd	Company Name	City	Max.exch.rate dev.
0001	SAP A.G.	Walldorf	10 %
0005	IDES AG NEW GL	Frankfurt	10 %
0006	IDES US INC New GL	New York	10 %
0007	IDES AG NEW GL 7	Frankfurt	10 %
0008	IDES US INC New GL 8	New York	10 %

Figure 4.82 Permitted Maximum Difference Between Exchange Rates for Each Company Code

To receive a balance of zero for each ledger (and account assignment), the system implements transfer postings specific to ledger groups. Afterwards, the system activates open item management and clears the

Transfer posting— clearing— reposting

currently existing open items. If you set the PERFORM REPOSTING indicator (see Figure 4.79), you are provided with an additional option because the amounts that were initially written off are reposted.

4.9.2 Sample Posting for the Switch to Open Item Management for G/L Accounts

The example is based on three posted documents on one account with three different amounts (2000, 3000, and 4000) and three different account assignments (X, Y, and Z). The account for the transfer posting is the dummy account with dummy account assignment D.

1. **Transfer posting**
   In the first step, a transfer posting is made in order to clear the account, which is now to be switched to open item management.

2. **Offsetting posting**
   The offsetting posting is made on the dummy account (account for transfer posting), as shown in Figure 4.83.

   Result: The account that is supposed to be switched is now cleared.

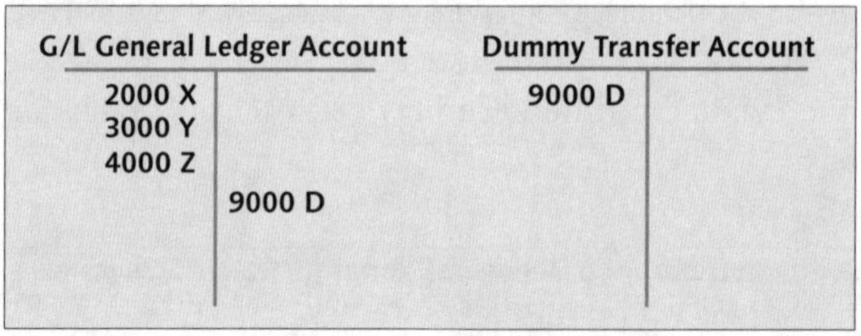

G/L General Ledger Account	Dummy Transfer Account
2000 X	9000 D
3000 Y	
4000 Z	
9000 D	

Figure 4.83 Transfer Posting for Clearing the Accounts to Be Switched

3. **Transfer postings according to account assignment features**
   In the next step, the transfer postings are made according to the account assignment features in order to obtain an account balanced to zero with regard to all account assignment features.

   Figure 4.84 illustrates these transfer postings.

```
 ┌─────────────────────────────┐
 │ G/L General Ledger Account  │
 │                             │
 │     2000 X  │               │
 │     3000 Y  │               │
 │     4000 Z  │               │
 │             │  9000 D       │
 │             │               │
 │             │               │
 │     2000 D  │  2000 X       │
 │     3000 D  │  3000 Y       │
 │     4000 D  │  4000 Z       │
 │             │               │
 └─────────────────────────────┘
```

Figure 4.84 Transfer Posting with Regard to Account Assignment Features

4. **Clearing**

   In the next step, the system clears all items. The switch on date (which you can find in the account data in the selection screen) determines how the items are handled:

   ▶ Items that were posted before or on this date are cleared.

   ▶ Items that were posted after this date are listed as open items.

   ▶ When switching from open item management to ledger group-specific open item management, the system ignores this date field because the open items already contain the ledger group as a blank. No postings are made here.

5. **Reposting**

   In the last step, the system reposts the amount (9000 in this example) from the dummy account to the switched G/L account.

4.10   Conclusion

Mapping parallel accounting in individual financial closings renders obsolete the Microsoft Excel-based solutions still used in many companies. SAP software with SAP ERP Financials supports several options for determining different valuation approaches. The accounts and ledger approaches are given equal status in New G/L. Customers still can choose their storage locations, based on some key points:

► **Accounts approach as storage location**
If you are already using the accounts approach to mapping parallel accounting and are happy with its implementation, there is no reason to switch to a ledger approach in New G/L. Some of the new scenarios, such as real-time document splitting, may make more sense for you.

► **Alternative to the accounts approach**
On the other hand, if you are about to roll out parallel accounting, New G/L contains two equally valid alternatives: the accounts approach and the ledger approach. The main criterion here is likely to be controlling and mapping parallel values in this component. In this case, the accounts approach is preferable because only the cost element values of the leading ledger are transferred.

► **Controlling aspect of integration**
If one valuation approach is enough in Controlling, and if there otherwise are many valuation variances, the new ledger approach in New G/L has significant benefits.

► **Leading valuation in Asset Accounting context**
If the leading valuation is IFRS, it will be included in depreciation area 01 in Asset Accounting as well as in Controlling. The delta posting logic in this subledger gives the auditor significant insights into the IFRS balance sheet and cost accounting.

► **Use in practice**
This new option for saving valuation approaches for parallel accounting is used by approximately 50 % of all companies that have introduced New G/L. The ledger approach in New G/L has some restrictions (OI management of provisions accounts) up to Enhancement Package 3. It must be mentioned at this point that you shouldn't reduce New G/L to the status of simply being a ledger approach for parallel accounting in General Ledger.

*If the perspective becomes blurred, it is sometimes sufficient sim-
ply to change it. Many things that were unclear then make sense
again.*

5   Document Splitting

Document splitting is an automatic process of splitting document line
items within a document according to selected dimensions. You can,
for example, split receivables line items according to profit centers. This
way, you can create segment reports for each document. Companies that
intend to carry out segment reporting based on high-quality data will
benefit substantially from this function. Based on various examples, this
chapter describes the SAP system configuration and the effects on operational posting processes.

You will first learn about the business context and the advantages of
using the document splitting function. The subsequent sections then
discuss different views of *Financial Accounting*. The goal of these sections
is to demonstrate the effects of this new function by means of real-life
posting examples. The focus of this chapter is on the section that deals
with configuration, where you obtain a description of the flexible and
hence complex options provided in Customizing. The chapter concludes
with a description of special G/L transactions, periodic activities, and the
innovations of Enhancement Package 4.

5.1   Reasons for Document Splitting

Online document splitting involves customizing, migration effort, and
system testing. The reason to implement this new function is that it
enables you to obtain transparent and detailed insight into the different
business activities (areas) of an enterprise. The principles of presenting
financial information according to business segments and geographical

Transparency and
detailedness

segments requirement for segment reporting are set forth in IAS 14, which therefore meets the requirement for segment reporting.

Companies must report on business or geographical segments if the majority of revenue originates from sales to external customers and the revenues of the segment in question amounts to at least 10 % of all external and internal revenues of all segments, the segment result amounts to at least 10 % of the results of all segments, or the fixed assets of the segment amount to at least 10 % of all fixed assets of all segments. (Source: http://www.ax-net.de/inhalt/standards/ias_14/_$ret_ias14_ inhalt.html)

Previously, the "business area" and "profit center" objects were usually used to create this type of report, provided that—and this often represented the actual challenge—the two objects did not have to meet any other reporting requirements.

Some postings, such as tax transactions, receivables, and payables cannot be enriched with these characteristics. For those cases, the closing activities in SAP R/3 included adjustments of balance sheet and P&L accounts or a totals posting using the SAPF180 and SAPF181 programs in order to obtain a balance of zero in the business area and profit center statements. Basically, there is no legal requirement for such detailed information that can be met by document splitting.

Internal corporate management

From an internal point of view, the approach of providing split documents to support corporate management is rather complex. In the context of closing procedures, high-quality figures represent a considerable added value, particularly if matrix consolidation is used. Moreover, developments of individual segments can be analyzed better, that is, at any time and in more detail. If you implement the document splitting concept consistently, you must consider that this will have a substantial impact on the operations carried out in your accounting department. The document splitting concept requires that posting transactions be entered generically for the purpose of future consolidation and reporting. This means that it must be possible to split each posting within a set of rules. If this is not possible, the process cannot be performed.

Practical Example of a Consistent Document-Splitting Conceptfrom Individual Financial Statements to Consolidation

Siemens was one of the first companies to implement this concept in 2004. Both legal consolidation and management consolidation use SAP SEM-BCS and are thus based on a uniform set of figures with different views. This means that the traditional adjustment tasks between these two areas have been made redundant. To improve the quality of data, profit-center-based document splitting was implemented in the feeder systems, and operational posting transactions were adjusted accordingly.

The topics of financial statements for segments and document splitting are relevant not only for large corporations. Mid-sized companies also see the benefits brought about by New General Ledger (New G/L) and the document splitting function.

Practical Example of the Implementation of New G/L

During migration of its IT systems to SAP solutions, a renowned plant construction enterprise implemented New G/L of SAP ERP Financials. In addition to cost-of-sales accounting, profit center accounting in the general ledger, and online document splitting for segments, parallel accounting in different ledgers based on HGB (Germany), IFRS, and US-GAAP provides the basis for fast close and, at the same time, for preparing the accounting data for segment reporting.

However, in order to reach this goal, operational transactions must not be modified too much or interfered with. Subledger accounts, for example, are entered only once, and despite the fact that document splitting is used, only one open item exists for receivables and payables. Thus, internal splitting of the generic transaction does not affect external business partners and is, in turn, only relevant for reporting purposes in general ledger accounting.

Operational transactions

5.2 Concept

This section describes the business background for creating financial statements for segments and delivering the high-quality data for matrix consolidation presented in Section 5.1, Reasons for Document Splitting, in more detail and with a special focus on the underlying concept. Apart

Functions of document splitting

from the data concept, we will describe the following three types of the Document Splitting function:

- ▶ Active (document) split
- ▶ Passive (document) split
- ▶ Clearing line items

5.2.1 Active Split

Configured set of rules

A stored set of rules that you must configure represents the basis of active document splits. If financial statements need to be available at profit-center level or for other entities, all business transactions must take this into account. Postings to subledger accounts involve the projection of P&L account characteristics to all other document line items. Figure 5.1 illustrates an active document split based on the sample business transaction of a vendor invoice. The Profit Center characteristic is derived from cost centers CC01/CC02, then transferred in real time to the payables line items, and, if necessary, to tax line items by means of active document splitting.

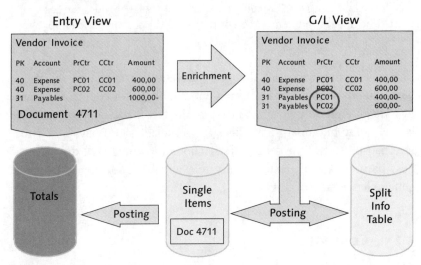

Figure 5.1 Document Splitting—Invoice

At this point, you should note that the data entry view for the accounts-payable accountant has not changed at all. Only in the G/L view will two customer line items and, if necessary, two tax-line items be stored. Splitting information is stored in a separate table that will be described in greater detail in Section 5.2.4, Data Concept. For valuations that are based on New G/L, such as financial statements for profit centers, this feature is very useful and desirable. Subledgers are not affected by this, as they will continue to contain an open item.

5.2.2 Passive Split

In clearing documents, a passive split ensures that the account itself is balanced, as well as the additional dimensions. As shown in Figure 5.2, the vendor invoice is assigned to the payment in which the bank and discount account assignments are split between profit centers at a ratio of 6 to 4 in accordance with the original document. The business transaction is recognized by the system, and the account assignments of the items to be cleared are automatically inherited by the clearing line items in the corresponding ratio. This transaction accesses the new table containing splitting information. In contrast to an active split, a passive split does not require detailed configuration, nor does it allow for such configuration.

Clearing according to original document

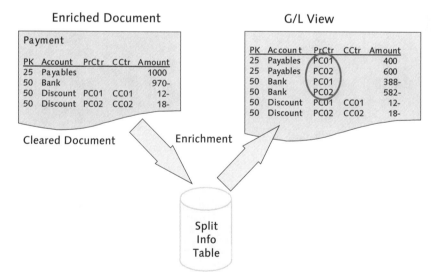

Figure 5.2 Document Splitting—Payment

5.2.3 Clearing Line Items

Zero balance for each dimension

Clearing line items ensure that the balances of the document itself and of the additional dimensions are zero. These clearing line items are used whenever you need to repost values between account assignment objects. Figure 5.2 shows a sample correction of a bank posting. As far as the accounting employee is concerned, the document-entry process does not change at all. The only difference from the previous way of entering the documents is that clearing line items are automatically produced for independent accounting units. Without the clearing line items, a financial statement for the Segment would no longer show a balance of zero. The zero balance by means of clearing line items makes sense and is necessary only if you want to generate a complete financial statement for the characteristic in question. Cost center and profit center repostings in the General Ledger would be similar.

Account	Description	Debit Amount	Credit Amount	Segment
113100	Bank	EUR 10,000.00		A
194500	Clearing account Segment		EUR 10,000.00	A
113100	Bank		EUR 10,000.00	B
194500	Clearing account Segment	EUR 10,000.00		B

Table 5.1 Clearing Line Items in the G/L View

5.2.4 Data Concept

New totals table

Several elements have changed with regard to saving document information. While the classic General Ledger with its totals table GLT0 originally represented the basis of all reporting activities, this table is replaced in New G/L by table FAGLFLEXT. Here, the final letter in the table name stands for *Totals*, which can form the basis of account balances and financial statements. In order to evaluate line items, tables continue to be available for the document header (BKPF) and document lines (BSEG). Because of the new split information, enrichments are stored in document table FAGLFLEXA. Here, the final letter in the table name stands for *Actuals*, that is, journal entry records.

If customer-specific fields are needed as financial statement items, you can add these fields at a later stage in tables FAGLFLEXA and FAGLFLEXT. Other characteristics, such as SEGMENT, are contained in the standard delivery package. A document that is to be split posts entries to tables BKPF, BSEG, FAGLFLEXA as well as to the new totals table FAGLFLEXT. Document splitting functions are carried out centrally prior to postings in Financial Accounting. The advantage of this design is that nothing really changes with regard to subledgers that may be integrated, such as Human Capital Management, Treasury, or Real Estate Management. Note that you always must be able to deliver the characteristics according to which documents are supposed to be split.

Customer-specific fields

5.3   Examples of Applying Active and Passive Splits

One of the main concepts behind document splitting is the principle of passing on or handing down information from the original document to all subsequent documents. Now that you have acquired a basic idea of the document splitting concept in Section 5.2, Concept, this section describes in greater detail an application example that details inheritance across different subjects.

Document splitting—handing down original information

> **Examples of Active and Passive Document Splits**
>
> We will manually enter a vendor invoice and split it by means of an active split. After that, the invoice will be settled by means of an outgoing payment, while a passive split is used on the basis of the information that's passed on.

[+]

5.3.1   Example of an Active Split

The system is configured in such a way that document splitting must be carried out according to the Profit Center and Segment characteristics. A vendor invoice amounting to EUR 11,000.00 is entered in accounts payable, which is supposed to be posted to different profit centers and segments. Figure 5.3 shows the data entry view.

Figure 5.3 does not yet show the corresponding settings that have been made in the system. Even at this stage, a check is run with regard to the set of rules that must be applied to a document split. Apart from the additional General Ledger View button, the user interface hasn't changed considerably, so the accounts-payable user shouldn't have any problem using it.

| Display Document: Data Entry View | | | | | | | | | | | |

Data Entry View											
Document Number	1900000007		Company Code	0005	Fiscal Year	2007					
Document Date	18.02.2007		Posting Date	18.02.2007	Period	2					
Reference			Cross-CC no.								
Currency	EUR		Texts exist	☐	Ledger Group						

Co	Item	PK	S	Account	Description	Amount	Curr.	Tx	BusA	Cost Center	Profit Center	Segment
0005	1	31		1000	C.E.B. BERLIN	11.000,00-	EUR	1I				
	2	40		476000	Office supplies	2.000,00	EUR	1I	9900	5_2200	9999	CONS
	3	40		476000	Office supplies	5.000,00	EUR	1I	9900	5_1000	ADMIN	SERV
	4	40		476000	Office supplies	3.000,00	EUR	1I	9900	5_2200	9999	PHAR
	5	40		154000	Input tax	1.000,00	EUR	1I				

Figure 5.3 Data Entry View for a Vendor Invoice

5.3.2 Simulating the General Ledger View

In addition to the simulation function, with which you should already be familiar, a new function specifically related to the General Ledger view is available as of SAP ERP 6.0. This view shows you how a document would actually be split (see Figure 5.4). The General Ledger simulation applies all rules as required. Payables and tax line items are split for both the profit center and the segment. The independent accounting units thus show a balance of zero. By clicking the EXPERT MODE button, you can obtain further information.

5.3.3 Document Simulation in Expert Mode

Splitting method and business transaction

Besides the General Ledger simulation, the *expert mode* can also answer the question of how a document splitting process is carried out. The expert mode provides additional information about the configuration of document splitting as soon as you post a document. Figure 5.5 shows that document type KR; based on this, business transaction 0300 (vendor invoice) was found in conjunction with splitting method 0000000012 and business transaction variant 0001. These sections will have a considerable impact on the splitting of document line items in the following step.

General Ledger Simulation

CoCd	Item	L.item	PK	S	G/L Account	G/L account name		Amount	Curr.	Profit Center	Segment
0005	1	000003	31		160000	AP-domestic		5.500,00-	EUR	ADMIN	SERV
0005	3	000005	40		476000	Office supplies		5.000,00	EUR	ADMIN	
0005	5	000009	40		154000	Input tax		500,00	EUR	ADMIN	
0005	1	000002	31		160000	AP-domestic		3.300,00-	EUR	9999	PHAR
0005	4	000006	40		476000	Office supplies		3.000,00	EUR	9999	
0005	5	000008	40		154000	Input tax		300,00	EUR	9999	
0005	1	000001	31		160000	AP-domestic		2.200,00-	EUR	9999	CONS
0005	2	000004	40		476000	Office supplies		2.000,00	EUR	9999	
0005	5	000007	40		154000	Input tax		200,00	EUR	9999	

Document Date: 18.02.2007 — Posting Date: 18.02.2007 — Fiscal Year: 2007 — Reference: — Cross-co. code no.: — Posting Period: 2 — Currency: EUR — Ledger Group: — Ledger: 0L

Figure 5.4 General Ledger Simulation

Configuration of Doc. Splitting

Parameter	Val.
Reference Transact.	BKPF
Splitting Method	0000000012
Business Transaction	0300
Business Transaction Variant	0001
Deriv. via Doc. Type	KR
Company Code of Leading Item	0005
Zero Balance Method	P

Document Display

Company Code / Item	Acct Assgmt Cat.	Assignment Origin	Item	Post	G/L Acc	Item cat.	Amount	Crcy	Profit Ctr	Segment
▽ ☐ 0005										
▽ ☐ 0000000001	Split According ...		1 31		160000	03000	2.200,00-	EUR	9999	CONS
		Base Line 0000000004								
		Base Line 0000000007								
▽ ☐ 0000000002	Split According ...		1 31		160000	03000	3.300,00-	EUR	9999	PHAR
		Base Line 0000000006								
		Base Line 0000000008								
▽ ☐ 0000000003	Split According ...		1 31		160000	03000	5.500,00-	EUR	ADMIN	SERV
		Base Line 0000000009								
		Base Line 0000000005								
0000000004	Base Line		2 40		476000	20000	2.000,00	EUR	9999	CONS
0000000005	Base Line		3 40		476000	20000	5.000,00	EUR	ADMIN	SERV
0000000006	Base Line		4 40		476000	20000	3.000,00	EUR	9999	PHAR
▽ ☐ 0000000007	Split According ...		5 40		154000	05100	200,00	EUR	9999	CONS
		Base Line 0000000004								
▽ ☐ 0000000008	Split According ...		5 40		154000	05100	300,00	EUR	9999	PHAR
		Base Line 0000000006								
▽ ☐ 0000000009	Split According ...		5 40		154000	05100	500,00	EUR	ADMIN	SERV
		Base Line 0000000005								

Figure 5.5 Expert Mode

Figure 5.5 also shows the basis on which the items of the payables account were created. Split 1 according to line items 4 and 7 results in a total amount of EUR 2,200.00 for segment CONS and profit center 9999. Splits 2 and 3 are displayed similarly. With regard to the flexible use and wide-ranging functions of document splitting, the expert mode provides a transparent and useful approach.

5.3.4 Example of a Passive Split

Outgoing payment

Passive splits are used in clearing transactions. Not only do the two accounts and several amount items need top be cleared but also the additional dimensions. In the following example, we'll pay the vendor. Figure 5.6 shows an outgoing payment of EUR 11,000.00 for the original vendor invoice minus a cash discount. There is only one open item. The splitting information of the original business transaction is imported from table FAGLSPLINFO.

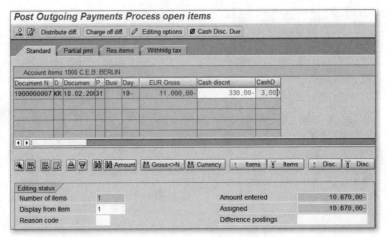

Figure 5.6 Outgoing Payment Minus 3 % Cash Discount

The total amount of EUR 10,670.00 is paid for the invoice, with EUR 300.00 of cash discount received and EUR 30.00 of cash discount adjustment. Both amounts must be split according to the original invoice. The simulation shown in Figure 5.7 already clearly shows that the amount of EUR 300.00 of cash discount received will be split. Because the vendor invoice was posted to three different segments, the cash discount amount is also applied to three different segments.

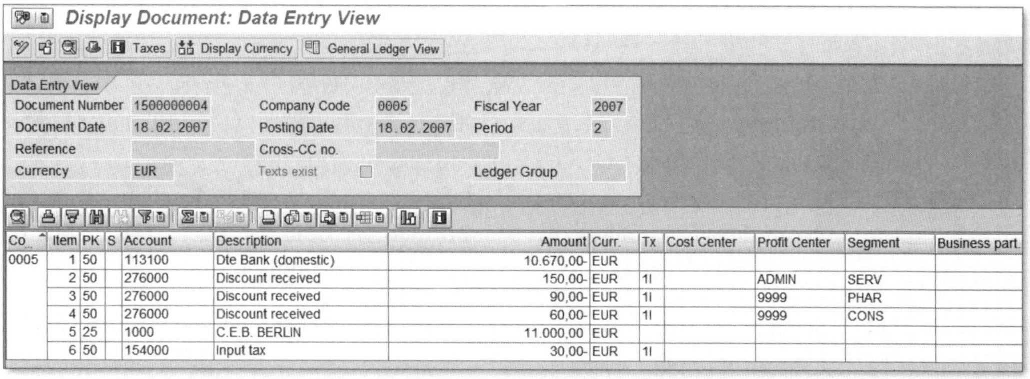

Display Document: Data Entry View

Taxes | Display Currency | General Ledger View

Data Entry View

Document Number	1500000004	Company Code	0005	Fiscal Year	2007
Document Date	18.02.2007	Posting Date	18.02.2007	Period	2
Reference		Cross-CC no.			
Currency	EUR	Texts exist		Ledger Group	

Co...	Item	PK	S	Account	Description	Amount	Curr.	Tx	Cost Center	Profit Center	Segment	Business part.
0005	1	50		113100	Dte Bank (domestic)	10.670,00-	EUR					
	2	50		276000	Discount received	150,00-	EUR	1I		ADMIN	SERV	
	3	50		276000	Discount received	90,00-	EUR	1I		9999	PHAR	
	4	50		276000	Discount received	60,00-	EUR	1I		9999	CONS	
	5	25		1000	C.E.B. BERLIN	11.000,00	EUR					
	6	50		154000	Input tax	30,00-	EUR	1I				

Figure 5.7 Simulating an Outgoing Payment Document

The General Ledger simulation function displays the outgoing payment account and the input tax as split in the same relation. A simple document can become very complex once document splitting has been applied in the General Ledger. For this reason, the six-digit L.ITEM (line item) was introduced. You can now avoid the limit of 999 line items so that a split document may contain up to 999999 line items in the General Ledger view.

General Ledger Simulation

As shown in Figure 5.8, financial statements based on segments and profit centers show a balance of zero.

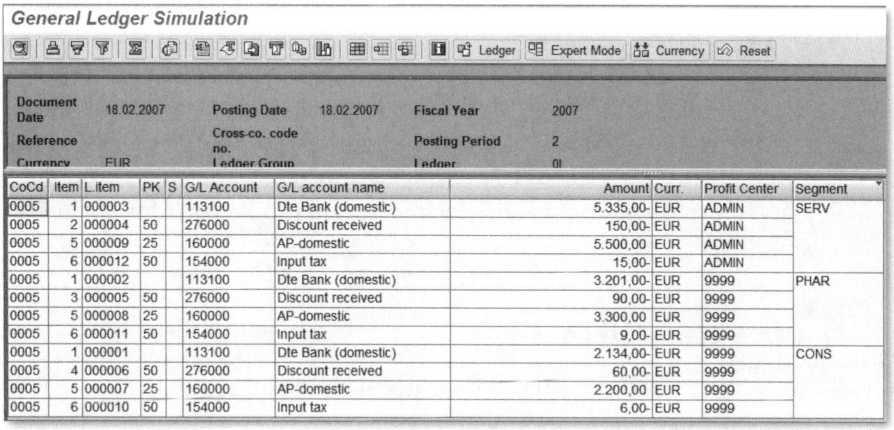

General Ledger Simulation

Ledger | Expert Mode | Currency | Reset

Document Date	18.02.2007	Posting Date	18.02.2007	Fiscal Year	2007
Reference		Cross-co. code no.		Posting Period	2
Currency	EUR	Ledger Group		Ledger	0L

CoCd	Item	L.item	PK	S	G/L Account	G/L account name	Amount	Curr.	Profit Center	Segment
0005	1	000003			113100	Dte Bank (domestic)	5.335,00-	EUR	ADMIN	SERV
0005	2	000004	50		276000	Discount received	150,00-	EUR	ADMIN	
0005	5	000009	25		160000	AP-domestic	5.500,00	EUR	ADMIN	
0005	6	000012	50		154000	Input tax	15,00-	EUR	ADMIN	
0005	1	000002			113100	Dte Bank (domestic)	3.201,00-	EUR	9999	PHAR
0005	3	000005	50		276000	Discount received	90,00-	EUR	9999	
0005	5	000008	25		160000	AP-domestic	3.300,00	EUR	9999	
0005	6	000011	50		154000	Input tax	9,00-	EUR	9999	
0005	1	000001			113100	Dte Bank (domestic)	2.134,00-	EUR	9999	CONS
0005	4	000006	50		276000	Discount received	60,00-	EUR	9999	
0005	5	000007	25		160000	AP-domestic	2.200,00	EUR	9999	
0005	6	000010	50		154000	Input tax	6,00-	EUR	9999	

Figure 5.8 General Ledger Simulation Function

5.4   Configuration

Now that you have seen real-life examples of the effects of document splitting in Section 5.3, Examples of Applying Active and Passive Splits, this section describes the Customizing options in greater detail. The configuration of document splitting is very flexible and therefore also very complex. The goal of this section is to provide you with an overview of how you can configure the document splitting function.

Configuration steps

The following configuration steps must be considered with regard to the splitting logic:

- ▶ Item category
- ▶ Business transaction
- ▶ Splitting method
- ▶ Definition of document splitting characteristics
- ▶ Default account assignment
- ▶ Inheritance
- ▶ Activation
- ▶ Splitting rules
- ▶ Wizards

Figure 5.9 shows where you can find the basic settings for document splitting in Customizing.

In Customizing, you are provided with a separate subfolder called Extended Document Splitting. It contains essential functions that are described in the course of this chapter. However, as a first step, you must classify the G/L accounts and document types to be used for document splitting.

5.4.1   Item Category

Classifying the line item

One of the basic prerequisites for document splitting is that you know how each individual document line item is structured. For this reason, you must assign each account to an *item category*. Some accounts, such as customer and vendor accounts, can be identified automatically by the system. Exchange rate differences and cash discount accounts are identified automatically by means of the associated posting transaction. However, this identification is not as easy when it come to other accounts, for instance, if repostings, bank-account postings, or goods receipt postings are involved. For this reason, a process is needed to clearly identify a posting based on the assignment of a G/L account to an item category. Figure 5.10 shows such a classification.

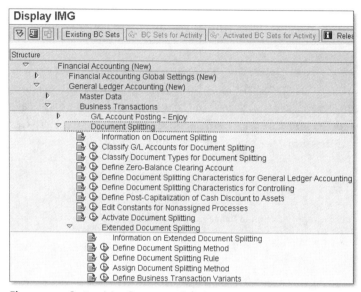

Figure 5.9 Customizing Document Splitting

Change View "Classify G/L Accounts for Document Splitting"

Chart of Accts   INT   Chart of accounts - international

Acct from	Account to	Overrd.	Cat.	Description
465010	465010	☐	20000	Expense
470000	476000	☐	20000	Expense
481000	481000	☐	20000	Expense
799999	799999	☐	06000	Material
800000	800999	☐	30000	Revenue
811000	811000	☐	20000	Expense
884010	884010	☐	30000	Revenue
888000	888000	☐	30000	Revenue
893015	893015	☐	06000	Material
894025	894025	☐	06000	Material
895000	895000	☐	06000	Material

Figure 5.10 Additional Information Based on the Account Number

You can access Customizing via the following menu path: Financial Accounting (New) • General Ledger Accounting (New) • Business Transactions • Document Splitting • Classify G/L Accounts for Document Splitting.

Deviating reconciliation accounts must be entered in the table for item categories 02100 (Customers) and 03100 (Vendors Special G/L). In addition, you must activate the column that contains the override option. Section 5.5, Special G/L Transactions, provides a detailed example of this topic.

Error message If not all document line items can be classified within a posting, an error message will occur. Figure 5.11 shows what happens when an account that has been posted to is not stored in Customizing: the document cannot be posted. As you can see, configuring the item category increases the organizational work for the accounting department.

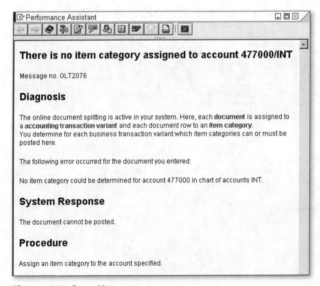

Figure 5.11 Error Message

5.4.2 Business Transaction

Assigning the document type The next step you need to carry out is to categorize all document types within the business transactions defined by SAP (see Figure 5.12). This process provides the SAP accounting system with additional information for document splitting. The document type is used to determine the business transaction.

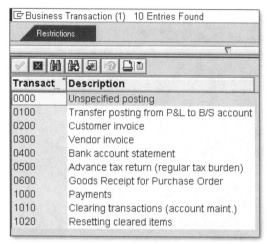

Transact	Description
0000	Unspecified posting
0100	Transfer posting from P&L to B/S account
0200	Customer invoice
0300	Vendor invoice
0400	Bank account statement
0500	Advance tax return (regular tax burden)
0600	Goods Receipt for Purchase Order
1000	Payments
1010	Clearing transactions (account maint.)
1020	Resetting cleared items

Figure 5.12 Business Transactions

Next, you must classify the document line items on the basis of the corresponding item categories. The "unspecified posting" business transaction provides the least information. In order to better understand this type of transaction, you may have to make some additional settings. This detailed assignment increases the significance of the Document Type characteristic enormously. If a unique classification based on existing document types is not possible, you must create additional document types. Keep in mind that document types are meant to reference actual business transactions (see Figure 5.13). If this is not the case, you must define other document types that can be used instead. Conversely, this means that you must categorize all posting transactions on the basis of specific rules. If there is an exception, the program cannot carry out the posting transaction if active document splits are used.

Classifying the line items

You can find this option in Customizing via the following menu path: FINANCIAL ACCOUNTING (NEW) • GENERAL LEDGER ACCOUNTING (NEW) • BUSINESS TRANSACTIONS • DOCUMENT SPLITTING • CLASSIFY G/L ACCOUNTS FOR DOCUMENT TYPES.

Display View "Classify FI Document Type for Document Splitting"

Type	Transactn.	Variant	Description	Name
AA	0000	0001	Unspecified posting	Standard
AB	0000	0001	Unspecified posting	Standard
AE				
AF	0000	0001	Unspecified posting	Standard
AN	0000	0001	Unspecified posting	Standard
C1				
CI				
CP				
DA	0200	0001	Customer invoice	Standard
DB				
DE				
DG	0200	0001	Customer invoice	Standard
DR	0200	0001	Customer invoice	Standard
DZ	1000	0001	Payments	Standard
EU				
EX	0000	0001	Unspecified posting	Standard
GF				
JE				
KA	0300	0001	Vendor invoice	Standard
KG	0300	0001	Vendor invoice	Standard
KN	0300	0001	Vendor invoice	Standard
KP	1010	0001	Clearing transactions (a	Standard
KR	0300	0001	Vendor invoice	Standard

Figure 5.13 Additional Information Based on the Document Type

5.4.3 Splitting Method

Splitting methods define the ways in which document splitting is to be carried out. Depending on the splitting method, the system makes a definition regarding the way that item categories are to be treated in individual business transactions. Figure 5.14 provides an overview of the splitting methods provided by SAP.

Display View "Splitting method": Overview

Method	Text
0000000001	Splitting: Customer, Vendor, Tax
0000000002	Splitting: Customer, Vendor, Tax, Money, Co.Code Clearing
0000000012	Splitting: Same as 0000000002 (Follow-Up Costs Online)
0000000101	Splitting for US Fund Accounting
0000000111	Splitting for US Fund Accounting (Follow-Up Costs Online)
BZ00000013	Splitting: Same as 0000000002 (Follow-Up Costs Online) Brazi

Figure 5.14 Splitting Methods

You will find splitting methods in Customizing by following the menu path: Financial Accounting (New) • General Ledger Accounting (New) • Business Transactions • Document Splitting • Extended Document Splitting • Define Splitting Methods.

Splitting method 0000000001 takes only specific business transactions into account, whereas splitting method 0000000002 considers all business transactions contained in splitting method 0000000001 including money and clearing accounts. Some of the processes include "follow-up costs online," and include functions that are described in Section 5.5, Special G/L Transactions. For the examples in this book, we used splitting method 0000000012. If the standard splitting methods provided by SAP are insufficient, you can also define new splitting methods.

Interaction of the different settings

Figure 5.15 illustrates the interaction between the different settings. Within splitting method 0000000012, business transaction 0300 (Vendor invoice) is assigned to document type KR. The corresponding business transaction variant contains information about the way individual item categories are supposed to be handled. Both the vendor line item and the sales tax item are automatically identified by the system, and the G/L account is stored in the Customizing for the Expense item category. As before, the expense is assigned to two different splitting characteristics for the amounts of 90 and 10 in the data entry view. The system realizes that the account assignments for payables and tax line items result from the expense line items.

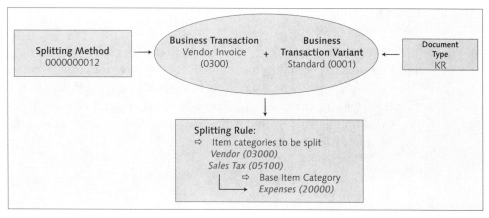

Figure 5.15 Interaction of the Different Settings

5.4.4 Definition of Document Splitting Characteristics

Defining
dimensions

You can define the dimensions you want to use for document splitting. In doing so, you can use both SAP-specific and customer-specific characteristics. In the example shown in Figure 5.16, three entities have been stored for document splitting:

▶ Business area

▶ Profit center

▶ Segment

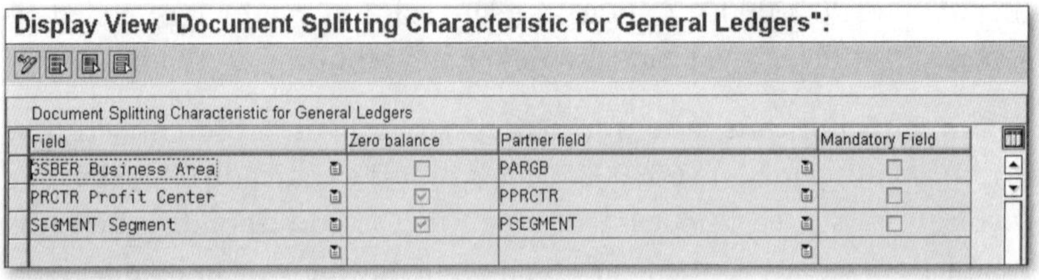

Figure 5.16 Document Splitting Characteristics

You can define the document splitting characteristics in Customizing via the following menu path: Financial Accounting (New) • General Ledger Accounting (New) • Business Transactions • Document Splitting • Define Document Splitting Characteristics for General Ledger Accounting. The Mandatory Field and Zero balance flags are essential for these settings.

Mandatory Field

The Mandatory Field flag represents an extension of the field status. If you set this flag, each document line item must have the corresponding characteristic when you assign it to an account. You can do that either by entering the characteristic manually or having the characteristics assigned on the basis of automatically determined values, for instance, by means of substitutions or splitting rules.

Zero Balance

If you want to maintain segment balances with a balance of zero because of a specific characteristic, you must set the ZERO BALANCE flag. All characteristics marked in this way are then included in the creation of a zero balance. Clearing line items are used correspondingly.

5.4.5 Default Account Assignment

Not every business transaction can be split right away. An intermediate solution may be needed, especially if a reference to the original document cannot be established immediately and the posting transaction must be carried out nonetheless. In this case, document splitting can use the default account assignment function. The following example demonstrates the posting logic and Customizing tasks.

Reference to original documents

Step 1: Cash Receipt

If a cash receipt is assigned to a house bank account, it is usually not known right away which invoices are supposed to be paid with the amount received. In order to enter the information about the available funds into the system as quickly as possible, you must first post the amount against a clearing account. Because you don't have any further information in this case, you must post the amount to a defined standard segment. In this example, that is segment 9999 (see Table 5.2).

Posting to a standard segment

Account	Segment	Debit	Credit
Bank account	9999	EUR 1,000.00	
Bank subaccount	9999		EUR 1,000.00

Table 5.2 Cash Receipt

Step 2: Bank Subaccount

Based on the bank subaccount, a search is performed for the customer who was supposed to pay the corresponding invoices. Only at this point can you determine the correct segments on the basis of the original invoice data (see Table 5.3).

Determining the correct segment

Account	Segment	Debit	Credit
Bank subaccount	SEG A	EUR 1,000.00	
Customer	SEG A		EUR 1,000.00

Table 5.3 Accounts Receivable Posting

Step 3: Clearing the Items in the Bank Subaccount

Clearing line items

Finally, you must clear the two items in the bank account and bank subaccount. Because the two items have been assigned to different segments, you must generate the corresponding clearing line items (see Table 5.4).

Account	Segment	Debit	Credit
Bank subaccount	9999	EUR 1,000.00	
Segment clearing account	9999		EUR 1,000.00
Bank subaccount	SEG A		EUR 1,000.00
Segment clearing account	SEG A	EUR 1,000.00	

Table 5.4 Clearing the Items in the Bank Subaccount

Zero balance

If a zero balance is required for the segment, additional document line items will be generated in a clearing account stored in Customizing. These document line items will ensure that the balance in each segment is set to zero. These clearing line items reflect the adjustment of segment information in the bank accounts. For this reason, the clearing account must be assigned to the bank accounts in the financial statement. Table 5.5 contains a list of values for a segment balance sheet. Values with a plus sign are debit postings, while those with a minus sign are credit postings.

Segment 9999 = default value

After final consideration of the three steps, you see that segment 9999 represents a default value. If the financial statement contains the bank account, bank subaccount, and the clearing account, the balance will be zero. The financial statement for SEG A, on the other hand, shows that a cash receipt of EUR 1,000.00 occurred in this segment. This method is certainly not simple, but it represents the only way to present bank data in accordance with the original document.

	9999	SEG A
Bank account	(1) + EUR 1,000.00	
Bank subaccount	(1) – EUR 1,000.00 (3) + EUR 1,000.00 = EUR 0.00	(2) + EUR 1,000.00 – (3) EUR 1,000.00 = EUR 0.00
Segment clearing account	(3) – EUR 1,000.00	(3) + EUR 1,000.00
Customer		(2) – EUR 1,000.00

Table 5.5   Segment Balance Sheet

To be able to use the default account assignment function, you must first create a constant. To do this, select the following Customizing path: Financial Accounting (New) • General Ledger Accounting (New) • Business Transactions • Document Splitting • Edit Constants for Non-Assigned Processes.

Constant for default account assignment

Figure 5.17 shows how you define the ZTEST constant. This constant must be stored in the document splitting process for default account assignments (see Figure 5.18). You can find the corresponding item in Customizing by following the menu path: Financial Accounting (New) • General Ledger Accounting (New) • Business Transactions • Document Splitting • Extended Document Splitting • Assign Document Splitting Methods.

Constant "ZTEST"

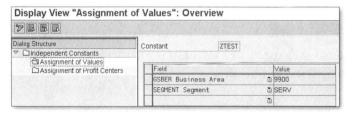

Figure 5.17   Defining Constants

Figure 5.18 Storing a Constant for Default Account Assignment

Defining clearing accounts

It is not only the postings in each account and company code that have to show zero balances. Financial statements based on any characteristic at line item level require all dimensions to have zero balances as well. For this reason, we need to use clearing accounts. Figure 5.19 shows clearing account 194601 for account key 000. To perform the assignment in the financial statement and also to make it easier to reproduce the transactions, you must create multiple clearing accounts.

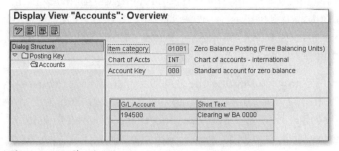

Figure 5.19 Clearing Account

You define clearing accounts in Customizing via the path: FINANCIAL ACCOUNTING (NEW) • GENERAL LEDGER ACCOUNTING (NEW) • BUSINESS TRANSACTIONS • DOCUMENT SPLITTING • DEFINE ZERO BALANCE CLEARING ACCOUNT.

Figure 5.20 shows the account key stored in the header data of the splitting rules for each business transaction.

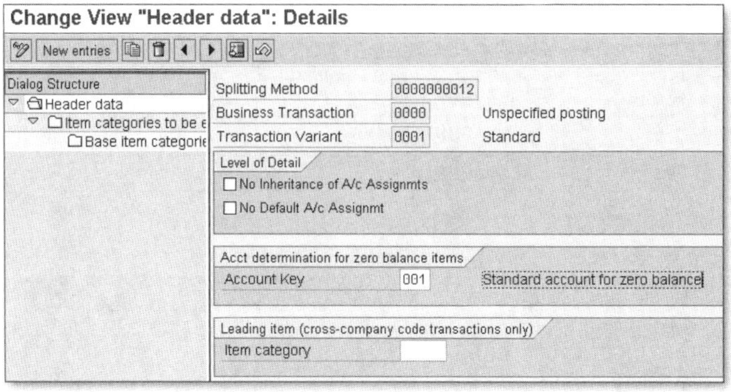

Figure 5.20 Assigning Clearing Accounts to Business Transactions

Each associated clearing account is used according to each specific requirement. This way, you make sure that dimensions included in the financial statement show a balance of zero for each document.

5.4.6 Inheritance

Usually, if document splitting is activated, the inheritance function is activated as well in the first step. In Figure 5.21, a G/L account posting with document type SA is entered. The posting record, OFFICE MATERIALS, INPUT TAX, and PETTY CASH, are illustrated for both inactive and active inheritance. If the Segment characteristic is a mandatory field and inheritance is deactivated, the document in Figure 5.21 (the lower left table ❶) cannot be posted. If you want to create financial statements for segments, you must first activate the inheritance function. You can find the corresponding item in Customizing by following the menu path: FINANCIAL ACCOUNTING (NEW) • GENERAL LEDGER ACCOUNTING (NEW) • BUSINESS TRANSACTIONS • DOCUMENT SPLITTING • EXTENDED DOCUMENT SPLITTING • ASSIGN DOCUMENT SPLITTING METHODS.

Let's suppose you want to create a financial statement for a profit center. As a prerequisite, you must assign all line items with this entity to accounts. In the case of incoming invoices, the system can derive the profit center based on the information provided by the expense line items and the cost center. It then can project the profit center into the payables and tax line items by means of inheritance.

Deactivating inheritance

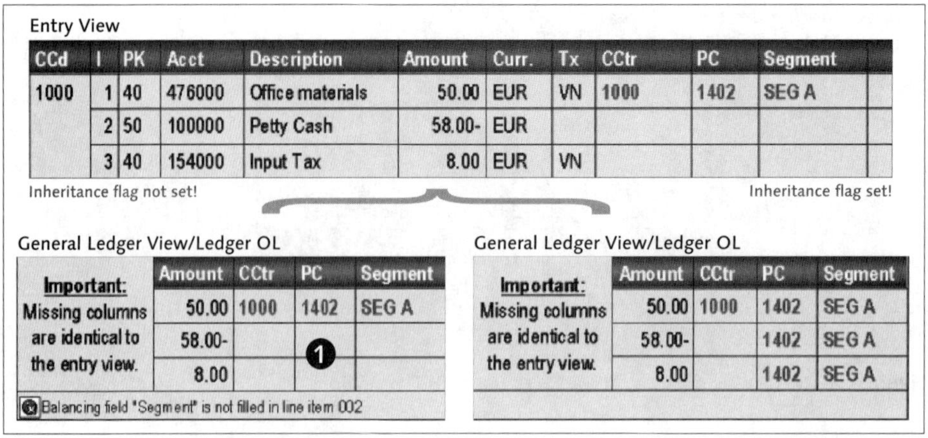

Figure 5.21 Inheritance

Regarding outgoing invoices, the process is identical. Thus, INHERI-TANCE works fine as long as it makes sense to use it. However, leaving the inheritance function activated doesn't make sense for all business transactions.

As a matter of fact, it may even be counterproductive in certain situations because incomplete configurations are not recognized and incorrect posting records are produced. You should still create a financial statement for a profit center, in which all postings contain this entity. Figure 5.22 shows a material master record for plant 1000. Here it makes sense to store the profit center for postings.

Stock transfer   The business transaction of a stock transfer between different plants may involve a change of profit centers, as shown in Table 5.6.

Stock Transfer From	Stock Transfer To
Plant 1000	Plant 1300
Profit center 1010	Profit center 2000

Table 5.6 Stock Transfer Between Plants 1000 and 1300

A separate view with a separate profit center is maintained for each plant, and these views are used for posting purposes. Profit centers are usually considered as companies within companies, which is why intermediate profits may arise in this process. Table 5.7 shows a posting record.

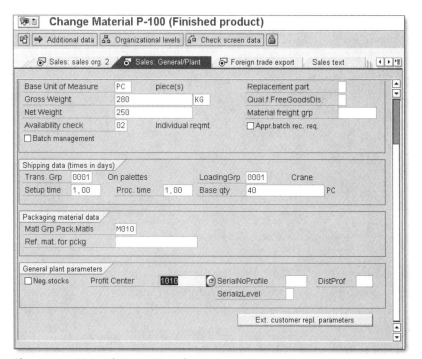

Figure 5.22 Material Master Record

Account	Account	Debit	Credit	Additional Account Assignment	Additional Account Assignment
Finished products		EUR 480.14		Profit center 1010	Plant 1010
Revenue from stock transfer		EUR 113.18		Profit center 1010	Plant 1010
To	Finished products		EUR 593.32	Profit center 2000	Plant 2000

Table 5.7 Stock Transfer

If no master data is maintained, the inheritance function causes an incorrect posting record to be generated automatically. Figure 5.23 shows the result if no profit center 2000 is maintained for the receiving plant 1300 and the inheritance function is activated for the business transaction.

Master data maintenance

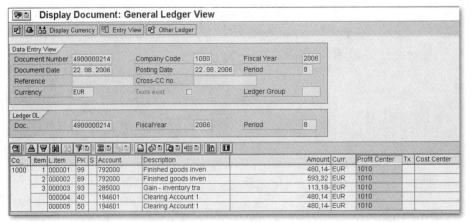

Figure 5.23 Inheritance Generates Incorrect Posting Record

This example clearly demonstrates the importance of having a complete and consistent document splitting concept. If fields of activity are identified, they can be configured efficiently in Customizing. Once the inheritance function has been generally activated in the document splitting process, it must be deactivated for specific business transactions. In practical use, you should configure business transaction 0000 (Unspecified posting). Figure 5.24 shows that header data of splitting rules contain this flag (Unspecified posting checkbox).

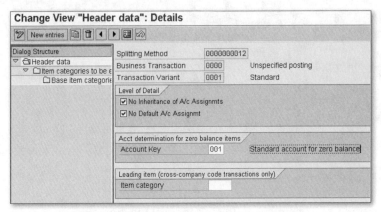

Figure 5.24 Document Splitting Rule—Deactivate Inheritance

Profit center in material master record

Once you have entered the changes in Customizing via the menu path: FINANCIAL ACCOUNTING (NEW) • GENERAL LEDGER ACCOUNTING (NEW) •

Business Transactions • Document Splitting • Extended Document Splitting • Define Document Splitting Rule, the application outputs an error message in the Stock Transfer business transaction (see Figure 5.25).

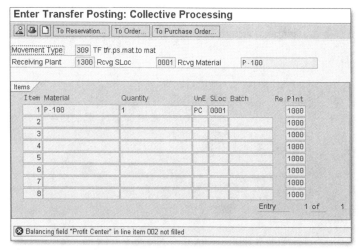

Figure 5.25 Stock Transfer—Error Message

The profit center does not exist in the material master record and there-fore is not inherited. However, because the profit center is an independent accounting unit, it is a mandatory field. The document is incomplete and therefore cannot be posted. In order to create a financial statement for a segment at line-item level based on exact profit center figures, you must now maintain material master data.

Error message

5.4.7 Activation

In principle, document splitting must be activated at the client level. After that, you can deactivate the document splitting function for indi-vidual company codes. Figure 5.26 shows how to do this for company codes 0100 through 1002.

In Customizing, you can deactivate document splitting by following the menu path: Financial Accounting (New) • General Ledger Account-ing (New) • Business Transactions • Document Splitting • Activate Document Splitting. As a result of the deactivation, business trans-

Consequences of the deactivation

actions such as assessments, distributions, or postings across several company codes only function in groups with activated or deactivated document splitting. If postings from company code 1000 to 0005, for example, are made, the system displays the error message shown in Figure 5.27.

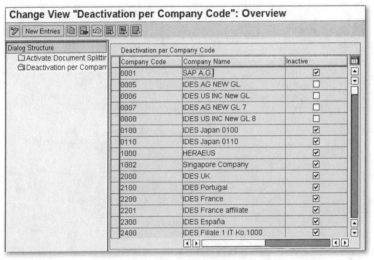

Figure 5.26 Deactivating Document Splitting for Individual Company Codes

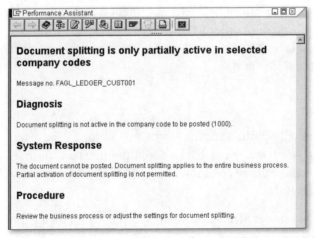

Figure 5.27 Error Message with Partially Activated Document Splitting Function

Because the activation process is not just a checkbox but an entire project that involves the enrichment of legacy data, you must consider this step, including all its advantages and disadvantages, as early as the design phase.

Before you implement an activation, you should check the expert settings.

5.4.8 Splitting Rules

The splitting rules involve the detailed functioning of the splitting method. Depending on the business transaction, you can adapt the logic of the document splitting within certain limits. In the configuration, you can find these rules by following the menu path: FINANCIAL ACCOUNTING (NEW) • GENERAL LEDGER ACCOUNTING (NEW) • BUSINESS TRANSACTIONS • DOCUMENT SPLITTING • EXTENDED DOCUMENT SPLITTING • DEFINE DOCUMENT SPLITTING RULE.

Functioning of the splitting method

Let's consider an example of using splitting rules: Section 5.4.6, Inheritance, presented a case where it doesn't make sense from a business point of view to project account assignment values from one line item to another. Such adaptations are made at splitting rule level for each business transaction. In other cases, you not only need to set a single switch, but to create a separate transaction variant as well.

Standard Configuration [+]

The standard configuration delivered is comprehensive and covers most business transactions. So, at first glance, there is no need for SAP consultants or customers to store own splitting rules within their defined transaction variants. If you test only the standard cases in a project, you may be able to implement up to 90 % of all document splittings correctly.

At a second glance, however, you recognize that precisely those 10 % of the cases not covered cause major problems. If, for example, the rules of the special G/L transactions are not configured correctly, a complete payment run (maybe with a down payment only) cannot be executed. Changes are time-critical in this case because this may involve a lost cash discount. Changing the configuration may require database changes for documents that are already posted or split "incorrectly." You can prevent this critical condition, including high follow-up costs, by comprehensively checking and supplementing the standard configuration for splitting rules.

Example of the Need for a Separate Splitting Rule

Example: business transaction FI-AA

This section presents a consistent example in which the configuration of the splitting rules is not initially correct. In Asset Accounting, two complex fixed assets need to be sold to a customer. You will encounter this sample process frequently in real life.

With regard to the document splitting rules, it is important that more than one complex fixed asset is to be sold within a posting document. In addition, the complex fixed assets are assigned to different profit centers and segments, according to which you are supposed to create balance sheets with a zero balance using document splitting. The following pages describe an example in which this case doesn't work correctly with the standard SAP delivery.

Initial Situation—Balance Sheet Values of Assets

The example starts with a business transaction or a posting document illustrating for 01/01/2009 that asset 3003 with a total value of EUR 500.00 was acquired in profit center 1402 or in segment SEGA (see Figure 5.28).

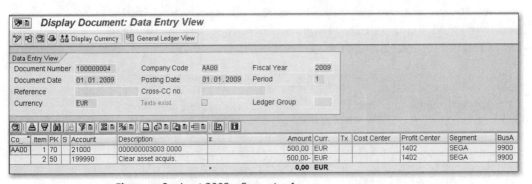

Figure 5.28 Asset 3003—Computer 1

Figure 5.29 illustrates the second asset 3004 with an acquisition value of EUR 700.00 and the additional account assignments, profit center 1000 and segment SEGB, respectively.

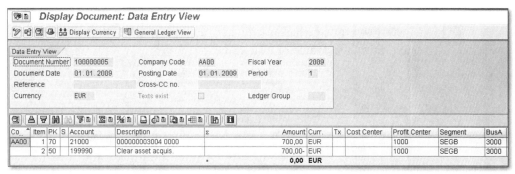

Figure 5.29 Asset 3004—Computer 2

In this example, the two computers are supposed to be depreciated over a period of three years. A full year is used as the period of examination. Accordingly, this depreciation results in a net book value of EUR 333.33 for the first computer, as illustrated in Figure 5.30.

Depreciation over a period of three years

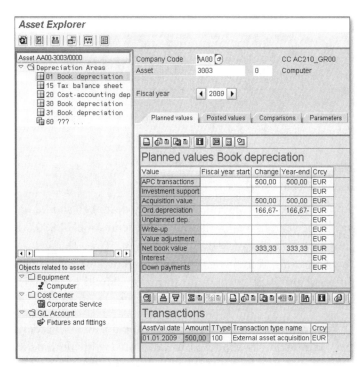

Figure 5.30 Net Book Value—Computer 1

With a higher acquisition value of EUR 700.00 and a useful life of three years, computer 2 has an annual ordinary depreciation of EUR 233.33 and a net book value of EUR 466.67.

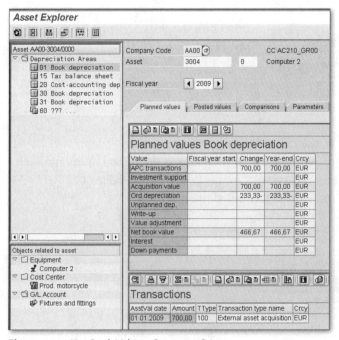

Figure 5.31 Net Book Value—Computer 2

Course of the Example—Asset Retirement through Sales with Customer

Revenue posting to different profit centers

Within a sales document, the computers previously described should be sold at the end of the year. In total, you achieve a revenue of EUR 880.00 gross including an output tax of EUR 80.00, that is, 10 %. This value, including the tax amount, is to be distributed to the two assets and the associated different profit centers. To do this, you should proceed as follows:

1. In the first step, you enter the information for the document header. The business transaction is supposed to be posted with document type DR (see Figure 5.32). In the configuration of the document splitting, this already implies both transaction 0200 (Customer invoice) and variant 0001, which is delivered in the standard.

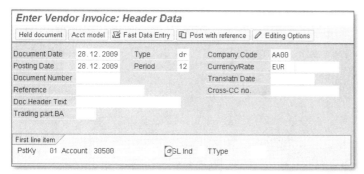

Figure 5.32 Entering the Document Header

2. In the next step, you enter the gross amount of EUR 880.00 and the tax code 10 for 10 % for customer 30500 Janning KgaA (see Figure 5.33). The document splitting function must split both the receivable and the proportionate tax amount according the profit centers found as well as the segments.

Proportionate tax amount

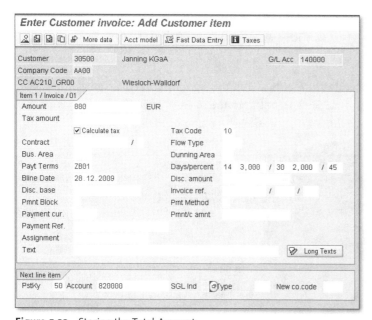

Figure 5.33 Storing the Total Amount

3. In the field status control, General Ledger account 820000 is designed in such a way that asset retirements can be posted. An additional input window is displayed in which you store the number of the

Retirement corresponds to complete retirement

complex fixed asset and the type of retirement (complete retirement here). The total amount of EUR 330.00 includes a net value for the complex fixed asset, computer 1, of EUR 300.00 and a tax portion of EUR 30.00 (see Figure 5.34).

4. On the basis of the net book value of EUR 333.33, this has a loss of EUR 33.33.

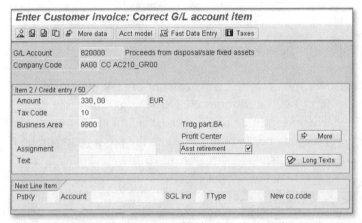

Figure 5.34 Proportionate Amount for the Complex Fixed Asset Computer 1

Computer 2 5. The procedure is identical for the complex fixed asset, computer 2 (see Figure 5.35). The net amount of EUR 500.00 balances with the net book value of EUR 466.67 to a gain of EUR 33.33.

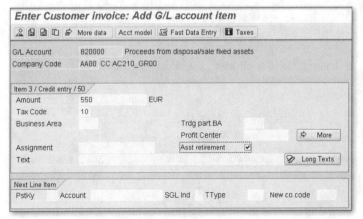

Figure 5.35 Proportionate Amount for the Complex Fixed Asset Computer 2

6. Figure 5.36 provides an overview of the comprehensive posting document. At this point, the user is still in the entry view.

```
Enter Customer invoice: Display Overview

  🔍 🏁 Display Currency   📋 Taxes   ✏ Reset

Document Date    28.12.2009    Type           DR      Company Code   AA00
Posting Date     28.12.2009    Period         12      Currency       EUR
Document Number  INTERNAL      Fiscal Year    2009    Translatn Date 28.12.2009
Reference                                             Cross-CC no.
Doc.Header Text                                       Trading part.BA

Items in document currency
     PK  BusA Acct                               EUR   Amount      Tax amnt
 001 01        0000030500 Janning KGaA                  880,00           10
 002 50  9900 0000820000 Proceeds from dispo            300,00-          10
 003 50  3000 0000820000 Proceeds from dispo            500,00-          10
 004 50        0000175000 Output tax                     80,00-          10
 005 75  9900 0000021000 000000003003 0000             500,00-
 006 70  9900 0000021010 000000003003 0000             166,67
 007 40  9900 0000825000 Suspense a/c · disp           300,00
 008 40  9900 0000200000 Loss·asset disposal            33,33
 009 75  3000 0000021000 000000003004 0000             700,00-
 010 70  3000 0000021010 000000003004 0000             233,33
 011 40  3000 0000825000 Suspense a/c · disp           500,00
 012 50  3000 0000250000 Profits on disposal            33,33-

 D 2.113,33         C 2.113,33                           0,00  *   12 Line Items
```

Figure 5.36 Document Overview

7. Not until you run a G/L view simulation, such as the one shown in Figure 5.37, does it become clear which additional account assignment information is available. You can also clearly see that the revenue rows with G/L account 820000 have no additional account assignments.

If you want to create a segment balance sheet with a balance of zero, as in this example, this constellation is not permitted.

Constellation not permitted

8. The expert mode in Figure 5.38 reveals that, as was already assumed, splitting method 0000000012 of business transaction 0200 (Customer invoice) including business transaction variant 0001 is used.

Analysis of the facts

In the Document Display area of Figure 5.38, you can see that it is not possible to project the account assignment features to line items 1, 2, 11, 12, 13, and 14 even if the inheritance rule is activated. It is striking that this involves balance sheet accounts.

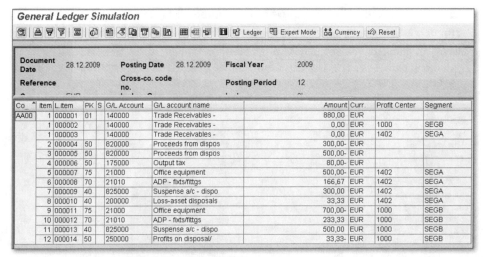

Figure 5.37 General Ledger Simulation

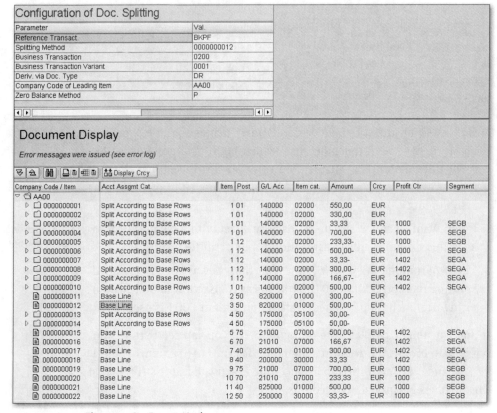

Figure 5.38 Expert Mode

Due to the present standard Customizing, the system displays the error message shown in Figure 5.39 for this business transaction.

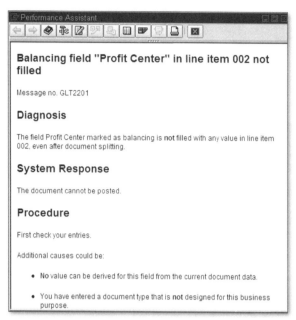

Figure 5.39 Error Message

To avoid such a message in live operation, you require not only extensive tests but also an adaptation of the standard Customizing, such as the one shown in this example.

Adapting the standard Customizing

Preventive Measure—Custom Configuration

Via Financial Accounting (New) • General Ledger Accounting (New) • Business Transactions • Document Splitting • Extended Document Splitting • Define Document Splitting Rule, you can have the system display the delivered rules individually or create your own rules.

The standard rule shown in Figure 5.40 can and should be used as a template for your own rules. To enable the system to correctly process

Create own transaction variant

the case previously presented, you must add the balance sheet account category within the transaction variant.

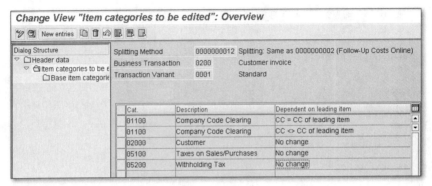

Figure 5.40 Standard Delivery of the Splitting Rule

The transaction variant Z001 that you've created yourself closes this gap because category 01000 (Balance Sheet Account) was added (see Figure 5.41).

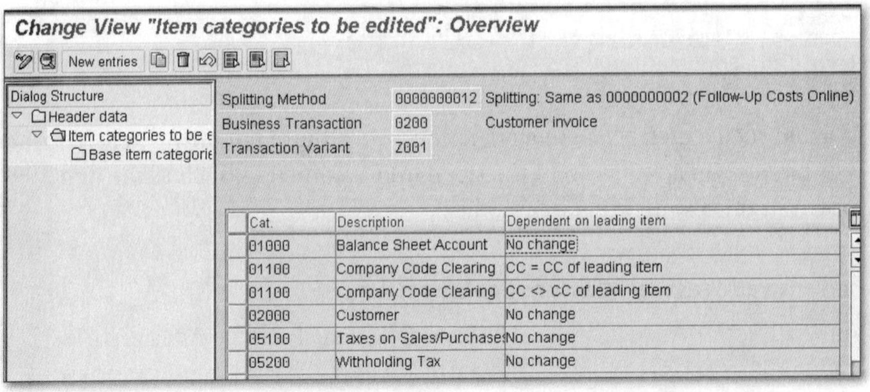

Figure 5.41 Custom Splitting Rule

If you double-click the processing of the item category, the system takes you to Figure 5.42. There you must store the processing category with specification 1, SPLITTING ACCORDING TO BASIS ITEM CATEGORIES.

Caution if you change the already active configuration

If you want to change a setting of document splitting in live operation, you must be extremely cautious. You must consider the already existing data. You can cause mass system crashes if you change the document splitting incorrectly.

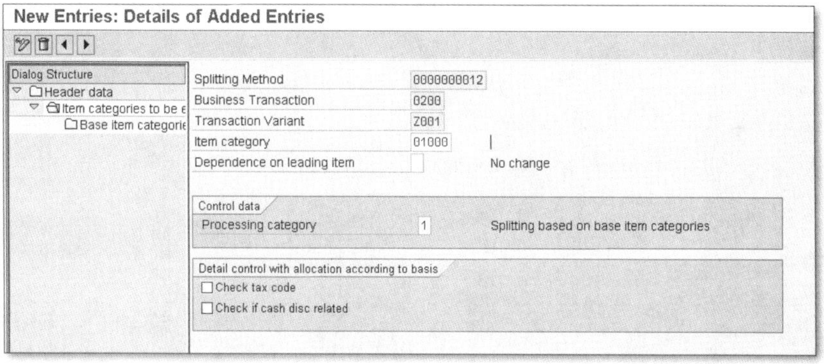

Figure 5.42 Splitting According to Basis Item Categories

If you are unsure about how to proceed, contact your consulting partner or SAP directly. Moreover, you must consider to which business cases the change is supposed to apply. In this example, the change applies only to the retirements in Asset Accounting. To be able to specify this in detail, it is recommended that you deploy a custom document type, or, as in this case, an exclusive use of document type DR in Asset Accounting (see Figure 5.43).

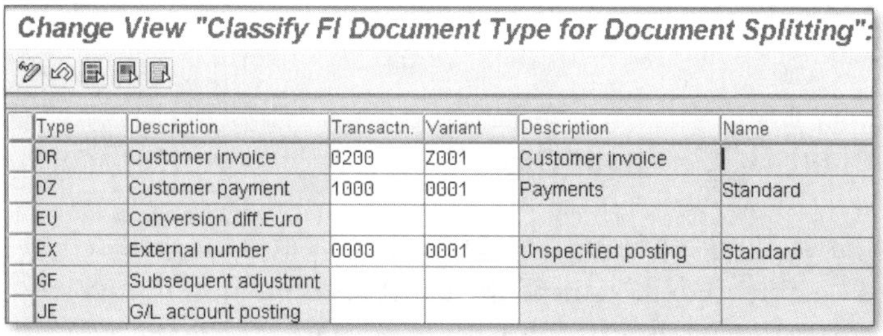
Change View "Classify FI Document Type for Document Splitting":

Type	Description	Transactn.	Variant	Description	Name
DR	Customer invoice	0200	Z001	Customer invoice	
DZ	Customer payment	1000	0001	Payments	Standard
EU	Conversion diff.Euro				
EX	External number	0000	0001	Unspecified posting	Standard
GF	Subsequent adjustmnt				
JE	G/L account posting				

Figure 5.43 Assigning to the Document Type

Once you've made these settings, the balance sheet items that were not split previously will be processed correctly (see Figure 5.44).

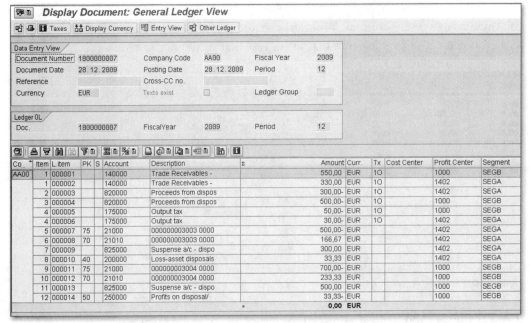

Figure 5.44 Correct Splitting of the Document

[+]

> **Wizard**
>
> Enhancement Package 4 includes a new wizard that supports you in making the right settings in chronological order. But you should not forget the already mentioned dependencies between existing data or the wide range of business transactions. For more information refer to Section 5.6, Wizards for Customizing the Document Splitting.

5.5 Special G/L Transactions

Down payment made

Special G/L transactions represent a separate specific area for certain business data. To be able to demonstrate the specific configuration involved here, the following example includes a down payment made of EUR 110,000.00. In the second process step, an incoming invoice for this amount is posted. Finally, posting documents are cleared against each other.

Document splitting is activated for the Segment characteristic. Table 5.8 shows the General Ledger view of a down payment made.

First step— down payment

Account	Account	Debit	Credit	Additional Account Assignment
Vendor SHB		EUR 110,000.00		Segment C
To	Bank account		EUR 110,000.00	Segment C
Tax		EUR 10,000.00		Segment C
To	Tax clearing		EUR 10,000.00	Segment C

Table 5.8 General Ledger View—Down Payment Made

This posting record already involves two specific features:

► The tax amount is posted against a clearing account.

► No useful information about the segment is available until the incoming invoice has been cleared.

Table 5.9 shows the incoming invoice as the second process step.

Second step— incoming invoice

Account	Account	Debit	Credit	Additional Account Assignment
Expense		EUR 60,000.00		Segment B
Expense		EUR 40,000.00		Segment A
Tax		EUR 6,000.00		Segment B
Tax		EUR 4,000.00		Segment A
To	Vendor		EUR 66,000.00	Segment B
	Vendor		EUR 44,000.00	Segment A

Table 5.9 General Ledger View for Vendor Invoice

Third step—
releasing the
down payment The next step in this process consists of releasing the down payment made by linking the two documents with each other. The document splitting function makes sure that the balance of each independent accounting unit is zero. As a result, we obtain the posting record shown in Table 5.10.

Account	Account	Debit	Credit	Additional Account Assignment
Vendor		EUR 44,000.00		Segment A
Vendor		EUR 66,000.00		Segment B
	Vendor SHB		EUR 110,000.00	Segment C
	Tax		EUR 10,000.00	Segment C
Tax clearing		EUR 10,000.00		Segment C
Segment clearing			EUR 44,000.00	Segment A
	Segment clearing	EUR 44,000.00		Segment C
Segment clearing			EUR 66,000.00	Segment B
	Segment clearing	EUR 66,000.00		Segment C

Table 5.10 Clearing the Vendor Invoice and Down Payment Made

Table 5.11 lists the changes in values for a financial statement for the Segment characteristic.

	Segment A	Segment B	Segment C
Vendor	– EUR 44,000.00 + EUR 44,000.00	– EUR 66,000.00 + EUR 66,000.00	
Vendor SHB			EUR 110,000.00 – EUR 110,000.00
Bank account			– EUR 110,000.00
Tax	EUR 4,000.00	EUR 6,000.00	EUR 10,000.00 – EUR 10,000.00
Tax clearing			– EUR 10,000.00 + EUR 10,000.00
Expense	EUR 40,000.00	EUR 60,000.00	
Segment clearing	– EUR 44,000.00	– EUR 66,000.00	EUR 110,000.00

Table 5.11 Development of the Financial Statement for the Segment

Only additional clearing line items generated when the down payment is cleared against the vendor invoice enable a zero balance for each segment. The following sections describe the Customizing options for document splitting in G/L transactions.

Items related to vendors or customers are usually identified by the system. However, special G/L transactions are an exception and must be defined for document splitting. As you can see in Figure 5.45, you must enter deviating reconciliation accounts for item categories 02100 (Customer special G/L transaction) and 03100 (Vendor special G/L transaction) in the table and activate these accounts by checking the Override flag. You can do this in Customizing via the menu path: FINANCIAL ACCOUNTING (NEW) • GENERAL LEDGER ACCOUNTING (NEW) • BUSINESS TRANSACTIONS • DOCUMENT SPLITTING • CLASSIFY G/L ACCOUNTS FOR DOCUMENT SPLITTING.

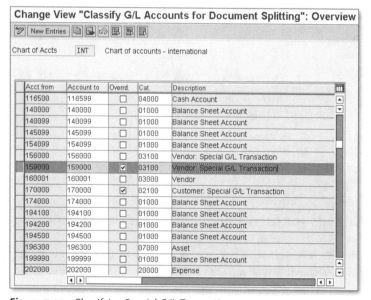

Figure 5.45 Classifying Special G/L Transactions

In addition, you must store the base item categories 02100 and 03100 for the unspecified business transaction 0000 in document splitting. To check whether these base item categories have been stored, select the following path in Customizing: FINANCIAL ACCOUNTING (NEW) • GENERAL

LEDGER ACCOUNTING (NEW) • BUSINESS TRANSACTIONS • DOCUMENT SPLITTING • EXTENDED DOCUMENT SPLITTING • DEFINE DOCUMENT SPLITTING RULE. If you select the relevant entry of your splitting method and click the printer icon, the screen shown in Figure 5.46 should be displayed.

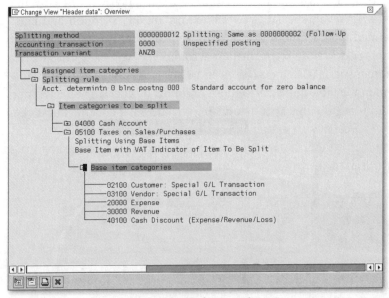

Figure 5.46 Configuring a Splitting Rule for Special G/L Transactions

Only if these settings have been made can special G/L transactions be mapped correctly for financial statements of segments.

5.6   Wizards for Customizing the Document Splitting

EHP4 includes two new wizards

Wizards are not new, but they are based on a basis technology of the SAP workflow. Wizards are also used in other areas of SAP Customizing, for instance, in Asset Accounting. The configuration of the document splitting comprises multiple tables and settings. To keep this procedure transparent and clear, two wizards for document splitting were added in Enhancement Package 4. You can find the these in Customizing by following the menu path: FINANCIAL ACCOUNTING (NEW) • GENERAL LEDGER

ACCOUNTING (NEW) • BUSINESS TRANSACTIONS • DOCUMENT SPLITTING •
WIZARDS FOR DOCUMENT SPLITTING.

In the context of document splitting, the new functions are at the beginning of the configuration settings (see Figure 5.47). A separate wizard is available both for the configuration of the complete document splitting and for the document splitting rules.

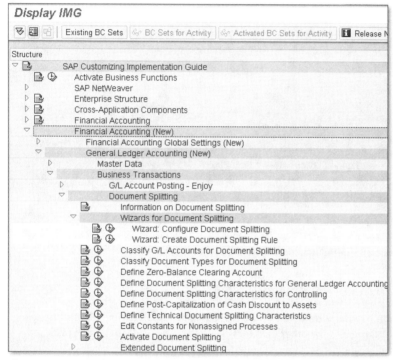

Figure 5.47 Wizards in SAP Customizing

The wizards entail a procedure that guides the SAP user through Customizing step by step; the various settings are made in a defined logical sequence. Figure 5.48 provides an overview of the ten steps to be carried out for the configuration of document splitting. The wizard for a new document splitting rule comprises eight configuration steps.

Step-by-step user guidance

The individual steps for table maintenance are linked and are directly updated within the wizard. In addition, help texts provide descriptions

Help texts and descriptions

on the technical and business purpose the respective settings pursue. Here, the standard SAP help texts are integrated which, in turn, provide navigation to further help texts or even Customizing tables.

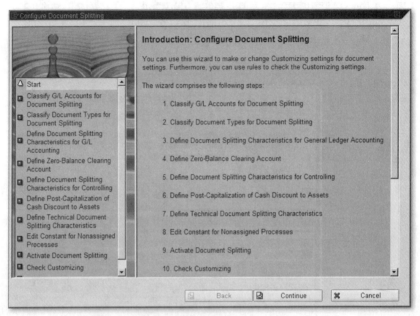

Figure 5.48 Introduction and Wizard Overview

Warning on Data Consistency

If you use the wizard to change the Customizing of document splitting, you must not make any other Customizing changes by navigating to an IMG activity via a link in a system documentation. Doing this could result in an inconsistent Customizing. The following pages describe the settings of document splitting in more detail.

Configuring the Wizard Document Splitting

The application screen is divided into three areas. The left-hand side shows the various steps, including their respective status. The upper right area provides a help text on the process. The lower right area contains the actual Customizing. Let's look at the required ten steps in chronological order.

Step 1 — Classify G/L Accounts for Document Splitting

Each G/L account of a chart of accounts must be assigned to an item category. This can be done as a single value or with intervals (see Figure 5.49). The logic of document splitting is based on this assignment.

G/L account and document type

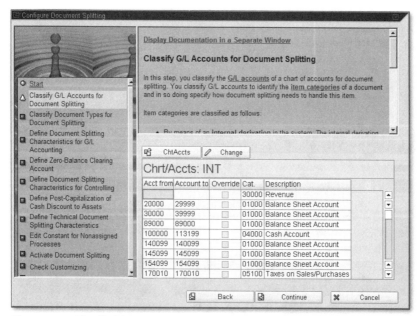

Figure 5.49 Classify G/L Accounts

Step 2 — Classify Document Types for Document Splitting

Similar to the classification for G/L accounts, you need to identify the business transaction based on the document type. Each document type must be assigned to a combination of business transaction and variant (see Figure 5.50).

Business transaction and document type

Step 3 — Define Document Splitting Characteristics for G/L Accounting

In this step, you define the characteristics that determine how the business transactions are to be split. Figure 5.51 shows an example in which the document splitting is made according to the characteristics Business Area and Profit Center.

Accounting assignment characteristics and their properties

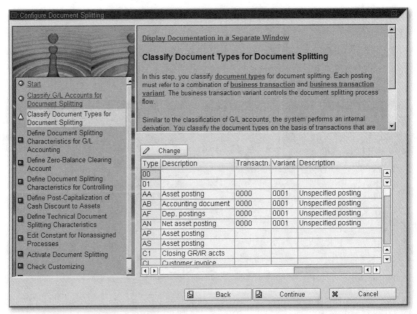

Figure 5.50 Classify Document Types

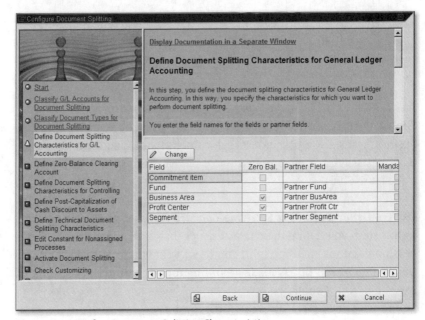

Figure 5.51 Define Document Splitting Characteristics

Step 4 — Define Zero-Balance Clearing Account

If you've defined a zero balance for the characteristics for document splitting as in the third step, this requires the clearing accounts that must be stored in Step 4. Account 194500 is used for the example shown in Figure 5.52.

Zero-balance and clearing account

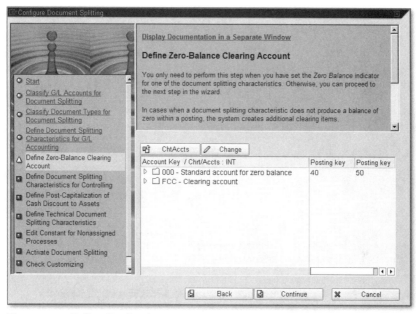

Figure 5.52 Define Clearing Accounts

Step 5 — Define Document Splitting Characteristics for Controlling

If you post line items for cash discount paid, cash discount received, lost cash discount, realized exchange rate differences, expense/revenue from foreign currency valuation or expense/revenue from single value adjustment in a business process, the characteristics defined in Step 5 are inherited by these line items and transferred to Controlling (if a cost element is defined). In the case shown in Figure 5.53, this process involves the Order und Cost Center fields.

Inherit account assignment characteristics

Step 6 — Define Post-Capitalization of Cash Discount to Assets

If you purchase a complex fixed asset on account and subsequently pay with a deduction of cash discount, then you need to reduce the actual acquisition value of the asset. Without New G/L, this situation was

Automatic adjustment

posted periodically using a program for balance sheet adjustment. With New G/L and a configuration similar to Figure 5.54, the process occurs in real time.

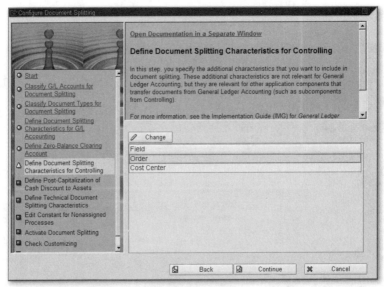

Figure 5.53 Characteristics for Controlling

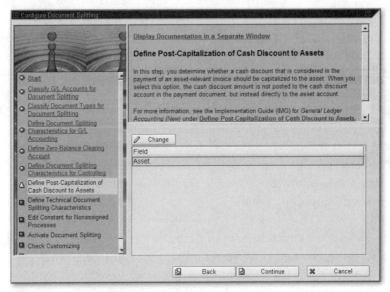

Figure 5.54 Post-Capitalization FI-AA

Step 7 — Define Technical Document Splitting Characteristics

Industries such as public administration can use the function of document splitting in additional areas, for instance, for online payment update or change in account assignment. For these situations it is possible to define technical document splitting characteristics.

Specifics for public administration

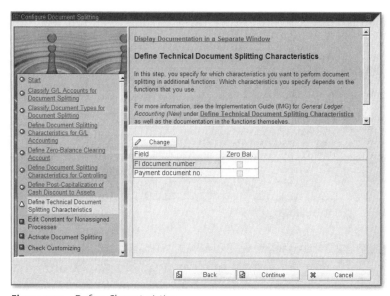

Figure 5.55 Define Characteristics

Step 8 — Edit Constant for Nonassigned Processes

Constants for nonassigned processes are an important element within the document splitting technology. It's not possible in all cases that you can split a document immediately and in real time into the correct characteristic specifications. In the case of down payments, for example, you initially use a constant value for each splitting characteristic until the actual invoice is available and cleared. Figure 5.56 indicates the different cases and characteristics for constants.

Define constants

Step 9 — Activate Document Splitting

You can activate the document splitting for each company code. Restrictions, such as the cross-company code postings, must be taken into account here. In this Customizing step, you additionally make specifications for a document splitting process.

Cross-company code configuration

343

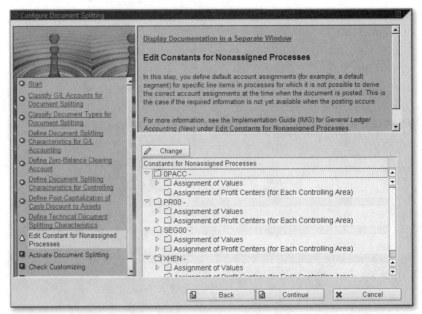

Figure 5.56 Edit Constant

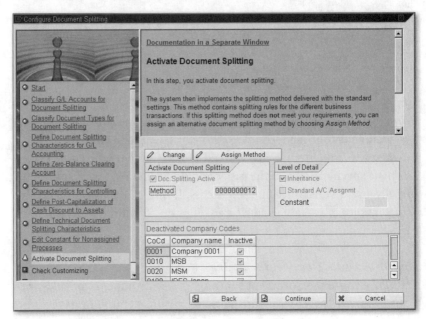

Figure 5.57 Activate Document Splitting

Step 10 — Check Customizing

The last step comprises a check of the settings made. Figure 5.58 illustrates some warning messages that result from incomplete processing of Step 2, Classify Document Types for Document Splitting.

Interpreting the log

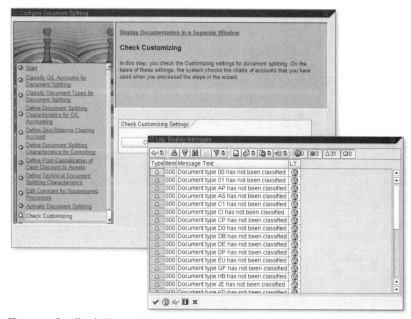

Figure 5.58 Check Customizing

Once you've completed the wizard, you can use the document splitting in principle. In the document splitting process, you can define your own document splitting rules as transaction variants. This is useful, for example, if the document splitting is required to behave differently for a business transaction, for instance, within the scope of accounts receivable accounting, than is defined in the SAP standard.

Defining transaction variants

Creating Wizard Document Splitting Rules

Because this configuration is a somewhat more comprehensive undertaking, you are provided with a separate wizard in EHP4. This wizard comprises eight steps, which are described next.

Step 1—Create Business Transaction Variant

In the first step, you create a custom transaction variant that starts with Z. Figure 5.59 shows an example for the business transaction, customer invoice.

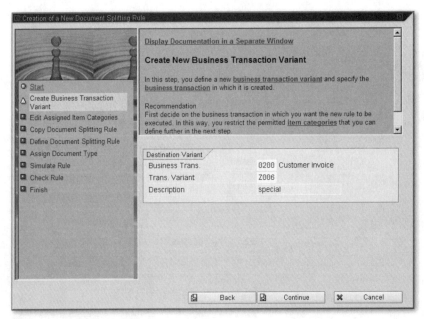

Figure 5.59 Create Variant

Step 2—Edit Assigned Item Categories

Customer-specific transaction variant
For the business transaction, customer invoice, the assigned item categories define the content of the customer-specific transaction variant. In this example, item category 20000 (Expense) is disallowed; that is, if a posting document for the customer invoice business transaction is identified with the customer-specific transaction variant, there must not be any line items with the expense item (see Figure 5.60).

Step 3—Copy Document Splitting Rule

Using the copy template
On the basis of document splitting rules, you can configure the document splitting process in the next step. So that you don't have to define the posting rules completely anew, it is useful to build on an existing basis. Here, a standard transaction variant is used as a copy template (see Figure 5.61).

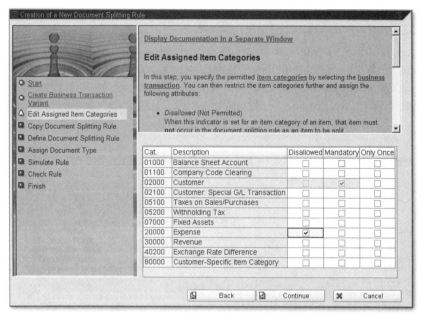

Figure 5.60 Edit Item Categories

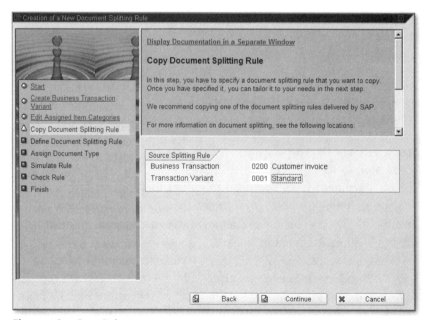

Figure 5.61 Copy Rule

Step 4—Define Document Splitting Rule

Custom adaptation   In this step, you can adapt the document splitting rules that you've copied in Step 3 to your requirements (see Figure 5.62). For example, you can make changes particularly for the company code clearing by setting the SPLIT AUTOMATICALLY option for balance sheet account item category. As a result, the system would implement an automatic document splitting for clearing, partial clearing, or reverse postings only.

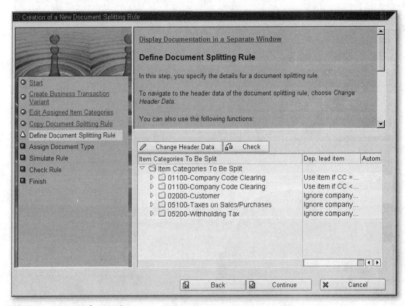

Figure 5.62   Define Rule

Step 5—Assign Document Type

Compatible document type   To be able to use a document splitting rule, it must be assigned to a specific document type. You need to ensure that the document type is compatible with the business transaction. Figure 5.63 shows that the document type DA (customer document) was assigned to the customer invoice business transaction.

Step 6—Simulate Document Splitting Rule

Simulation options   In this step, you can simulate the effects of configuration on an already existing document (see Figure 5.64). Provided that further SAP systems are connected via Remote Function Call (RFC), you can also access their documents for simulation purposes.

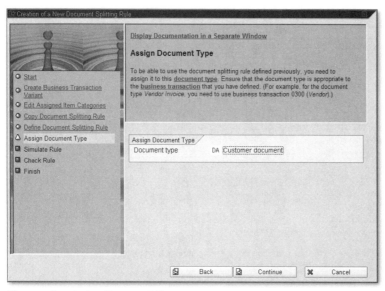

Figure 5.63 Assign Document Type

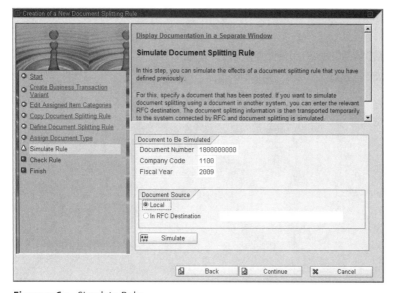

Figure 5.64 Simulate Rule

The result of the simulation corresponds to the expert mode, which is also available for each online posting. Figure 5.65 illustrates that the newly defined Z variant was used here.

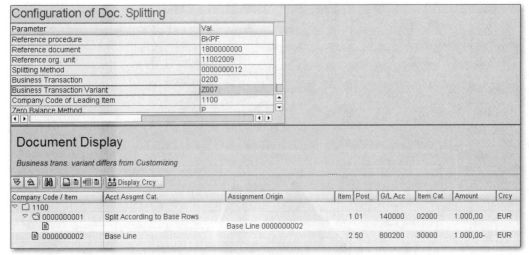

Figure 5.65 Result of the Simulation

Step 7 — Check Document Splitting Rule

This step ensures a complete and consistent configuration because it checks all settings.

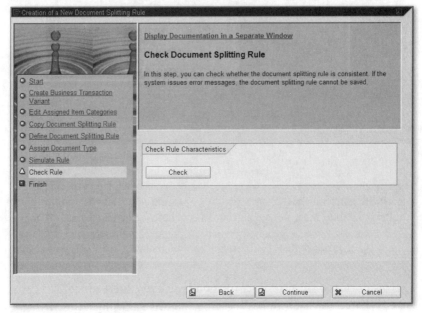

Figure 5.66 Check Rule

Step 8 — Finish

The last step of the configuration wizard for document splitting rules provides an overview to document the settings made.

Overview of configuration

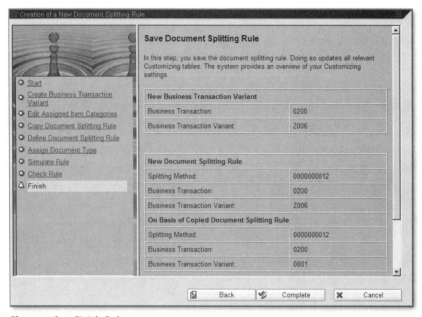

Figure 5.67 Finish Rule

Once the configuration for document splitting is finished, you can create transaction data. In this process, recurring activities at the end of a month, quarter, or year must also be considered in the context of a multidimensional financial statement.

5.7 Periodic Processing

Balance carryforwards are performed not only for balance sheet accounts but for individual entities, such as "segment" or "profit center." Computer-based evaluation programs must consider the splitting ratios of the original document and create valuation postings for all dimensions.

Balance carryforwards

The process of a foreign currency valuation is a good example to demonstrate the effects of document splitting. In Table 5.12, an incoming

Foreign currency valuation

351

invoice of USD 10,000.00 is posted to different profit centers with an indirect quotation of EUR 1.50.

At the end of the period, the invoice is valuated at the current exchange rate of EUR/USD 1.29. In accordance with the original document, the exchange rate difference must be split into the different independent accounting units: in this case, "profit center" and "segment." Figure 5.68 shows the generated posting records of the foreign currency program.

Debit Item	Credit Item	Transaction currency	Local Currency	Additional Account Assignment	Additional Account Assignment
Vendor		USE 7,000.00	EUR 4,666.00	Profit center: ADMIN	Segment: SERV
Vendor		USE 3,000.00	EUR 2,000.00	Profit center: 9999	Segment: SERV
To	Expense	USE 7,000.00	EUR 4,666.00	Profit center: ADMIN	Segment: SERV
To	Expense	USE 3,000.00	EUR 2,000.00	Profit center: 9999	Segment: SERV

Table 5.12 General Ledger View of Vendor Invoice

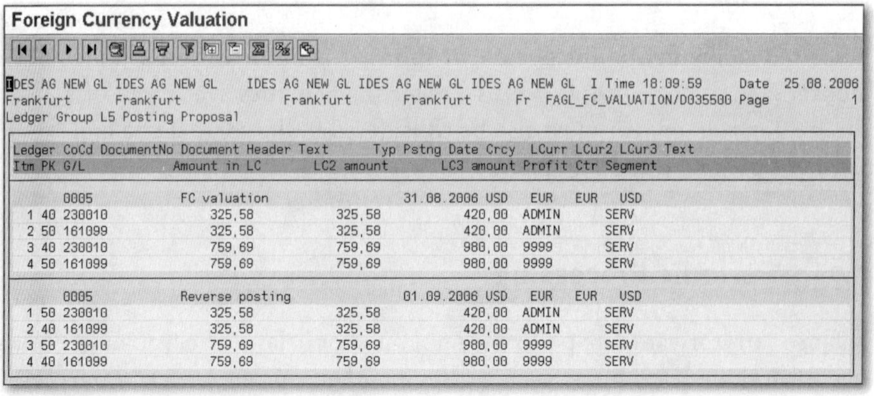

Figure 5.68 Foreign Currency Valuation—Profit Center

In contrast to a valuation without document splitting, posting records are carried out on the key date for each independent accounting unit.

5.8   Conclusion

Document splitting enhances the quality of data in individual financial statements. Flexible splits and the resulting financial statements can be created on the basis of freely selectable old and new characteristics. This option is particularly advantageous for the consolidation department, where legal consolidation and management consolidation can now be combined in one step. The highly granular data enables exact analyses and conclusions. Naturally, external reporting also benefits from a more accurate presentation of financial statements for individual segments. As an organizational unit, the company code will continue to be of key importance. In future, activities for controlling operations—such as payment, dunning, or advance return for tax on sales/purchases—will continue to be closely related to the dominant company code criteria.

Before you can benefit from the manifold options of New G/L, migration is required. It must be planned, designed, and implemented carefully.

6 Migration

In the previous chapters you have learned how important solid planning and design are in switching to New General Ledger (New G/L). Further, having a solid conceptual basis on which to base the plan for the switch also affects the migration itself.

In this chapter you will first learn how you can activate New G/L. The treatment of the migration project, especially with respect to the migration scenario and the migration cockpit, is based on this activation. You will also learn about the SAP Migration Service.

Chapter 7, Practical Reports, discusses some examples of migration experiences drawn from real life.

6.1 Activating New General Ledger

Let's first look at the situation in which you as a customer find yourself before we look at new transactions and reports and compare totals records in the classic General Ledger with those in New G/L. Activation of New G/L will be carried out differently depending on whether you are a new customer or an existing customer. **Default delivery**

During a new installation, New G/L accounting in the standard system is set to active. While the use of the classic General Ledger is theoretically also possible for new customers, SAP advises against using it because doing so will necessitate an additional, and avoidable, migration effort later on. The expense involved in a migration is significant. **New installation**

Upgrade

In contrast, during the release upgrade for an SAP R/3 system to SAP ERP, the classic General Ledger initially continues to remain active. Totals table GLT0 remains in effect. If you want to switch from the classic General Ledger to New G/L, you can do this in the course of a project in a second step, after the upgrade. In that step you have the choice (so it is not absolutely necessary) of activating and using New G/L.

The checkbox for activating New General Ledger Accounting is Active (see Figure 6.1) is set for each client. The Customizing menu path is Financial Accounting • Basic Settings Financial Accounting • New General Ledger Accounting.

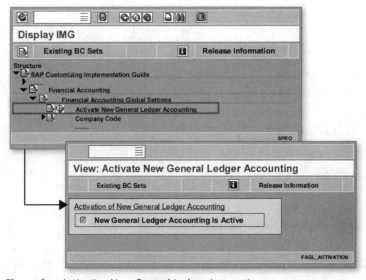

Figure 6.1 Activating New General Ledger Accounting

[+]

Various Production Clients

If there are no data flows between the production clients, you can configure, migrate, and activate in the individual clients without any dependencies.

Table FAGL_ACTIVEC with the FAGL_ACTIVE field (checkbox: New General Ledger Accounting is Active) is client-independent. All other tables that are relevant for New G/L (FAGL*) are also client-independent.

Activation also produces cross-client changes. These changes affect the paths in the application and in Customizing for the SAP ERP system. After activating New G/L, in addition to the classic paths in Customizing, you will now also find new paths for New G/L accounting (see Figure 6.2).

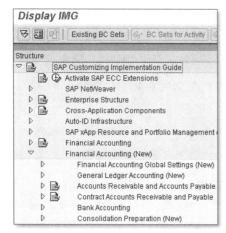

Figure 6.2 New Paths in Customizing after Activating New General Ledger

The already known classic financial accounting paths continue to remain available for better orientation. You will also see new menu paths in the application and in the SAP Easy Access menu, as a result of the activation of New G/L. New transactions appear, such as FB50L (enter G/L account document for ledger group (enjoy transaction)), or FB01L (enter general posting for ledger group) (see Figure 6.3).

New paths in Customizing and application

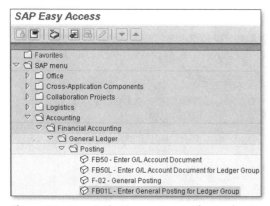

Figure 6.3 New Paths/Transactions in the Application

Showing and
hiding Customizing
and menu paths
If, after activating New G/L, you want to work exclusively with the paths of New G/L accounting, you can hide the classic financial accounting paths using the RFAGL_SWAP_IMG_OLD program.

In Transaction SA38 you are provided with four small programs to display Customizing and menu paths for classic and New G/L (see Table 6.1):

Report	Name
RFAGL_SWAP_IMG_NEW	Show and hide new implementation guide
RFAGL_SWAP_IMG_OLD	Show and hide old implementation guide
RFAGL_SWAP_MENU_NEW	Show and hide old menu
RFAGL_SWAP_MENU_OLD	Show and hide old menu

Table 6.1 Programs for Showing or Hiding Customizing and Menu Paths

Let's look again at the transition from the classic to New G/L. In the standard system, when you activate New G/L accounting, the balances are also updated in the tables of the classic General Ledger accounting (totals table GLT0) in addition to the tables of New G/L accounting. This parallel updating may be useful for a period of time, from a security point of view.

Update totals in
totals tables
A comparative report can give you the guarantee that New G/L accounting is capable of delivering the right results. The menu path to the report for comparing data is FINANCIAL ACCOUNTING (NEW) • FINANCIAL ACCOUNTING BASIC SETTINGS (NEW) • TOOLS • COMPARE LEDGERS.

Comparing the
totals records
You can use Transaction GCAC (Ledger Comparison) to compare the totals records of any two ledgers; you can see the corresponding selection screen in Figure 6.4. Here you can also compare local and global ledgers with each other, as well as those ledgers with differing fiscal year variants and charts of accounts.

In the standard system, the comparison is made at the level of the organizational unit (company code or company) and of the account, but you can also incorporate further fields into the comparison, such as the business area, functional area, and cost center. Among other options, you also have the option to compare currency amounts and quantities.

Using this report called by Transaction GCAC, you can compare the totals records in the tables of New G/L accounting with the totals records in the tables of the classic General Ledger accounting (GLT0). Without a data migration, the differences shown are those arising from transactions prior to the activation of New G/L.

Transaction GCAC

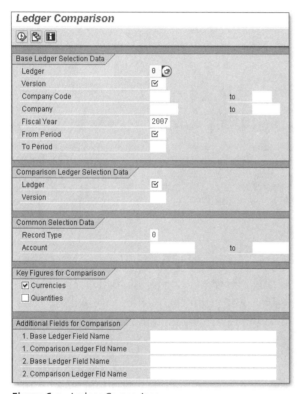

Figure 6.4 Ledger Comparison

If you are a technical consultant and work with Transactions SE38 or SA38, you must be aware that this RGUCOMP4 program called in the IMG as an activity is called only by Transaction GCAC. Transactions SE38 and SA38 are not supported, for technical reasons (see Figure 6.5).

Program RGUCOMP4

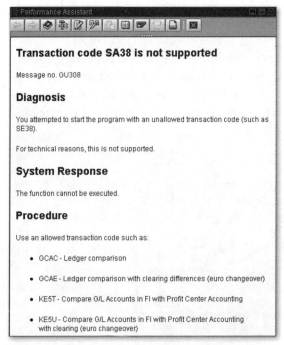

Figure 6.5 Transaction Code SA38 is Not Supported

6.2 Migration Projects

Naturally, activating New G/L is not simply a question of flicking a switch. Migration always involves a project. In this section, we will describe what you must take into account during a migration project.

Particularly if you are an existing customer, New G/L may under no circumstances simply be switched on. If a document is updated during the start-up process, the activity can not be undone and, in the worst case, may lead to data inconsistencies.

6.2.1 Migration as a Discrete (Sub)Project

Various migration scenarios are possible during the transition from the classic to New G/L, depending on whether you primarily want New G/L to achieve the integration of your internal and external bookkeeping (including segment reporting), to boost transparency, to provide parallel accounting, or to speed up period-end closing. These scenarios range from a simple summary of existing ledgers to a complete reworking of your accounting system.

During redesign in particular, the transition to New G/L accounting consists of a *conceptual* business element and a technical element, where the existing financial accounting data must be migrated into the new structures of the general accounting. The improvements in and complexity of the transition to New G/L accounting and the affected data volume can be very extensive. Comprehensive analysis of your initial position and detailed planning are important *success factors* for the migration. We therefore recommend that within the New G/L implementation project you provide for a separate sub-project for migrating the financial accounting data. Figure 6.6 illustrates the chronological sequence of individual sub-projects.

Redesigning the accounting system

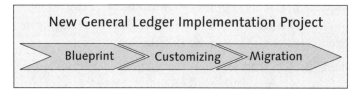

Figure 6.6 Sub-Projects Within Migration Project

A migration should always be begun as a project, with all of the elements of a project: phases, milestones, tests, and so on. Here, the *migration* project represents only a sub-project of the larger project for New G/L.

Migration = Project

A basic prerequisite for performing the migration is that the technical upgrade to an SAP ERP system first has been successfully performed. New G/L is implemented in a second, separate project.

Prerequisites

[+]

Upgrade to SAP ERP and Migration to New G/L — Distribution to Two Fiscal Years

Irrespective of the migration scenario, it is recommended that you implement the release upgrade and migration to New G/L in separate fiscal years. So if you plan to use document splitting, you should activate the VALIDATION OF DOCUMENT SPLITTING function well in advance of the migration date. Another example concerns the replacement of the accounts approach with the ledger approach. Here as well you have activities (valuation postings) that need to be done prior to the migration date.

Before the obligatory *New G/L Migration Service* becomes active, the implementation project has already begun, and the design and Customizing of New G/L, in particular, have been completed. An exact and complete configuration of New G/L is required before New G/L accounting is set to active. In parallel with the configuration of New G/L, work continues in the classic General Ledger.

Project duration

We cannot generalize about the duration of a project because it depends on various factors. You can accelerate the project by addressing the following issues:

▸ Can test systems be quickly built, and are transports immediately available? In any case, the parties concerned should have the opportunity to familiarize themselves with the procedure in a test system so that the affected areas (department and consulting) can assess existing challenges.

▸ How does the *staffing* for the project look from the customer side? What background experience do members bring to the project team, and is the company prepared to invest in training?

▸ The customer's project team or the implementation partner's team should consist of members with well-grounded expertise in the area of SAP ERP Financials and Migration. You can find an important link related to the transfer of expertise on SAP's service page (*http://service.sap.com/GLMIG*).

Assessing the project duration

To better assess the project duration, you also should ask yourself the following questions:

▸ How familiar are the project team members with the systems/processes? How complex are these systems/processes?

▸ How large is the number of migration objects or the scope of the document volume?

▸ What migration scenario has been chosen? (Section 6.5, Migration Scenarios, discusses migration scenarios in detail).

▶ What efforts are being made to reach the defined milestones on time? Any delay will necessitate extra effort during testing!

6.2.2 Other Independent Projects

The following projects are self-contained and are not part of a migration project:

▶ Introduction of a parallel accounting system

▶ Introduction of segment reporting

▶ Adjustment of the leading valuation, if a parallel valuation is already performed

▶ Adjustment of the leading valuation area in the asset accounting (FI-AA)

▶ Change to or conversion of the chart of accounts

▶ Consolidation of company codes

▶ Currency conversion, such as introduction of new currencies

SAP supports the last four projects mentioned using the Operations Service System Landscape Optimization (SLO). Even if there may be interdependencies between these projects and the migration project, these projects are closed insofar as they must be performed decoupled from the migration project.

System landscape optimization

Restrictions for Local Currency Changeover and Document Splitting   **[+]**

The tools for a local currency changeover in New G/L are available both for SAP ERP 6.0 and for SAP ERP 2004 (5.0). If you activate the document splitting in New G/L, you cannot change over the local currency in the same fiscal year. You have two options to avoid this situation:

▶ **Option 1**
Local currency changeover in the classic G/L, migration to New G/L (including document splitting)

▶ **Option 2**
Migration to New G/L (without document splitting), local currency changeover to New G/L, activation of document splitting (scenario 6)

6.3   The Phase Model of Migration

Three phases The phase model for migration consists of three phases. When you look at migration, you must differentiate between the activities in each phase and the posting data. Two dates play an important role here:

▸ **Migration date**
The migration date with the beginning of migration: between Phase 0 and Phase 1 of the migration

▸ **Activation date**
The activation date of New G/L, described in Section 6.1, Activating New General Ledger: the date that separates Phase 1 and Phase 2

Figure 6.7 provides an overview of the migration phases.

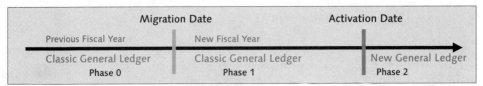

Figure 6.7 Phase Model of Migration

Phase 0—design In Phase 0, you implement the design and Customizing of New G/L. and Customizing These activities are followed by functional and integration tests in a (separate) test system. Additionally, you start to plan and design the subsequent migration. If you use a scenario including document splitting, you must implement the Customizing (without activation) in the production system. Besides these activities, you must also consider the posting data. No single documents are copied from Phase 0 prior to the migration date. For non-open item (OI)-managed accounts, such as the G/L account that you see in Figure 6.8, a carryforward is made into the migration year.

Phase 1— In contrast to non-OI-managed accounts where you copy only a balance, validation OI-managed accounts are migrated individually from documents that are not yet balanced.

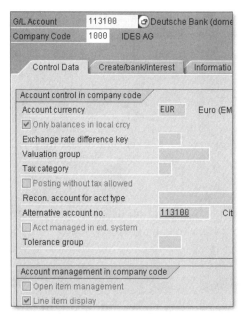

Figure 6.8 Non-OI-Managed Account

Within the scope of the project, the activities of Phase 1 entail the closing of the old fiscal year. At this point, you need to run an analysis from the results of the validation of document splitting and you can change the configuration for the last time. Documents from Phase 1 are completely posted subsequently as part of the migration. Any document splitting is postprocessed in this phase.

For planned active document splitting, the documents of this phase should be checked the first time they are entered to see whether they are "fit" for New G/L. This check is performed through a validation, which is described in detail later (see Section 6.6.2, Setup Phase).

Transaction FBRA—Reset Clearing   [+]

In Phase 1, clearing documents are not provided with document splitting characteristics. Due to the clearing reset using Transaction FBRA, the original information is lost completely. Such documents must be enhanced or handled specifically for the migration using a BAdI. To avoid this situation, this transaction in Phase 1 should not be used.

Test migration—
live migration

Customizing of New G/L and migration are now complete. Both the functional and the integration tests were finalized in the test system, and test migrations have been implemented. The actual live migration occurs at the end of Phase 1.

[Ex] **Example of the Migration's Time Flow**

If you assume a current date of 4/1/2010, a recommended migration date could be 1/1/2010. The activation date of New G/L could be 5/1/2010. This scheme would put the activation date of the validation at 1/1/2010, perhaps even earlier.

Phase 1—
document volume

The farther apart the migration date and activation date are, the greater the volume of Phase 1 documents that must be subsequently posted tends to be.

[+] **Activation Date**

There is no binding date for the activation. It can be the first or the last day of a month/a period.

Phase 2—use
in production

Phase 2 entails the use of New G/L Accounting in production. After a transition period, you deactivate the classic G/L Accounting after updating values in totals table GLT0 or other functions of the classic environment such as profit center accounting with totals table GLPCT.

6.4 SAP Service for Migration

Project assistance from the migration service SAP General Ledger Migration can significantly contribute to the success of a migration project. The following sections describe general conditions, content, and the migration scenarios supported by the service.

6.4.1 Content of the SAP General Ledger Migration Service

Orderliness

Central components of the migration sub-project are the preparation and performance of a technical migration of the source data from the classic applications into New G/L. The top priority here is to preserve the orderliness of the accounting during the migration. To guarantee maximum security, SAP accompanies each of these migration (sub)projects with a migration service. This compulsory technical service is based on standard migration scenarios and contains a scenario-specific Migration Cockpit and two service sessions aimed at quality assurance for the data and for the migration project. The migration service has the following specific content:

► Migration Cockpit for performing the migration

► Remote service session for scenario validation

► Remote service session for test validation

► Development support by the General Ledger Migration Back Office

This content relates to support during the technical migration of the source data from the classic application into New G/L. For support with the blueprint and Customizing of New G/L, you can use SAP Consulting from an appropriate local company or consulting partners. They offer consultancy support, for instance, in designing New G/L as well as planning the implementation project and individual reviews. The individual service content will be described in further detail in the following.

Support of technical migration

6.4.2 Migration Cockpit

The Migration Cockpit is a tool for performing the migration. It consists of three parts that support a structured and efficient processing of migration activities: the migration overview, a flow structure, and a monitor.

Reducing complexity

> **Additional Information on the Migration Cockpit**
>
> The following discusses the migration overview and the flow structure. Section 6.6 provides more detailed information on the Migration Cockpit.

[+]

Migration Overview

You navigate to the migration overview using Transaction CNV_MBT_NGLM, which you may store in your favorites in the SAP Easy Access menu (see Figure 6.9).

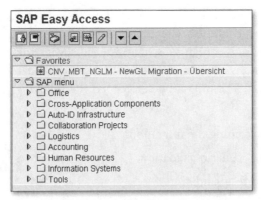

Figure 6.9 SAP Easy Access Navigation Menu

From here, you implement all activities that are not directly part of a specific migration package. For example, you can create a project or package or register selected users.

Flow Structure (Process Tree)

Activities of migration—split by scenarios

The flow structure provides a scenario-based management. It contains a process tree showing the individual activities of the migration, which are tailored to your specific scenario. These activities involve either steps that must be performed manually or programs that must be started.

Monitor

The Cockpit also contains a *monitor* that you can use to trace the processing and status of the individual steps. You can view the programs' system logs here, and you have the option of storing project-internal notes or additional documents as annexes. Other migration-specific information, such as the start and end times of the programs and the number of migrated datasets, is also stored. This information helps improve the transparency and traceability of the migration process, which are also important in auditing. The main advantage of the Cockpit is scenario-specific management through the migration process. It simplifies handling and execution of migration and reduces its complexity.

6.4.3   SAP System Landscape

Customers usually have a three-stage SAP ERP system architecture, which comprises development, quality assurance, and production systems. These systems generally involve separate SAP installations, which are each connected to a transport system. With regard to migration, the individual systems assume the following functions:

Three-Stage Architecture

1. **Development system**
   In the development system, you configure New G/L Development of BAPIs or your own programs also occurs in this system.

2. **Quality assurance system**
   The quality assurance system is a copy of the production system at time X; that is, representative master and transaction data is available. Additionally, the new configuration and programming is transported from the test system to the quality assurance system. So, in principle, this system is suitable for test migrations to New G/L.

> **SAP's Recommendation: Set Up Your Own Test System**   **[+]**
>
> However, SAP recommends setting up your own independent test system for this purpose. Particularly if you need to test follow-on processes after the migration for an active New G/L, it is worthwhile to have a test system independent of the actual test system.

3. **Production system**
   In the production system, you can access the configuration only to a very limited extent. Only when the last test migration has been completed successfully should you change to the live operation.

During the migration project, you must ensure that the Customizing for New G/L Accounting has no negative effects on your current day-to-day activities. You must prevent an "accidental activation" by all means. If you use a scenario with document splitting, it is necessary and useful to transport the configuration (without activating New G/L) before the migration to the production system. Only under these conditions can validation and logging of document splitting rules be performed. An identical procedure needs to be considered for the scenario *migration from accounts approach to ledger approach.*

6.4.4 Remote Service Session for Scenario Validation

Valid scenario   The first remote service session takes place at the beginning of the migration project. It validates the migration scenario, which is identified in advance of the project via a questionnaire and is commissioned by the customer or partner. We examine whether the migration scenario is suitable for the configuration of the system and for the purpose of activating New G/L. Relatedly, a migration-related system analysis is performed for the dataset and configuration. Application-specific checks are also performed, depending on the migration scenario. At this time, the Customizing of New G/L is not a prerequisite. The service session is run according to the procedure described in the following section.

6.4.5 Remote Service Session for Test Validation

Data quality   The second service session takes place after one of the last test migrations and validates the migrated test data. Technical plausibility checks are performed in the migrated test data, as well as application-specific compatibility checks with regard to the migration scenario. Business-related checks, such as validations of segment-reporting structure according to IFRS, must be done by the customer or partner as part of the user testing after the test migrations. The session should take place after a test migration that delivers valid results, but it also must not occur too close to the production migration, so that there still will be time to clear up any new problems that arise. This session is also performed according to the procedure described next.

6.4.6 Delivery of Service Sessions

Overall process of the service sessions   The service sessions are performed by a Migration Back Office (BO) especially set up for this purpose. For the service sessions, an employee in the back office logs onto his or her SAP ERP production system or into a current copy of it (scenario validation) or into the migration test system (test validation), extracts data, and then loads it into SAP systems, where it is analyzed and evaluated. The employee then launches test programs for the evaluation. These programs will be explained in detail later. The results are summarized in a final report that will be made available to you. After the service sessions, a so-called feedback session takes place, where you can discuss the report results with the back-office employee. This exchange may reveal the need for an additional consulting session, which can be directed toward the local SAP subsidiary. This applies in particular to business questions regarding the design and Customizing of New G/L or cleaning up any data inconsistencies in the system's source data.

Figure 6.10 shows the timing of service session delivery within the migration project.

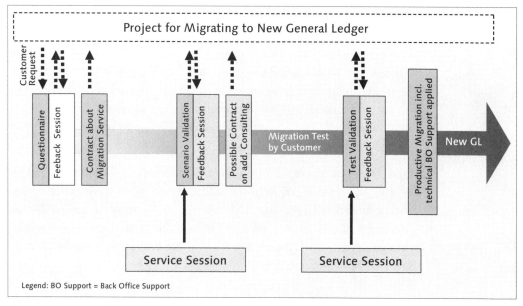

Figure 6.10 Timing of the Service Sessions

In addition to supplying the service sessions, the Migration Back Office offers the following support during the migration project:

▶ Support for test migrations during normal office hours

▶ 24/7 support during production migration on weekends

This support relates exclusively to technical problems during the migrations, both in tests and during the production migration.

[!]

Support for the Production Weekend
Support for the production weekend can be guaranteed only if SAP receives adequate advance notice of the migration. Please refer to the information provided in SAP Note 1014369.

6.4.7 Booking the Service

You can send queries about the migration service by e-mailing *NewGL-Migration@sap.com* or by sending a message under the OSS component, FI-GL-MIG-BO. SAP also plans to include the migration service in the SAP service catalog under *http://www.service.sap.com/servicecatalog*. You also can obtain price information from this site. Alternatively, please contact your local SAP subsidiary. Following your query, you will receive a questionnaire from Migration Back Office in order to establish your migration scenario. Fill out the questionnaire and return it to the Migration Back Office, and you will receive an offer based on the information you have provided.

Once the offer is accepted, you are provided with the Migration Cockpit on the SAP Service Marketplace, and the Migration Back Office agrees appointments with you for the service sessions. You can find additional information, such as presentation documentation on the service, a migration guide, as well as a questionnaire on the SAP Service Marketplace at *http://service.sap.com/GLMIG*.

6.5 Migration Scenarios

Migrations primarily involve moving existing data. For example, if you want an existing classic profit center accounting to be mapped in New G/L in the future, data must be copied from table GLPCT into the new totals table FAGLFLEXT. Standardized methods and program packages therefore must be delivered with the scenarios created by SAP in order to provide secure and effective support for the migration within a project.

This section differentiates between the terms *service-based* and *project-based* migration and introduces you to the scenarios of service-based migration.

6.5.1 Overview of the Scenarios

In real life, there is a wide variety of requirements for a migration. We must therefore distinguish between two different approaches:

► Service-based migration
► Project-based migration

We choose service-based migration if predefined scenarios are used within a customer project. In all cases, data is copied from previously existing applications. Various scenarios are covered, each having an increasing degree of complexity:

Service-based migration

► **Scenario 1**
Merging of FI ledgers

► **Scenario 2**
Scenario 1 + profit center and/or special ledger

► **Scenario 3**
Scenario 2 + introduction of document splitting

► **Scenario 4**
Scenario 2 + switch from accounts approach to ledger approach

► **Scenario 5**
Scenario 3 + switch from accounts approach to ledger approach

► **Scenario 6**
Retroactive implementation of document splitting in New G/L

► **Scenario 7**
Retroactive implementation of the ledger approach in New G/L

These scenarios are each offered at a fixed price by the migration service, depending on the degree of complexity and the number of production clients. The content of the individual scenarios will be described in more detail in the following sections.

A migration is described as being project-based if none of the standard scenarios covers 100 % of the requirements. In these cases, the migration programs can be used; however, additional programming is required in the course of a consultants' solution. For example, the basic introduction of profit center accounting is not a service-based migration. In this case,

Project-based migration

Scenario 2 or 3 will be used, but, because there are no initial values from the classic profit center calculation, additional manual or automatic activities would be required. Another example of a project-based migration is a plan to map your parallel accounting with the Special Ledger (FI-SL) and switch to the ledger approach in New G/L. There is no scenario defined by SAP for this case. A migration to New G/L is certainly technically possible, though with programs that are developed individually within a customer project.

After differentiating between individual customer/project-based migration and standardized/service-based migration, let's look at the content of the scenarios offered in more detail.

6.5.2 Scenario 1

Possible data sources ledger 00, 0F, 09

In Scenario 1, various FI books are merged in New G/L. Primarily, this involves the migration of three possible data sources into New G/L:

▶ Table GLT0 of the classic General Ledger (Ledger 00) is migrated. As a result, the business area may be available for evaluations in New G/L accounting.

▶ Table GLFUNCT of the cost of sales book (Ledger 0F) is migrated. As a result, the functional area may be available for evaluations in New G/L accounting.

▶ Table GLT3 of the consolidation preparation book (Ledger 09) is migrated. In this way the company, trading partner and transaction type may be available for valuations.

You can decide for each account from what data source the new totals table FAGLFLEXT and the leading ledger 0L should be built. It may be useful to copy P&L accounts from the source ledger 8A including the profit center. Values for balance sheet accounts are copied from the classic General Ledger, Ledger 00. Specifically, this means that a balance carryforward is made for non-OI-managed accounts prior to the migration date (Phase 0). Individual documents for OI-managed accounts are completely migrated. Documents after the migration date (Phase 1) are posted subsequently as a best practice.

If there are customer-specific FI-SL fields, these are subsequently available in Scenario 1 for valuations at individual item level. If you need valuations at totals level, Scenario 2 is appropriate.

6.5.3 Scenario 2

Scenario 2 offers options in addition to all of the issues covered in Scenario 1. Values relating to customer-specific fields can be copied from special ledgers (FI-SL) into New G/L accounting and are available there for valuations at totals level. Besides an enhancement of the totals table FAGLFLEXT, you can read values for customer-specific characteristics such as REGION, PRODUCT GROUP, and so on from the FI-SL and migrate them.

Customer-specific fields

Table ZZ.... of FI-SL (Ledger XY) is migrated. In this way, customer-specific fields are available for valuations.

You should note that this procedure does not involve transfer of parallel ledgers or values for parallel accounting.

[!]

Additional Currencies in FI-SL

Values can be transferred only if Special Ledger (FI-SL) is led in compliance with General Ledger. For example, you cannot migrate data in parallel currency fields that exist in FI-SL but are not available in the original document. In such a case, if the data is still relevant, you must keep Special Ledger after the successful migration.

Also provided in Scenario 2 is the transfer of the classic profit center accounting into New G/L. Table GLPCT of profit center accounting (Ledger 8A) is migrated. In this way, the fields PROFIT CENTER and PARTNER PROFIT CENTER are available for valuations. In addition to the profit center accounting in New G/L, the new SEGMENT field can be used. Values are derived for a migration from the relevant master record of the profit center accounting. If this rule does not apply in your case, an alternative solution is possible by derivation using a Business Add-In (BAdI). However, programming and implementation is not a component of service-based migration.

Profit center accounting

6.5.4 Scenario 3

Document
Online Split

Scenario 3 uses the function of document splitting. In New G/L, the document split allows balance sheet evaluations for fields such as PROFIT CENTER, BUSINESS AREA, or SEGMENT, as well as customer-specific fields. Even before a migration, having a validation running in the background will help identify problematic transactions. The future function can be checked in the classic General Ledger, thereby improving the data quality. During a subsequent data transfer, you must be able to augment every individual document to be copied with information for document splitting.

6.5.5 Scenarios 4 and 5

Parallel accounting

In addition to Scenario 2, Scenario 4 also contains a conversion from the accounts approach to the ledger approach in New G/L. As explained in Chapter 4, Parallel Accounting—IFRS on the Advance, both storage locations are classified as equal; nevertheless, there are customers who want to convert their existing architecture. Scenario 5 comprises Scenario 4 and the additional document-splitting function.

[+]

Restrictions in the Context of SAP Treasury

For Scenarios 4 and 5, there is currently no standard solution for migrating the Treasury components CFM and CML. Please consult SAP directly in the blueprint phase.

Accounts approach

The basis of the accounts approach includes the use of absolute posting values (no delta method), for which there are two types of posting transactions:

► Valuation variances are not posted to joint accounts (0xxxxx).

► Valuations occur in a separate account range (1xxxxx or 2xxxxx) respectively.

Migration Scenarios 4 and 5 follow the approach that all joint accounts are posted as usual. Without a Special Ledger group, these values are identical for all valuation areas in a ledger approach. During Phase 1 of the migration project, however, you must provide valuation postings and standardizing entries with information on a target ledger. This is done, for example, using Transaction FB01L or the automatic valuation program, RAPERP2000. Postings that don't include the leading ledger must additionally be provided with a separate new document number interval.

To continue to report monthly and quarterly figures during the transition period in the current fiscal year, you must still use own account ranges for variances.

Own account ranges are retained initially

> **Workaround—Use Own Account Reports**
>
> If these report requirements don't exist in your project, you have the option of not posting the valuation variances in migration Phase 1 and implementing them later on in the active General Ledger accounting in Phase 2.

[+]

6.5.6 Scenario 6

In Scenario 6, New G/L is already used in production, and the function of document splitting is reimplemented retroactively. A change in the existing document splitting is not covered with this scenario. If these prerequisites exist, the technical conditions described in SAP Note 1086181 must be met additionally.

6.5.7 Scenario 7

Scenario 7 is also based on New G/L that is used in production. In this scenario, the accounts approach is to be replaced by a ledger approach for parallel accounting. To map various accounting principles, enhancement by non-leading ledgers must be carried out.

6.5.8 Looking Ahead

You can see that the complexity increases with each scenario. In the early days of the migration at the beginning of 2007, the Migration Back Office received many queries about Scenarios 1 and 2. Sometimes the document splitting with Scenario 3 was also queried. During this time, there were an unexpectedly low number of queries about Scenarios 4 and 5.

Development

Today, this must be considered in a more differentiated manner. According to a survey of the Internet platform, *http://www.fico-forum.de*, which was performed in March 2009, there is a wide need for migration scenarios (see Figure 6.11). The additional scenarios, which require an already active General Ledger that is used in production, attend upon the ever-growing group of customers who already use New G/L.

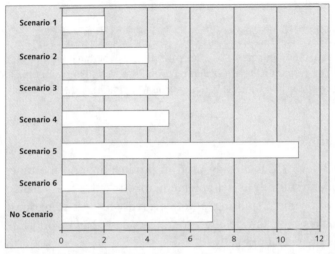

Figure 6.11 Survey of www.fico-forum.de

Any other scenario that differs from those mentioned above is considered a project solution. Further standardized scenarios are conceivable, but are not being focused on or planned at present. An example would be a migration of FI-SL into New G/L or a migration from New G/L into New G/L. Demand from SAP customers will have the most important influence on the services offered by SAP.

6.6 Migration Cockpit

Process trees and migration programs

As well as the various scenarios, the Migration Cockpit is a key element of scenario-based migration. It is provided to you as part of the SAP General Ledger Migration Services, which must be paid for. It contains predefined, scenario-dependent process trees and migration programs (see Section 6.4.2, Migration Cockpit). If you have opted for scenarios 1 or 2, for example, activities relating to document splitting in the Migration Cockpit are hidden. This procedure helps in structuring all of a project's necessary activities in a logical sequence. The monitor also allows you to get status information and view the project progress at a glance. Furthermore, in a later review you can completely and comprehensively manage logs, attachments, and notes.

6.6.1 Overview

In Customizing for New G/L you will find a separate folder for the migration by following the menu path: FINANCIAL ACCOUNTING (NEW) • GENERAL LEDGER ACCOUNTING (NEW) • PREPARATION FOR PRODUCTIVE START • MIGRATION OF EXISTING DATA. Figure 6.12 shows that a number of functions are already delivered in the standard system. With ERP 2004, this is the case as of Support Package 10.

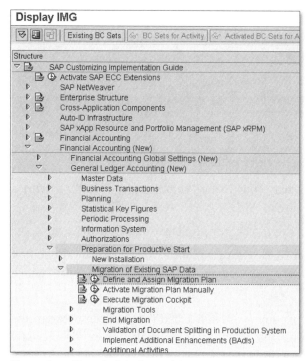

Figure 6.12 Menu Path in Customizing

In the past, without an authorized registration, the notification MIGRA-
TION INTO NEW G/L NOT ALLOWED was displayed.

As of SAP ERP 2004 Support Package 13 or SAP ERP 6.0, most of these
migration programs are completely locked. Figure 6.13 shows that you
are immediately asked for a license key and referred to the important
SAP Note 812919.

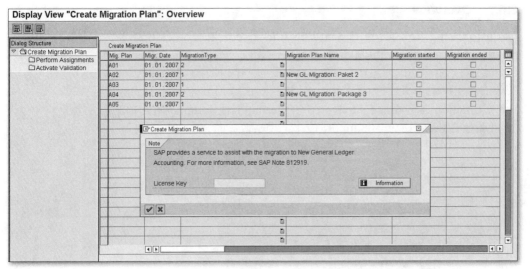

Figure 6.13   License Key—SAP Note 812919

SAP Note 812919   SAP Note 812919 covers three main issues:

- ▶ SAP recommends that you do not combine the migration with a
  technical upgrade to SAP ERP.

- ▶ The migration is a sub-project for implementing New G/L.

- ▶ The SAP Migration Back Office supports you during the migration
  through an obligatory SAP General Ledger Migration Service, which
  carries a fee.

License key   Since March 2007, customers are still asked for the license key in the
Customizing; however, the actual migration takes place via the new
Migration Cockpit. As a result, SAP will no longer issue a license key but
will provide the Migration Cockpit following a contractual agreement on
the use of the New G/L Migration service.

Technical Infrastructure

To be able to work with the Cockpit, a certain technical infrastructure is required in advance. Check in the SAP application menu path: SYSTEM • STATUS • COMPONENTS (see Figure 6.14) to see whether the basic component DMIS with the latest Support Package version is available. You may already have this add-on installed because it is a technical component of other SAP products such as Test Data Migration Server. If you do not yet have the DMIS, you will find the software in the SAP Service Marketplace (*http://service.sap.com*) and an installation guide in SAP Note 970531.

Basic component DMIS

ERECRUIT	600	0006	SAPK · 6000¢	E-Recruiting
ECC-DIMP	600	0006	SAPK · 6000¢	DIMP
DMIS	2006_1_700	0002	SAPK · 6170;	DMIS 2006_1_700 : Add-On Installation
CPRXRPM	400	0000	·	CPRXRPM 400 Upgrade: Meta-Commandfile (C
IS-UT	600	0006	SAPK · 6000¢	SAP Utilities/Telecommunication
WFMCORE	200	0002	SAPK · 2000;	WFMCORE 200 Upgrade: Meta-Commandfile (
LSOFE	600	0006	SAPK · 6000¢	SAP Learning Solution Front-End
SLL-LEG	7.00	0000	·	SLL-LEG 700 : Add-On Supplement

Figure 6.14 Overview of Add-Ons

The DMIS basis provides an initially content-free framework for the Migration Cockpit. Subsequently, importing the second add-on NMI_CONT delivers content in the form of process trees and migration programs.

Operation

If all of the technical prerequisites have been met, you can start the Migration Cockpit using Transaction CNV_MBT_NGLM. Because of the transaction's long name and the fact that the Migration Cockpit is frequently used, it is recommended that you store the transaction in your personal favorites.

Transaction CNV_MBT_NGLM

Once you have started the Migration Cockpit, you will see a user-related overview of the migration projects (see Figure 6.15). In this example, no project has been created or assigned yet for the user New_GL.

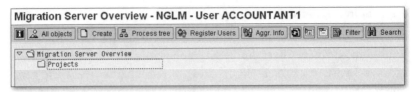

Figure 6.15   Project Overview

When you create a new project, it is defined within a client with the specified type NGLM (New GL Migration; see Figure 6.16).

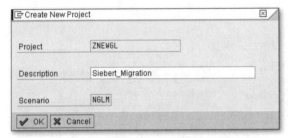

Figure 6.16   New Project

Packages/ Migration plan

A project can contain several packages. Subsequently, a package will be uniquely assigned to a migration plan. This organizational object appears several times and must be chosen with care. In principle, you can assign several company codes to a package /migration plan provided that these have identical fiscal year variants and use the same migration scenario.

[+]

Inactive Company Codes

You don't need to take into account inactive company codes for the migration. This type of company code is used only for information purposes for data archiving. An inactive company code exists if no open items, balance carryforwards, or new FI documents are present at the beginning of the current fiscal year.

One active company code per package

However, it is conceivable that each (active) company code may be reflected individually in a package/migration plan. This increases flexibility when you reset the test data that is produced for each migration plan.

Figure 6.17 shows two packages/migration plans that are assigned to user SIEBERTJO. You can see that this is technically necessary because you are working with two different migration scenarios.

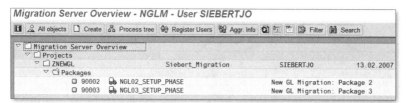

Figure 6.17 Migration Plan

When you create a new package/migration plan, the system firsts asks you what scenario you want to use. The process tree is built on this basis. Figure 6.18 shows this tree being created. Scenario

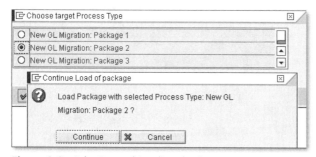

Figure 6.18 Selecting and Loading the Scenario

The Migration Cockpit shown in Figure 6.19 includes the following six milestones/project phases: Milestones project phases

- Setup phase
- Checkup phase
- Preparation phase

383

▶ Migration phase

▶ Validation phase

▶ Activation phase

Moreover, it includes other tools that support the project, for example, by automatically documenting every single step with time stamps and users.

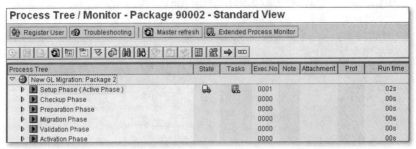

Figure 6.19 Phases in the Migration Cockpit

Relating phases 0, 1, and 2 of the migration project to the phases of the Migration Cockpit results in the following matrix (see Table 6.2).

Migration Cockpit	Project Phase 0	Project Phase 1	Project Phase 2
Setup phase	X	X	
Checkup phase	X	X	
Preparation phase		X	
Migration phase		X	
Validation phase		X	
Activation phase			X

Table 6.2 Overview of the Milestones/Project Phases in the Migration Cockpit

SAP_NGLM_
MASTER role

Users registered only for the project can work with the relevant migration plan. A separate role SAP_NGLM_MASTER is stored for this task in the authorization concept. Additional persons can be assigned with the Register User button. Users with the role SAP_ALL always have access to all transactions and thus also to the Migration Cockpit, as well as all migration plans created. However, there should be few, if any, SAP_ALL users.

Activities

The process trees of the individual phases are arranged differently depending on the scenario. Figure 6.20 illustrates two different migration scenarios (❶ and ❷). Additional activities for document splitting are necessary at certain useful times and thus lengthen the process tree shown in ❷.

Different process trees

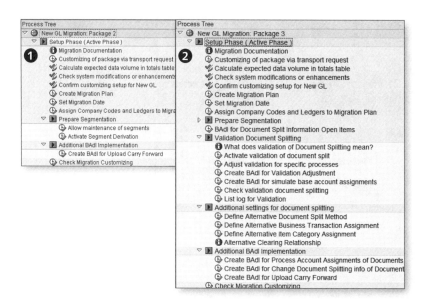

Figure 6.20 Different Process Trees

Generally, the activities can be divided into three categories:

- Manual confirmations
- Transactions
- Check programs

Manual confirmations are found most frequently in the first phases. For instance, in one of the first steps a question is asked about the future data volume in the FAGLFLEXT. The corresponding help text outlines the

Manual confirmation

problems by referring you to SAP Note 820495. This results in manual checking of the architecture (see Section 2.2, Scenarios) and calculation of the data volume.

External documents can be stored in the Migration Cockpit (see Figure 6.21).

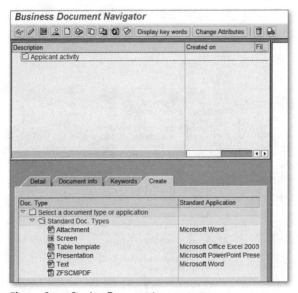

Figure 6.21 Storing Documents

The activity is then confirmed manually (see Figure 6.22).

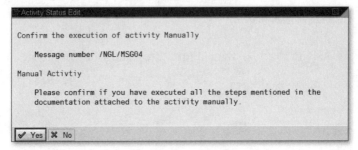

Figure 6.22 Manual Confirmation

The transactions stored in the process tree are required, for example, to maintain the migration date in the system or post a balance carryforward.

Transactions

Many activities are based on check programs that check the consistency of the current Customizing and the dataset. For example, if an update of the new SEGMENT field is defined for the configuration of New G/L, you also need to define at least one master record for segments in Customizing. The system also checks whether the new field can be derived from all profit centers.

Check programs

The sequence of the manual confirmations, transactions, and check programs is not random. Because of dependencies, we differentiate between *optional* and *obligatory* steps. The Migration Process Monitor (see Figure 6.23) shows all processed mandatory activities for the relevant phase.

Migration Process Monitor

Package : 90003

Phase : Setup Phase

Phase overview

Node Text	State	%	Tasks	Exec.No.	Prot	Start date	Start time	End date	End time	Run time
Calculate expected data volume in totals table	CCO	100		1		14.02.2007	16:14:33	14.02.2007	16:14:34	01s
Check system modifications or enhancements	CCO	100		1		14.02.2007	16:18:26	14.02.2007	16:18:27	01s
Confirm customizing setup for New GL	CCO	100		1		14.02.2007	16:18:32	14.02.2007	16:18:33	01s
Create Migration Plan	CCO	100		1		14.02.2007	16:18:38	14.02.2007	16:18:39	01s
Set Migration Date	CXO	100		1		14.02.2007	16:19:03	14.02.2007	16:19:04	01s
Assign Company Codes and Ledgers to Migration Plan	CCO	100		1		14.02.2007	16:19:44	14.02.2007	16:19:45	01s
BAdI for Document Split Information Open Items	CCO	100		1		14.02.2007	16:49:17	14.02.2007	16:49:18	01s
Activate validation of document split	CCO	100		1		14.02.2007	16:30:27	14.02.2007	16:30:28	01s
Adjust validation for specific processes	CCO	100		1		14.02.2007	16:31:55	14.02.2007	16:31:56	01s
Create BAdI for Validation Adjustment	CCO	100		1		14.02.2007	16:32:14	14.02.2007	16:32:15	01s
Create BAdI for simulate base account assignments	CCO	100		1		14.02.2007	16:32:25	14.02.2007	16:32:26	01s
Check validation document splitting	CCO	100		1		14.02.2007	16:32:36	14.02.2007	16:32:37	01s
Check Migration Customizing	CXO	100		3		14.02.2007	16:49:23	14.02.2007	16:49:24	01s
Creation of package	CCO	100		1		14.02.2007	16:13:35	14.02.2007	16:13:38	03s

Figure 6.23 Migration Process Monitor

Some activities can be repeated as often as you like; others are possible only at a particular time. The icon highlighted in the top left of Figure 6.24 shows the following interdependencies:

▸ Is there a predecessor or successor relationship?

▸ Is a repeat run possible?

Figure 6.24 shows that optional steps are not joined to a status management.

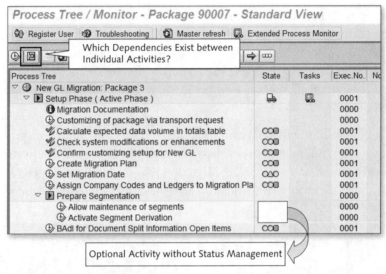

Figure 6.24 Properties of the Activities

Now that you have learned the basics of using the Migration Cockpit, let's look at the individual milestones and project phases in more detail.

6.6.2 Setup Phase

The content shown relates to Migration Scenario 3, a migration service that comprises document splitting. Figure 6.25 provides an overview of all activities in the setup phase. The next phase cannot start until all mandatory activities have been run correctly.

Customizing via Transport Request

First activity We begin with the first activity: package Customizing via transport request. This optional operation depends on the design of your system landscape. If you have a typical environment with development, quality assurance, and production systems, all these systems require Customizing settings and developments must be transported for BAdIs. If the Migration Cockpit is executed when the system goes live in the production system, the activity is no longer required.

Figure 6.25 Overview of the Setup Phase

Manual Confirmations

The three following steps must be confirmed manually:

1. **Data volume**

   In the context of SAP Note 820495, you need to answer the question about data volume. If you can foresee that the number of data-sets in the FAGLFLEXT totals table may be too high, a separate totals table may be required for each defined ledger. You can also question whether all fields to be copied are really needed in New G/L for valuations.

2. **Modifications**

   Another important aspect involves modifications/extensions and their effects in the context of New G/L. Are they still needed, in principle? What test methods will subsequently allow you to ensure that they function correctly?

3. **Target concept completed**

   In confirming the configuration of New G/L, you declare the individual arrangement to be completed. The target concept is finished and stored in the system.

389

The data volume, and consequently the number of totals records, have major impacts on the performance of evaluations. A previous version of the Migration Cockpit required only a simple manual confirmation. Now an analysis program supports you to give the correct answer to this question.

This new analysis program is to be described based on an example. The first step shows a selection screen (see Figure 6.26) that starts with document row table BSEG as the analysis focus. In addition to the selections already made here, fiscal year 2009 and company code AA20, there are also alternatives.

If you already use a profit center accounting or Special Ledger approach and the data in the new totals table that exists there will be very similar in New G/L, you can consult this data.

[+] **Profit Center and Segment**

Usually, the Segment characteristic derives from the Profit Center characteristic. But the update of the segment doesn't increase the data volume.

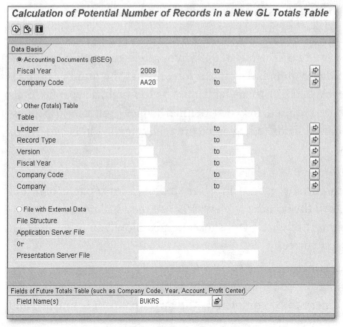

Figure 6.26 Calculation of the Potential Number of Records

One of the next steps is to define the fields of the future totals tables in the selection screen. An input field with the option for multiple selection (icon) is available. After you've activated this field, the system displays the selection of single values, as illustrated in Figure 6.27.

Defining fields of the totals table

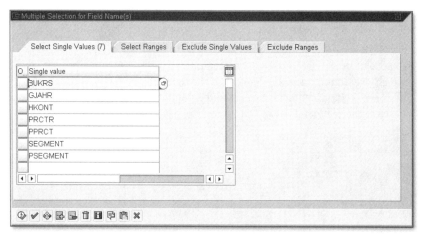

Figure 6.27 Selecting Characteristics

In this example, you selected the characteristics COMPANY CODE, FISCAL YEAR, PROFIT CENTER, PARTNER PROFIT CENTER, SEGMENT, and PARTNER SEGMENT. If you run the analysis report by pressing the F8 key, the system takes you to a results overview similar to the one shown in Figure 6.28.

Run analysis report

Result of the Analysis of the Table BSEG (24.03.2009) :
No. Calculated Totals Records: 9

Fld	Description	Number of Different Values
HKONT	G/L	9
BUKRS	Company Code	1
GJAHR	Fiscal Year	1
PRCTR	Profit Center	1
PPRCT	Partner PC	1
SEGMENT	Segment	1
PSEGMENT	Partner Segment	1

Figure 6.28 Analysis Report of Table BSEG

The sample data is far too low due to the test system and so cannot be compared with normal accounting. Nevertheless, you can assess how many totals records you can expect per fiscal year for your largest company code.

[+]

Determining the Number of Totals Records

A general formula for determining totals records does not exist. For example, multiplying the characteristics COMPANY CODE, FISCAL YEAR, PROFIT CENTER, PARTNER PROFIT CENTER, SEGMENT, and PARTNER SEGMENT results in a value that is far too high and therefore in an unrealistic result.

One solution is to find out which accounts/account groups are posted with which characteristics. Experience has shown that not every account posts with every profit center or business area definition. Figure 6.28 is intended to make the context clear.

Account	Amount	Business Area	Profit Center
4711	EUR 1.00	A	1
4711	EUR 2.00	A	2
4711	EUR 3.00	B	2
0815	EUR 4.00	A	1
0815	EUR 5.00	A	1

Table 6.3 Document Row Table BSEG

These five document rows of table BSEG generate the following entries in the totals tables (see Tables 6.4, 6.5, and 6.6).

Account	Amount	Business Area
4711	EUR 3.00	A
4711	EUR 3.00	B
0815	EUR 9.00	A

Table 6.4 Classic General Ledger—GLT0

Account	Amount	Profit Center
4711	EUR 1.00	1
4711	EUR 5.00	2
0815	EUR 9.00	1

Table 6.5 Classic Profit Center Accounting—GLPCT

Account	Amount	Business Area	Profit Center
4711	EUR 1.00	A	1
4711	EUR 2.00	A	2
4711	EUR 3.00	B	3
0815	EUR 9.00	A	1

Table 6.6 New General Ledger—FAGLFLEXT

If you can foresee that the number of datasets in the FAGLFLEXT totals table may be too high, a separate totals table may be required for each defined ledger. You could also question whether all fields to be copied are really needed in New G/L for valuations.

If the architecture is assessed conclusively with the number of totals records to be expected, you manually confirm and document this in the Migration Cockpit.

Final confirmation

Migration Plan

Once these steps of manual confirmation are completed, the migration plan will be stored technically. In Figure 6.29, the package 90020 is uniquely assigned to migration plan A12, and a migration date is maintained. In each case, the system will propose the first day of the fiscal year variants configured in the system—in Figure 6.29 this date is 01/01/2009.

All data that is posted before this date (Phase 0) is copied only as a balance carryforward. OI-managed customers constitute an exception to this. As of this date (Phase 1), the complete posting data is posted and thus assembled in the tables of New G/L accounting.

Maintaining the migration date

If you choose the start of the current year as your migration date, you will get an amber traffic light in the status bar. This should make it clear that when you are already well into the fiscal year, it may be useful to push the migration date further into the future. If you choose the current fiscal year plus one as your migration date, the status bar shows a green traffic light.

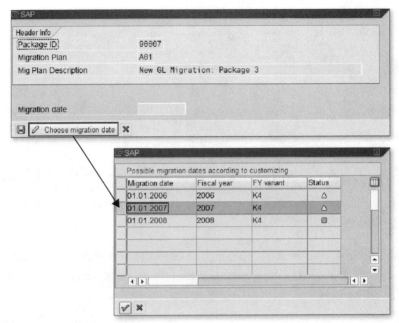

Figure 6.29 Defining Migration Plan and Specifying Migration Date

Assigning Company Codes

The next activity is the assigning of the company codes and ledgers to the migration plan (see Figure 6.30). Here you can assign only company codes whose fiscal year variant is identical to that of the chosen migration date (in this example, this is the fiscal year variant with the migration date 01/01/2009). Furthermore, a company code cannot be included in several migration plans.

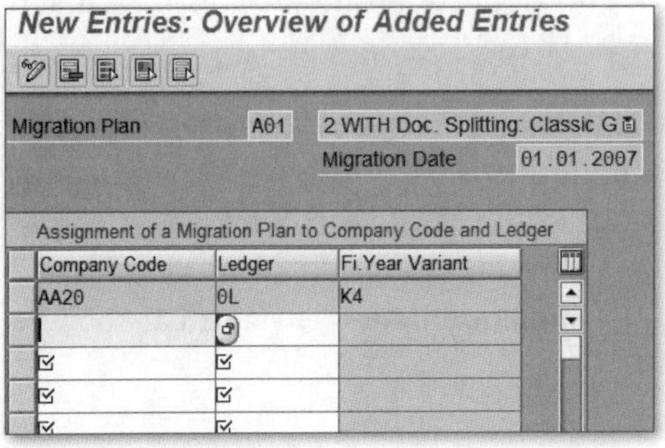

Figure 6.30 Assigning Company Codes, Migration Plan

Assigning the Source Ledgers

One special feature of scenarios 4 and 5 is migrating the previous accounts approach to a ledger approach of New G/L. This requires an assignment of the individual account areas to the respective ledger groups. Accounts within a company code, source ledger, and currency code are assigned to the target ledger, or other accounts are excluded explicitly. Figure 6.31 illustrates the target ledger 0L, for which you must assign the accounts. The worklist in the upper part of the screen must be processed completely. This worklist forms the basis for a subsequent data transfer of the respective local accounting rules (for instance, IFRS and local GAAP).

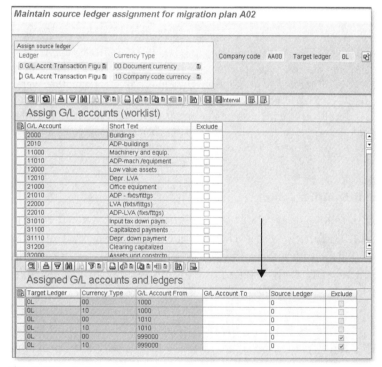

Figure 6.31 Assigning Accounts

Segment

An optional step is then available in which settings can be made for the new SEGMENT field. This activity will be relevant only if you want to use the characteristic in New G/L and subsequently generate information

Deriving the profit center/segment

as part of the migration. If you have segment derivation activated (see Figure 6.32), you can use the standard process using the profit center derivation even prior to activation of New G/L.

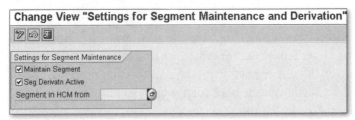

Figure 6.32 Preparing the Segment Maintenance

Sample Presentation of a Migration

1/1/2009 is set as the migration date. The data transfer into New G/L is to occur following the end of the previous fiscal year on the weekend beginning on 3/24/2009. If the segment derivation is active, all documents that were posted between 01/01 and 03/24 contain a segment based on the profit center at the document level. These documents from Phase 1 are subsequently posted for New G/L, which is why the SEGMENT characteristic is subsequently available to you at the totals record level for valuations.

Document Splitting—BAdI

Derivation for balance carryforwards and open items

An activity follows that relates specially to Scenario 3 with the Document Splitting function. In each case, you will need a BAdI in order to enrich balance carryforwards (FAGL_UPLOAD_CF) and documents (FAGL_MIGR_SUBST) from Phase 0 with information. In our example, New G/L is used with document splitting in order to create a separate balance sheet for the SEGMENT field. The ability to subsequently enhance documents is thus a mandatory activity for later subsequent steps. This ability cannot be standardized, which is why BAdI programming becomes necessary.

Figure 6.33 shows an example of balance carryforwards. Similar BAdI programming has already been discussed in Chapter 2, Design and Features of the Ledgers. A fundamental derivation of the segment (FAGL_DERIVE_SEGMENT) was also described there.

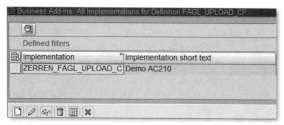

Figure 6.33 Assigning the BAdI—Technical Name and Description

Figure 6.34 provides additional fundamental information about the BAdI. In particular you should note the reference to the source code IF_EX_FAGL_UPLOAD_CF.

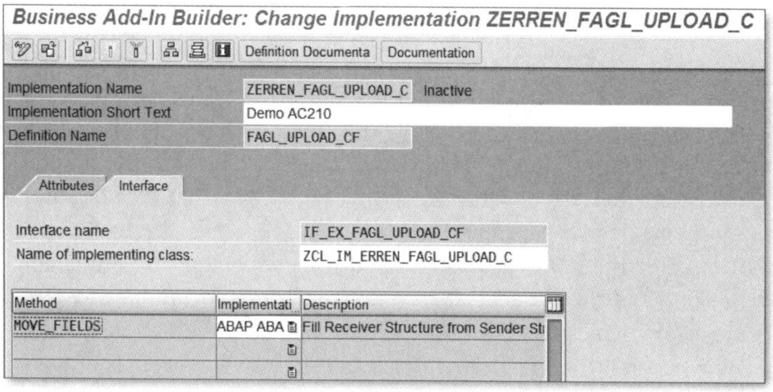

Figure 6.34 Assigning BAdI—Attributes

Figure 6.35 shows a sample program. A derivation of field information can be stored here for each customer.

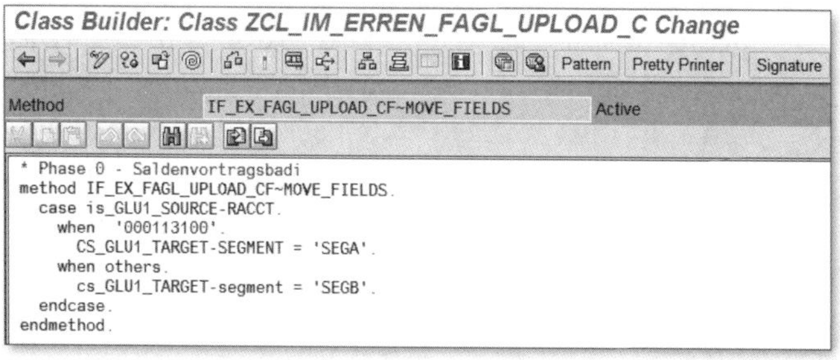

Figure 6.35 Assigning BAdI—Source Code

A certain blurring will always remain, despite flexible programming. If singular assigning was always used in the past, not all information can be generated for documents of Phase 0, that is, the balance carryforward and open items prior to the migration date.

This blurring can be kept to a minimum through a programmed arrangement of rules, for instance, by copying the segment with the greatest posting amount into the singular rows. You also could take a pragmatic approach by starting with a default value for the new fields to be balanced. Over time, the open items from Phase 0 will cancel each other out. The new split logic is already applied in the migration to documents from Phase 1, and these are available with the complete information.

[Ex]

The Given Data Quality Can be Improved Only Partly

Your migration date is 1/1/2010. On 12/24/2009, a receivable was posted in the amount of EUR 10,000.00 with the revenue rows EUR 8,000 in profit center A, and EUR 2,000 in profit center B. This document is still open at the migration time of 3/24/2010. The BAdI (FAGL_MIGR_SUBST) can derive the new accounting characteristic, SEGMENT, from the information profit center and save it in the respective revenue rows. This is possible because two document rows exist for the revenue postings, both of which can be enriched. For the receivable and tax, if necessary, there is only one document row and thus one piece of segment information. The complete information on the respective new segment would require two line items, however. The BAdI cannot change this requirement. These documents remain blurred because only one feature of the segment can be updated in the line item "receivables and tax."

Document Splitting—Validation

To ensure that the document-splitting function can work as smoothly as possible within the migration, we advise using the validation. A check of the future document splitting running in the background helps identify problematic transactions in advance. The future Document Splitting function can thus be simulated in the classic General Ledger. Figure 6.36 shows the various time-dependent validation options.

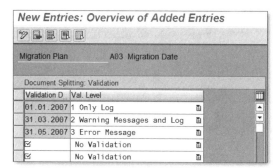

Figure 6.36 Activation

Sample Data Migration with Active Document Splitting [Ex]

Your migration date is 1/1/2010. Documents that are posted as of this time in the classic General Ledger again undergo the complete posting logic as Phase 1 data before they are updated in New G/L.

During a later data transfer, each document to be copied is enriched for document splitting. With validation active as of 1/1/2010, problematic transactions are disclosed in a log. As of 3/31/2010, the system already penalizes these documents with a warning notification (see Figure 6.37) in the classic General Ledger. Roughly one month prior to the actual migration, the "real thing" is rehearsed with an error message.

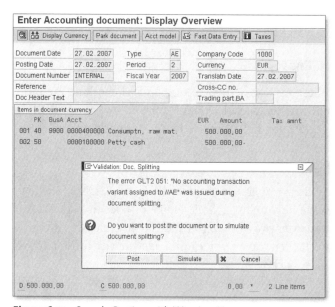

Figure 6.37 Sample Posting with Warning Message

With this approach, certain transactions can initially be omitted (see Figure 6.38). This is useful if a clarification is initiated for certain issues and if the log is to be arranged more clearly. This situation could occur if the interface to the HR/HCM system still has to be adjusted or the material master records have not yet been maintained.

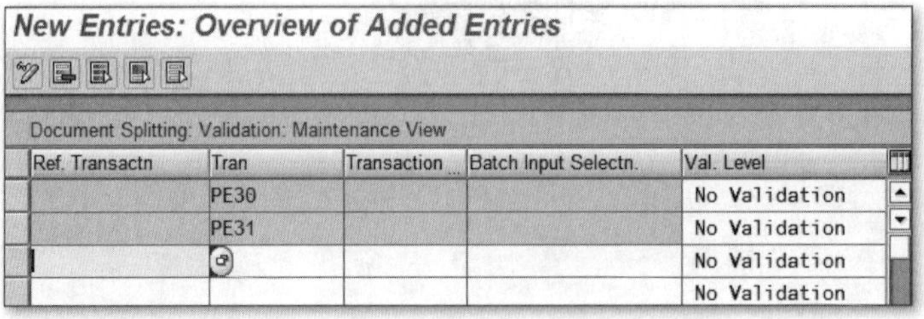

Figure 6.38 Adjusting Validation for Special Processes

Enhancing data quality

The validation that is available from SAP ERP 2005 onwards allows you to test Customizing of document splitting under real conditions and to enhance the data quality of the documents to be copied. Further document enrichment options will later be discussed in the migration phase (see Section 6.6.5).

The setup phase ends once you have successfully checked the migration Customizing. You cannot continue to work in the checkup phase until this milestone has been successfully completed.

6.6.3 Checkup Phase

Configuration

After the setup phase has focused on setting up and checking the basic migration Customizing, the checkup phase concentrates on configuring New G/L. Figure 6.39 shows all of the activities in this context.

Is New G/L Still Inactive?

Totals table FAGLFLEXT is empty

In the first step, a check program ensures that New G/L is still inactive. This ensures that the new totals table FAGLFLEXT does not yet contain any entries. Transactions are updated in the classic tables as before. If this basic prerequisite is not met, you cannot execute any further activities in the Migration Cockpit.

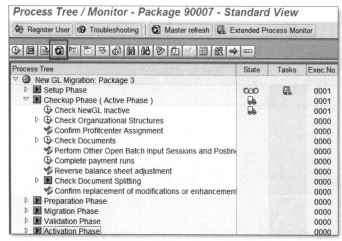

Figure 6.39 Overview of the Checkup Phase

Checking the Organizational Objects

The next step comprises a range of check programs at the level of the organizational objects:

- Company
- Company code
- Functional area
- Controlling area
- Business area
- Consolidation
- Segment
- Profit center
- Assigning the profit center to the segment

Figure 6.40 shows the result of such checking.

Check Organizational Structures			
Check Company Code Parameters	⊗○○	0001	
Check Controlling Area	○○□	0001	
Check Business Areas	○△○	0001	
Check Segmentation	⊗○○	0001	
Check Profit Center	○○□	0001	
Check Assignment Profit Center and Segment	⊗○○	0001	

Figure 6.40 Checking the Organizational Structures

"Business area" object

The yellow traffic light with the "business area" object in Figure 6.41 indicates that this scenario is not assigned for New G/L, although there are account assignments with the characteristic in the classic General Ledger. Only a warning appears because it may not necessarily involve an error. There may be a switch in principle from the organizational object "business area" towards the much more flexible entity "profit center."

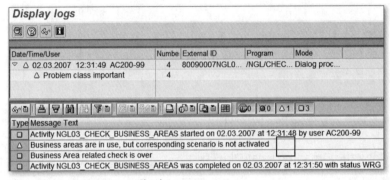

Figure 6.41 Business Area Check Log

"Segment" object

The *red traffic light* indicates an error in the configuration. The message's log explains that there is an active scenario segment, but that no segment information has been defined. This configuration gap can be closed in the section CORPORATE STRUCTURE • DEFINITION • FINANCIAL ACCOUNTING • DEFINE SEGMENT. Figure 6.42 shows the definition of the segments.

Segment	Description
SEG-A	Segment A
SEG-B	Segment B
SEG-C	Segment C

New Entries: Overview of Added Entries

Segments for Segment Reporting

Figure 6.42 Defining Segments

Mass maintenance

Assignments are also missing for profit centers and the segment. With Transaction KE55 you can run a mass maintenance of the profit center master data and store the new SEGMENT characteristic (see Figure 6.43).

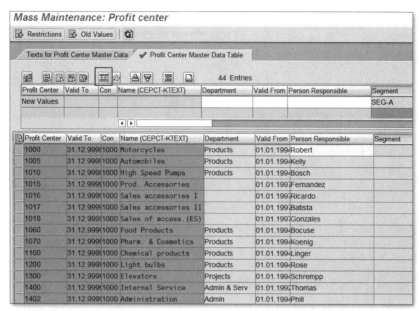

Figure 6.43 Mass Maintenance of the Profit Center

If all organizational objects are assigned green, or at least amber, traffic lights, the obligatory higher-level composite activity is also given a corresponding status.

In the next activity, you confirm the mandatory assignment of the profit center to other data objects such as the "cost center," "internal order," or "material master." You find a complete list by following the Customizing menu path: FINANCIAL ACCOUNTING (NEW) • GENERAL LEDGER ACCOUNTING (NEW) • MASTER DATA • PROFIT CENTER • ASSIGN ACCOUNT ASSIGNMENT OBJECTS TO PROFIT CENTERS. If a segment balance is derived from this object, a simple change after the migration may no longer be possible. In the past, you may have had similar experiences with business-area financial statements. If these are active, you can no longer manually change assignments of business areas and complex fixed assets in FI-AA, for example. If you still need to switch business areas, a transfer posting will take place. Only in this way can a correct divestiture or receipt be documented for each business area.

Mandatory profit center assignment

Once you manually confirm the profit center assignment, two check programs take over to complete an additional step in order to ensure the quality and consistency of the data to be copied.

Archived Documents

Securing data consistency begins by checking for documents archived after the migration date. You see that migration, that is, the subsequent posting of archive documents, is not possible. If you encounter a red traffic light here, open a problem notification for the component FI-GL-MIG. Before you reload the data from the archive into the operational system, note that reload programs for the FI_DOCUMNT archiving object are no longer part of the standard SAP system since the release of Support Package SAPKH50007 (see SAP Note 877439).

Operations for All Company Codes

Consistency check In addition to data quality, a consistency check is run at the level of the "company code" organizational object. The system determines whether you have used postings for all company codes in the past. You must be able to find corresponding company codes in the migration plans. If there are different fiscal year start and finish dates, the activity determines whether there are FI documents for all company codes in the fiscal year of the migration (Phase 1). In this case, you would receive an error message and have to create a customer notification under FI-GL-MIG. Furthermore, the configuration is checked for the document-splitting function. There may be postings for all company codes only if those involved each use the document split or have each deactivated it. There is no mixed solution.

Once the data quality and consistency have been checked at company code level, the next step entails a manual activity. You must confirm that all open batch-input sessions have been performed in full. From this time onward, there may no longer be any batch-input sessions with the following statuses:

- New
- Faulty

- In process

- In the background

- Is being created

Particularly if you use document splitting, the documents contained in the batch input sessions must be completely assigned in the classic General Ledger so that they are then also available for migration. In a separate manual activity this also applies for open payment runs.

Resetting Balance Sheet Adjustments

The next step, the resetting of the balance sheet adjustments, originates in the changed architecture of New G/L. We will therefore look at two aspects more closely in the following pages:

- Balance sheet adjustment

- Foreign currency valuation

In the classic General Ledger you used the SAPF180 program for balance sheet adjustments, for instance, in order to enable a zero balance for the BUSINESS AREA characteristic. Generally, these summary postings are a component of the end-of-month accounts. With New G/L, the subsequent debit technique was replaced by document splitting.

Balance sheet adjustment

In the future, you will no longer be able to execute the SAPF180 program. As a result, the document-splitting technique must be used if you continue to need balance sheets based on business areas. In Phase 1, that is, after the migration date, all documents undergo the document split and allow a zero balance at document level for the BUSINESS AREA characteristic. Summary postings made by the SAPF180 program in Phase 1 in the classic General Ledger must therefore be manually undone using Transaction F.80.

Another aspect of the activity "Undoing the balance sheet adjustments" relates to the changed architecture of the foreign currency conversion. In most cases, a valuation of foreign currency documents is posted at month's end and is then cancelled at the start of the new period.

Foreign currency valuation

However, some countries have general legal conditions forbidding an undoing of the valuation posting in this way and demanding a *delta posting technique*. This was mapped in the classic General Ledger with the so-called BDIFF logic. In New G/L, the architecture is arranged in a differentiated way. Here, the information is stored in valuation areas. The new program for foreign currency valuations exclusively works with the new architecture.

The subject "Foreign currency valuation – delta technique" is problematic because the SAP system cannot produce an error message. This involves a logical breach that can lead in extreme cases to a false valuation of the foreign currencies.

[Ex]

Problem: Foreign Currency Conversion—Delta Technique

A European company buys products at an exchange rate of EUR/USD 1.25 from an American company. This purchase has a receivable in the amount of USD 100,000.00 or EUR 80,000. As of the balance sheet date 12/31/2009 the exchange rate is EUR/USD 1.35. Because the dollar has lost value, now only approximately EUR 74,000.00 are to be balanced. An adjusting entry using the delta technique is performed in Table 6.1. The valued amount of EUR 6,000.00 is saved in table BDIFF (see Table 6.7).

Account	Name	Debit	Credit
230010	Capital loss	EUR 6,000.00	
140099	Receivables adjustment account		EUR 6,000.00

Table 6.7 Foreign Currency Valuation—Delta Technique

In most countries and cases, the delta technique is not applied. Instead, the amount would be cancelled as of 1/1/2010. If there is a payment receipt or a renewed foreign currency valuation, the entire price gain or loss is realized based on the exchange rate of EUR/USD 1.25. In our example, only the delta is posted based on the valued exchange rate of EUR/USD 1.35. Let us continue this example further, with a migration taking place on 3/24/2010. In New G/L, the balances of the P&L accounts are reflected in the retained earnings account. The balance of the adjustment account is migrated and open items are copied individually (see Table 6.8).

Account	Name	Debit	Credit
900000	Retained earnings		EUR 74,000.00
140099	Receivables adjustment account		EUR 6,000.00
140000	Receivables	EUR 80,000.00	

Table 6.8 Foreign Currency Valuation—Complete Posting

When you activate New G/L you must work with the FAGL_FC_VALUATION program for the foreign currency valuation. This program cannot access the "old document information" and, in this delta example, with a stable exchange rate of EUR/USD 1.35, it would create the posting record shown in Table 6.9.

Account	Name	Debit	Credit
230010	Capital loss	EUR 6,000.00	
140099	Receivables adjustment account		EUR 6,000.00

Table 6.9 Foreign Currency Valuation—Delta Technique

This invalid allocation can be avoided only if you perform an inverse posting in migration Phase 1 for the delta valuations. You can define a valuation method as a reset method using Transaction OB59. In this example, you must resolve all remaining datasets in the classic General Ledger on 3/1/2010 with the program SAPF100, a valuation for the balance sheet preparation and the defined reset method (see Table 6.10).

Account	Name	Debit	Credit
230010	Capital loss		EUR 6,000.00
140099	Receivables adjustment account	EUR 6,000.00	

Table 6.10 Foreign Currency Valuation—Reset Method

In Phase 1, capital gains and losses can be posted as usual by the old method for the months of January and February. A correction does not take place before the final transfer of the data in March, thereby avoiding an invalid posting based on the new architecture.

In summary, the manual activity "Resetting the balance sheet adjustments" is of particular interest in those cases where business area balances are used or in which the delta technique is used as part of the foreign currency valuation.

Document Splitting — Optimizing the Configuration

If you have opted for a scenario with document splitting, the process tree contains four activities to optimize your existing database in the classic General Ledger with the configuration of the future document splitting.

Assigning account/
item category

During the data migration, and also for later postings in Phase 2, it is vital that the G/L accounts be known as the item type in the configuration of document splitting, as described in Chapter 5, Document Splitting. In Figure 6.44, you can see the result of a Customizing check. Accounts not assigned to date are presented with a default value for an item type and flagged with a red traffic light.

Assigning
document
type/business
transaction

Following the first check, there is a validation based on the used and correctly configured document types (see Figure 6.45). If you look at the document type VI (Vendor Invoices), there are documents there that are to be migrated. A configuration was stored for the assignment of document type and document splitting, which is why a green traffic light is displayed. Section 5.4.2, Business Transaction, provides details on this subject. A yellow traffic light generally indicates that the Customizing for this document type is missing, but there are no documents waiting for transfer. These cases are not critical for a migration of the Phase 1 documents. Error messages appear if these document types are used with manual postings in Phase 2. A red traffic light should be interpreted as an error message indicating that there are documents to be migrated but a gap in the configuration will prevent successful transfer.

Assignment Between G/L Account and Item Category

	Chart of Accts	CoCode	G/L Account	Name	Default Item	Item category	Status
	INT	AA19	0000476000	Office supplies	20000	20000	✱◯◯
	INT	AA19	0000476100	Data processing supplies expenses	20000	20000	✱◯◯
	INT	AA19	0000476300	External Services	20000	20000	✱◯◯
	INT	AA19	0000476500	Other administrative expenses	20000	20000	✱◯◯
	INT	AA19	0000476900	Other general expenses	20000	20000	✱◯◯
	INT	AA19	0000477000	Advertising and Sales costs	20000	20000	✱◯◯
	INT	AA19	0000477100	Marketing Presents (see Account Assignme	20000	20000	✱◯◯
	INT	AA19	0000478000	Marketing/Sales Rep. costs	20000	20000	✱◯◯
	INT	AA19	0000479000	Bank Charges	20000	20000	✱◯◯
	INT	AA19	0000479100	TR-TM: Other expense - financial transacti	20000	20000	✱◯◯
	INT	AA19	0000481000	Cost-accounting depreciation	20000	20000	✱◯◯
	INT	AA19	0000481100	Minor assets - direct method	20000	20000	✱◯◯
	INT	AA19	0000482000	Taxbased depreciation	20000	20000	✱◯◯
	INT	AA19	0000483000	Imputed interest	20000	20000	✱◯◯
	INT	AA19	0000484000	Estimated depreciation - other	20000	20000	✱◯◯
	INT	AA19	0000489000	Other estimated costs	20000	20000	✱◯◯
	INT	AA19	0000499998	Reconciliation FI-CO (internal postings)	20000	20000	✱◯◯
	INT	AA19	0000499999	Reconciliation FI-CO (external postings)	20000	20000	✱◯◯
	INT	AA19	0000609080	Transfer Marketing Costs	20000		✱◯◯
	INT	AA19	0000698000	Internal revenue (profit center)	20000		✱◯◯
	INT	AA19	0000698100	Internal stock changes	20000		✱◯◯
	INT	AA19	0000698200	Internal transfers	20000		✱◯◯
	INT	AA19	0000699999	Function area bill of exchange	20000		✱◯◯
	INT	AA19	0000790000	Unfinished products	06000		✱◯◯
	INT	AA19	0000790010	Work in process from external procuremen	06000		✱◯◯
	INT	AA19	0000791000	Products being processed	01000		✱◯◯
	INT	AA19	0000792000	Finished goods inventory	06000		✱◯◯

Figure 6.44 Accounts—Item Types

Check on Business Transaction Assignment for Document Type

Display Definition

Status	Ty.	Tran.	Varia	Description	DocsBefore	Docs.After	Message (Customizing settings OK?)
◯◯◯	DR	0200	0001	Customer invoice	0	0	OK
◯◯◯	DZ	1000	0001	Payments	0	0	OK
◯△◯	EU				0	0	No assignment
◯◯◯	EX	0000	0001	Unspecified posting	0	0	OK
◯△◯	GF				0	0	No assignment
◯△◯	JE				0	0	No assignment
◯◯◯	KA	0000	0002	Unspecified posting	0	0	OK
◯△◯	KE				0	0	No assignment
◯◯◯	KG	0300	0001	Vendor invoice	0	0	OK
◯◯◯	KN	0300	0001	Vendor invoice	0	0	OK
◯◯◯	KP	1010	0001	Clearing transactions (account maint.)	0	0	OK
◯◯◯	KR	0300	0001	Vendor invoice	1	1	OK
◯◯◯	KZ	1000	0001	Payments	0	0	OK
◯◯◯	ML	0000	0001	Unspecified posting	0	0	OK
◯△◯	NB				0	0	No assignment

Figure 6.45 Document Types—Business Transaction

The next check program looks at documents from Phases 0 and 1 that would no longer be postable due to the current configuration of document splitting. This would be the case, for instance, if the document type KR is now to be used exclusively for vendor invoices, even though

Documents of
Phase 0 and
Phase 1

in the past pure G/L account postings also took place. Figure 6.46 shows options for selecting the company code, document number interval, and period and document type.

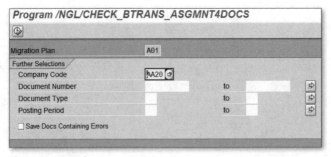

Figure 6.46 Selection

Special migration cases

The resulting log can be used to check the current configuration or to define exceptions in the migration for certain documents. In the example illustrated in Figure 6.47, the business transaction 0300 (Vendor Invoice) was not run in the split logic, unlike all other business transactions with document type KR. Figure 6.47 defines an alternative operation that controls the document 1900000002 for migration in such a way that business transaction 1000 (Payment) is processed as the business transaction.

Change View "Document-Specific Business Transaction Assignment": Overv

New Entries

Document-Specific Business Transaction Assignment

CoCd	Year	Document Number	Business Transaction	Transaction Variant	Ref. Transactn	Reference Key	Status
1000	2007	1900000002	1000	0001	BKPF	190000000210002007	1 Active

Figure 6.47 Defining Alternative Operation

In this way, the migration will also work for former special cases beyond the document-splitting rules that are otherwise defined.

Modifications and Enhancements

The checkup phase ends with a manual activity. If you are using modifications and enhancements that could impact New G/L, you confirm their adjustment with this step.

6.6.4 Preparation Phase

Once you've successfully processed all of the mandatory activities in the setup and checkup phase, there are only a few steps left in the preparation phase between you and the actual migration (see Figure 6.48).

Once this phase begins, you may no longer post into the old fiscal year. The periods must be closed accordingly. With the CHECK RESET CLEARING CONTROL activity, from now on clearing documents are no longer possible prior to the migration date. These steps end the operational work for the previous year. The activities that follow are mainly directed at analyzing and ensuring the quality of the available posting data.

Closing periods

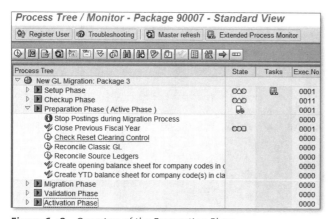

Figure 6.48 Overview of the Preparation Phase

Major Sales Check

This activity is started by the SAPF190 program (comparative financial accounting analysis). For example, the total of the individual items must tally with the transaction figures for the relevant period. This is the case in Figure 6.49 for Period 2 with an amount of EUR 1,100.00.

Program SAPF190

From the point of view of the log, the step that has been successfully performed must be confirmed manually.

Ledger Comparison

Another option for ensuring the quality of the data to be copied is offered by Transaction GCAC (Ledger Comparison). Figure 6.44 shows the flexible options this program offers. You select the classic General Ledger,

Transaction GCAC

Ledger 00, for company code AA11 and the entire fiscal year 2008 (see Figure 6.50).

A CoCd Local FY FP T curcy FP	Item debit total	Account debit total	Debit difference	Item credit total	Account credit total	Credit difference
K AA20 EUR 07 01	0,00	0,00	0,00	0,00	0,00	0,00
K AA20 EUR 07 02	0,00	0,00	0,00	1.100,00	1.100,00	0,00
K AA20 EUR 07 03	0,00	0,00	0,00	0,00	0,00	0,00
K AA20 EUR 07 04	0,00	0,00	0,00	0,00	0,00	0,00
K AA20 EUR 07 05	0,00	0,00	0,00	0,00	0,00	0,00
K AA20 EUR 07 06	0,00	0,00	0,00	0,00	0,00	0,00
K AA20 EUR 07 07	0,00	0,00	0,00	0,00	0,00	0,00
K AA20 EUR 07 08	0,00	0,00	0,00	0,00	0,00	0,00
K AA20 EUR 07 09	0,00	0,00	0,00	0,00	0,00	0,00
K AA20 EUR 07 10	0,00	0,00	0,00	0,00	0,00	0,00
K AA20 EUR 07 11	0,00	0,00	0,00	0,00	0,00	0,00
K AA20 EUR 07 12	0,00	0,00	0,00	0,00	0,00	0,00
K AA20 EUR 07 13	0,00	0,00	0,00	0,00	0,00	0,00
K AA20 EUR 07 14	0,00	0,00	0,00	0,00	0,00	0,00
K AA20 EUR 07 15	0,00	0,00	0,00	0,00	0,00	0,00
K AA20 EUR 07 16	0,00	0,00	0,00	0,00	0,00	0,00
K AA20 EUR 07 **	0,00	0,00	0,00	1.100,00	1.100,00	0,00

Recon. in company code currency   EUR

Figure 6.49 Reconciliation of Financial Accounting

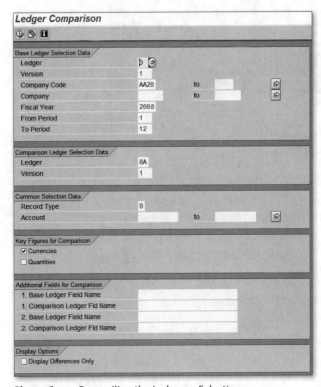

Figure 6.50 Reconciling the Ledgers—Selection

If no costing-based values are offered in the ledgers, there should not be any differences between the books (see Figure 6.51). Any inconsistencies can be identified and analyzed for each account. Before you copy balances carried forward and documents from the world of the classic General Ledger, your top priority is to ensure the original data consistency.

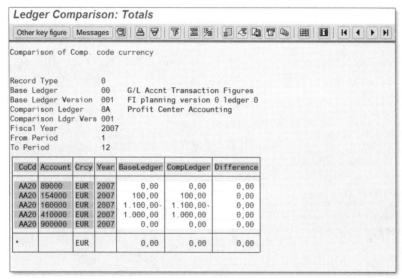

Figure 6.51 Reconciling the Ledgers—Result

Documentation

If all mandatory activities have been successfully run, the preparation phase concludes with a documentation of the actual status. Balance sheets are created and saved for the classic General Ledger. Nothing stands in the way of the migration. The migration phase follows.

Documenting the actual status

6.6.5 Migration Phase

Various preparatory steps have been successfully concluded, and data is now copied from the classic General Ledger into New G/L. Figure 6.52 shows an overview of the process tree for this phase.

Actual data transfer

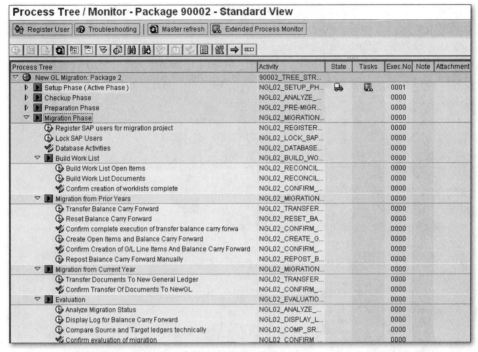

Figure 6.52 Overview of the Migration Phase

We must differentiate between five different work areas:

- ▸ Backing up the system
- ▸ Building a worklist
- ▸ Migration from the previous year (Phase 0 data)
- ▸ Migration From the Current Year (Phase 1 Data)
- ▸ Evaluation of the Migration That Has Been Performed

On the next few pages, we look at the work areas and their respective activities in more detail.

Backing Up the System

Taking precautionary measures

In backing up the system, a number of precautionary measures need to be taken before data can be migrated. First, the users who are essential must be must be completely registered for the project. This means that users who are not registered are locked in the system for the duration of the migration. This is necessary to guarantee the consistency of the data to be migrated. You can easily take this measure through the activity LOCK SAP USER (see Figure 6.53).

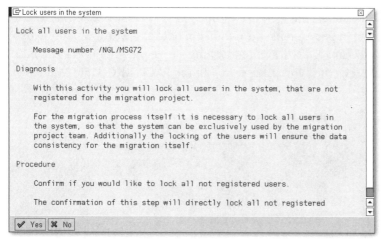

Figure 6.53 Locking Users

Prior to starting migration, we recommend that you perform a complete data backup. If problems or errors occur during migration, you can restart again in an emergency by returning to this original dataset.

To optimize the performance and runtime of the data transfer, you can deactivate the database logging. Your system or database administrator can help you here. There are various ways to do this, depending on the database used.

Optimizing the database

Once you have locked out the users, performed a data backup, and optimized the database for the migration, the next of the five work areas can begin.

Building a Worklist

Documents from the classic General Ledger must be included in a worklist for a later data transfer. There are two different worklists:

Two types

415

- One worklist for open items of Phase 0, that is, before the migration date

- One worklist for all documents of Phase 1, that is, after the migration date

The first step begins when you build the worklists for the migration.

Figure 6.54 shows the worklist for open items in Phase 0. You can see in the log that in this example the number of objects—with a vendor invoice and an OI-managed G/L account posting—is very clear. From a technical point of view, this worklist is stored in the FAGL_MIG_OPITEMS table.

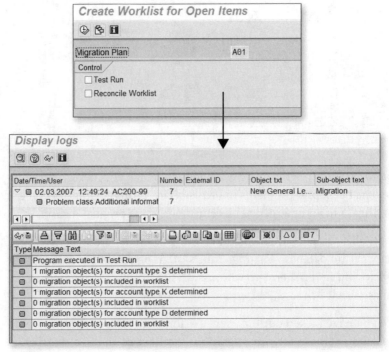

Figure 6.54 Creating a Worklist for Open Items

In a second step, you create a worklist for all documents from Phase 1 (see Figure 6.55).

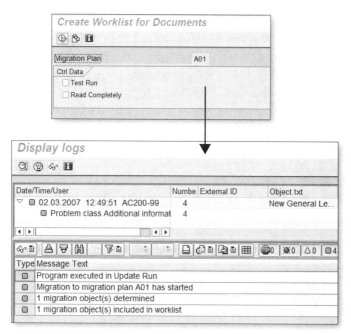

Figure 6.55 Worklist for Documents

If the program is executed more than once, the system takes only the additional documents into account. When you confirm the completeness of the worklists as shown in Figure 6.56, the next work area—the migration of the Phase 0 data—can begin.

Figure 6.56 Confirmation

Migration of Previous Years (Phase 0)

The system is backed up and the worklists have been created. Now the actual migration begins with Step 3. However, before the balance carryforwards and open items of Phase 0 are copied, a ledger comparison between the classic General Ledger (00) and New G/L (0L) shows the current status. There are no values yet in totals table FAGLFLEXT, and there is a difference for each account (see Figure 6.57).

```
Comparison of Comp. code currency

Record Type            0
Base Ledger            00      G/L Accnt Transaction Figures
Base Ledger Version    001     FI planning version 0 ledger 0
Comparison Ledger      0L      Leading Ledger
Comparison Ldgr Vers   001
Fiscal Year            2007
From Period            0
To Period              0
```

CoCd	Account	Crcy	Year	Base ledger	CompLedger	Difference
AA20	89000	EUR	2007	100.000,00-	0,00	100.000,00-
AA20	154000	EUR	2007	500,00	0,00	500,00
AA20	160000	EUR	2007	5.500,00-	0,00	5.500,00-
AA20	900000	EUR	2007	105.000,00	0,00	105.000,00
AA20	410000	EUR	2007	0,00	0,00	0,00
*		EUR		0,00	0,00	0,00

Figure 6.57 Ledger Comparison 00/0L

Once you begin the migration, the status of table FAGLFLEXT changes. In the first activity, the balance carryforward is copied for each account or company code (see Figure 6.52). You define which original ledger values are to be copied into a defined target ledger, in this example 0L (see Figure 6.58).

In addition to the values, you can migrate the characteristics of the relevant source ledger. For example, ledger 8A allows the retained earnings account to be copied broken down by profit centers. Figure 6.59 shows the log for a balance carryforward performed for source ledger 0.

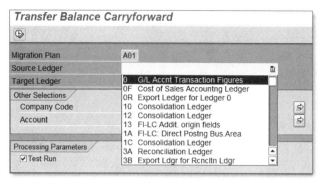

Figure 6.58 Balance Carryforward—Selection

Year	Tran	Ref. Tran.	COAr	Crcy	BUn	R	Ver	LogSystem	CoCd	Account	Cost Elem.	D/C	Tr.Prt	TTy	Partner PC	Profit Ctr	Ptnr Segm.	Segment	Trans.cur.	Co.cd.curr
2007				1000	EUR		0	1		AA20	154000		S								500,00	500,00
2007				1000	EUR		0	1		AA20	900000		S								105.000,00	105.000,00
*					EUR															105.500,00	105.500,00

Update Run: Transfer Balance Carryforward to Ledger 0L

Figure 6.59 Balance Carryforward Log

Unlike the classic balance carryforward program, multiple execution also means a cumulated writing of the values into totals table FAGLFLEXT. The system indicates these issues with a warning message, as shown in Figure 6.60.

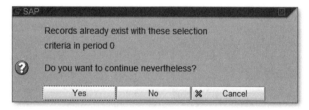

Figure 6.60 Warning Message

You can use the additional activity Reset Balance Carryforward to correct the balance carryforward again for each company code and account. Figure 6.61 shows the program's selection criteria. Resetting the balance carryforward does not delete the entries in totals table FAGLFLEXT, but simply sets them to zero.

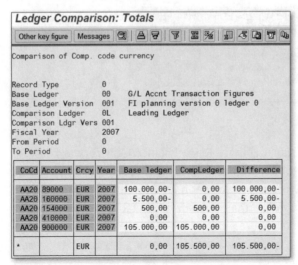

Figure 6.61 Resetting the Balance Carryforward

Figure 6.62 shows a ledger comparison after the balance transfer. The retained earnings account 900000 and the G/L account 154000 have been copied in their entirety into New G/L.

Enhancing the "Segment" field

If you want to use the new SEGMENT field, it cannot be enriched by default by the balance carryforward program. This is also the case if you copy data from Ledger 8A, the profit center accounting. There are two general options for obtaining a characteristic assignment in the balance carryforward: You can perform an automatic enhancement with the FAGL_UPLOAD_CF BadI stored in the setup phase, or you can post manually with Transaction FBCB into Period 0.

Ledger Comparison: Totals

```
Other key figure   Messages

Comparison of Comp. code currency

Record Type          0
Base Ledger          00      G/L Accnt Transaction Figures
Base Ledger Version  001     FI planning version 0 ledger 0
Comparison Ledger    0L      Leading Ledger
Comparison Ldgr Vers 001
Fiscal Year          2007
From Period          0
To Period            0
```

CoCd	Account	Crcy	Year	Base ledger	CompLedger	Difference
AA20	89000	EUR	2007	100.000,00-	0,00	100.000,00-
AA20	160000	EUR	2007	5.500,00-	0,00	5.500,00-
AA20	154000	EUR	2007	500,00	500,00	0,00
AA20	410000	EUR	2007	0,00	0,00	0,00
AA20	900000	EUR	2007	105.000,00	105.000,00	0,00
*		EUR		0,00	105.500,00	105.500,00-

Figure 6.62 Ledger Comparison 00/0L, Following Balance Transfer

As a matter of principle, the system copies the characteristics into New G/L only if the corresponding scenario is also assigned. As an example, let's take the consolidation transaction type, which is used by many customers for provision postings and creating provision lists. If the *consolidation preparation* scenario is not assigned to the Ledger 0L, no transfer of this characteristic takes place. Even if you choose table GLT3 as the source ledger for the balance carryforward, a Report Painter report based on FAGLFLEXT cannot show any values.

In the next activity, split information must be built for the open items of Phase 0. Because this is an automatic step, it is best if you display the results with Transaction SE16N in table FAGL_SPLINFO (see Figure 6.63). At this time, this activity does not have any effects on tables FAGL-FLEXA and FAGLFLEXT.

Display of Entries Found

Table to be searched	FAGL_SPLINFO	Splittling Information of Open Items
Number of hits	6	
Runtime	0	Maximum no. of hits 500

DocumentNo	Year	CoCd	Itm	SeqNo	Log.System	Ref. Tran.	Ref.Doc.No	Ref.Org Un	BusA	Profit Ctr	Segment	TPBA
100000000	2006	AA20	2	1		BKPF	100000000	AA202006	9900	1402	SEG-A	
1900000000	2006	AA20	1	1		BKPF	1900000000	AA202006	9900	1402	SEG-A	
1900000001	2007	AA20	1	1		BKPF	1900000001	AA202007		1000	SEG-A	
1900000001	2007	AA20	1	4		BKPF	1900000001	AA202007		1402	SEG-A	
1900000001	2007	AA20	4	2		BKPF	1900000001	AA202007		1000	SEG-A	
1900000001	2007	AA20	4	3		BKPF	1900000001	AA202007		1402	SEG-A	

Figure 6.63 Table FAGL_SPLINFO

The BAdI FAGL_MIGR_SUBST already stored in the setup phase is run in this activity and generates information in our example on the new SEGMENT FIELD. As already mentioned, a certain fuzziness remains concerning singular postings. If the BAdI works correctly and delivers satisfactory information for the individual characteristics, the OI-managed accounts can be copied in the subsequent step (see Figure 6.64). Table FAGLFLEXA and the balance carryforward in the FAGLFLEXT are updated.

BAdI FAGL_
MIGR_SUBST

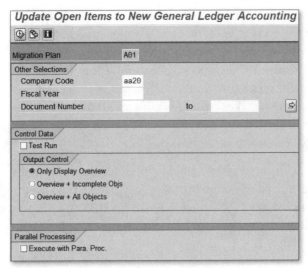

Figure 6.64 Copying Open Items—Selection

Log In the log (see Figure 6.65), you can see that two documents were copied from table FAGL_SPLINFO.

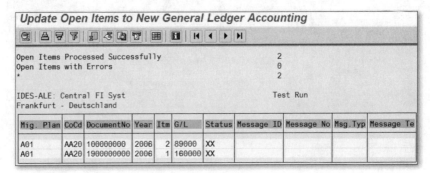

Figure 6.65 Copying Open Items—Log

Ledger Comparison A ledger comparison between the classic General Ledger, Ledger 00, and New G/L, Ledger 0L, may now no longer display any differences in Period 0 (see Figure 6.66).

Once you confirm, the data transfer for Phase 0 is complete. Migration of the documents from Phase 1 begins.

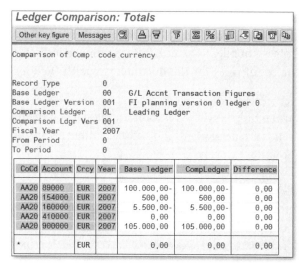

Figure 6.66 Ledger Comparison

Migration From the Current Year (Phase 1)

Documents posted after the migration date are posted subsequently in their entirety. By now it should be clear that the time allowed for Phase 1—that is, from the migration date to the activation date—must be as small as possible. In large enterprises, a document volume of several tens of thousands of documents per month is by no means unusual. The greater the number of documents, the more likely it is that problems will arise. From a technical point of view, it must be possible to enrich all documents with new information in tables FAGL_SPLINFO, FAGL-FLEXA, and FAGLFLEXT. Unlike open items in Phase 0, no BAdI is ever required. When you build the split information, an error log helps you analyze the causes (see Figure 6.67).

Transferring the documents from Phase 1

Log Output: Validation: Document Splitting

IDES-ALE: Central FI Syst
Frankfurt · Deutschland

Time 16:16:34 Date
Page

CoCd	Year	DocumentNo	Message text	Type	Transaction Code
1000	2007	500000000	No accounting transaction variant assigned to FBR2//AE	AE	FBR2
1000	2007	500000001	No accounting transaction variant assigned to FB01//AE	AE	FB01
1000	2007	1400000000	Balancing field "Segment" in line item 001 not filled	DZ	FBZ1
1000	2007	1800000003	Balancing field "Segment" in line item 001 not filled	DR	FBR2
1000	2007	1900000002	Item category 04000 not allowed in accounting transaction 0300/0001	KR	FB50

Figure 6.67 Error Log

The first two entries are caused by a document type AE that is not configured for document splitting. In the next two documents, the new mandatory field SEGMENT is not filled. The fifth entry in the log indicates a document beyond the set of rules for the document type VI (Vendor Invoice).

Error categories

By double-clicking, you can branch to the relevant individual document and can thus analyze it in more detail. Let's look at these three error categories and their solution more closely.

Configuring Document Type AE

This error can be eliminated with an entry in the Customizing via the menu path FINANCIAL ACCOUNTING (NEW) • GENERAL LEDGER ACCOUNTING (NEW) • BUSINESS TRANSACTIONS • DOCUMENT SPLITTING • CLASSIFY DOCUMENT TYPES FOR DOCUMENT SPLITTING.

The Mandatory "Segment" Field is Not Filled

Enriching documents manually

A supplementary account assignment for Phase 1 documents is possible as part of the migration into New G/L. This activity, which is quite risky, is not stored in the Migration Cockpit. In a two-step procedure, documents containing at least one OI-managed account can be enriched with additional information. The change of the original document is logged in a change document.

With Transaction FAGL_MIG_FICHAN you build a worklist in a first step. The selection screen in Figure 6.68 allows you to restrict the company code, the fiscal year, and the document numbers. You can enrich the characteristics PROFIT CENTER, PARTNER PROFIT CENTER, SEGMENT, and PARTNER SEGMENT with a default value.

You can also have the segment subsequently derived from an existing profit center account assignment. This option is very useful if not all profit center master data has been maintained with a segment (see Figure 6.69) during the previous document posting.

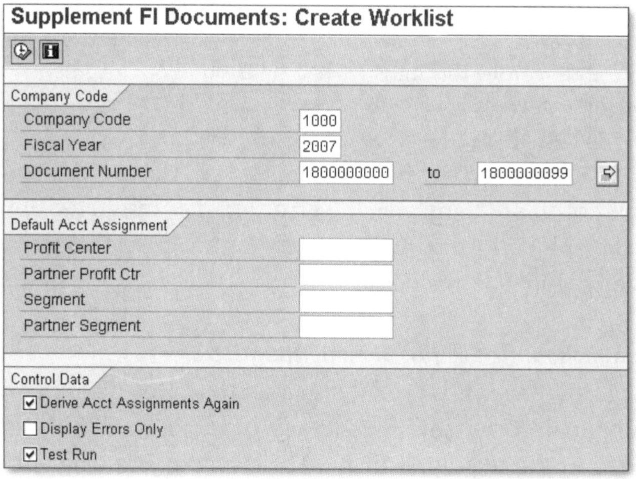

Supplement FI Documents: Create Worklist

Company Code
Company Code	1000
Fiscal Year	2007
Document Number	1800000000 to 1800000099

Default Acct Assignment
Profit Center	
Partner Profit Ctr	
Segment	
Partner Segment	

Control Data
- ☑ Derive Acct Assignments Again
- ☐ Display Errors Only
- ☑ Test Run

Figure 6.68 Worklist—Selection

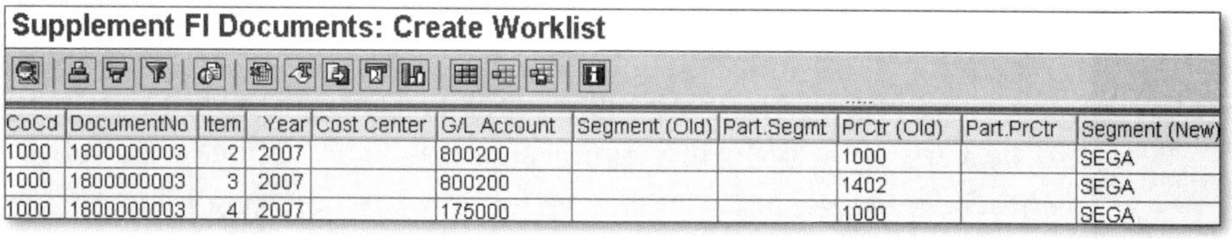

Supplement FI Documents: Create Worklist

CoCd	DocumentNo	Item	Year	Cost Center	G/L Account	Segment (Old)	Part.Segmt	PrCtr (Old)	Part.PrCtr	Segment (New)
1000	1800000003	2	2007		800200			1000		SEGA
1000	1800000003	3	2007		800200			1402		SEGA
1000	1800000003	4	2007		175000			1000		SEGA

Figure 6.69 Worklist—Overview

Once the worklist is built, you need to use Transaction FAGL_MIG_
FICHAT to perform a document change (see Figure 6.70).

**Transaction FAGL_
MIG_FICHAT**

Supplement FI Documents: Implement Worklist

Selection
Company Code	1000

Control Parameters
- ☐ Block Documents
- ☐ Display Errors Only
- ☑ Test Run

Parallel Proc.
Number of Parallel Processes	
ServGrp: Backgrnd, in Parallel	

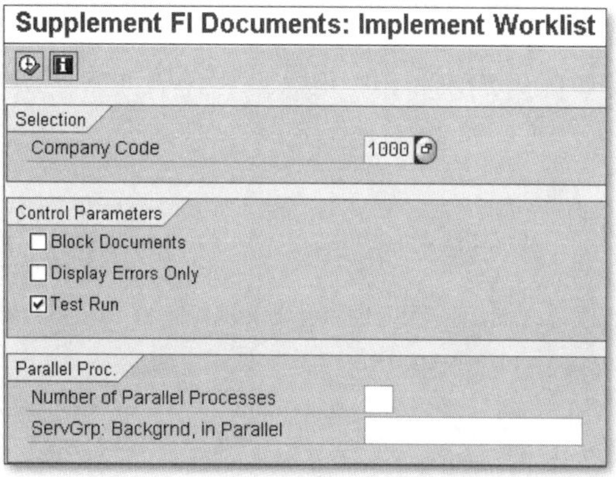

Figure 6.70 Performing a Change

[!]

> **Cautious Handling of Mass Change Transactions**
>
> We stress again how dangerous this mass change transaction is. Documents from Phase 1 that were previously correctly posted could subsequently contain incorrect information.

The source element of this activity was the error log that resulted from the building of the split information. Two of the three error sources could have been eliminated at this point.

A Document Beyond the Rule Set for Document Splitting

In the checkup phase, the validity of the configuration of document splitting and individual documents has already been checked. Such a method is also used in the migration phase. For example, if a payment was accidentally posted with document type KR, an exception rule can be specially defined for this document. There is therefore nothing left to hinder enrichment of this document.

Transaction FAGL_
MIG_SIM_SPL

Transaction FAGL_MIG_SIM_SPL (Simulate Document Splitting) may also be very helpful during troubleshooting. The data cannot subsequently be migrated unless you have found a solution for all documents shown in the error log.

Evaluation of the Migration That Has Been Performed

In this step you confirm that all migration objects have been completely transferred into New G/L. Balance carryforwards were built and reconciled, in scenario 3, Document Splitting, all open items were enriched with additional information. A status log provides you with a current overview (see Figure 6.71).

Analysis: Migration Status

| Message Statistics | Analyze Transferred Documents |

Status Overview

Status Overview

	Status	Status Name	≡ Number of	≡ Percentage
	00	Not processed	8.955	15,19
	01	Processing started	0	0,00
	10	Split information built	49.997	84,81
	XX	Completely processed	0	0,00
		≡	58.952 ≡	100,00

Figure 6.71 Migration Status—Log

If the migration is subsequently confirmed as successful, activities can no longer be performed in conjunction with the migration phase.

6.6.6 Validation Phase

Important validation steps take place after the migration phase (see Figure 6.72).

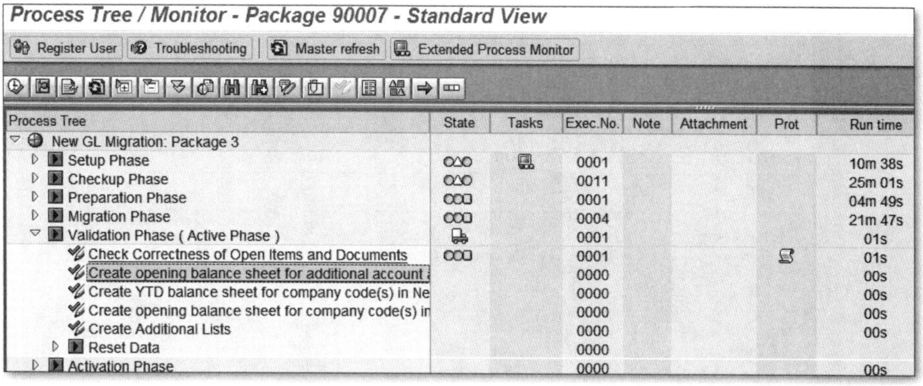

Figure 6.72 Overview of the Validation Phase

If you assume that you perform several test migrations, you have to turn your attention to more than a reconciled balance sheet and a completed process tree.

Testing follow-on processes

Specifying G/L Accounts Prior to Test Migration   **[+]**

There are three fields in G/L Account Master Record that you should check and, if required, adapt with regard to the test migration:

▶ Totals only in Local Currency field
If this switch is not set, all currencies are updated. Ask yourself whether this is necessary in all cases. In a migration, totals table FAGLFLEXT is enriched with many unnecessary data records otherwise.

▶ Open Item Management field
Check for which accounts an OI management is truly useful. For example, accounts that are used for the foreign currency evaluation should not be OI-managed (SAP Note 318399).

▶ Reconciliation Account for Account Type field
If you use document splitting, the reconciliation accounts of an account type have identical specifications, for example, for vendors in each company code.

For Scenario 3, follow-on processes that access information from the open items that are subsequently enriched must be extensively tested. Suppose, for example, that you want to pay open expense invoices in a payment run. If only one document is contained with incomplete document-splitting information, you may not be able to post the complete payment run (see Figure 6.73).

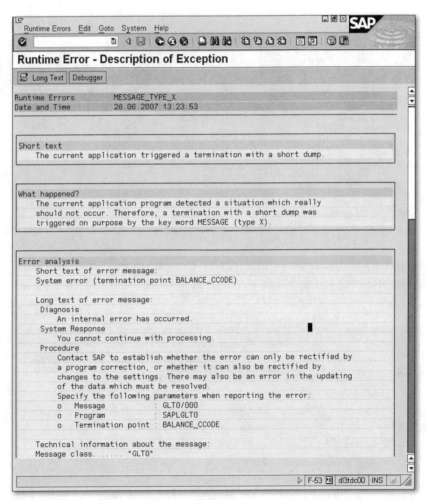

Figure 6.73 Error Message—Outgoing Payment

In another test scenario, it is useful to post a number of electronic bank statements. Financial accounting with the Document Splitting function has become somewhat more complex. The system cannot always refer to the issue with clear error messages, as shown in Figure 6.73, and, in the worst case scenario, you get a program termination with an ABAP short dump.

Experience shows that approximately 50 % of all customers use the Document Splitting function and have performed three to four test migrations prior to the start of production. The front runner is an IT company that uses a document splitting for 238 company codes based on SAP ERP 2005 and has copied 1,500,000 open items from Phase 0 and 300,000 documents from Phase 1. Because of potential BAdI enhancements during the migration, a random test for documents in each category and derivation rule is essential.

Project experiences

If you use New G/L to introduce additional financial characteristics such as Profit Center and Segment, you should ensure sufficient data quality with opening balances and transaction balances. We recommend that you use the Migration Cockpit to store this documentation.

In this phase you have a last chance to reset a complete migration. The prerequisite is an inactive New G/L and cancellation of the manually posted balance carryforwards using Transaction FBCB. The RESET AND DELETE indicator deletes the following tables for all company codes belonging to the migration plan:

Last chance to reset migration

- ▶ Worklists
- ▶ Journal entry table (FAGLFLEXA)
- ▶ Totals table (FAGLFLEXT)
- ▶ Document-splitting table (FAGL_SPLINFO)
- ▶ Other migration tables

If no additional test migration takes place and if the data quality corresponds to the target position, then you no longer need to reset the migration. The activation phase can begin.

6.6.7　Activation Phase

In principle, you must migrate all company codes and documents completely and without any errors. With the activation phase you terminate the migration; resetting the data is now no longer necessary.

Figure 6.74 shows a number of activities that must be run in this phase.

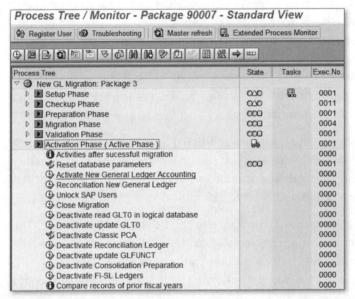

Figure 6.74　Overview of the Activation Phase

[+] **Deactivating the Update in Table GLT0**

The function of parallel updating values in table GLT0 should be used only for a short period of time (several months at most). In the case of a planned local currency changeover, chart of accounts changeover, or any other cross-application activities, you must inevitably make a deactivation for this fiscal year. You can access this switch in Customizing independent of the Migration Cockpit: FINANCIAL ACCOUNTING (NEW) • FINANCIAL ACCOUNTING BASIC SETTINGS (NEW) • TOOLS • DEACTIVATE UPDATE OF CLASSIC GENERAL LEDGER.

Database parameters were optimized for the period of the migration; your database or system administrator should now set them again for operational work. Before you release the locked users, the activation of New G/L must take place (see Figure 6.75).

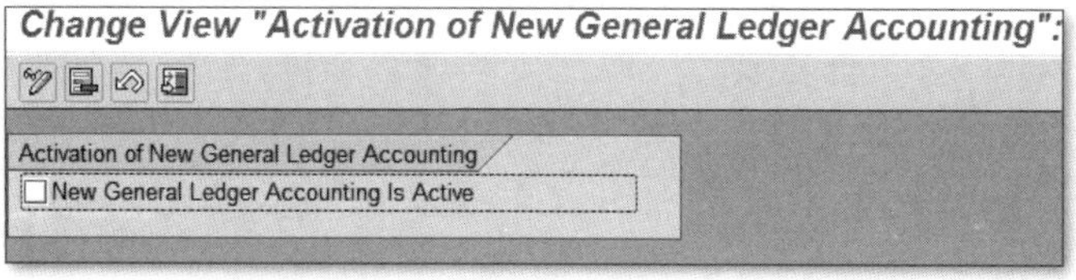

Figure 6.75 Activating New General Ledger

You should also check whether specific work in the production system could now be useful. This work would include, for example, deactivating the profit center accounting and the reconciliation ledger. However, you can also perform these optional steps at a later time using a separate transport request. You terminate all activities in the migration plan using the activity COMPLETE MIGRATION.

6.7   Conclusion

Detailed design of New G/L and planning of migration form the basis for a successful project. The migration service ensures the quality of the data and minimizes possible risks associated with the project. The Migration Cockpit simplifies the handling of the migration and significantly reduces its complexity. The migrations that already have been performed and the related experience that has been gained allow you to minimize risk and successfully implement the functional added value of New G/L.

7 Practical Reports

Chapter 6, Migration, described the functions and implementation of New G/L; this chapter offers you five extensive practical examples. Here you will learn about the experience of consultancy firms during migration to New G/L, find out how other customers use it, and read about the lessons learned in the projects.

7.1 SAP Consulting

Today's demands on accounting systems are complex. As well as various different requirements for external accounting, many internal reporting requirements must also be met. New G/L and document splitting offer high-performance tools to enable you to meet these requirements.

SAP Consulting has been involved in several projects since 2004 in which systems were implemented based on New G/L. This experience report concentrates on entirely new systems that have been set up. This is known as the *greenfield approach*. Customers either were looking to comprehensively harmonize heterogeneous SAP environments or were newly implementing SAP ERP.

Two key questions apply to your project work for projects based on New G/L:

Fundamental orientation

▶ Is parallel accounting to be mapped through the accounts approach or the ledger approach?

▶ Are balance sheets required for additional account assignment features under the company code (for instance, profit center balance sheets)?

7.1.1 Parallel Accounting

In current projects, IFRS is generally used as the leading accounting standard. In addition, financial statements in accordance with national GAAPs are, of course, required. It is not possible to give general recommendations for technically mapping parallel accounting. In the ledger approach, only the leading ledger (usually IFRS) updates in the Controlling module (CO), so that customers who need both IFRS and local GAAP valuation approaches there must rely on the classic accounts approach. Another problem with the ledger approach is that OI-managed accounts always update into all ledgers. Enhancement Package 3 for SAP ERP 6.0 allows ledger-related OI management, so that the ledger approach will become more attractive.

Because many experts anticipate a gradual divergence between commercial balance sheets and tax balance sheets, there is also growing demand for a complete tax balance sheet system in the SAP system. Technically meeting this demand does not present any problem; nevertheless, in individual cases you must weigh very carefully whether the additional operational effort involved in creating an additional account layer, or a ledger in the ledger approach, is worth the benefit it brings. Organizational aspects must also be assessed. For example, does the accounting staff know enough about differing tax valuations?

7.1.2 Balance Sheets for Subaccount Assignments

Cash Generating Unit (CGU)

A key question for the project is whether complete balance sheets are required on additional account assignment features under the company code. Today, financial controlling purely on the basis of the P&L statement is usually no longer sufficient; the corresponding capital tie-up must also be identifiable. IFRS requirements (evaluation of the *Cash Generating Unit*) also include balance sheets for subaccount assignments. In the past, SAP customers used business areas for this or consolidated the legal unit from several company codes, with corresponding maintenance expenses. However, this practice had a massive impact on operational processes such that business transactions that were actually contiguous (for instance, billing documents for material and working time) had to be artificially separated in order to divide the receivables and revenues into the corresponding subaccount assignments.

With ERP, SAP offers a new procedure of document splitting through the online splitter for creating balance sheets on subaccount assignments. The following information on document splitting relates to document splitting by profit center. Segment reporting could be derived from this. In this context we would like to point out that use of the new Segment characteristic is released only in conjunction with the use of profit centers (see SAP Note 1035140).

7.1.3 Selected Aspects of Implementation

Many projects today use process modeling. The usual process models generally have the character of a flowchart. They show process steps and their course sequences, but they do not show when particular reporting dimensions are added or where these are derived from. It is therefore advisable to begin with an intensive reporting analysis. The process modeling must therefore be accompanied by formulating the corresponding posting logic, taking into account the relevant subaccount assignments such as profit center, functional area, or partner account assignment. The tried and tested T-account display has been and remains effective, although now it is enhanced with additional account-assignment features.

Taking reporting dimensions into account in the process model

7.1.4 Additional Fields in New General Ledger

As well as the standard General Ledger scenario, you can also update customer-specific fields in the system in the FAGLFLEXT totals table. This option is especially useful if you need additional subaccount assignments in group reporting. As a prerequisite, you must first include the additional fields in the account assignment block and in FAGLFLEXT. The additional fields must either be entered manually during posting or filled via substitution. FI substitutions are not processed in the standard system for postings through the accounting interface (including postings from MM and SD), so additional implementation steps are required to do this. With manual entries, we recommend that you ensure the data quality through corresponding validation steps. The problem is that there is as yet no option to fill fields by substitution in the document lines that have been created by document splitting on the zero-balance clearing account.

Data quality of customer-specific fields

Usually, most customers' existing special ledger scenarios are replaced in current projects by New G/L. Special Ledger (SL) is now used only as a tool for special cases.

7.1.5   Using Document Splitting

Reconciliation   Document splitting was a major influencing factor for all posting processes in projects. The following points must be reconciled with each other and applied correctly so that the online splitter returns the desired results:

▸ Processes

▸ Document types

▸ Account classifications

▸ Open Item management

[!]   Changing Customizing Retroactively

It is vital that you consider that much of the Customizing of document splitting cannot subsequently be changed or can be changed only by taking major risks (see SAP Note 891144).

We therefore urgently advise you to thoroughly test all processes: much more thoroughly than would be necessary without document splitting!

Testing   The tests must include the complete operation, including all follow-on processes; for instance, it is no longer sufficient to test only the classic order-to-cash process chain. Later, you must also test whether the sales tax transfer (Report RFUMSV00) is working correctly in terms of document splitting. Often, the method with the account-balance-related splitting of the tax payable posting does not lead to the desired result. You are therefore strongly urged to use the new split-related splitting method (see SAP Notes 877045 and 889150).

Account assignment handbook   Because accounting staffs have to consider more than they did without document splitting, a detailed account-assignment handbook is very strongly advised for end users. However, this cannot replace a fundamental understanding of the document splitting technique; this is still vital, at least for power-users. To be on the safe side, any processes or settings not yet used should be locked for the moment, in order to avoid errors. For example, it is better if you delete any document types that are not needed.

If you have active document splitting, OI management is no longer only an operational processing aid; it also carries account assignment information into subsequent documents (clearing, interest calculation, and value adjustment). The decision to equip an account with OI management therefore also determines the posting logic. More detailed knowledge of the technical processes in the system seems advisable for the future, at least for power users.

OI management also determines the posting logic

Up to Enhancement Package 3, when you use document splitting it is not possible to subsequently build an OI management as was otherwise still possible—with restrictions—with special programs like RFSEPA02 (see SAP Note 175960). For some constellations, there are several setting options, each of which has different advantages and disadvantages. SAP Note 922743 clearly explains this, using the example of the cash account book.

As of Enhancement Package 3, Transaction FAGL_ACTIVATE_OP provides you with the option to retroactively build an OI management.

The use of document splitting has significantly increased complexity of projects. We can only urgently advise all those involved in the projects to develop the requisite expertise in a timely manner.

[!]

Recommendation: Early Prototyping

It is also recommended that you build a prototype early so that critical points can be identified early. If document splitting is repeatedly deactivated in the prototyping phase (completely or for important test company codes), the project management should regard this as a warning signal because it indicates a lack of New G/L knowledge on the part of the project team.

7.1.6 Limits and Constraints on the Profit-Center Balance Sheet

In order to obtain a profit-center balance sheet, constraints must also be taken into account, in addition to document splitting. The Cost Center assignment in the asset master record may not be outsorted time-dependently. Only in this way will the stock values of the attachment be rebooked to the new profit center during a Cost Center switch (with profit center switch) from Asset Accounting.

Generally speaking, an increased level of detail in the reporting goes hand in hand with higher expenses for the accounting department. In practice, we create an asset master record only for important central complex fixed assets for Asset Accounting (for instance, licenses or patents). We do not split these into different asset master records (for each profit center); rather, we only distribute the write-downs.

7.1.7 Reporting vs. Operational Management

No authorization check of the profit center during postings

Currently, document splitting has a primarily reporting-oriented design. The authorization checks for the profit center or segment access the financial accounting only during the reporting but not during posting. In order to obtain an authorization check for the profit center during posting as well, validations had to be implemented with user exits or a BAdI. Corresponding BAdIs could also be used for the document display and the single item lists. The *Business Transaction Event* (BTE) 950 is available (see SAP Note 961509) for accessing the item selection of Transaction F-03, which may helpful for decentralized bookkeeping.

Managing operational jobs via subaccount assignments

In practice, we also often want to use the subaccount assignments in order to manage operational processes (for instance, dunning or payments). Dunning and payment runs currently only evaluate the data entry view of the document and cannot access the General Ledger view. Solution approaches were also developed for this in projects. This situation was aggravated by the fact that a different organizational unit (master market) is sometimes responsible for the follow-on processes rather than the market in which a receivable arises.

SAP Development is also investigating the subject area of "Managing operational processes via subaccount assignments."

7.1.8 Further SAP Developments

SAP Consulting always maintains close contact with SAP Development throughout all phases of the projects. Sometimes, three hours spent in

Walldorf or St. Leon-Rot were of more benefit to projects than three days spend on-site. Many functional gaps that occurred in the early prototyping stage of New G/L projects have since been closed by further development (for instance, item-interest calculation according to split information, split simulation, and other gaps mentioned in many of the SAP Notes).

7.1.9 Legacy Data Transfer

Because various document characteristics are updated in New G/L, during legacy data transfer you should ensure that the values are reported correctly for all reporting dimensions. Consequently, more attention should be paid to the migration's quality control and acceptance. It is not enough to simply compare "old balance" and "new balance" with each other; the reconciliation must also encompass the subaccount assignment level. Any fields not identified during the migration because of incorrect or missing subaccount assignments can only be rectified later at great expense.

Reconciliation at subaccount assignment level

With active document splitting, the corresponding split information must additionally be correctly assembled during the OI transfer, so that the derivation of the follow-up costs (for instance, during payment with cash discounts) can function in the new system. This requirement can increase both the time involved for reading the data from the legacy system (readout including offsetting postings is required) and the complexity of the import interface at the SAP ERP end.

Migration with split information becomes more complex

Overall, we observe that even with conventional legacy data transfer, the complexity increases significantly if document splitting in the target system is active. New tools are not required; the classic "toolbox" (for instance, LSMW) is enough. However, the transition from a business point of view must allow for all of the dimensions of the target system.

7.1.10 Lessons Learned

Posting logic and technology affect each other, especially when document splitting is used. A dualism from a subject/technical point of view is therefore out of place in New G/L projects.

Early development of New G/L expertise among all those involved in the project is urgently advised. This can be accomplished, for example, by attending the corresponding SAP training course AC 210, for the change-over of an SAP system that is already running, plus course AC 212.

Limits of conventional process modeling

Conventional process modeling reaches its limits with the design of modern accounting systems. It is also advisable from a financial application point of view that you start with the reporting requirements, then tailor the data model to it, and only then include the processes. The posting logic should be developed at the same time as the process.

There is no doubt that New G/L should be obligatory today for all new SAP ERP implementations. Many settings determine the system's fundamental direction and cannot subsequently be changed, or only at great expense. For this reason, much more time should be invested in the design phase, especially where document splitting is used. The return on investment will be worth it.

[+]

Author of the Sample Case

Lars Gartenschlaeger works as a Senior Architect for SAP Consulting. His consulting focuses on design and implementation expertise for SAP ERP Financials systems at C-level, the optimization of financials processes, parallel accounting HGB/IFRS/US-GAAP, migration, GDPdU, system shutdowns, audits, and compliance. He also runs several DSAG groups on behalf of SAP.

Contact: *lars.gartenschlaeger@sap.com*

7.2 Accenture GmbH

The basis for implementing the New General Ledger successfully involves selecting and allocating the use of the new functions correctly. The following considers a report from Accenture GmbH about an implementation project involving the use of New G/L for one of the enterprise's customers.

7.2.1 Customer Description and Initial Situation

The project we conducted was initiated by the corporate accounting department of a world-leading retail and services group (with approximately 11.5 billion Euro turnover and about 53,000 employees in the 2007/2008 fiscal year). As part of harmonizing the corporate chart of accounts worldwide, a decision was made to replace the traditional third-party software with SAP ERP Central Component (ECC) 6.0 for the German/Dutch accounting system group (approximately 550 future SAP users). The scope of the project involved 84 legal entities in 13 locations (mainly in Germany) with their main field of business in the area of multichannel retail (catalog, Internet, stationary retail).

The enterprise

7.2.2 Challenges of the Project

One of the complex challenges of the project involved harmonizing the accounting carried out at 13 locations to facilitate implementing the information from corporate accounting uniformly across the locations.

The new harmonized corporate chart of accounts had to be detailed further to map a global, operationally usable chart of accounts in SAP ECC 6.0. The new processes also had to increase efficiency potential considerably because the decision to implement an SAP system was based on a preinvestment analysis.

The new global requirements also included mapping parallel accounting in accordance with local accounting standards (for example, German, UK, and U.S.-GAAP) and IFRS, which meant reimplementing the P&L statement based on cost of sales accounting. The implementation of transferring both accounting standards to the SAP EC-CS corporate reporting system every month and the need to take into account other already emerging international system rollouts completed the requirements.

Global requirements

7.2.3 Constitutional Project Decisions

From the perspective of Accenture, the introduction of New G/L (with its new functions) meets the needs of the market, which, given the

Market requirements

441

heightened requirements in accounting, requires more flexibility when accounting is being mapped using standard software. Examples of heightened requirements include managing different parallel accounting standards owing to a globalization of systems and the creation of complete financial statements at the segment level.

Design phase

The introduction of New G/L to the market by SAP essentially did not change the need to identify constitutional questions early in the design phase, develop possible solutions for them, and ultimately choose an alternative option. Many of these decisions occur in the same way for all customers but may have completely different results, depending on the customer's circumstances and the required debit situation.

Individual consideration of each project

New G/L offers additional alternatives, each with its own advantages and disadvantages, to the toolbox of the project team, specifically for these constitutional decisions. Because each of these alternatives has advantages and disadvantages, we recommend that you carefully weigh traditional solution alternatives again for each project and assess them against New G/L.

Especially for customers who migrate from systems other than SAP, the choice to move to a new function of New G/L may be only the second-best alternative from a procedural point of view.

The implementation project described here was formed based on the constitutional decisions to make use of New G/L, which are discussed in the following.

Parallel Accounting

Primary requirement

The primary requirement from the very beginning of the project was to be able to map two parallel valuations simultaneously. Depending on the subsidiary company, these valuations were the relevant country-specific accounting standard (for example, in accordance with German GAAP, UK GAAP, Dutch closing statement) and the accounting standard in accordance with IFRS for group reporting.

Secondary requirement

Secondary objectives were to minimize operational expenses in accounting for entering accounting material and creating closing statements, to comply with generally accepted accounting principles, to maximize the transparency of implemented solutions, and to maximize functions in all accounting methods (ledgers). The following activities were analyzed and evaluated with a view to their feasibility:

- Mapping using account logic
- Mapping using account delta logic[1]
- Mapping using the new functions of parallel ledgers

When you map using account logic, there is a single general ledger, in other words, a single data store where you post the information in accordance with local accounting standards (for the sake of simplicity, abbreviated to GAAP from here on) and information in accordance with IFRS.

One general ledger

The customer also mapped this variant in the original accounting system with what is known in the project as the "Mickey Mouse" model (see Figure 7.1).

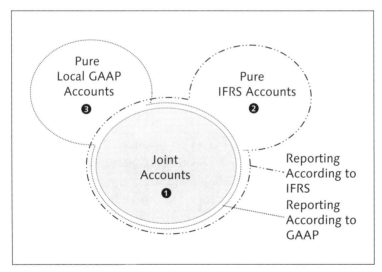

Figure 7.1 "Mickey Mouse" Model [2]

Let's consider the individual elements:

---

1 This alternative was not further pursued owing to its higher complexity.
2 Source: Hölzlwimmer, *Optimizing Value Flows with SAP ERP, SAP PRESS 2009*

- Most information is posted in accordance with IFRS and GAAP, that is, in Mickey Mouse's head. This information is posted on the G/L accounts that are allowed only for common information ❶.

- The left ear is reserved for GAAP information only (for example, tax-based adjustments) ❷.

- The right ear is reserved for IFRS information only (for example, the activation of software created in-house) ❸.

Disadvantages of the "Mickey Mouse" solution

Therefore, postings only have to be entered twice for information that must be updated differently between the two accounting standards. The main disadvantages of this solution are adding duplicate accounts to the chart of accounts presenting the same contents in the different ears and the possibility of creating value shifts owing to inadvertent postings between the accounting standards.

Advantages of parallel ledgers

Considering these disadvantages, the analysis of mapping using parallel ledgers was carried out with great interest. Obvious benefits of this method include the clear separation of accounting into two different data stores and the prevention of duplicate accounts if the same information is to be posted in a different amount. The information can therefore no longer be mixed up. We can compare the operational posting expenditure with that of the "Mickey Mouse" accounts approach because it enables New G/L to update the same information simultaneously in both ledgers.

Improvement potential

However, in an ECC 6.0 Release without Enhancement Package 3 (EHP3 was still in the ramp-up phase), the restrictions that open items could be managed only in the leading ledger (for example, clearing provision accounts) and that the Controlling ledger (for example, for cost of sales accounting) could be compared only in the leading ledger proved to be disadvantageous.

Decision

Because of these disadvantages (which SAP partially removed in Enhancement Package 3) and the convenience of not having to change the posting logic during the implementation, the tried-and-tested accounts approach was eventually chosen.

**Introducing the P&L Statement According to Cost of Sales
Accounting with Real-Time Integration of CO/FI**

When a P&L statement is introduced in accordance with cost of sales accounting, it immediately raises the question in retail as to which reporting dimensions, such as customer group, article, material group, distribution channel or branches, are to be used for reporting.

Reporting
dimensions

Customer analysis showed that a solution developed in-house already existed for the detailed contribution margin accounting and profitability analysis, and this is why the requested reporting dimensions were limited to the company code. All other dimensions of the customer-specific profitability analysis were filled by other operational systems. Therefore, the alternative to mapping using the profitability analysis (SAP CO-PA) that was suitable for the customer-specific multidimensionality of the reporting dimensions was discarded because of the considerable implementation effort required and the process changes needed when entering posting data.

In addition to the number of reporting dimensions, the requirement to manage a subfunctional area had to be met. This meant that the type of costs incurred had to be taken into account under the actual functional area, for example, sales and administration costs. This requirement could be mapped using a multiplication of the relevant income statement accounts with the functions and through the classic variant using the functional areas object.

Managing a
subfunctional area

The variant to multiply out accounts would inevitably have extended the chart of accounts. Therefore, this variant was rejected because the necessary extension of the chart of accounts clashed with the project's objective to reduce the number of accounts.

Furthermore, the previously exclusive benefit of this variant no longer exists owing to the new CO-FI real-time integration of the new General Ledger. The benefit in question was that, by posting to accounts that had been multiplied out, the P&L statement in accordance with cost of sales accounting was also in real time when the classic general ledger was used (thus there was no waiting for the postings from the reconciliation ledger).

Decision In the end, the customer chose in favor of mapping using functional areas and of using the new CO-FI real-time integration, for which the functional areas are stored in the material costs master or cost center master and all relevant information for cost of sales accounting can therefore be derived automatically in the background without additional operational effort when accounting documents are entered. The information for the subfunctional area already mentioned is contained in the FI G/L account or CO cost element to ensure that the combination of G/L account and cost element and functional area meets the content-related requirements of cost of sales accounting.

Customer-Specific Fields of New G/L

Evaluation variety versus performance When customer-specific fields are used, the requirement to obtain all financial evaluations from one data source, in accordance with the "one truth" basic principle, competes with the objective to minimize the complexity of the accounting system and ensure that it operates efficiently. Every additional reporting dimension also has to be entered, which adds an extra level to the summary record tables. Consequently, every customer can again weigh these two objectives against each other during the design phase.

Decision The requirement that emerged in our case was that Financial Accounting had to enter data relating to article numbers and the material group and forward the data to a downstream profitability analysis. However, a transfer of the "article" and "material group" master data into Financial Accounting and a consequent synchronization between these two systems was ruled out because of the complexity of the master data. Nevertheless, the existence of suitable master data stored in the SAP system is a useful prerequisite for customer-specific fields. In this situation, therefore, the best alternative remaining for the customer was to use a free text field (in this case, ASSIGNMENT) where the article number or material group can be entered. This approach is in no way a solution to be recommended for the vast majority of SAP customers, but it is intended to show that an unconventional solution can also be productive.

Profit Center Accounting, Segment Reporting, and Online Document Split

The integrated profit center accounting in New G/L offered the greatest benefit for our customer. It fulfills a wide range of requirements, and the customer was able to use it to map the defined branch and shop network, and to make its own P&L statement, and the most important balance sheet items such as material stock, available for each location. Profit center accounting was also used as the basis for segment reporting, in particular for companies that hold shares in different segments. Furthermore, foreign commission companies were mapped through profit centers.

With future requirements in mind, the online document split was activated when the system was configured, and the ZERO BALANCE FOR PROFIT CENTER setting was selected when the document splitting characteristics were set. These technical functions, which run in the background, completed an important preparatory step for future requirements such as activity reporting: The SAP system can now map complete financial statements at the profit center level. As a result, new business models can be mapped separately and reported without creating a separate legal entity and therefore without creating a new company code based on profit centers. This enables the customer to "control" new activities based on the same profitability key figures, even before divestment, and therefore reduces investment costs when developing new business areas.

Online document split

Empirical data from this and other projects conducted by Accenture and information from SAP itself show that the online document split initially requires a high level of configuration effort during the project phase, which must be considered when planning the project within the framework of creating the business case and planning resources. Mechanisms must also be implemented for the subsequent operation in order to prevent problems from occurring if, for example, there is a lack of profit center information that necessitates carrying out postprocessing when updating documents, which would involve significantly higher operating costs.

Special Ledger and SAP CO-OM as Enhancement to New G/L

In principle, the structure of New G/L is similar to that of a special ledger. There are two cases that deviate from the basic principle of mapping only one truth if possible and consequently mapping all accounting-relevant information in the general ledger:

▶ The cost center and internal order accounting was mapped in SAP CO-OM in the classic way owing to allocations across company codes, the use of established CO standard reporting, and planning functions.

▶ A special ledger that represents the data basis for EC-CS interface was also introduced despite New G/L.

Reason for decision

There were two main reasons for this decision:

▶ As required by corporate accounting, the (sub)functional area was able to be implemented into a "real" G/L account posting on the group account using special ledger derivation rules.

▶ This ability enabled the customer to achieve greater flexibility when mapping the segment assignment of profit centers. This could no longer be changed in the profit center master record (in the standard SAP system of New G/L) as soon as postings took place.

Project experience shows that New G/L integrates superbly with traditional techniques such as a special ledger or overhead cost controlling, which represents unprecedented flexibility in the development of the accounting solution.

Excursus Liquidity Planner

Financial Supply Chain Management

The Liquidity Planner is another relatively new function that has been provided since Release mySAP ERP 2004 within Financial Supply Chain Management (FSCM). It[3] replaces the cash budget management. Although the Liquidity Planner is not part of New G/L and belongs to FSCM, a brief discussion of the Liquidity Planner is helpful at this point, given the close link between actual LP accounting and Financial Accounting.

---

3 Source: Kerber, Warntje, *Cash Accounting and Cash Flow Planning with SAP Liquidity Planner,* SAP PRESS 2005

In the actual accounting of the Liquidity Planner, you can trace the enterprise's payments from the enterprise's bank and cash accounts, to the closed document chains, to the P&L account or balance sheet account containing the information. Based on the information on the payment cause obtained this way, the Liquidity Planner prepares direct cash flow accounting. Because document chains lay the foundation for Liquidity Planner processes, the introduction of the Liquidity Planner affects the definition as to which accounts are supposed to be managed using open items. You should include the main document chains (customer payments, vendor payments for goods or cost accounting, intercompany payments, and so on) during the project so that no changes need to be made to the account configuration later on for already existing operational posting data.

7.2.4 Conclusion

The functions of New G/L considerably extend the wide range of tools provided by the SAP system and offer a project team greater flexibility when mapping customer requirements. From the perspective of Accenture, with the introduction of New G/L, the focus is still on the processes and on determining the most important future reporting requirements. System functions, regardless of whether you select the new or classic version, must support these requirements in the best possible way. From our point of view, it is therefore extremely important in the design phase to carefully consider the customer requirements and how the new functions can be used effectively.

In particular, enhanced options (such as customer-specific fields and the online document split) to add additional account assignment information to the posting data create a need for greater discipline when entering posting data. All feeder systems and users must be able to access the additional information to enable them to specify it for the relevant posting. It is essential that these requirements are taken into account when interfaces, processes, and training are being designed.

Future improvements
Overall, it is also worthwhile to introduce New G/L from another perspective. There is still a lot of activity involved in the development of New G/L by SAP, which means you will be able to benefit from future improvements and enhancements to functions without great effort. This circumstance will facilitate SAP's strategy to provide new functions in enhancement packages that can be gradually implemented with little effort.

[+]

Authors of the Sample Case
This report was written by Timo Accardo and Stefan Bronzel, employees of Accenture GmbH.
Contact: *timo.accardo@accenture.com, stefan.d.bronzel@accenture.com*

7.3 Siemens IT Solutions and Services

"Process efficiency and evaluation options have significantly increased in our rapidly growing enterprise through the benefits of SAP's New G/L. We've waited for this solution!" We'd like to start this project report with this quotation from Rainer Krug, Head of Accounting and Controlling, SMA Solar Technology AG. New G/L is an SAP solution that comprehensively accommodates globalization requirements as an engine of an integrated value flow. We—Siemens IT Solutions and Services—support our customers in setting up and implementing their own value adding programs.

Because the success of our customers is our benchmark of success, we'd like to report on the implementation of New G/L and the use of the Migration Cockpit with SAP ECC 6.0 with a practical orientation.

The enterprise
This short field report relates to a project that we implemented in cooperation with and for SMA Solar Technology AG, a market-leading manufacturer of solar inverters, which is represented on four continents with eight subsidiaries. With a workforce of approximately 2,500 employees, SMA Solar Technology AG generated earnings of about EUR 330 million in fiscal year 2007. This highly innovative enterprise

is characterized by global growth and a consistent internationalization strategy.

7.3.1 Initial Situation

Because of SMA's initial public offering in June 2008 and a strongly growing international business as well as the desire to master future challenges better, faster, and more reliably, SMA and Siemens IT Solutions and Services implemented an integrated SAP solution for the individual and consolidated financial statements, planning (uniform demand, sales revenue, balance sheet, and P&L planning throughout the group on a consolidated basis), and reporting.

Prerequisites

Prerequisites for the consolidation requirements were the mapping of a uniform cost of sales accounting and segmentation at an individual financial statement level. The consolidated financial statements needed to be made according to IFRS and the individual financial statements according to the local legislation, which requires parallel valuation at the individual financial statements level. Thus, the project "Implementation of New G/L" and the migration of existing data were born.

Goal of the Overall Project: An Integrated Financials Application

The goals of the overall project were the harmonization of financial processes, the optimization of internal and external reporting on the basis of shared structures, and the integration of the SAP ERP system with the SAP NetWeaver BW system, which had to be newly implemented. Figure 7.2 provides an overview of the four subprojects:

▸ NGLA—New General Ledger Accounting

▸ BI—Business Intelligence

▸ BI-IP—Integrated Planning

▸ BCS—Consolidation

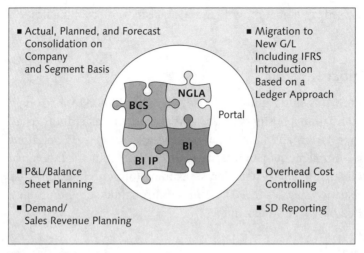

Figure 7.2 Subprojects

Requirements on the "New G/L" Subproject

At SMA Solar Technology AG, New G/L is the integrative driver of the process and value flow (see Figure 7.3).

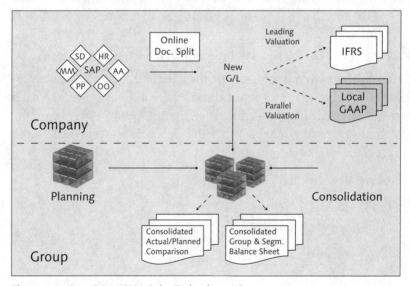

Figure 7.3 New G/L at SMA Solar Technology AG

New G/L was designed and implemented on the basis of requirements and customer requests. These requirements and requests can be summarized as follows:

- ▶ International accounting with an innovative design

- ▶ A transparent mapping of parallel accounting according to International Financial Reporting Standards (IFRS), according to local valuation rules (HGB/US-GAAP), and according to tax law

- ▶ Formatted balance sheet and P&L data specific to segments for consolidation

- ▶ A central component for universal and integrated reporting and planning structures that are developed on the basis of BI/BW components

7.3.2 The "New G/L" Project

The following challenges had to be faced:

- ▶ Implementation of parallel valuation according to various valuation rules (IFRS and HGB) on the basis of a ledger approach

- ▶ Implementation of SAP's New G/L and migration of existing data using the Migration Cockpit

- ▶ Switching the leading valuation to IFRS

- ▶ Implementation of a uniform cost of sales accounting throughout the group

- ▶ Provision of individual financial statements for a consolidated financial statement at the company and segment level

- ▶ Integration of New G/L with BI planning and consolidation for a uniform reporting throughout the group

All requirements had to be implemented for fiscal year 2008 so that the migration date of New G/L was set as 01/01/2008.

Scope, Organization, and Progress of the Project

The "New G/L" project started in August 2007 and was closely coordinated with other subprojects from the very beginning because its focus was on mapping shared structures and lean processes.

Design phase
Due to the use of transfer prices, the SLO service was already requested during the three-month design phase in order to switch to the parallel local currency. Using transfer prices in the classic General edger and transferring New G/L was problematic because the profit center valuation was solely updated in table GLPCT and not in the General Ledger. Thus, the values could not be migrated. The SLO service set up the new currency type, 12, so that the profit center valuation could be updated in the General Ledger and could therefore be migrated.

Implementation
At the same time, a harmonized sales method was implemented. The derivation criteria for the functional areas and the requirements for master and organizational data (for example, order type and material type) were analyzed, designed, and implemented until December 2007. Uniform cost of sales accounting was planned to be used in production starting January 1, 2008.

At the end of December 2007, the first user training was conducted in order to establish an understanding of the project background, to clarify possible validation messages, and to allay users' fears regarding the start of production. A second training session was carried out just before the start of production to introduce the functionality of New G/L as well as the new reports and transactions.

Test migration
The first test migration was planned at an early stage, in the first quarter of 2008, to be able to make valid statements regarding system platform, data quality, and development status of the "brand new" Migration Cockpit. The date for the second test migration was set for the end of April, keeping in mind the end-of-quarter closing. Ultimately, production migration was implemented for May 31, 2008.

Switching to IFRS
The process of switching the leading valuation to IFRS was addressed directly after the migration. For the migration, identical valuation approaches were assumed for each ledger; after the migration's acceptance, standardizing entries were made for the current fiscal year

according to the ledger-specific posting method so that the correct valuation approaches were mapped for the individual valuation views.

Parallel Accounting

The decision to introduce parallel accounting according to IFRS, HGB, or U.S.-GAAP and in favor of fiscal valuation principles also involved a decision in favor of an implementation of SAP's ledger approach in New G/L. It was determined that IFRS presented the leading valuation approach as of fiscal year 2008. The leading depreciation area in Asset Accounting therefore had to be switched from 01 to IFRS, and new depreciation areas for local GAAP and fiscal laws as well as the corresponding ledger-specific posting methods had to be set up.

Segmentation

The consolidation requirements mandatorily involved the implementation of the additional "segment" account assignment object. To be able to provide profit center and segment financial statements, document splitting was implemented for the profit center and segment. Within the scope of the design and implementation of New G/L, the derivation criteria for all business transactions on the individual segments—ex ante and ex post—had to be specified and defined in postings. In this context, the enterprise additionally had to adapt and redesign its processes.

Cost of Sales Accounting

The implementation of uniform cost of sales accounting due to legal consolidation requirements was characterized by this initial situation: In addition to reporting according to period accounting, the U.S. company code already used cost of sales accounting, but in a way that did not correspond to the corporate group standard. Consequently, this step focused on designing corporate cost of sales accounting considering the locally required structures. In addition to the new implementation of cost of sales accounting for the companies that had used period accounting for reporting, the U.S. company code had to switch to the corporate group standard.

Harmonized Individual and Consolidated Financial Statement

One of the main goals of the project was the harmonization of the individual and consolidated financial statements. In parallel with the "New G/L" project, this consolidation was implemented on the basis of SAP SEM-BCS (consolidated financial statements—in plan and forecast as well—at the segment and company level). SAP SEM-BCS and SAP NetWeaver BW had to be supplied with data from New G/L. This meant that the preparation for consolidation—that is, partner profit center determination and company determination as well as the derivation of the consolidation transaction types—had to be implemented. The uniform group item plan was the key for this integration.

Integration

FI – CO   The periodic reconciliation of FI and CO was very complex in terms of the use of the classic General Ledger. Numerous assessment and distribution cycles were used intensively. Consequently, the project additionally focused on the implementation of the CO-FI real-time integration. Reconciliation measures between external and internal accounting were therefore no longer necessary so that period-end closing could be done more quickly and fast closes were ensured.

HR   In the Human Resources area, the payroll processes were switched to a resource-related distribution of payables so that the postings from this area could be correctly distributed across profit centers and segments.

Both implementations—the real-time integration of CO with FI and the automatic resource-related distribution of payables from the HR system—considerably contributed to the data quality and accelerated closing operations.

Migration

Scenario 3   The enterprise was guided throughout the migration process by SAP's Migration Service, which was available as of October 2007. The customer selected Migration Scenario 3, which includes document splitting as well as merging of FI and PCA ledger data for data migration.

The Migration Cockpit was a helpful guide for the migration of the classic General Ledger to New G/L. It contains phase-related descriptions of the necessary steps. Scenario and test validation include various check programs that provide valuable information on the required steps in advance.

In the planning phase of the two test migrations, we decided to carry out two test validations. This procedure proved itself because the Cockpit's development status was enhanced during the project, and the second test validation included check steps that hadn't been implemented in the first test validation.

Test validations

The time window for the temporary system shut-down for data migration, data validation, acceptance and activation of New G/L during the production migration was quite narrow because SMA Solar Technology AG operates in three shifts over the weekend. We therefore decided to transfer the balance carryforwards and most of the document volume from the current fiscal year in advance, in parallel with running operations.

Production migration

7.3.3 Success Factors and Lessons Learned from the Project

This demanding and innovative project successfully reached its objectives. The main success factors were the customer's flexibility and willingness to make decisions, qualified and motivated key users, fast decision processes, the positive expectations of the management, as well as the personal experience and IT competence of the sponsor. The experience gained was very versatile and comprehensive. We want to share this experience with you.

The *SAP Migration Service* is an obligatory technical service, which had been considerably further developed by SAP at the time the project was conducted. Within the scope of the project, we carried out two test migrations and also requested an additional validation, which had to be paid for. This was a good decision: due to enhanced event reports by SAP, errors emerged during the second test migration that had not been identified during the first test migration.

SAP Migration Service

You should determine in advance which support packages, notes, and so on need to be imported into the various systems. Furthermore, you should carefully analyze which dependencies and time conditions are

System platform and technical environment

needed for the test migration system and NGLA system set-up and whether the required hardware resources are available.

Process changes and organizational changes

It must be mentioned for process changes and organizational changes in user departments that the document splitting process ultimately checks all business transactions. Because the automatic document split information is derived using account and document type, the document types need to be maintained carefully in the future, and some processes need to be changed. In the context of the CO-FI real-time integration, process changes cannot be excluded.

Test management

Well-organized *test management* for the test migrations saves you from time-consuming postprocessing during the production migration and during production operation later on. The more detailed the test cases, the more error sources can be eliminated in advance. The test cases were supposed to reflect operational activities, closing activities, and reporting requirements up to the segment level. When defining and detailing the test cases, it may make sense to use document types and their interpretation algorithms for orientation.

Employee training

For this project, it was helpful to include two training sessions:

- At the time of the activation of the validation for the fiscal year change (providing background information on New G/L, on the new SEG-MENT field, explaining the use of the document types, discussing document splitting and validation, CO-FI real-time integration)
- At the time of the production start of New G/L (providing information on new transactions, ledger-specific postings, ledger-specific evaluations, new reports for New G/L)

This way, the enterprise could ensure that the users were not afraid of using the new system and the new mode of operation; rather, the users had a positive attitude.

Production migration

Because the time frames for shut-down of the production system are usually very narrow and the individual migration steps may have very long run times depending on the quantity structure and hardware resources, you should plan carefully and shouldn't perform certain migration steps during shut-down periods.

Author of the Sample Case   **[+]**

Siemens IT Solutions and Services is an experienced, reliable, and globally active business partner for all IT concerns, with a focus on a comprehensive and wide solution and software competence.

Contact: *dorothea.baumann@siemens.com*

7.4   ConVista Consulting AG

Since the beginning of the introduction of New G/L in SAP ERP Financials, ConVista Consulting AG has played a pioneering role in its implementation, both internationally and across the industries. ConVista Consulting AG focuses on the financial services and energy supply sector with the first, and most intensive, users of New G/L. Since the first production installation of SAP ERP 5.0 worldwide, ConVista Consulting AG has helped numerous customers with the introduction of New G/L and the corresponding migration projects. These were enterprises with workforces from 100 to 10,000 employees, often with hundreds of company codes and users as well as a document volume on the order of millions. More than 50% of all implementations were new installations using SAP ERP Financials for the first time; the other projects involved technical upgrades from Release SAP ERP 5.0 to SAP ERP 6.0.

The enterprise

Number of Customers	Number of Company Codes	Number of Users	Document Volume	New Implementation of New GL	Migration of New GL
3	>500	>500	>10 mio.	100 %	0 %
5	>100	>300	>5 mio.	20 %	80 %
4	<100	<100	>3 mio.	75 %	25 %
3	<100	>100	>5 mio.	0 %	0 %

Table 7.1   Overview of the Conducted SAP ERP/New GL Projects Sorted by Size

Table 7.1 indicates that only a few customers changed their SAP ERP release without implementing New G/L, which demonstrates the wide acceptance of New G/L.

459

7.4.1 Motivation and Implementation of Technical Requirements

Reasons for the implementation

As Table 7.2 shows, the reasons for implementing New G/L were diverse but showed astoundingly similar focuses despite the differing technical requirements of the customers (multiple choices were possible).

Ranking	Main Motivators	Percentage	Tendency
1	Mapping of parallel accounting according to IFRS	70 %	⇨
2	Mapping of industry-specific reporting requirements in New G/L	30 %	⇨
3	New installation/redesign of the system landscape	25 %	⇨
4	Mapping of a tax balance sheet (as a result of the German Accounting Law Modernization Act)	20 %	⬈
5	Segment reporting	15 %	⬈
6	Account balancing on additional reporting dimensions using document splitting	10 %	⬈
7	Standardization of the data basis for the entire financial reporting	5 %	⬈

Table 7.2 Ranking of the Main Motivators for the Use of New G/L

Parallel Accounting

Main motivators

Parallel management of various accounting methods was the primary incentive for implementing New G/L. Most of the customers planned additional ledgers for mapping at least one additional accounting system (mainly IAS/IFRS) from the very beginning.

Since the German Accounting Law Modernization Act became effective, customers have been increasingly interested in the use of a further parallel evaluation area for mapping taxation valuation approaches in addition to the implementing parallel valuation areas for IFRS and US-GAAP.

Where an IFRS report or tax balance sheet was already prepared prior to the implementation of New G/L, this was done using manual transfer calculations in Excel, which involved a great deal of manual effort for data retrieval and evaluation on the basis of the legacy solutions.

Using Default and Customer-Specific Fields

The option of including the transaction type and trading partner in the totals table in order to perform a comprehensive intercompany reconciliation and prepare the consolidated financial statement is a great benefit of New G/L.

However, all customers also needed to use additional customer-specific fields (additional account assignment) on top of the account assignments provided in the standard SAP system.

The primary customer motivation was to avoid the encryption of technical differentiation characteristics in the companies' charts of accounts. In real life, the posting data is supposed to be differentiated according to the following aspects:

Different valuation of the posting data

▶ Organizational aspects (sales organizations, branches, and so on)

▶ Product-related aspects (product lines, product groups, and so on)

▶ External reporting requirements (German directive on the presentation of accounts of insurance companies and so on)

▶ Time selection of the posting data (IFRS 1 and so on)

If these differentiation characteristics are mapped using separate accounts, the chart of accounts inflates considerably. However, it is appropriate to introduce a customer-specific field only if this is relevant for a significant number of accounts. The mapping of business transactions through accounts corresponds to the accountant's "natural way of thinking" and is easy to maintain. However, it maximizes the number of accounts and can be systematically evaluated only to a limited extent. With all of the projects in this environment, the customers opted to use additional account assignments in the form of customer-specific fields or the standard SAP additional account assignments of the industry solutions.

Segment Reporting and Document Splitting

Due to the provisioning of segment account assignment and its consistent integration with standard reporting, a very good segment reporting function is available, which has proven itself in real life.

Document splitting further supports segment reporting, which considerably affects the complexity of the New G/L integration. From a technical perspective, a priori determining of the splitting rules was a major challenge. Prior to implementation of the splitting, you had to clarify whether the prerequisites required for all manual or automated postings for a technically appropriate object key determination had been met at the time of the posting. Even for data migrations, subsequently determining the split information considerably increased the work and complexity involved. Document splitting is especially useful if the keys at the time of the posting are known and no further subsequent adjustment must be performed. In this regard, subsequently enriching the posting data at the end of the period or at the time of the reporting may represent an alternative to the document split that is transparent and easier to realize from a technical perspective.

The technical question still arises as to whether complete segment balances and income statements really have to be prepared. In the case of insurance companies, for instance, these can often already be evaluated through the company code because of the line separation required by law. Additional differentiation of the lines by customer groups, for example, is currently not required. In the case of energy suppliers, for example, consequent segmentation of so-called "zebra" companies (a company that can be assigned to multiple segments) is very complex and can hardly be justified from the technical perspective.

Ultimately, all of our customers refrained from directly implementing document splitting. Because of the technical complexity and the scope of the processes resulting from the document split, as well as the technical adjustments, in our view the implementation of document splitting should be taken on as a separate (sub)project. The requirement for a subsequent implementation of document splitting for New G/L that is already being used was covered in Migration Scenario 6.

In general, it must be mentioned that in real life the challenge lies primarily in the content rather than in the system-related functionality.

7.4.2 Experiences Gained from the Projects

The projects supported by ConVista comprise smaller, mainly technically oriented migration projects up to highly complex new implementations, so-called green field approaches.

New Implementation

In the context of the SAP ERP implementation, some customers recognized the potential for revising and restructuring existing processes and systems. These are naturally significantly larger projects and can hardly be compared to seemingly "simple" migration projects, where totals data is transferred from the "old" to the "new" world.

Migration

Considering the migration within an existing SAP system, SAP has further developed the New General Ledger Migration service (NGLM service) considerably during the last few years. The programs, as well as the Migration Cockpit, have been enhanced significantly. The standard migration scenarios have proven effective and practical. It is almost impossible (and in most cases it is not required) to imagine migration without tried-and-tested migration programs and the Migration Cockpit.

However, the NGLM service also includes restrictions. Due to these restrictions, many customer requests had to be implemented as special developments. The restrictions comprise re-postings to the fiscal year before the migration date or migration scenarios that go beyond a specific fiscal year, for example. The service does not cover a simultaneous implementation of parallel accounting or the option of migrating from CO-PA. This kind of additional requirements may have to be addressed in cooperation with the consultant.

In general, the migration becomes much more demanding if the components of Asset Accounting (FI-AA), Consumer Mortgage Loans (CML) and Financial Asset Management (FAM) are used. You must pay particular attention to the CML and FAM components in implementing New

G/L and introducing parallel evaluation areas, because postings for these components have a special position in New G/L.

7.4.3 Experiences from Live Operation and Functional Aspects

Some of the new SAP ERP and New G/L functions that are now used by our customers can be differentiated according to their rate of capacity utilization based on the empirical data obtained from live operation. Besides parallel accounting, ledger group-specific OI management is used to a great extent (see Table 7.3). For example, the use of intercompany reconciliation and document splitting has increased.

Functions	Use	Tendency
Parallel ledgers	>80 %	⬈
Ledger group-specific OI management	>50 %	⬈
Intercompany reconciliation	>40 %	⬈
CO-FI real-time integration	<30 %	⇨
Closing Cockpit	<10 %	⬈
Document splitting	>10 %	⬈

Table 7.3 Rate Of Capacity Utilization for Individual SAP ERP and New G/L Functions

Ledger Group-Specific OI Management

With EHP 3, SAP met the customer requirement for providing open item management specific to ledger groups for G/L accounts, which is required for clearing provision accounts, for example. However, it is still not possible to clear an account across the ledger groups. A possible enhancement here would be the generation of automatic clearing postings between the ledgers, similar to the process used for cross-company code postings. But the standard version does not provide any function for this purpose.

Database Growth

In terms of performance and database growth, a general rule is that the overall size of the New G/L totals table should not exceed twelve million data records. When deciding how many ledgers are supposed to be managed for the various accounting purposes in New G/L, you have to consider the consequences of the data volume arising from the technical definitions. For example, with every additional accounting method, the data volume relating to a single local GAAP ledger is potentially doubled. Similar to the number of ledgers, the type and number of additional account assignments used have a significant impact on the data volume and thus on the necessary system environment. Some of the customer projects involved overdimendional database growths of the single record table, which is continuously updated and, in contrast to the classic special ledger, cannot be deactivated. This problem can be eased quickly by deactivating indices that are not needed.

CO-FI Real-Time Integration

All customers discussed the CO-FI real-time integration. One of the limitations was the technical separation of financial and controlling area, which still exists in many enterprises. Direct through-postings to FI company codes were therefore not always wanted. Instead, the customers considered a summary transfer analogous to the reconciliation ledger function a benefit. This meant that the conversion requirement was seen as small. It was to some extent kept separate from an immediate implementation of the CO real-time integration, although the technical demands and requirements, based on previous experience, would have been easily derivable and definitely useful. The additional increase of the data volume from CO-FI real-time documents due to intensive CO correction runs was considered an additional disadvantage and ultimately emerged as the main reason for not using the function.

Integration of Contract Accounts Receivable and Payable (FI-CA, FS-CD, IS-U, IS-M, IS-T, and so on), Asset Accounting and Controlling

The FI-CA component, which is used in many industry solutions, provides you with the option to make ledger group-specific postings. Consequently, it supports the supply of parallel valuation approaches according to IFRS and so on. However, automatic document splitting from FI-CA is currently not supported and won't be supported in the future. Moreover, the automatic transfer of additional account assignments needs to be further adapted and developed.

Customers still consider the technical need for mapping parallel valuation approaches within Asset Accounting using delta depreciation areas a disadvantage of the general ledger transfer. In CO, the standard version solely provides you with the option to make through-postings for the leading valuation; currently, there are no plans to include the ledger group in the FI-AA and CO tables.

7.4.4 Conclusion

SAP's New G/L component has proven itself in real life. Although it is still a relatively young component, we experienced hardly any "teething problems." When implementing the new functions, you should consult the corresponding experts. We sense our customer's strong urge to migrate to New G/L, and we assume that New G/L will be the standard component for the financial accounting area in a few years.

[+]

Authors of the Sample Case

Formed in 1999 in Cologne, ConVista Consulting AG currently (as of June 2009) has 150 employees in Germany and 240 employees worldwide and is poised to grow further. As a special expertise partner for SAP, ConVista has particular process, methodological, and technology expertise in the area of financial services and energy industries.

Contact: Oliver Kewes, Managing Partner, and Samuel Gonzalez, Process Manager Financials

Email: *info@convista.com*

7.5 J&M Management Consulting

The implementation of New G/L with SAP ERP provides an enterprise that uses SAP with numerous new options for designing processes in Financial Accounting and Controlling. Although the use of New G/L does not directly lead to monetary benefits, the business case of a migration to New G/L can pay off due to the enhanced reporting options. The following sections describe a migration project that involved the redesign of the reporting and accounting processes. Within the scope of this project, classic G/L accounting and classic profit center accounting (EC-PCA) were migrated to New G/L, and account balancing was set up at the segment level.

7.5.1 Initial Situation

The enterprise for which the described project was conducted belongs to the largest, internationally active IT service provider. Its field of activity comprises hardware trading as well as consulting and outsourcing in the IT environment. Its regional focus is on Europe. Over the last few years, parts of the enterprise have grown rapidly: growth that has been achieved especially through acquisitions. The acquired parts of the enterprise were usually not completely integrated with the entire enterprise. The company code was always transferred to the existing SAP system, but the processes and mapping of the system was not standardized.

To map its own business activities, the enterprise worked with Release 6.0 for the SAP ERP system in which the FI and CO components for accounting as well as the SD and MM components were actively used. In addition, the enterprise deployed various third-party systems having interfaces with the SAP system.

Grown system landscape

In the SAP system that was relevant for the project, approximately 15 company codes were used. There were additional company codes that contained data but that hadn't actually been used for several years. These were not considered for migration.

In accounting, the continuous growth and the missing harmonization entailed a great deal of effort and thus personnel overhead. In this context, the reconciliation of the figures between FI and CO as well as the explanation of possible differences in the month-end closing were particularly time-consuming. In addition, new reporting requirements, such as mandatory segment reporting in balance sheet quality, forced the user departments such as IT to find a future-oriented solution for mapping accounting together. Here, New G/L presented a promising option. The enterprise expected the following benefits:

Project charter

- ► Creation of Financial Accounting and Controlling reports, based on a shared dataset, through integration of the cost of sales accounting ledger and classic profit center accounting (EC-PCA) with New G/L

- ► Reduction of the reconciliation effort, thanks to the shared data basis

- ► Cleansing of the account assignment element in Controlling by simplifying the account assignment logic

- ► Segment reporting in balance sheet quality by activating the zero balance for the new account assignment object, "segment"

This was a challenging task for the project team, consisting of employees from the Financial Accounting department, employees from the Controlling department, employees from the internal IT department, and consultants. So as not to jeopardize the success of the project, the customer decided against a larger project scope. The mapping of parallel accounting was discussed in particular. Because a solution with parallel accounts was established in the enterprise and did not lead to problems, the customer decided against parallel ledgers.

Project organization To reach the enterprise's goals, New G/L including document splitting had to be configured at the profit center and segment level. In addition, a migration to New G/L had to be implemented. For these tasks, about 15 months was allocated, from the project initialization to the first month-end closing in New G/L.

Backward scheduling The subsequent schedule was determined using backward scheduling. By organizing the year-end closing more strictly and preponing the auditing period with the auditors, the start of the production migration could be scheduled for February 6, 2009. The data of the fiscal year to be migrated was also supposed to be used for a dry run in order to obtain more detailed information on the expected technical runtimes during the migration. It had to be considered in this dry run that a Slovakian company code had to be migrated and that the European Union decided to introduce the Euro into Slovakia on January 1, 2009. In the production system, the Euro was supposed to be introduced before the data was extracted for the dry run. The customer decided to introduce the Euro on January 10, 2009 so that a copy of the production system could be created the next weekend in order to start the dry run on January 18. All function and integration tests were carried out in 2008.

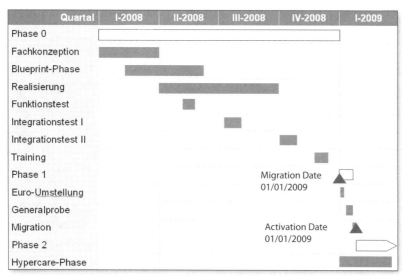

Figure 7.4 Project Plan

The project plan illustrated in Figure 7.4 shows that the phase for the creation of the technical concept and blueprint and the implementation phase overlap. The reason for this overlap is the complexity of the implementation of New G/L. Many decisions could be made only in interdisciplinary workshops involving the Financial Accounting department, the Controlling department, the IT department, and consultants. The overlapping project phases also considered the employees' learning curve.

Overlapping phases

The hypercare phase or after go-live support, that is, the increased availability of the IT employees and consultants in case of problems or questions regarding the application, did not start with the live migration process but earlier, during phase 1 (01/01/2009). In phase 1, the document splitting rules already applied to all postings in the General Ledger. Consequently, problems occurred, especially in the posting of documents. The posting logic was not changed after the migration. Directly after the migration, the focus of the user support was on explaining the figures resulting from the migration. In particular, the differentiation between data entry view and General Ledger view was not easy for the user to see and thus led to many questions.

Long hypercare phase

The function and integration tests were separated into three subphases:

- Testing of phase 1 (period: migration date to activation date)
- Testing of the actual migration
- Testing of phase 2 (after the migration and activation of New G/L)

The testing of phase 1 explicitly ensured that all transactions could be posted. At this time, correct segment derivation was not necessary because New G/L had not been activated yet. Testing phase 1 also ensured that sufficient and meaningful data was available for the test migration. During the subsequent technical migration, the functions of the Migration Cockpit as well as the account assignment derivation used for this purpose were tested. The reconciliation was always made by comparing the classic General Ledger and New G/L. No deviations were allowed here. This is different when you compare profit center accounting and the cost of sales accounting ledger: Because the general derivation logic for the profit center and functional area was revised, the balances at these levels between classic ledgers and New G/L could not be identical. In addition, only the P&L statement was mapped in classic profit center accounting.

Before the system behavior was tested for the activated New G/L component (phase 2) by posting all transactions in Financial Accounting and Controlling and a representative selection of the logistics processes was tested, the migration was reconciled first. This was always done in two steps. First, a technical check was carried out using Transaction GCAC (Ledger Comparison) at the company code level. Only then were the details reconciled at the G/L account, functional area, profit center, and segment level. The detailed reconciliation was difficult because of the already mentioned new derivation of functional area, profit center, and segment in the documents of the current fiscal year. This is not possible in the standard version of the Migration Cockpit. If a document already contains one of the mentioned account assignments in the data entry view, this entry is copied to the general ledger view. A modification here enabled the enterprise to newly derive the account assignment in the General Ledger view. Due to the modification, the currently valid assignment of cost center data and order master data was used instead of the historical assignment. This choice "cleansed" the assignment changes that were implemented in phase 1. The disadvantage of this procedure is that the data entry view and General Ledger view of the documents from phase 1 have different account assignments. However, this was the only way to cleanse the posting data with the 01/01/2009 key date.

7.5.2 Updating Master Data

It has already been mentioned that the mapped matrix organization of classic profit center accounting was supposed to be broken down. For this purpose, the content of the segments had to be defined first. The main point for discussion was the use of a dummy segment. This segment can be derived in the standard SAP system if no other segment was determined from the posting data. The enterprise finally decided to include a dummy segment in the first tests only. Particularly in the production system, this entry was not supposed to exist. Instead, missing segments were supposed to trigger an error message when the respective document was posted in order to minimize the effort needed to make corrections for the month-end closing. However, a so-called "auxiliary segment" was introduced. Such a segment is always used when facts cannot be clearly or reasonably assigned to a segment. Examples include postings in the stockholders' equity or incoming electronic bank statements.

Using a dummy segment

The correct segment assignment of cost centers and internal orders could usually be derived from the profit centers that were specified in the master data. For quality assurance, the enterprise also took the opportunity to have the persons responsible for the cost centers check to see whether the assignments were correct. This way, the master data could be significantly cleansed. The number of profit center could be reduced by a factor of five.

Cleansing master data

7.5.3 Configuring New General Ledger

For the design of New G/L, workshops involving the user department, IT, and consultants were conducted for several weeks. Based on these workshops, it was decided to use a single ledger, default ledger 0L, and continue to map the parallel accounting methods using the accounts approach. In accordance with the project goals mentioned above, the following scenarios were activated:

Activated scenarios

- FIN_CONS (Preparations for Consolidation)
- FIN_PCA (Profit Center Update)
- FIN_SEGM (Segmentation)
- FIN_UKV (Cost of Sales Accounting)

The implementation of document splitting involved considerably more problems than having to make decisions about the number of ledgers and scenarios. In particular, in contract accounting, the use of document types had to be modified significantly. There were numerous document types that were used for various business transactions, for example. With document splitting, this was no longer possible. Consequently, additional document types had to be set up. While the tests had been carried out, individual accounts, especially clearing accounts that were managed via open items, were also used for various transactions. To ensure the correct processing of the posting data by document splitting across all subsidiaries and locations affected, a detailed account assignment manual was created. It described the derivation logic for functional area, profit center, and segment in detail. It also provided information on the document splitting functionality in a user-friendly way. Finally, this manual defined rules that specified which document types and G/L accounts were supposed to be used to post individual business transactions. The customer also implemented numerous validations in the system for quality assurance.

Specific document splitting procedure

According to SAP's recommendations, the Customizing of document splitting was done using a specific document splitting procedure as a reference. This procedure was a copy of the standard procedure but had been enhanced significantly during the project. Some transactions or document types used special accounts as zero balance clearing accounts. This was necessary, for example, for accounting-specific postings with segment switch because this also required accounting-specific clearing accounts in order to obtain a balance of zero for all financial statements.

Account determination for real-time integration

The accounts to which postings were supposed to be made were also discussed in the context of real-time integration. At this point, a conflict of goals arose between Accounting and Controlling. There was no question that real-time integration for CO transactions with primary cost elements should use not account determination but the G/L account for the primary cost element to transfer data to FI. When transferring posting data to secondary cost elements, the Accounting department preferred to use as few clearing accounts in FI as possible. In contrast, the Controlling department had concerns about the informative value of profit center accounting in case the secondary elements got lost in reporting. A compromise had to be reached. The compromise stated that, in the future, the Controlling department had to clearly differentiate between the levels at which reports were supposed to be created. All parties agreed that a differentiated mapping of secondary cost elements in operational cost center and order controlling was inevitable. At management level, that is, for reporting by profit center, this mapping was no longer required to the full extent.

When transferring profit center accounting to New G/L, all transactions that had been mapped in EC-PCA had to be integrated with the General Ledger.

Particularly the reduction of the account assignment elements in CO, which was requested in the project charter, could not be achieved in the standard SAP system. The problem was that profit center accounting was used to map a matrix organization and displayed both the divisions and the organizational structure. In classic profit center accounting, this made it necessary to multiply the profit center because the sales and distribution area, for example, can be found in every division. The organizational structure was supposed to be mapped via the segment in the future so that profit centers map divisions only. In the standard SAP system, the segments are defined in the profit center master data. Therefore, it would not have been possible to cleanse and thus reduce the organizational structure information from the profit centers. The enterprise consequently decided to derive the segments not from the profit centers but directly from the cost centers, internal orders, and sales orders as well as from the WBS elements, that is, from all actively used CO account assignment objects. For this purpose, the SEGMENT field was added to the respective master data. In addition, dependencies to individual document types or G/L accounts were implemented. For the derivation itself, the corresponding BAdIs were used.

Specific segment derivation

473

Mapping of
reorganizations In EC-PCA, the customer already used a custom development that carried out postings at the profit center level in case of reorganizations. This feature enabled the enterprise, for example, to include the profit center assignment of cost centers retroactively in the posting data. The custom development was based on the default transaction, KEND, which can be used to map reorganizations in CO-PA. The goal of this development was to make profit center accounting and CO-PA reconcilable even after reorganizations. When the project was conducted, SAP did not provide an appropriate solution for New G/L, so the enterprise decided to program a solution itself. Due to activated document splitting, the process was difficult—from both the functional perspective and the technical perspective. The customer thus decided, for example, to make adjustment postings only to P&L accounts but not to balance sheet accounts.

7.5.4 Reporting

Because New G/L uses specific table structures, reporting had to be revised too. Here, as well, the customer took the opportunity to focus on the current reporting requirements of the user departments. As a result, only some of the previously used drill-down and report painter reports were transferred from the classic General Ledger, cost of sales accounting ledger, and profit center accounting to New G/L and adapted if required. The reporting with segment reference had to be restructured. The structure of balance sheet and P&L statement played a particularly important role here. Consequently, numerous new clearing accounts, for example, for zero balances in the case of segment switches, were added to the existing structure. To be able to use the data from the previous years for comparison, the last five fiscal years were copied from the cost of sales accounting ledger to a rollup ledger in New G/L.

7.5.5 Migration Project

Selecting the
migration scenario For the necessary migration to New G/L, the customer decided to use the service provided by SAP and hence the Migration Cockpit. First, all company codes were supposed to be migrated using migration scenario 3 (merging General Ledger, cost of sales accounting ledger, and profit center accounting as well as implementing document splitting). Due to the introduction of the Euro, one special aspect had to be considered

for the Slovakian company code: Technical restrictions did not allow the activation of document splitting for this company code. This fact facilitated the migration because migration Scenario 2 (merging General Ledger, cost of sales accounting ledger, and profit center accounting but without document splitting) had to be used.

The company codes that were migrated using Scenario 3 could be distributed across three packages. Any further subdivision would be desirable from the perspective of the migration team but was not possible due to cross-company code transactions. The advantages of smaller packages were shorter runtimes of the migration programs and—based on the project team's experience—fewer problems when deleting and setting up migrated data during the technical migration. Classic General Ledger accounting was used for all G/L accounts as the basis for the migration. Because the functional area and profit center were newly derived during the migration, it would not have made sense to copy the data from the cost of sales accounting ledger or from EC-PCA.

Defining the set-up phase

Experience has shown that problems with open items and clearing documents without line items can still occur in phase 1, even when the correct system settings have been made. The accounts and documents involved, however, were already identified during the dry run. So while these errors also occurred during the live migration, the corresponding solutions were already considered in the cut-over plan.

All steps of the set-up phase were performed before the migration weekend.

The migration weekend started with the backup process for the live system. Afterwards, on Friday around 8 p.m., the technical migration could be initiated. The migration packages were processed by several consultants in parallel so that nearly all packages were completely migrated by lunch time the next day. While the last and most comprehensive packages were still being migrated, the user departments were already able to start reconciling the figures. Thanks to good organization, the close cooperation of all parties involved, and the swift decision-making process on the part of the project management, the migration was successfully released for all company codes both by the Accounting department and Controlling department on Sunday. The system could therefore be released for

Schedule of the migration weekend

all users early on Sunday evening, in accordance with the schedule. This point was critical because the system couldn't be locked any longer. So the migration would had to have been canceled and the system backup reactivated if problems occurred.

Postprocessing

To keep the period during which the system was locked as short as possible, numerous uncritical postprocessing processes were implemented over the next few days. These included setting up the rollup ledgers based on the data of the cost of sales accounting ledger and clearing reversed zero-balance documents again. The activation of New G/L did not lead to any problems outside of financial accounting during the following days. The Accounting and Controlling departments also reported only a few errors after the migration, so no acceptance problems among the employees occurred in the last project phase.

7.5.6 Conclusion

Future-oriented and cross-component decisions

An inevitable prerequisite for the successful implementation of New G/L is a detailed concept. In this context, the IT department and consultants are responsible for demonstrating the functions of New G/L as well as the consequences of the decisions made, for example, the activation of document splitting and real-time integration. The decision makers of the user department must therefore take a future-oriented and cross-component approach.

High testing effort

The customer initially underestimated the testing effort resulting from the activation of document splitting. Compared to the company code that was migrated in migration Scenario 2 (without document splitting), the testing and reconciliation effort for company codes with document splitting (Migration Scenario 3) had to be multiplied by a factor of about five.

Information value of reports

After New G/L had been activated, some of the data from old, closed, and thus unmigrated fiscal years could no longer be evaluated using the existing reports. To compare fiscal years, you had to use custom developments or a BW system. This fact, as well as the changed table structure in SAP, required the early involvement of the BW team in the project.

After the month-end and end-of-quarter closings had been created and the initial application problems in New G/L were resolved, the implementation was reported as a great success. Both the General Ledger Accounting department and the Controlling department stated that reporting had been facilitated and that differences between FI and CO had been reduced to a large extent. However, this outcome also resulted in part from a consequent redesign of the account assignment derivation and the subsequent value flow. Therefore, you cannot consider a case of a migration to New G/L in isolation but must always take into account the intentionally created side effects.

Author of the Sample Case   **[+]**

J&M Management Consulting AG specializes in the following industries: process industry (chemical and pharmaceutical), consumer goods and retail, high-tech and electronics, telecommunications, machine and plant construction, as well as automotive industry.

As a partner for leading technology providers, J&M collaborates particularly closely with SAP AG.

Contact: Lars Eickmann, Partner J&M Management Consulting AG

Email: *l.eickmann@jnm.com*

7.6 Conclusion

The five practical reports demonstrate that many different aspects need to be considered in migration projects. Critical success factors are a general knowledge of New G/L, a good concept of future accounting requirements as well as experience with data migration and the necessary diligence. You should ensure that sufficient time is allowed for this kind of project and cooperate with the appropriate consulting partner.

A   Frequently Asked Questions

This appendix discusses some questions that are frequently asked in the context of New G/L.

A.1   Technology

► **What is the maximum number of segments in the key of the new totals table FAGLFLEXT?**
In Special Ledger there are 45 object number tables, each with 15 key fields. The SL totals table can contain a maximum of 45 key fields. These 45 key fields also contain some fixed standard fields such as COMPANY CODE, GENERAL LEDGER ACCOUNT, PROFIT CENTER, and SEGMENT.

In New General Ledger, fields like COMPANY CODE, ACCOUNT, PROFIT CENTER, and SEGMENT are standard in the table key. In addition, two customer includes are available where the customer can include an additional 15 fields (other SAP standard fields such as the plant or customer-defined fields). Keep in mind that many additional fields can result in high data volume, which causes performance problems in processes such as reporting, foreign currency valuation, and allocation.

► **What are the sizing impacts if New General Ledger is used and what impact does turning on New G/L have on performance issues?**
The impact depends on the implemented functions. Sizing and performance remain the same if no additional functions are used. Mainly

it is "additional ledgers for parallel accounting" or "document split" that have an impact.

▶ **Can line items and totals be managed together?**
No. Line items and totals are managed in different tables. There is no option to manage them all in one table.

▶ **When table logic has changed (FAGLXX replaces GLT0), how does the data source for SAP NetWeaver BI evolve in turn?**
The data sources have to be created first. There will be the technical name 3FI_GL_XX_TT, which is a placeholder (naming convention), where XX has to be replaced by the ledger description. For a ledger "LL," the data source would be 3FI_GL_LL_TT if it has been created before. The transaction for creating your own data sources in New General Ledger is FAGLBW03.

The only data source for the New General Ledger delivered by SAP is 0FI_GL_10, which extracts data only from the leading ledger. If data from the non-leading ledger is requested, the procedure described previously occurs.

In some cases, an extract structure is required to create a data source. This structure has to be generated using Transaction FAGLBW01. This structure has to be created if the ledger for which the data source is needed is not based on the delivered standard totals table FAGL-FLEXT.

▶ **Extending fields in New General Ledger tables**

  ▶ *How is the enhancement with customer-defined fields technically mapped? Can a customer who has enhanced the BSEG using COBL up to now continue to use COBL in New General Ledger, or is there another procedure?*
The procedure is identical. Technically, the customer field is inserted using an include (CI_COBL in COBL).

  ▶ *Does SAP give recommendations on how many customer dimensions with how many characteristics customers should have?*
SAP offers no recommendation on this issue. It must be decided at the project level. The important parameter is performance during data evaluation. It is also possible to work with a few different ledgers, each with one characteristic.

▶ *When fields are extended in New General Ledger tables, does this extension easily allow for tasks such as reporting (line item detail and balances, and SAP processes such as year-end balance carry-forwards, including the extended field, and so on?*

All customer-defined fields are extended within the line-item structures and are available in the entry view for general inquiry/reporting. Fields can also be customized for inclusion in the totals table, making them available in the ledger view. Only fields included in the totals table have balances carried forward.

▶ *Can only customer-defined extensible fields be included, or can existing SAP fields be included as well (for instance, material number)?*

A limited number of standard fields can be included in New General Ledger totals table via normal Customizing. Fields that are not available can be installed as customer fields; however, it is necessary to make the derivation in order for the values to be populated.

▶ *Is there any functionality that extending fields in the tables won't allow for?*

Customer fields must have substitution or derivation logic and/or be available for input in order to receive values.

▶ *Is there anything to be considered when extending fields within New General Ledger tables?*

There will be impacts on table growth within summary tables for each extended field. According to SAP's development department (see Note 820495), having five to six million rows in summary tables create a situation in which performance degradation may be apparent for activities including allocations, month-end processes, reporting, and SAP NetWeaver BI extracts. Splitting and zero-balancing on extended fields will affect table growth as well.

▶ *What other considerations will impact system performance?*

Document-splitting functionality and zero-balancing functionality create additional line items.

A.2   Document Online Split

▶ **How is the online split in New General Ledger different from the online split in FI-SL in SAP R/3 Enterprise?**

The split function has been enhanced with additional functions from SAPF181, such as POST-CAPITALIZATION OF ASSETS AND THE SPLITTING OF FOLLOW-UP COSTS (discount, currency differences, and so on).

The split information is also available for the closing activity in FI (foreign currency valuation, regrouping, and so on, and therefore also at the segment level).

CO-relevant valuation postings (for instance, expense from exchange rate differences) can be transferred to CO in split form.

▶ **What is the impact and use of activating and defining the "Define Document-Splitting Characteristics for Controlling" in the Customizing settings?**
This action concerns characteristics supplied by SAP and the characteristics of the customer. Characteristics that are stored here can be transferred in splitting from Controlling in connection with determining follow-up cost (foreign currency valuation, realized exchange rate difference, discount, and so on). The precondition is that the GL account has been created as a cost element. However, you should remember that the characteristics cannot be used for balancing.

▶ **Are there any concerns regarding document-splitting and zero-balancing functionality on financial postings generated by highly customized applications?**
All cost flows require analysis to determine derivation logic or data-entry requirements. Any mandatory field not derived or entered will create errors.

▶ **For balance-sheet-only entries, how does profit center and/or segment splitting occur?**
The value for profit center/segment must be entered or derived in order to produce an offsetting split or zero-balancing transaction item in the G/L view of the document. Splitting rules can be configured to assist with this process, provided the process is clearly defined and appropriate accounts and document types are consistently used.

▶ **Are there any considerations or cautions concerning document splitting on residual postings? What happens if the profit center or segment is changed in the system prior to a residual posting being completely cleared?**

All clearing postings use a passive split, whereby the original split information about the item is used as the basis for the clearing update. For migration purposes only, customers must assign each open item to a single characteristic for conversion.

▶ **Assuming segments are assigned via standard SAP (from profit center), can the segment assignment be overridden by the user on a financial posting? How is this accomplished?**
During data entry, it is possible to over-type and override the segment relationship. This may or may not be desirable. A substitution routine can enforce the relationship if this should not be permitted.

A.3 Comparing Special Ledger with New General Ledger

▶ **Is there ledger selection in New General Ledger as there is in FI-SL?**
Ledger selection like that in FI-SL does not exist in New General Ledger because New General Ledger deals with general ledgers that are used for legal reporting. The validation function can be used for validation checks (for instance, profit center 1 can be assigned only with account 5).

▶ **What is the future role of the Special Purpose Ledger?**
If the customer uses New General Ledger, FI-SL again assumes its original role as an additional internal reporting tool. All customers who until now have used FI-SL as a General Ledger substitute should be able to do without FI-SL by changing over to New General Ledger. However, each customer should evaluate individually whether he or she wants to stay with FI-SL for "special purposes."

The ledger approach for mapping parallel financial reporting, introduced with SAP R/3 Enterprise as an alternative to the accounts approach, is replaced by the complete parallelism in New General Ledger. Customers who upgrade to SAP ERP and do not want to implement New General Ledger can, however, use the classic approach.

A.4 Parallel Financial Accounting and Ledgers

▸ **What strategy does SAP recommend for technical mapping of parallel financial reporting (parallel ledgers in general ledger, accounts approach, company code solution)?**
Customer requirements determine whether using parallel General Ledgers or the accounts approach is more appropriate with only one leading General Ledger. The use of parallel company codes is not recommended by SAP. SAP will not develop this solution further because of the significant disadvantages caused by a high proportion of manual postings.

▸ **Are the parallel ledgers already defined for mapping of parallel financial accounting when they are shipped, or do customers have to create them in their entirety themselves?**
The standard ledger/leading ledger 0L is shipped. Customers themselves need to create further ledgers.

▸ **Can separate currencies be assigned to the different parallel ledgers?**
No. You cannot create new currencies in the parallel ledgers if they are not defined in the leading ledger.

▸ **Suppose a customer decides to use New General Ledger but initially uses only a single parallel ledger (the leading Ledger). The customer processes some transactions for a few months and then decides to use an additional ledger in the system. Is there a program that the customer can run to enable retrospective posting to a new non-leading ledger?**
SAP offers a migration service. For more information, refer to Section A.8, Miscellaneous.

▸ **When a New Leading Ledger is created for LX without any posting, can the customer delete the Ledger 0L?**
If it is really necessary, the customer can delete ledger 0L. But SAP may deliver ledger 0L again, and then the customer would have it again. In this case, though, it would not be a leading ledger, so it should not cause significant problems.

▶ **Are direct postings to a parallel ledger readily identifiable in New General Ledger? What is the best means of doing this?**

The easiest way would be via the ledger group.

▶ **Do the Operating Chart of Accounts (CoA) and Statutory CoA automatically apply to the parallel ledgers or can a different Operating CoA be used in parallel ledgers? What about the Group CoA? In other words, if parallel ledgers are not applicable to SAP Consolidations functionality, is it correct that Group CoA functionality in SAP is not applicable to parallel ledgers?**

If the country-specific chart of accounts or group chart of accounts is required for reporting within the totals table, these would be realized through the implementation of customer-specific fields. The standard Financial Statement Version allows for output according to the alternative chart (country-specific) at runtime. This option generally satisfies local reporting requirements without having to include them in the summary table. Advantages of run-time determination are that assignments are flexible and can be retroactively adapted.

▶ **Can FI allocations, assessments, or distributions be performed directly within a parallel ledger?**

Yes, it is possible to do this in a parallel ledger. They won't flow to CO. In ECC 5.0 this is possible only on a percentage or amounts basis, not as statistical key figures (SKF). SKFs are possible with release ECC 6.0.

A.5   Segment/Profit Center/Business Area/Customer Fields

▶ **On what level is the segment defined?**

Segments are maintained at the client level; that is, they are valid throughout the entire group and do not depend on the controlling area.

▶ **What procedure is used to derive the segment in posting transactions?**

In SAP ERP, segments can be used only with profit centers. In FI postings, where profit centers information is not relevant, the segment can be derived using a BAdI, or it can be entered manually.

▶ **What is the future status of the business area?**
For installed-base customers, the business area will be retained in its present form. Data and functions will still be available in the future.

▶ **Why is the segment derived from the profit center? Why not from the business area? Why does the segment not stand alone? Is there a particular reason for this, or is it a technical issue?**
The segment is derived from the profit center because the derivation rules of the Materials Management (MM) and Sales and Distribution (SD) "feeder systems" are based on the profit center and not on the business area.

▶ **When will the segment be better than the business area? Should business-area customers retain the business area for now or is the tendency toward the segment? Or, should customers run both in parallel during the transition period?**
There are different recommendations for new customers and installed-base customers:

  ▶ *New customers*
    SAP recommends that new customers start with the segment immediately because this corresponds to its development strategy.

  ▶ *Installed-base customers*
    Installed-base customers who work with highly specific business areas should retain them for now because existing derivation rules/substitutions for determining the business area can still be used.

▶ **In New General Ledger, can the customer-specific fields be picked up from transactions initiated in other components?**
If a customer wants to insert his or her own dimension, he or she first has to extend the coding block (as before) and then he or she can use it in New General Ledger. This means that he or she has to insert it into the specific New G/L ledger in which it will be a key field. Feeder systems have to deliver this field.

▶ **What is the situation for allocations and settlement in CO with respect to the additional fields, such as customer-defined fields?**
CO doesn't keep the additional fields in their totals. So allocations based on those totals cannot take into consideration additional fields.

Settlements based on single items keep the additional field because additional fields are kept in the CO items.

▶ **What is the logic behind graying out the segment field in the profit center master after it is saved?**
A change of the allocation of the profit center to segment is very critical after the data has been posted. Checking to see whether a profit center already has been posted is extremely performance-critical. Therefore, the SEGMENT field in the profit center master is grayed out and not editable after it has been saved.

▶ **SAP Business Area functionality continues to exist in New General Ledger.**

  ▶ *Has SAP enhanced the functionality? If yes, in what ways?*
  No: the functionality is the same.

  ▶ *Does SAP provide a general recommendation regarding the use of business areas as part of New General Ledger functionality if they are not being used in classic GL?*
  There are no general recommendations either way, other than that the functionality is not being enhanced. If there is a business requirement that cannot be met via other alternatives, SAP advises that business areas should be considered because they are native fields (that is, in cost centers and assets) and cross company-code boundaries.

  ▶ *Are there certain applications where business areas should be used in addition to New General Ledger functionality, or where it may be a better alternative to profit center or document-splitting and zero-balancing functionality?*
  SAP recommends analyzing which method is appropriate in the context of a New General Ledger implementation project.

  ▶ *Is business-area balancing in New General Ledger automatic as a function of document splitting (assuming a business area can be pulled in as a field to split on), or is this still performed via a program?*
  Yes: Business area balance sheets are available by customizing splitting rules and real-time zero-balancing when posting within New General Ledger. Subsequent program runs such as SAPF180 and SAPF181 are no longer used.

▶ **What drives zero-balancing for a profit center during profit center posting? Is this configuration where it sends the difference to an inter-company balancing account?**
This logic is very similar to current company-code functionality. Before posting, the document is checked if the balance of the profit center is zero. If it is unbalanced, additional clearing items are created if zero-balancing is required for profit centers in the Customizing settings of New General Ledger. Therefore, clearing account(s) must be determined in the Customizing settings, too.

A.6   Integration

A.6.1   Integration of New General Ledger—SAP Consolidation

▶ **How does New General Ledger Parallel-Ledger functionality work in relation to SAP consolidation functionality?**

    ▶ *SAP consolidation—parallel ledgers*
    Can SAP Consolidation take into account New General Ledger parallel ledgers, or does it consider only New General Ledger Leading Ledger?

    ▶ *SAP consolidation—only leading ledgers*
    If only the Leading Ledger is used in SAP Consolidation, then is it correct to assume that the Leading Ledger must be maintained in a single corporate accounting principle in order to allow for appropriate consolidations to take place under one accounting principle, and that the parallel ledgers must be used for local accounting principles?

SAP's experience so far is that companies using SAP Consolidation treat the leading ledger the corporate accounting ledger and that local accounting GAAP is performed in parallel ledgers. The primary reason for this is the leading ledger integration throughout SAP (such as CO), whereas parallel ledgers are associated only with FI.

SAP's recommendation is to configure the leading ledger according to corporate GAAP standards and parallel ledgers in accordance with local GAAP.

A.6.2 Integration New General Ledger—Asset Accounting

▸ **Can certain transactions/types of postings in the leading ledger be blocked from flowing to any one or more parallel ledgers (for example, depreciation postings)? If so, how is this accomplished?**
Parallel ledgers are assigned to ledger groups and ledger groups to a depreciation area. Typically, a different parallel ledger would be set up for each country. Therefore, in effect this setup can prevent 01 depreciation area postings from being represented in a parallel ledger if this is desired.

The asset transactions from the leading area (01) are posted to all ledgers. In general, asset transactions are posted without a ledger group. If the valuation of an asset acquisition is different in an additional ledger, then manual posting must be made for this area. During APC posting, the derived area (30 or 31) is calculated and the difference is posted to the additional ledger.

In general, most automated processes (depreciation, FX revaluation, and so on) are controlled by the mechanism of the ledger group. In assets, the chart of depreciation is the level at which depreciation areas are assigned to ledger groups. For other processes, a valuation area is assigned to an accounting principle, which in turn is assigned to a ledger group.

▸ **How do depreciation areas work in New General Ledger parallel-ledger functionality?**
Depreciation Area 01 is assigned to the leading ledger and leading ledger postings flow to the parallel ledgers.

▸ **How is a different depreciation area for localized accounting requirements accounted for in the parallel ledger functionality? Can depreciation for a non-01 depreciation area be run independently within a parallel ledger?**
Yes: Non-01 depreciation areas can update specific parallel ledgers.

▸ **How is it assured that depreciation is not double-counted in the parallel ledger? Depreciation-area 01 postings would theoretically flow from the Leading Ledger to the parallel ledger, but accounting principles in a parallel ledger require depreciation to be run using another depreciation area.**

Delta depreciation areas are used to capture the differences between corporate and local GAAP. These are derived areas that are used to post differences to the local GAAP ledgers only.

A.6.3 Integration GL-CO, Allocations

▸ **Is the FI functionality in New General Ledger the only way to get allocations, assessments, and distributions postings to the parallel ledgers (assuming parallel ledgers are not updated with CO information)? Do New General Ledger FI allocation, assessment, and distribution postings flow to the parallel ledgers?**
CO-only postings (allocations and so on) can be set up to flow to a parallel ledger via ledger group assignments. CO-only postings can flow to parallel ledgers through the ledger group assignments, but they have also to flow to the leading ledger as well. You cannot set the CO postings up to flow only to the parallel ledger and not the leading ledger.

▸ **How is the FI allocations functionality different than CO in New General Ledger; that is, is it more limited, and, if so, in what way? Can you run allocations between balance sheet and P&L accounts? Can you run them specifically for balance sheet reclasses between profit centers?**
In some ways, New General Ledger has more functionality than CO and in some ways less. As an example, Statistical Key Figures don't exist in ECC 5.0 (only in ECC 6.0). Therefore, FI allocations based on statistical key figures are not possible. But it is possible to do allocations on a percentage base or absolute amount basis. Another option to consider is recurring entries or account assignment templates. Therefore, FI allocations on the basis of statistic key figures are possible only as of SAP ERP 2005. GL doesn't use secondary cost elements.

▸ **Does something similar to CO assessments and distributions functionality exist in New General Ledger FI? If so, how is it different?**
It is possible to do FI allocations using extended fields. It is important to note that it is not possible to do cross-company FI allocations in New General Ledger.

▶ **Will secondary cost element postings—such as WIP settlements and labor transfers for editorial costs to the balance sheet—still post to PCA now that PCA is part of FI? Secondary cost elements reside in CO, but PCA is now in FI. Do settlements need to be performed separately in both New General Ledger and CO now? How does New General Ledger impact these processes?**

There are no changes from the current functionality other than that updates are automatically performed in FI in New General Ledger. The reconciliation ledger is no longer used. The integration is now on a real-time basis. CO integration is customized using a variant. All defined cost flows must be configured for the complete integration to work properly. Secondary cost elements are not taken into consideration in New General Ledger.

▶ **Are the FI and CO allocations now broken out or separated in New General Ledger?**

 ▶ *Do you have to run allocations or distributions separately now: once in FI and once in CO?*

 No: You don't need to run two allocations in New General Ledger. CO allocations cover costs. FI allocations are not meant to cover costs. Here you can allocate values, such as default-posted profit centers for internal profit center reporting purposes. CO is not updated.

 ▶ *How is it assured that data is kept in sync, given that the reconciliation ledger no longer exists?*

 Automatically. Technically, the same internal structure is used to track cross-characteristic cost flows originating in CO. Only the posting update has been enhanced to allow real-time integration (if desired).

A.7 Reporting

▶ **Is standard reporting in New General Ledger available, as in Ppofit center accounting?**

New General Ledger is available for all standard reporting tools (Drill Down; Report Painter, Business Warehouse). SAP delivers some example standard reports for Drill Down and NetWeaver BI reports: there, a selection for profit center is possible.

▶ **Can profit center groups be used in New General Ledger reports?**
In drill-down reports, you can use profit center groups in the display list. You cannot use them as a selection criterion.

▶ **Is it possible to use Customizing fairly easily to create an effective-dated hierarchy structure for segment reporting (similar to the standard and alternate hierarchy concept in PCA)?**
SAP recommends that if hierarchy reporting of segment is needed, it should be performed within SAP NetWeaver BI.

▶ **Is it difficult to implement the segment functionality at a later date after New General Ledger goes live?**
If segment were implemented later, you would get only segment information for go-forward transactions after activation; it would not be retroactive to historical postings. In any case, this is not a solution that can be implemented at the click of a button; it has to be done within the framework of a separate project.

▶ **Why isn't segment setup similar to the PCA standard and alternate hierarchy structure for reporting purposes?**
It's intended to be a flat, non-dimensional field.

▶ **Is SAP considering, or would they be willing to consider, setting up segment hierarchies?**
Not as of SAP ERP 2004/2005.

▶ **Can the PCA profit center hierarchy (both standard and alternate hierarchies) be used in New General Ledger for balance sheet reporting now that PCA is in the FI component of New General Ledger?**
PCA profit center hierarchies are not applicable to FI, meaning that reporting is available only at the profit-center level not at the node level for FI reporting in New General Ledger. Profit center is available in some SAP standard reports (such as the Financial Statement Version), but node reporting is not possible in standard reports. SAP indicates that this may be possible through custom reports and Report Painter. SAP also notes that it is possible to do this in SAP NetWeaver BI.

Hierarchies are available in G/L drill-down reports. If a functional area is used in the Financial Statement Version for P&L reporting, drill-down reporting (vs. standard delivered version) reports must be used.

▶ **Is there a way in SAP to run a query, report, or variant of only postings directly to a parallel ledger vs. those postings flowing from the Leading Ledger vs. all postings affecting the parallel ledger?**
It is possible to obtain a line-items report for direct parallel-ledger posting by document number (separate document number range for parallel ledger entries) or via other means if the ledger group is part of the document header.

It would not be possible to get a balance report for direct parallel ledger postings because the document type is not included as a characteristic in the standard totals table.

▶ **Can data be as easily extracted out of SAP Parallel Accounts as out of parallel ledgers for the purposes of loading into another application? For example, is it possible to extract from SAP tables only postings directly made to a parallel ledger as well as both leading ledger and flow-through postings? How is this best accomplished?**
It depends on the volume of parallel accounts that would be created. It would be possible either way but more easily if using parallel accounts. SAP offers various document-selection reports that allow detailed selection. Create a flat output file and transfer this information into the target system. Determining whether to use a parallel ledger vs. parallel accounts approach must be done as part of the migration scoping and blueprint.

A.8   Miscellaneous

▶ **How does a customer proceed if he or she wants to perform a migration of the data from the classic General Ledger to New General Ledger?**
The path for migration will differ from customer to customer. To ensure a high degree of safety when carrying out this process, SAP accompanies each migration project with a migration service. This

technical service relates to standard migration scenarios and is provided in the form of migration packages. More information regarding New General Ledger Migration Service can be accessed using the quick link GLMIG on the SAP Service Marketplace (*http://service.sap.com/GLMIG*). See Note 812919.

▶ **Can customers continue with Classic General Ledger accounting in SAP ERP?**
Implementation of New General Ledger is not compulsory. But if a customer decides to use New General Ledger, the data must be migrated from the classic General Ledger.

▶ **If customers upgrade to SAP ERP 2004, can they work in parallel in the different company codes with the classic General Ledger and New General Ledger?**
This is not possible with SAP ERP 2004. Customers must use New General Ledger either for all or none of the company codes.

▶ **Can an upgrade to SAP ERP 2004 and migration to New General Ledger be combined without risk in one project or should these procedures follow one another in two projects?**
SAP recommends two projects: first the technical upgrade to SAP ERP, and then migration to New General Ledger.

▶ **Is transfer pricing available in New General Ledger?**
It is not available in SAP ERP 2004 but is in SAP ERP 2005.

▶ **Can average balancing be done for banks to calculate the money flow and average balance based on the balance of Assets and liability?**
This function is available. See SAP Note 848111.

▶ **How can I stop an update in PCA?**
If an update in classic PCA is no longer required, you can deactivate the customizing of the basic settings of PCA.

▶ **Can the reconciliation ledger simply be switched off once New General Ledger is in use?**
If New General Ledger is active, the reconciliation ledger is not available, so the customer does not need to take any extra steps.

▶ **Is the Account Group function available in New General Ledger?**
There is no change in the Account Group function. It can be used in New General Ledger.

▶ **How many currencies are available in a parallel ledger?**
It is the same functionality as in classic GL: Up to four currencies are available within the leading ledger:

  ▶ Transaction currency

  ▶ Company code/local currency

  ▶ Up to two parallel reporting currencies as assigned in FI

Parallel ledgers can use at maximum the same or, if sufficient, only some of the currencies defined in the leading ledgers.

▶ **Is it possible to get gross margin reports out of New General Ledger extensible fields rather than using the component "Profitability Analysis" (PA)?**
New General Ledger should be used to produce a full complement of financial statements. It is not intended to be used for detailed analysis, nor is it designed to be a replacement for PA.

▶ **What are the important OSS notes/SAP notes concerning New General Ledger in SAP ERP?**

  ▶ 741821 Release limitations concerning SAP ERP 2004

  ▶ 756146 SAP ERP New G/L: General Information

  ▶ 779251 SAP ERP New G/L: Parallel Accounting

  ▶ 862523 SAP ERP New G/L: New Functions as of SP 10

  ▶ 890237 New G/L With Document Splitting: Legacy Data Transfer

  ▶ 891144 New G/L/Document Split: Risks of Subsequent Changes

  ▶ 918675 Basic Architecture of the New G/L Accounting

  ▶ 812919 SAP ERP New G/L: Migration

  ▶ 826357 Profit Center Acc. and New G/L in mySAP ERP

  ▶ 852971 SEM-BCS: Integration with the New G/L

  ▶ 820495 SAP ERP New G/L: Data volume and Parallel Ledgers

B   The Authors

Eric Bauer studied Business and Economics Education at the University of Mannheim, Germany, where he majored in Financial Accounting and Financing. His thesis was awarded the Barbara-Hopf-Stiftung Prize. He then completed a two-year internship while also working as a freelance trainer providing both basic and advanced training programs for a variety of banking, insurance, and retail companies. Eric joined SAP in 1998, first as an Education Consultant in Financial Accounting, then as an Education Development Coordinator in the Financials application area with responsibility for international training development. In 2004, he was active in the Financials and Human Capital Management areas as a Director of Education Training Delivery with responsibility for the design, creation, and delivery of global education solution portfolios. Eric has worked in EMEA Regional Solution for Sales Financials since 2006.

Jörg Siebert began working as a consultant, trainer, and customer sales advisor in the Financial Accounting area in 1996. In 2009, he joined SAP AG's product management team. His work focuses on the SAP ERP Financials solution. His certification as a consultant for the SAP ERP Financials components, FI, CO, and SAP SEM, his degree in Information Management, and his qualification as a CPA are the basis of Jörg's extensive technical competence. You can visit his blog at *http://www.hauptbuch.info*.

Index

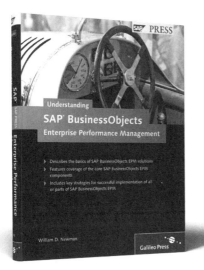

Provides key stakeholders and decision-makers with a practical functional overview of SAP BusinessObjects EPM solutions

Features coverage of the core EPM components, including BPC, FIM, SM, and SPM

Includes key strategies for successful implementation of all or parts of EPM

William D. Newman

Understanding SAP BusinessObjects Enterprise Performance Management

This book provides decision-makers with guidance on implementing and using the SAP BusinessObjects Enterprise Performance Management solutions, including Strategy Management, Financial Information Management, Spend Analytics, XBRL and more. Readers will benefit from the strategic, high-level overviews of the various products in the EPM application, and develop an understanding of the best practices for implementation, integration, and use. The scenario-based approach should appeal to a broad range of stakeholders, from executives to functional department heads and managers.

282 pp., 2010, 69,95 Euro / US$ 69.95
ISBN 978-1-59229-348-3

>> www.sap-press.com

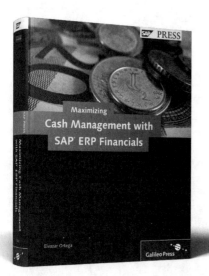

Includes real-world strategies for implementing and integrating SAP ERP Cash Management components

Provides business users with an overview of SAP's liquidity management solutions

Features practical coverage of Cash Management, In-House Cash, SWIFT integration, and more

Eleazar Ortega

Maximizing Cash Management with SAP ERP Financials

This book provides an overview of the functionality for all key cash management components, including best practices, real-world business scenarios, and key configuration and master data information. It explains how all the components can be integrated, and how both the individual components and the integrated solution can be maximized for optimal performance. Topics covered include SAP ERP Cash Management, Electronic Banking, Liquidity Planner, In-House Cash, Bank Communications Management, and integration with SAP ERP Financials and other components.

approx. 400 pp., 79,95 Euro / US$ 79.95
ISBN 978-1-59229-324-7, Sept 2010

>> www.sap-press.com

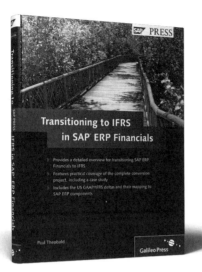

Provides a detailed overview for transitioning SAP ERP Financials to IFRS

Features practical coverage of the complete conversion project, including a case study

Includes the US GAAP/IFRS deltas and their mapping to SAP ERP components

Paul Theobald

Transitioning to IFRS in SAP ERP Financials

This book is the roadmap your conversion project team needs to prepare your SAP ERP Financials systems for conversion to IFRS. It includes detailed coverage of the transition process, an overview of the US GAAP/IFRS deltas and how they are mapped in ERP Financials, and real-world advice from an IFRS conversion project at a large petrochemical company. With this concise guide, you'll give your finance professionals, executives, technical staff, project managers, and consultants a real jumpstart to IFRS projects in upgrade or non-upgrade scenarios.

209 pp., 2010, 79,95 Euro / US$ 79.95
ISBN 978-1-59229-319-3

>> www.sap-press.com

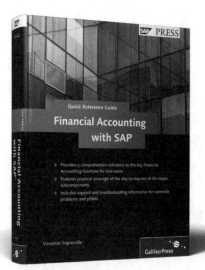

Provides a comprehensive reference to the key Financial

Accounting functions for end-users

Features practical coverage of the day-to-day use of the major sub-components

Includes support and troubleshooting information for common problems and pitfalls

Vincenzo Sopracolle

Quick Reference Guide: Financial Accounting with SAP

If you use SAP ERP Financials on a daily basis, this definitive, comprehensive guide is a must-have resource. You'll find practical, detailed guidance to all of the key functions of the Financial Accounting component, including troubleshooting and problem-solving information. You'll find easy-to-use answers to frequently asked questions in the core areas of the SAP General Ledger, Asset Accounting (AA), Accounts Payable (AP), Accounts Receivable (AR), Banking (BK), and Special Purpose Ledger (SPL). In addition, the book includes quick-reference material such as lists of transaction codes, tables, and menu paths.

665 pp., 2010, 69,95 Euro / US$ 69.95
ISBN 978-1-59229-313-1

>> www.sap-press.com

 **PRESS**

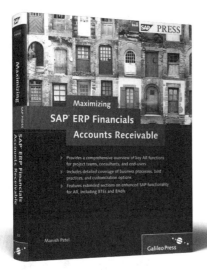

Provides a comprehensive overview of key AR functions for implementation teams, consultants, and end-users

Includes detailed coverage of business processes, best practices, and customization options

Features extended sections on enhanced SAP functionality for AR, including BTEs and BAdIs, among others.

Manish Patel

Maximizing SAP ERP Financials Accounts Receivable

Are you using SAP ERP Financials Accounts Receivables to its maximum capability? If not, this book will give you a roadmap for ensuring that you are, whether you're an implementation team member, executive, functional or technical user, or an end-user. The book will teach you how to maximize the use and potential of the Accounts Receivable component and increase the ROI of your implementation. You'll also develop knowledge and strategies for enhancing the use of the AR component and integrating it with other SAP services and components.

505 pp., 2010, 79,95 Euro / US$ 79.95
ISBN 978-1-59229-303-2

>> www.sap-press.com

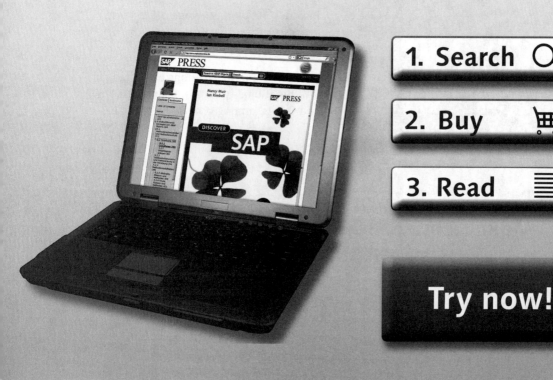